Return migration is discussed a lot but remains poorly understood in both academic and policy contexts. Engaging with the multi-faceted realities of 'return', this book offers a much-needed critical view to return migration. Focusing on the psychosocial wellbeing of the returning migrant the book challenges the dominant myth that return is a 'good thing'. Contributions to this volume cover four continents and very different contexts of return (voluntary and forced, assisted and spontaneous) pointing to the agency of the migrant and to the role of volition in both returning and in seeking to escape (forced) return.

Anna Triandafyllidou, *Professor, Global Governance Programme, Robert Schuman Centre for Advanced Studies, European University Institute, Italy*

Return Migration and Psychosocial Wellbeing sheds new light on classical themes in the study of migration, such as agency, home, and the life course. The book connects these themes with current theoretical turns and policy contexts. The focus on psychosocial wellbeing weaves together forms of migration that are usually studies in isolation from each other.

Jørgen Carling, *Peace Research Institute Oslo, Norway*

Readers who want to *understand* the policy and societal relevance of returnees' wellbeing will find much in this volume co-edited by Russell King and Zana Vathi. The authors' contributions accurately identify the various psychosocial dimensions inherent in returnees' patterns of reintegration as well as their implications. To be sure, this volume clearly shows that it is still possible to reflect on return migration by critically examining and deconstructing predominant assumptions with grounded scientific evidence.

Jean-Pierre Cassarino, *Institut de Recherche sur le Maghreb Contemporain (IRMC), Tunisia*

Return Migration and Psychosocial Wellbeing

Return migration is a topic of growing interest among academics and policy-makers. Nonetheless, issues of psychosocial wellbeing are rarely discussed in its context.

Return Migration and Psychosocial Wellbeing problematises the widely held assumption that return to the country of origin, especially in the context of voluntary migrations, is a psychologically safe process. By exploding the forced–voluntary dichotomy, it analyses the continuum of experiences of return and the effect of time, the factors that affect the return process and associated mobilities, and their multiple links with returned migrants' wellbeing or psychosocial issues.

Drawing on research encompassing four different continents – Europe, North America, Africa and Asia – to offer a blend of studies, this timely volume contrasts with previous research which is heavily informed by clinical approaches and concepts, as the contributions in this book come from various disciplinary approaches such as sociology, geography, psychology, politics and anthropology. Indeed, this title will appeal to academics, NGOs and policy-makers working on migration and psychosocial wellbeing; and undergraduate and postgraduate students who are interested in the fields of migration, social policy, ethnicity studies, health studies, human geography, sociology and anthropology.

Zana Vathi is Reader in Social Sciences at Edge Hill University.

Russell King is Professor of Geography at the University of Sussex and Visiting Professor of Migration Studies at Malmö University.

Routledge Research in Race and Ethnicity

Return Migration and Psychosocial Wellbeing

Discourses, Policy-Making and Outcomes for Migrants and Their Families

Edited by Zana Vathi and Russell King

Routledge
Taylor & Francis Group

LONDON AND NEW YORK

First published 2017
by Routledge
2 Park Square, Milton Park, Abingdon, Oxon OX14 4RN

and by Routledge
711 Third Avenue, New York, NY 10017

Routledge is an imprint of the Taylor & Francis Group, an informa business

British Library Cataloguing in Publication Data
A catalogue record for this book is available from the British Library

Library of Congress Cataloging in Publication Data
A catalog record for this book has been requested

ISBN: 978-1-138-67750-0 (hbk)
ISBN: 978-1-315-61961-3 (ebk)

Typeset in Galliard
by Wearset Ltd, Boldon, Tyne and Wear

Contents

Contributors

Zana Vathi is Reader in Social Sciences at Edge Hill University. She specialises in migration studies and has been conducting interdisciplinary research in this field since 2005. As a member of the Sussex Centre for Migration Research from 2005 to 2012, she worked on projects concerning the integration of migrants and their descendants, migration and development, new immigration into Britain and transnationalism. Her doctoral research consisted of a comparative qualitative study with the children of migrants, first-generation migrants and key informants in three different cities: London (UK), Thessaloniki (Greece) and Florence (Italy). This research was awarded the 2012 IMISCOE Maria Ioannis Baganha Prize as the best PhD project in migration studies in Europe. She has served as an international expert on migration for organisations such as the Migration Policy Centre at the European University Institute, *Terre des Hommes* and the International Organization for Migration (IOM). Currently, her research focuses on the complex links between the spatial and the psychosocial in the context of migration.

Synnøve Bendixsen is a postdoctoral research fellow in the Department of Social Anthropology, University of Bergen, and Head of International Migration and Ethnic Relations at Uni Research Rokkansenteret, Norway. Her research interests include irregular migration, political mobilisation, Islam and Muslims in Europe, the study of inclusion and exclusion, and processes of marginalisation. She has published a number of articles and book chapters, and one monograph: *The Religious Identity of Young Muslim Women in Berlin* (Brill 2013). She has consulted for the Department of International Migration and Urbanization at UNESCO and The Ministry of Justice and Public Security and The Norwegian Directorate of Immigration in Norway. She has also been a visiting scholar at COMPAS, Oxford University, and at New York University. Since 2013, she has been co-editor of the *Nordic Journal of Migration Research.*

Hilde Lidén is a research professor at the Institute for Social Research (ISF), Oslo. Her research interests are transnational migration, mobility, childhood and family studies, gender, national minorities, immigration policy and family policy. She has carried out research on transnational childhoods and on unaccompanied and trafficked minors. In recent years, her research has focused on the dilemmas concerning migrants' rights in international and national policies and regulations, discussing migration, family life and citizenship from the children's point of view, as well as the parents' and the authorities' interests and perspectives.

Marta Bivand Erdal is senior researcher at the Peace Research Institute Oslo (PRIO), Norway. She is a human geographer and has conducted research in Norway, Poland and South Asia. Her research focuses on migrant transnationalism, including remittances, diaspora development engagements and Islamic charity, and on processes of migrant integration and citizenship practices in diverse contexts. She has recently been focusing on return migration, including return considerations among migrants living in Norway, experiences of return migration to Pakistan and Poland, and the question of sustained return mobilities and transnational living, as part of the 'Possibilities and Realities of Return Migration' (PREMIG) project.

Ceri Oeppen is lecturer in Human Geography at the University of Sussex and a global fellow of the Peace Research Institute Oslo (PRIO). Her research explores the ways in which migrants adapt to the new environments in which they find themselves, with a special interest in the interactions between transnationalism and integration. Her current research focuses on return migration, working with colleagues at PRIO to disseminate findings from the 'Possibilities and Realities of Return Migration' (PREMIG) project. Her particular expertise is in researching the experiences of Afghan asylum-seekers and refugees living in Europe and North America, and of those who have returned to Afghanistan.

Barak Kalir is an associate professor in the Department of Anthropology, University of Amsterdam. He is the co-director of the Institute for Migration and Ethnic Studies (IMES) and programme director of the research group 'Moving Matters: People, Goods, Power and Ideas'. His research interests revolve around the interface between legality and illegality in the social dynamics that shape human mobility across (state) borders. He is currently leading a five-year European Research Council (ERC)-funded project, 'The Social Life of State Deportation Regimes', in which the implementation of these latter is ethnographically examined in six countries: Greece, Spain, Belgium, Israel, Ecuador and Indonesia. His most recent publications include 'The Jewish state of anxiety: between moral obligation and fearism in the treatment of African asylum seekers in Israel', *Journal of Ethnic and Migration Studies* (2014), and the edited volume *Transnational Flows and Permissive Polities: Ethnographies of Human Mobilities in Asia* (Amsterdam University Press 2012).

Marcin Gońda is a research assistant in the Department of Sociology of Culture, Institute of Sociology of the University of Łódź, Poland. His PhD thesis (2016) examines biographical dimensions of educational migration of people of Polish origin from the former Soviet Union. In his qualitatively oriented research, he predominantly utilises a biographical method of data collection and analysis. Gońda is the author of a number of papers on migration, multiculturalism, ethnic minorities and the internationalisation of higher education in Poland. His research interests also revolve around individuals' perspectives on transformation in post-socialist societies. He is a member of the Polish National Science Centre-funded project 'Poles in the World of Late Capitalism: Changes of Biographical Processes in Terms of Professional Careers, Social Relations and Identity at the Time of System Transformation in Poland'.

João Sardinha is a research fellow in the Institute of Geography and Spatial Planning (IGOT) at the University of Lisbon, Portugal. His research interests centre on the descendants of first-generation migrants and their return migrations and identity, on belonging and transnationalism, lifestyle migrations, migrant youth, sports and music, and migrant associations. He has coordinated and participated in a number of projects funded by national and international institutions, among them the European Commission, the Portuguese Sciences and Technologies Foundation, the International Council for Canadian Studies and the International Migration, Integration and Social Cohesion (IMISCOE) Network of Excellence. He has published in *Ethnic and Racial Studies, Journal of International Migration and Integration, Diasporas* and *Journal of Mediterranean Studies,* and is the author of the book *Immigrant Associations, Integration and Identity: Angolan, Brazilian and Eastern European Communities in Portugal,* published by Amsterdam University Press.

David Cairns is a researcher in the Centre for Research and Studies in Sociology, Instituto Universitário de Lisboa (ISCTE)-University Institute of Lisbon, Portugal. His research interests include youth, geographical and social mobility, education and political participation. He has participated in numerous projects, including two large-scale EC-funded studies and work funded by the governments of Portugal, Ireland and the UK. To date, he has over 100 publications, including four books and a forthcoming title, *The Consequences of Mobility* (Palgrave Macmillan). He has also published in *International Migration, British Journal of Sociology of Education, Journal of the Royal Anthropological Institute, Social and Cultural Geography, Journal of Youth Studies* and *Young.* At present, he is working on a project exploring student mobility from a socio-demographic perspective, funded by the Portuguese Foundation for Science and Technology.

Selma Porobić is the director of the United Nations High Commissioner for Refugees (UNHCR)-initiated Centre for Refugee and IDP Studies at the University of Sarajevo and Assistant Professor of Psychology at the International University of Sarajevo. Her PhD, from Lund University, focused on the religiosity of Bosnian war refugees in Sweden. In 2006, she was a visiting fellow at the Refugee Studies Centre, Oxford University. She has published articles and book chapters on refugee protection, returnee reintegration practices, and the wellbeing and health of forced migrants in the Western Balkans. Her work mainly focuses on the mental health of displaced persons and their social and cultural resources for dealing with adversity. She is currently coordinating a Fribourg University-funded project investigating the long-term effects of displacement on the psychosocial wellbeing of female forced migrants in Bosnia, Serbia and Kosovo.

Daniela DeBono is Marie Skłodowska-Curie COFAS Fellow at the European University Institute (EUI), Senior Lecturer in Migration Studies at Malmö University and a member of the Malmo Institute for Studies of Migration, Diversity and Welfare (MIM). She is also country expert for Malta at the European Union Democracy Observatory (EUDO) housed at the European University Institute (EUI). Her research revolves around the migration–human rights nexus. She has conducted research on deportation, detention, reception and irregular migration in Sweden, Malta and Italy, as well as citizenship in Malta. In 2014–2015, she led a qualitative study of forced returns from Sweden. Her PhD, from the University of Sussex, was a qualitative study that explored, using human rights culture as a theoretical framework, the cultural and socio-political practices that form attitudes towards irregular migration in Malta. She is currently engaged in an ethnographic project studying the reception of irregularly arriving maritime migrants into the EU. Her recent publications include the co-authored volume *Humane and Dignified? Migrants' Experiences of Living in a 'State of Deportability' in Sweden* (Malmö University 2015).

Nassim Majidi is an affiliate researcher at Sciences Po's Centre for International Studies, specialising in return migration. She teaches a graduate course on *Refugees and Migration* as part of Sciences Po Lille's Conflict and Development Programme. She is the co-founder of Samuel Hall, a think-tank of the Global South, where she leads evidence-based research and policy development on migration. Her cross-cutting skills have led her to interview refugees, migrants and returnees in border areas, conflict settings, and countries of origin and transit. She has developed strategic programmes, national policies on migration, and monitoring reviews that have had a lasting impact. She was nominated in 2015 by the Norwegian Refugee Council for the Nansen Refugee Award for her work on behalf of Afghanistan's displaced population.

Ine Lietaert is a postdoctoral researcher in the Department of Social Work and Social Pedagogy, Faculty of Psychology and Educational Sciences at Ghent University. Her PhD project was on the return process and experiences of migrants returning on an Assisted Voluntary Return and Reintegration (AVRR) programme, with a main focus on returnees' lived experiences, subjective evaluations, and return and reintegration support. She has published in journals, including *International Migration, Global Networks, Population, Space and Place* and *Social Policy and Administration*, on the topics of return experiences, perspectives of migrants in detention centres and the Belgian AVRR programme. She is also a research member of the Centre for the Social Study of Migration and Refugees (CESSMIR).

Eric Broekaert was full professor in the Department of Special Education, Faculty of Psychology and Educational Sciences, Ghent University. He had extensive experience with a variety of national and international research projects on educational interventions for adults with substance abuse problems and children with emotional and behavioural disorders, and has published numerous scientific articles, books and book chapters. He was co-editor of the *International Journal of Therapeutic Communities* and co-founder of the European Working Group on Drugs Oriented Research (EWODOR) and the European Federation of Therapeutic Communities (EFTC). Finally, he was chairman of the Orthopedagogical Observation and Treatment Centre in Ghent and of EWODOR.

Ilse Derluyn is Lecturer in Intercultural Pedagogics in the Department of Social Work and Social Pedagogy, Faculty of Psychology and Educational Sciences, Ghent University. She has been involved in several research projects in the field of intercultural pedagogics and the wellbeing of refugee children in host countries and youths living in vulnerable situations, particularly unaccompanied refugee minors and war-affected youth in Uganda, Congo and Colombia. She is head of the interdisciplinary interfaculty research centre for the Social Study of Migration and Refugees at Ghent University, where she teaches courses on migration, intercultural pedagogics, diversity and social policies.

Aija Lulle is a research fellow at both the University of Sussex and the University of Eastern Finland. She was also the founding director of the Centre for Diaspora and Migration Research at the University of Latvia. Her current interests are related to youth mobilities, ageing and migration, transnational families and inequalities within families, especially through broader notions of identity. Her research also focuses on 'new diasporas' in the European Union as a result of intra-European migration. She serves as a national expert in the Organisation for Economic Co-operation and Development (OECD) Network of International Migration Experts and as an expert on migration for various European and Latvian teaching or research programmes. She has published papers in, *inter alia, Geografiska Annaler, Women's Studies International Forum, Population, Space and Place, Social and Cultural Geography* and *Sociology of Development*.

Eralba Cela is a postdoctoral research fellow in the Department of Economics and Social Sciences, Faculty of Economics at the Università Politecnica delle Marche, Italy. She completed a PhD in Demography at the University of Bari (Italy) in 2008. Since then, she has held a number of research and teaching positions at the Università Politecnica delle Marche. Her research interests focus on migration, remittances, family studies, gender, ageing and well-being. She has published in several Italian and international journals, including *Rivista Italiana di Economia, Demografia e Statistica, International Migration Review, Journal of Mediterranean Studies* and *Population, Space and Place*.

Kelly Hall is Lecturer in Social Policy at the University of Birmingham. Her research interests include migration, ageing, health/social care and the third sector. Her research into international retirement migration focuses on the migration and return of vulnerable, older British people within the EU. Over the last few years, she has undertaken a number of studies in collaboration with Age UK, Age Concern España and the British Consulate to explore the lived experiences of older British people in Spain and their access to informal and formal care and support. She has also undertaken research into health and social care and micro-enterprises. Her research has been published in journals such as *Ageing and Society* and *Public Management Review*, and as book chapters and a co-authored book.

Charles Betty obtained an MPhil from the University of Nottingham in 1977. Later in his career, he was Senior Inspector for Research and Development in Nottinghamshire, UK, and wrote several academic articles about the impact of social deprivation on young children and their learning. After retirement to Spain, he wrote a thesis on the retirement of older British people in Benalmadena for his MPhil at the University of Brighton. He is presently in the later stages of a PhD at the University of Northampton on the lived experiences of British retirees living in Spain who return to the UK, and has co-authored a number of academic papers relating to this work.

Jordi Giner is a PhD student in the University of València (Spain). He is a lecturer in the Sociology Department in the University of València and also in Florida Universitària. He co-wrote the book *Un peu dins, un peu fora* and has also published papers on migration in Spain in journals such as *Revista Internacional de Sociología* and *Papers de Turisme*. He is now preparing his PhD thesis on the return process of British retired citizens living on the northern coast of Alicante. In 2014, he was a visiting academic at the University of Birmingham.

Dora Sampaio is currently a PhD candidate at the University of Sussex. She previously worked at the Centre for Geographical Studies of the University of Lisbon, where she was involved in a number of projects on national and international migration, including the European projects Theorizing the Evolution of European Migration Systems (THEMIS) and Generating Inter-Ethnic Tolerance and Neighbourhood Integration in European Urban Spaces (GEITONIES). She trained as a human geographer at the University of Lisbon (BA, MA), and her main research interests lie in the intersection between international migration and later-life mobilities, with a particular focus on islands and local/rural contexts. In her doctoral research she is looking at later-life migration in the Azores.

Russell King is Professor of Geography at the University of Sussex and Visiting Professor of Migration Studies at Malmö University. Most of his research has been Europe based, with a special focus on migration processes and transitions in Southern Europe and the Balkan region. He has directed major research projects on international retirement migration, international student migration and return migration. He was editor of the *Journal of Ethnic and Migration Studies* from 2000 to 2013. Among his recent books are *The Atlas of Human Migration* (Earthscan 2010), *Remittances, Gender and Development* (I.B. Tauris 2011) and *Counter-diaspora: The Greek Second Generation Returns 'Home'* (Harvard University Press 2014), all co-authored. He has recently published papers in *Transactions of the Institute of British Geographers, Geoforum, Population, Space and Place, Gender, Place and Culture, Global Networks, Diaspora, Mobilities, International Migration, Social and Cultural Geography* and *Ethnic and Racial Studies*.

Preface and acknowledgements

Return migration is a topic of growing interest for academics and policy-makers. Nonetheless, the issue of return migrants' psychosocial wellbeing is rarely given much attention. This book problematises the widely held assumption that, compared with out-migration, return to the country of origin is a psychologically safe process. By reassessing the forced–voluntary dichotomy, the chapters in the volume analyse the continuum of experiences of return and the effects of time on the process, the actors who affect the return and associated mobilities, and the multiple links with returned migrants' wellbeing and/or psychosocial issues. The research presented distinguishes between, on the one hand, the positioning of states and migrants in the discourse on return and, on the other, the actual processes and experiences of return. Chapters in the book also analyse the way in which migrants' vulnerability and psychosocial wellbeing are positioned in immigration policies, neoliberal state organisations and service provision. In the context of critiques of 'groupism' in migration studies, the book covers within-group differences, with the role of power and positionality being considered in the context of return to the country of origin. In this vein, the authors also consider the effect of gender in various contexts and stages of return, and analyse the intersections of these variables with age and their implications for migrants' experiences of return.

The book arose out of a major European network on research on migration – International Migration, Integration and Social Cohesion in Europe (IMISCOE) – and especially the IMISCOE annual conference in Geneva in June 2015, at which first drafts of the chapters were presented and discussed in a multi-session panel convened by us as editors. The chapters draw on research encompassing four different continents – Europe, North America, Africa and Asia, with an arguably stronger focus on Europe – to offer a collection of studies that pay close attention to contextual differences that affect migrants' wellbeing in the context of return. Contributions to this volume integrate various disciplinary approaches, including sociology, geography, psychology, politics and anthropology.

The volume is organised into four sections:

- the forced–voluntary continuum in return migration;

- ancestral returns, adaptation and re-migration;
- asylum systems, assisted returns and post-return mobilities;
- the life course, family and health.

In considering psychosocial wellbeing as an empirical question investigated through different methodological approaches, the book offers a holistic perspective on how wellbeing is affected during the return process and its associated mobilities, enabling academics and policy-makers to understand the repercussions of return and not merely the clinical symptoms deriving from mental illness.

Therefore, the overall approach of the book and the data presented in the contributions fulfil an important function in suggesting preventive action and proactive policy-making on return migration. Since return is considered as a stage in an individual's migration history or trajectory, and since all chapters problematise the equation between country of birth/origin and home, the book will inform its diverse readerships about the link between migration and wellbeing in general, especially as the contributors do not see return as a specific end-point of migration, with only isolated psychosocial issues. This makes the book relevant to a wide range of scholars, practitioners and activists. Furthermore, the volume aims to inform policy-makers and migrants themselves on the variety of 'outcomes' available to these latter and their families. The chapters contain discussions on policy recommendations, while the variety of settings, types of migrants and returnees, and the geographical diversity they cover make the book relevant to a plurality of professionals and actors in the field of migration and return.

The chapters have benefited from discussion and generous comments by members of the multi-session panel at the 2015 IMISCOE conference in Geneva. We are also grateful for the encouraging remarks from three reviewers of the detailed book proposal. At Sussex, we thank Samantha Wannop for excellent editorial assistance throughout the process of compiling the volume, and Jenny Money for her crucial input at the eleventh hour. As editors, we acknowledge the cooperation and responsiveness of the chapter authors in revising their texts and accepting our suggestions and changes. Maybe at times they thought we were harsh and pedantic editors, but they never complained, and the end result is a product that we can all sign up to and even feel a little proud of.

The motivation for the volume is as much about the very essential human experience of home-making in the context of migration and return as it is about the overlooked injustice on which migration systems are still based in the twenty-first century: the all-encompassing state power over migrants' human right to home and belonging.

Zana Vathi, Edge Hill University, Ormskirk
Russell King, University of Sussex, Brighton

1 Introduction

The interface between return migration and psychosocial wellbeing

Zana Vathi

Introduction

This book brings into conversation with each other two concepts which have thus far received little attention as a duality: return migration as a subset of migration studies; and psychosocial wellbeing, part of an overall shift in social science towards emotionalities, relationalities, subjectivities and 'affect'. Migration, and mobility more broadly, has become a defining feature of contemporary Western societies (Cresswell 2006; Urry 2000, 2007), breaking down the sedentary containers of nation, state, class and residential community. Not only are more and more people 'on the move', some voluntarily but others with little choice in the matter, but migration and mobility reveal how some of the core features of human nature are enabled, contested, reshaped and reproduced. However, this very same mobility and change trigger a multiple need for relating, belonging and home-making; indeed, 'where home is' becomes one of the transformative discoveries and dilemmas of the overall migration experience.

The hegemonic notion of 'homeland' and the associated phenomenon of going or returning 'home' are based on the assumption that home is 'where one is originally from', where one was born (Malkki 1995). Indeed, place of birth can have huge symbolic (and citizenship) importance for some people, but those who attribute overriding importance to this definition of identity and belonging ignore abundant evidence on the importance of integration, adjustment and assimilation in the migrants' host countries. Socio-economic and cultural discontinuities and political and personal ruptures in the context of migration can erode this naturalistic and teleological sense of home, and instead lead to a rebuilding of home in another place, distinct from the presumed homeland.

Only recently has the literature on return migration acknowledged the problematic aspects of the simplistic idea of 'returning home'. As Gmelch (1980) pointed out in his seminal paper on return migration, this phase of the migration process has tended to be historically downplayed in the literature. This remains true, though arguably less so, today. Recent major studies of return or 'counter-diasporic' migration (Christou and King 2014; Conway and Potter 2009; Harper 2005; Long and Oxfeld 2004; Markowitz and Stefansson 2004; Tsuda 2009) have begun to document the emotional complexities of the 'return journey'. To repeat some revealing phrases in the titles of these books and their constituent chapters, the return home may be an 'illusion' (Janzen 2004), 'bittersweet' (Connell 2009) and 'an unsettling path' (Markowitz and Stefansson 2004). Anticipated as a 'welcoming embrace', the return might be an experience of 'rupture and disillusionment' (Christou and King 2014), and the non-migrant relatives may be 'brothers only in name' (Song 2009). In some contexts, returning to the country of origin is characterised by 'reverse culture shock – a new incarnation of social marginalization at "home" and a myriad of practical and psychological problems' (Stefansson 2004: 56).

Return migrants' psychosocial reactions to such complex and challenging processes are rarely studied or regarded as a cause for concern; the focus has been primarily on integration in the receiving countries and the effect of ethnicity and discrimination on migrants' mental health. Two significant changes in social sciences prefigure the need for research on this topic of return migration's psychosocial effects: first, a general turn towards holistic analyses; and second, a stronger focus in migration studies on issues of subjectivity and affect. In this context, this book problematises the widely held assumption that return to the country of origin, especially in the context of voluntary migrations, is a psychologically safer process than the one of migrating to another country. The book draws on research encompassing four different continents – Europe, North America, Africa and Asia – to offer a blend of studies that pay close attention to the many differences that affect wellbeing in the context of return. Existing research on migration, wellbeing and mental health is heavily informed by clinical approaches and concepts. We consider psychosocial wellbeing as an empirical question to be investigated through various methodological and (inter)disciplinary approaches; hence, we offer a holistic perspective on wellbeing in the return process and associated mobilities. Where possible, the chapters that follow include policy implications to enable academics and policy-makers to understand the wider repercussions of return and not just the clinical symptoms deriving from mental illness. This book is also for migrants themselves; recent evidence shows that return migrants are unaware of the readjustment challenges faced during and upon return, and preparedness prior to return rarely involves thinking about their psychosocial wellbeing (Barrett and Mosca 2013; Vathi *et al.* 2016).

As research presented in this book shows, the nexus between return and psychosocial wellbeing is fraught with tensions. This is not just because of radical policies and programmes that aim to encourage or enforce return migration (e.g. visa regimes, assisted voluntary return, deportation, etc.), but also because of the socio-cultural dissonance that return exposes. In order to unpack the outcomes of return migration and show sensitivity towards the effect of time, return is seen as a multi-phased process and as part of ongoing and future migration trajectories; hence, it may be more appropriate to speak of return *mobilities* rather than return migration. This book further expands the focus to include various actors and stakeholders who may impact migrants' wellbeing in the process of return in different stages as well as various contexts of return. It also shows how unilinear migration models have played a major role in obscuring the impact of return migration on psychosocial wellbeing and the overall complexity of the return experience, not least in overlooking the positive outcomes and failing to provide some analysis on how to harness these.

One of the major 'sins' of the existing literature is its simplistic focus in terms of the types of migration that give rise to psychosocial issues. A division is observable between 'voluntary' migration, considered as psychosocially safe, and a concentration of research on forced migration and migrants' war-related traumas (Vathi and Duci 2016). This distinction conceptualises force and volition with a strong reference to states' action and macro-level factors, consequently leaving 'voluntary' migrants out of the policy-making focus, and, at the same time, 'relieving' the countries of origin that receive returning migrants from responsibility for their wellbeing. The chapters that follow unpack the forced–voluntary dichotomy and illustrate the complexity found in the return spectrum, as well as factors that operate at community, personal and intimate levels.

Another important aspect of this book is the analysis of wellbeing in a continuum, as a developing, non-linear experience of migrants, conditioned by circumstantial as well as structural factors. Chapters look at the causal relationships between various contextual variables and wellbeing, considering historicity and contemporary configurations of multiple factors, as well as temporal dimensions of return. The negative outcomes researched include emotionalities of return, sensorial and bodily pain, adaptation difficulties and cultural dissonance, and mental health issues or other clinical health disorders. Wellbeing is researched through a relationality approach, analysing how return migration is experienced by both migrants and their nuclear and extended families, without overlooking the effect of the receiving communities on returnees. Additionally, a consideration of life course uncovers how return migration as well as associated mobilities can be propelled by different drivers and can have different consequences for people according to the stage in the life cycle. The evidence provided by different chapters on both the first and the second generation of migrants adds to these dimensions.

After a critical analysis of the existing literature on migration, mental health and psychosocial wellbeing, this chapter continues with an analysis of the innovative aspects of this book, taking in turn the themes of context, volition, post-return mobilities and enabling citizenships, and the intersections of age and gender.

Migration and psychosocial wellbeing

Issues of psychosocial wellbeing are often overlooked in research on migration. In most studies, the main foci are the 'drivers' of migration itself, or, post-migration, attention is focused on structural issues of integration, or the more cultural and political issues of identity. Research trends such as these reflect agendas of policy-making on migration in receiving countries, primarily concerned with migrants' economic viability and their impact on the welfare system, or their challenge to national identity. The policies of sending countries focus primarily on the benefits of migration for the country's economy and on advocacy on migrants' rights abroad, but not much, if anything at all, is said about their psychosocial wellbeing. However, a twin-track new trend is evident, first, with the incorporation of notions of general (and psychosocial) wellbeing into migration research (IOM 2013; Wright 2012), and second, with the 'emotionalities turn' in migration (Boccagni and Baldassar 2015; Gray 2008; Svašek 2010, 2012). But it is important to recognise the multifaceted nature of human wellbeing, comprising both the material and relational, and the objective and subjective, dimensions, as well as the essential complementarity between the economic-material on the one hand, and the subjective-emotional sphere on the other. In the words of Boccagni and Baldassar (2015: 73), 'far from being the opposite of the instrumental (i.e. economically-driven) dimension of migrant life, the emotional dimension is its inescapable complement ...'

Nonetheless, research on the link between migration and psychosocial wellbeing maintains that different stages of migration – pre-migration, initial state of migration and post-migration – entail different mental health outcomes for migrants. Other classifications distinguish between forced and voluntary migration – a division based on the pull and push factors that give rise to migration, but one that needs to be problematised, as we do later. Important demographics, such as ethnicity, gender and age, also matter. Adolescents, females and 'visible minorities' are found more at risk of developing psychosocial problems because of migration. Less prominent in the literature have been the effects of geographical distance and of time, mostly referred to as 'the period of adjustment' (Bhugra 2004), while there is hardly any mention of return migration.

It is, therefore, not a coincidence that the process of acculturation in the host society and the effects of discrimination in the post-migration stage have received the predominant attention. In this vein, research on migration and psychosocial wellbeing has mostly looked at the experience of the second generation and the effect of ethnicity, and mainly from a quantitative perspective (Stevens and Vollebergh 2008). However, existing research has paid little attention to 'confounding' variables and contextual differences. Indeed, a great deal of research has focused on pre-defined aspects of wellbeing, and not much is said about the causal relationships between different health and wellbeing aspects affected by migration (but see Karlsen and Nazroo 2002; Mirdal 2006; Wright 2012). Another bias of literature is the focus on the Global North.

With all their faults, studies of the effect of migration on psychosocial wellbeing and mental health reflect a general pattern that has for a long time characterised migration studies: migration seen as a one-way journey. The exclusion of return migration may have to do with the fact that this aspect of migration only came to the full attention of researchers in the 1970s and is often romanticised (Gmelch 1980). The limited literature on the psychosocial issues returnees face is dominated by research with 'forced' migrants. In these cases, a reverse culture shock takes place, due to a mismatch between (return) migrants' expectations and the actual experiences faced upon return, coupled with the effects of war and trauma. Discrimination by co-nationals upon return is not uncommon either; such was the case of Bosnian refugees returning after the war (Black and Gent 2004; Davids and Van Houte 2008; Stefansson 2004). Similar themes are reported by 'voluntary' returnees; among the first generation, rejection by co-nationals and a feeling of failure are common, whereas second-generation returnees often experience exclusion and even stigmatisation (Potter and Phillips 2008; Tsuda 2004; Vathi and Duci 2016).

Wellbeing is a complex concept; the literature gives a variety of definitions and, at the same time, notes the difficulty of adequately capturing its meaning (Dodge *et al.* 2012). Gough and McGregor (2007) maintain that human wellbeing refers to a relational state of being with others that enables the pursuance of one's goals and ultimately the achievement of an enhanced quality of life. As a more narrowly defined, and yet more complex, concept, psychosocial wellbeing (as opposed to clinical mental health) is deemed more suitable in the context of migration, being more considerate of the emotional, social and cultural aspects of migration (Wessells 1999). In the context of return, psychosocial wellbeing allows an exploration of the experience of 'going home' by addressing the multiscalar and temporal aspects of return that may affect wellbeing. As such, human wellbeing refers to a *state*, whereas psychosocial wellbeing refers more to a *process*. Paying close attention to the interlinkages between psychological and social experiences, psychosocial wellbeing is a person-centred concept that emphasises the value of interactions and social and emotional consonance, and the individual experience.

Nonetheless, a conflation of *factors* that affect wellbeing with *outcomes* for wellbeing is evident in the literature, while evidence in this book shows that there can be a two-way or circular relationship between the two. This interactional nature of wellbeing is addressed in various chapters, which look at the physical, health, socio-cultural and economic factors that affect and are affected by wellbeing in different contexts and at various scales. The definition of psychosocial wellbeing in this book, therefore, encompasses both the subjective and the objective aspects of wellbeing (Wright 2012), but the general stance is that these two aspects interact, contingent on context, making wellbeing a highly cultural and situational experience.

In line with Wright (2012: 469), focusing on wellbeing allows us to broaden our focus to the social narratives that permeate migration processes through a study of how human wellbeing is constructed in different settings and how it 'travels'. And yet another dimension overlooked is the *transnational* dimension of the return process. The 'simultaneity' of migrants' lives – their ongoing ties with the receiving society and the country of origin (Levitt and Glick Schiller 2004) – does not end as a result of the return process; how the maintenance or disruption of these ties affects psychosocial wellbeing has not been part of research on return and wellbeing. By looking at contextual factors in different time lags of the return process, this book extends the structural approach (Cerase 1974) to all stages of the return process.

As well as simultaneity, another important concept that is left unexplored by the return migration literature is relationality, both to people and to place. Return migrants are deeply affected by relationality, and crucially, their wellbeing is often seen as a function of significant others, with the concept of linked lives (Elder 1994) being an important dimension of their migration and return decision-making. Therefore, the interface between return and psychosocial wellbeing cannot be discussed separately from home, belonging and home-making. Belonging is widely understood as the sense of feeling at home through a degree of attachment to place over time (Huot et al. 2014). As well as these feelings being made or remade by the return experience, place is important in building and maintaining such notions among migrants.

Yet, return is referred to as 'homecoming', which in itself rests on the presumption that home is in the country of birth and origin. Paradoxically, home in the context of migration is associated with fixity, despite theoretical developments on transnationality and mobility. The fixity notion is stronger in the context of return migration, first, because of a rarely questioned assumption about the country of origin as the ultimate home (Malkki 1995), and second, because of broader governmental and institutional agendas on the desired sustainability of return (Black and Gent 2004). These assumptions are especially problematic in the case of the children of migrants, who may never have lived in the parents' country of origin. The few studies that exist on this topic see the migration of children to their parents' country of origin as 'returning home' and, as such, as psychologically 'safe' (e.g. Koliatis et al. 2003), whereas the reality may be quite different.

In the context of return, the issue of psychosocial wellbeing, even though pertinent to social protection and overall social policy and welfare systems, has not been treated as a priority by either the receiving or the sending states. Indeed, combining migration with wellbeing exposes the human rights deficit of migration systems and discourses (Gough and McGregor 2007). Especially in the case of irregular migrants (Drotbohm and Hasselberg 2015) – in terms of both their migration into and their expulsion or deportation from the territories of receiving countries – the disregard of states towards migrants' wellbeing shows how sovereignty, security and national identity in the case of receiving states, and acute issues of economic deficit and unemployment in the case of countries of origin, take priority over human rights.

Contextualising return migration and psychosocial wellbeing

In a bid to do justice to the role of context, this book puts return migration in a space-time frame. Consideration is given to the different scales of analysis, as well as to the temporal dimensions of return, aiming for a historical-spatial analysis of return processes. Holistic studies consider migrants' life histories, aiming to capture life in the country of origin, migration history in the receiving country and the complex experiences of return. Multi-sited and transnational designs are among the most innovative aspects of research presented in this book (e.g. chapters by Cela; Erdal and Oeppen; Hall *et al.*; Lulle; Majidi). Furthermore, different stages of the return process are researched: state of deportability and pending return (DeBono), decision-making, logistics and split returns (Majidi), programmes of return and repatriation and the experience of migrants who engage with these programmes (Bendixsen and Lidén; Kalir), voluntary and ancestral returns (Erdal and Oeppen; Gońda), return of refugees and internally displaced persons (IDPs) (Majidi; Porobić), return of economic migrants at a late stage in life (Cela; Hall *et al.*; Sampaio), back-and-forth mobilities and youth (Lulle), outcomes of return and post-return adaptation (Erdal and Oeppen; Lietaert *et al.*), and post-return mobilities and re-migration (Erdal and Oeppen; Lulle; Sardinha and Cairns).

Return migration and migrants' psychosocial wellbeing are contingent on contextual configurations; return may impact wellbeing, often by harming it, especially in the short term, or by enhancing it, particularly if migrants manage to re-establish a social life and access networks and support upon return. These generalised 'outcomes' of return appear to apply to different categories of migrants analysed, such as labour migrants (Erdal and Oeppen; Kalir), refugees (Majidi; Porobić), irregular migrants (DeBono), second-generation returnees (Sardinha and Cairns), women returnees (Majidi), students (Gońda), children and youth (Lulle; Majidi), split returns and children and partners left behind (Majidi), and elderly migrants (Cela; Hall *et al.*; Sampaio). Psychosocial wellbeing is seen in a continuum and as a developing non-linear experience for migrants (Lietaert *et al.*), conditioned by circumstantial factors, as well as structural ones (Hall *et al.*). Psychosocial wellbeing is also linked to other aspects of health and wellbeing; for example, Hall *et al.* look at health and psychosocial wellbeing of elderly migrants/returnees in the context of intra-EU differences and personal circumstances, while Cela extends this to other European contexts (Albania). Porobić looks at psychosocial wellbeing as an important aspect in a broader approach to mental health. In the context of young people's involuntary mobilities, Lulle discusses the psychosomatic issues that Latvian youth experienced in the course of their out-migration, return to Latvia and re-migration.

According to the evidence presented in several chapters, institutional barriers and the low quality of services negatively affect returnees' psychosocial wellbeing. DeBono looks at the impact of asylum-seeking regimes and the precarious living conditions of rejected asylum-seekers on their wellbeing. Little research has been conducted so far on migrants' accessibility to and the availability of mental health provisions in general, or their interaction with institutions. Porobić offers insights into the role of services in the particular context of return of refugees to Bosnia and Herzegovina (BiH): first, this is analysed taking into account the nature of migration and return; second, BiH, like other Balkan countries, has a weak social protection system, which complicates the process of adaptation.

Furthermore, adaptation upon return links to environment and space – be it because of memory and pre-migration experiences, or due to the aesthetic and environmental qualities of space and changes in spatial configurations that affect returnees' coping and resilience. In Sampaio's chapter, the beauty of the Azores eases the adaptation process upon return and perceptions of wellbeing, while young students moving to their ancestral 'homeland' of Poland experience the post-communist grey city spaces as emotionally degrading (Gońda). In the context of post-refugee return and adaptation, Porobić exemplifies how memory and sensory experiences with space are intertwined in the readjustment experiences of Bosnian refugees. The spatial divisions that aimed to 'rehabilitate' the ethnic conflict appear to act as reminders of war's legacy and hostility. And yet again, DeBono's chapter shows how dimensions of space and confinement define the looming prospect of undesirable return for rejected asylum-seekers in Sweden. Cela gives an extra spin to this discussion, maintaining that *place* determines wellbeing, as many forms of capital (economic, social) and other assets (such as social benefits, environment, climate and other natural amenities) are place specific, while others may be transnationally located (e.g. social capital).

An important aspect of contextual analysis is the observation of many chapters that the return context is not necessarily the same as the one the migrants left behind. There is a strong tendency among policy-makers to view return as a return to the situation before migration. Yet, psychosocial wellbeing is very much contingent on the subjective evaluation of experiences upon return and the overall migration (and return) project. It also, very importantly, depends on the attitudes towards returnees and overall wellbeing among the extended family and local community (Majidi; Sampaio). In some contexts, such as Bosnia, emigration is prioritised as the most rational life-improving strategy by local people who have not (yet) emigrated, so that returnees face scepticism or even ridicule from the local community (Porobić). In other return contexts, the intersections of societal conceptions of migration with political, security and economic realities give rise to different outcomes for individuals and families, as well as further mobility to better their personal situation (Erdal and Oeppen).

Post-return adaptation consists of a variety of experiences. Very rightly, Porobić distinguishes between the role of programmes of return and migrants' own agency in the process of home-making and adaptation. Erdal and Oeppen reason along similar lines, arguing that agency, coupled with the effects of the context of return, has a major influence on the way adaptation pans out. Another broad division that appears is the difference between return to a developing and to a developed 'homeland'. In both cases, return migration can pose various psychosocial challenges to returnees. While preparedness before return appears to play a role in adjustment (Cassarino 2008), the context of post-return and the evolving sense of belongingness play an important role in the process of readjustment (Erdal and Oeppen; Lulle; Sampaio). In the case of return to developing countries, however, the initial period is characterised by significant adjustment stress and even trauma (Erdal and Oeppen; Majidi).

In various case studies, the link between return migration and psychosocial wellbeing emerges as a two-way relationship: return affects migrants' wellbeing, but often concerns over wellbeing or the incidence of mental health issues are among the reasons for return. Kalir found that many users of assisted voluntary return (AVR) in Spain were already experiencing psychosocial problems, which made return the last resort. Lulle explains how the return of Latvian young people to the country of origin is driven by issues of health and wellbeing emerging in the course of settlement in the country to which their parents have migrated. Majidi also emphasises issues of wellbeing as a driver for return migration: Somalian female refugees embrace the return decision of their partners in order to escape the stress and anxiety they experience in the refugee camps in Kenya. Bendixsen and Lidén encountered cases of returnees from Norway who were part of AVR constrained by the psychological problems of family members, exacerbated by irregular migrant status. Health problems experienced by migrants or their partners and other family members affect not only the decision to return (DeBono), but also the evaluation of their post-return experiences (Lietaert *et al.*).

Reassessing volition in the context of return

While volition in the context of migration and the dichotomy between 'voluntary' and 'forced' migration have been critically examined (Van Hear 1998), hardly any consideration has been given to the different psychosocial outcomes of this dichotomy for returnees (Blitz *et al.* 2005). Referring to the traditional dichotomy that qualifies forced versus voluntary migrations based on the use (or not) of state power and coercion towards migrants, different types of returnees have been discussed in this book, ranging from irregular migrants or rejected asylum-seekers (DeBono) to refugees, voluntary migrants and circular migrants (Cela; Sardinha and Cairns), and AVR (Bendixsen and Lidén; Kalir). Psychosocial wellbeing is impacted by the policies and practices of migration, such as detention and deportation (De Bono), and by actors such as states (Bendixsen and Lidén), organisations and practitioners (Kalir). In particular, De Bono examines the (lack of) human rights in the legal provisions and the regulation of return migration and deportation from Sweden, and the significant bearing this has on rejected asylum-seekers.

The pressure to demonstrate the success of return programmes following military intervention is particularly strong, but the growing incidence of voluntary repatriation and the growing trend of removing unsuccessful asylum-seekers from Western countries have effectively narrowed the distinction between voluntary and forced returns (Blitz *et al.* 2005). However, in the existing literature, the question of volition has been primarily discussed in terms of state policies – an approach that reinforces the importance of the nation-state's sovereignty in the context of migration. In relation to forced migrants, wellbeing is part of the humanitarian discourse, which presents AVR as the safe and dignified way of managing return migration. In the case of 'voluntary' economic return migrants, AVR is presented as a 'return to sunshine' (Kalir). And yet, there is so much more to say about the 'blurry middle' – migrants who are neither repatriated nor accommodated through so-called 'voluntary' return programmes, but who take the trip to the country of origin for various reasons that link to their migration project and their personal and familial circumstances (Erdal and Oeppen). Volition itself is subject to empirical scrutiny in most chapters, and evidence shows that forced returns took place also because of power imbalances due to age, political agency and gender (Erdal and Oeppen; Lulle).

Therefore, volition is seen as a continuum. Porobić's chapter is purposefully focused on those Bosnian refugees who naturalised in the receiving countries and returned 'voluntarily' to Bosnia because of nostalgia. Lietaert *et al.* emphasise a diversity of grades of 'voluntariness' among returnees, and reject the clear-cut dichotomy that has characterised studies of return, returnees' vulnerability and policies that concern their wellbeing. Kalir problematises the very notion of voluntarism itself and its application to AVR programmes in Europe. The irony behind this term is stronger when we consider the situation of failed asylum-seekers (DeBono) who go 'underground' in desperate attempts to escape return and the so-called assisted 'voluntary' schemes, even though overstaying causes serious psychosocial issues. While some migrants resort to these schemes to fulfil the preparatory phase of return, which facilitates the arrival and settlement in the country of origin (Cassarino 2008), a good number of 'service users' oscillate between desperation, limbo, and yet another tried and failed life in the homeland. Kalir discusses this in the context of neoliberalism and the immigration policies of Western European nations, which assume little responsibility for vulnerable migrants who cannot contribute to their host-country economies.

Indeed, policies of return and reintegration often seem to overlook what happens after return. In this vein, Bendixsen and Lidén analyse the contrast and contradictions between the Norwegian government's policy and discourse on assisted return, and migrants' experiences. They explain how managerial rationality trumps the actual consideration of complex real-life issues, such as that of psychosocial wellbeing in the context of state-managed returns. Porobić links return policies with the urban and rural planning strategies of the areas where returnees settle, which appear to overlook the importance of developing their livelihoods in the long run in order to ensure sustainability of return. Research is showing, furthermore, that even though there are various programmes on AVR, the data collected by governments on returnees do not include wellbeing. Indeed, asylum systems often exert extreme pressure on asylum-seekers, who react by developing psychological and mental health issues. Failed asylumseekers in Sweden live in extreme precarity and gamble with their mental wellbeing as they refuse to return to their countries of origin in the hope of regularisation one day (DeBono). Post-return assistance is seen as 'going somewhere to solve a problem', and often the focus of developed countries is on preventing re-migration of returnees (Bendixsen and Lidén).

In turn, in the African context, the notions of vulnerability and protection are over-emphasised in the process of return of women refugees and their children from Kenya to Somalia (Majidi). And here lies an important assumption held strongly among policy-makers and a chunk of academia – that vulnerability and psychosocial issues are a predominant issue among 'forced' migrants whose categorisation involves those who were subjected to state-related violence. Other forms of violence (intimate, cultural) are ineligible for justifying the vulnerability of migrants.

Crucial to the discussion of volition is the decision-making process; here, power, agency and capital interrelate to determine not only the dimensions of return, but also the psychosocial outcomes for migrants. Return decision-making is an important aspect of the theorisation of return migration (Cassarino 2004). In this volume, chapters unpack the decision-making process, starting with the drivers or motivators of return. Lulle establishes links between imaginative return as a driver of psychosocial wellbeing for young people of Latvian origin. One shortcoming of existing literature on return is that decision-making is seen primarily in economic terms, for instance, the accumulation of economic capital or the existence of established networks. Research in this book shows that decision-making is highly contextual and contingent upon different factors, often fairly intimate ones operating at a micro level (e.g. Cela). Porobić discusses how the 'unit' of decision-making for the return to BiH is rarely the individual. Rather, the household (headed by men) and often the wider kin networks play a decisive role in these decisions. Meanwhile, return itself can be 'voluntarily forced' in some cases (Kalir), while evidence also shows that long-desired and well-prepared return can still result in psychosocial issues for the returnees. So does re-migration, or 'twice returns'; some returnees see re-migration as a route out of severe dissatisfaction and psychosocial issues upon return (Cela; Lulle; Sardinha and Cairns); others are apprehensive about re-migration due to bitter and unsuccessful experience with paperwork and failure to gain permanent settlement in their previous attempts (Lietaert *et al.*).

Evidence across various chapters, furthermore, shows that decision-making itself is directly linked to wellbeing. First, making decisions on return imposes significant stress upon migrants, with major life dilemmas permeating the discussions and emotionalities of return (DeBono; Hall *et al.*). Second, when return outcomes are unsatisfactory, decision-making leads to guilt, shame and a sense of failure (Erdal and Oeppen; Sampaio). However, in the context of AVR and deportation, the emotional and social disenfranchisement of migrants as decision-makers for their own lives appears to lie right at the centre of their trauma and psychosocial distress (see DeBono; Erdal and Oeppen). States and immigration policies remove political and personal agency from migrants, disabling them from their body-space autonomy. Choice and force in these cases, therefore, are linked to the dislocation of human agency from the migrant bodies; since migrants are characterised by strong drive and agency, this dislocation is a humiliation of the human right of being, belonging and residence.

Post-return mobilities and enabling citizenships

An important contribution this book makes is the exploration of various forms of mobilities of return, as well as the constraints on being mobile that returnees face before, during and after relocating to their country of origin. Indeed, mobilities appear not only as crucial to the actual realisation of the return process, but as directly affecting the psychosocial outcomes of return. One of the main tenets is the finding that access to and experience with mobilities post return are key to the psychosocial wellbeing of returnees (Erdal and Oeppen), making the country of origin rather like an 'optional home'. Porobić, for example, found that ongoing transnational mobilities are a coping strategy of households aiming to achieve satisfactory life conditions post return.

Mobility possibilities and practices, however, may often be correlated with stress and anxiety, as figuring out the logistics takes its toll on migrants and their families, and the struggle of adjustment post return is a common experience across the board. There is, therefore, a difference between *mobility as an option* and *mobility as actual practice*, and each has a different psychosocial impact on the returnees. While the option exists, prospects for mobility generally enhance the psychosocial wellbeing of the returnees. But on the other hand, the anticipation and logistics of mobility appear to heighten stress and negatively affect psychosocial wellbeing. Although they are individuals who enjoy freedom of movement (unlike other returnees in this volume), the inclination and desire to be mobile is not stress-free for the Portuguese second-generation returnees researched by Sardinha and Cairns. Therefore, while mobility has been celebrated for the resources on which it is based and which it further enhances, little is said about the emotional and psychosocial costs that mobile individuals experience.

Unilinear models see migration as a one-way journey towards another country. Literature on return migration may take a similar approach, seeing return as the end of the migratory journey and putting a strong emphasis on the sustainability of return. In this book, returning to the country of origin is presented as just one stage of often complex migratory trajectories. Sampaio points to the apprehension of elderly returnees to the Azores when considering re-migration, whereas Majidi explores this in the context of forced migration and voluntary returns of Somalian refugees in Kenya. For many of them, return is not permanent, and there are various mobilities linked to the temporary returns, not least because of split families and children left behind during the course of return to Somalia.

Crucial to the decision and the overall experience of return and its intersection with psychosocial wellbeing is the *citizenship* of returnees. Returnees who hold 'enabling citizenships' of developed nations, which allow further mobility if needed, are less likely to experience trauma and negative psychosocial outcomes upon return (Sardinha and Cairns). Return is experienced as open-ended for those who hold 'enabling citizenships' (cf. Porobić on Bosnians returning from various North-western European countries), and options are perceived as open for those who move within the EU (Hall *et al.*; Lulle; Sardinha and Cairns), or for those who have acquired the citizenship of the country where they resided for many years (e.g. Norway; Oeppen and Bivand). Enabling citizenships are, therefore, positively correlated with wellbeing during and post return; the opposite may happen when returnees hold 'disabling citizenships' (see Vathi and Duci 2016 on Albanian-origin children relocating to Albania from Greece).

The dimension of transnationality and how it affects wellbeing in the context of return mobilities opens up a new and unexplored avenue of research. Strategies of home-making upon return vary across geographical settings and circumstances of return at an individual and family level. In the context of BiH, Porobić talks about open-ended returns and practices of straddling, which consist of transgenerational and transnational home-making in different countries in order to optimise the outcomes of migration. For migrants in later life, Cela shows that the transnational lifestyle has an important positive impact on both the emotional and physical wellbeing of the so-called 'zero generation' (i.e. the parents of the first-generation Albanian migrants), whose 'home' is located in the transnational space of Italy–Albania due to their mobile lives.

For asylum-seekers and those who go through detention, prospective and actual return impact significantly on their spatial mobility. Those living in a state of deportability are confined and suffer severe limits on their daily movements and inter-country mobilities (DeBono). For those migrants who move back to their country of origin, however, return restores their spatial mobilities. In different chapters, the voices of adult migrants and those of their partners and children are vivid in explaining how they were happy to have left confinement behind and went on to restore their social identities as parents or as relatives when they returned. Children were able to play and spend time with relations. Lietaert *et al.* show the longer-term aspects of the evolving feelings and perceptions of wellbeing post return, and the links of wellbeing to internal and international mobility. Therefore, support is needed for a long time for migrants upon return, and wellbeing is not simply commensurate to a sum of money awarded before or immediately after return. Positive outcomes for those returning voluntarily and holding citizenship of a receiving developed country also relate to the more community- and family-focused lifestyle in their countries of origin, as opposed to the frenetic pace of life in the North-western countries where they had migrated (Porobić).

Age, gender and intersectionalities

The return process, the associated mobilities and their outcomes in terms of psychosocial wellbeing are all likely to be significantly impacted by gender, age and their intersections. Particularly in the Global South, female returnees are found not to enjoy unlimited access to mobilities. In the context of assisted returns in Kenya, Majidi highlights how the process of migration – be it to the receiving country, or towards the country of origin – alters the family experience of women and children by posing challenges of adaptation that often result in stress and other negative psychological symptoms. Other authors show how return can be less welcomed by men (Hall *et al.*) or by women (Sampaio), and this difference in attitudes towards return puts strain on couples and families.

Gender becomes particularly relevant due to the cultural backgrounds of migrants, and through transnational relations with extended family in the country of origin. Erdal and Oeppen show how ethnic-minority-origin women living in the Global North face a forced return to their countries of origin in order to fulfil traditional expectations as carers of elderly family members there. Porobić points to the role of gender in the employment of both intra-national and transnational mobilities as coping strategies by returned refugees. Similarly, Bendixsen and Lidén found that preparedness and AVR were correlated with different psychosocial outcomes for migrant men and women in Norway; however, gender was not a matter of concern in the context of non-governmental organisations' involvement in the AVR process in Spain (Kalir). Thus, although most of the return migration literature is gender blind, gender matters in the context of return, though certain situations make gender irrelevant (e.g. state of deportability; DeBono). In the absence of differential power and the lack of significant cultural differences, such as intra-EU migrations or movements between different developed countries, gender appears to play a smaller role in the return process, and its impact on psychosocial wellbeing is less evident (e.g. Sardinha and Cairns).

Much stronger is the role of life course. Life-course theory maintains that transitions and life events are worth investigating, since they significantly shape the form and meaning of an individual's life (Kulu and Milewski 2007); therefore, return may be propelled by different events in a migrant's life trajectory. Transitions to adulthood were seen as occasions to make the return to Latvia by teenagers who had reluctantly moved to Western Europe with their parents (Lulle), whereas elderly migrants from the Azores decided to move back from North America once they retired (Sampaio). Health issues in later life were the main return drivers for British older expats in Spain (Hall *et al.*).

Of particular importance is the study of the return experience of those at the extremes of age, since the migration literature, including that on return, has mostly focused on those in the active economic age band. In this book, age-specific mobilities also refer to the differential access to and experience of mobility of children and youth, and the elderly. Lulle shows how the adolescent children of Latvian migrants face forced mobilities when moving abroad with their parents, and voluntary, yet ambivalent, mobilities when they choose to return to Latvia in adulthood. Cela takes a generational perspective in demonstrating that age and generation matter to the way migrants are motivated to return and experience their life in their country of origin. And even in the case of enabling citizenships and intra-EU return/migration, structural differences between EU member states, and, more specifically, different health and care provisions for those in the later stage of life, impact on the 'outcomes' of return for many British older people returning from Spain (Hall *et al.*).

There are, however, different experiences in the 'ageing segment of life', with return experiences varying between those still economically active and the elderly returning post retirement (Cela; Sampaio), making the nexus of ageing–return a dynamic one. Among ageing migrants, psychosocial wellbeing is often perceived in the context of being able to offer intergenerational care to their grandchildren, while their co-habitation with their migrant children enables the latter to offer care towards their ageing parents, showing that a two-way concern over health and wellbeing underlies such migrations (Cela). Age is therefore an important theoretical term in understanding migration and return, as well as an important notion around which policies on the wellbeing of returnees ought to be framed.

Especially in the case of child migration, the focus on the family has obscured the actual experience of children. But even though the family and relationality are aspects that affect migrants' wellbeing, very little research has considered their effects on return migration. Majidi considers the effects of nuclear and extended family in shaping the return process and the post-return experiences of women and children refugees relocating to Somalia. Psychosocial issues experienced by migrants and/or their families across borders, according to her, affect and are affected by their preparedness (Cassarino 2008), and thereby determine the 'outcomes' of return migration for women and children. Cela maintains that the principle of linked lives (Elder 1994) is highly contextual and of particular relevance for migrants who come from countries characterised by a strong collective culture based on family and kin ties, such as Albania.

However, relationality is marked by power imbalances and cultural differences in the conception and experience of age and gender. Majidi explains the centrality of women in the process of return: while women are not key decision-makers, they play the most important role in organising return in terms of logistics, as well as in the overall functioning of family and kin geographies during and after return. Return migration, therefore, appears as a sophisticated process in which gender and age hierarchies and power positionalities materialise to determine the process of return in its dimensions: timing, logistics, location of settlement upon return, re-migration. These innovative findings on return migration have implications for migration theory, which King elaborates on in the final chapter.

Conclusions

The links between return migration and psychosocial wellbeing are not straightforward. While research and policy increasingly dismiss the classic linear migration models that present migration as a one-way journey (Cassarino 2008), neither does a two-way understanding of migration do justice to the complexities of international mobility. Return scenarios in this book are multidimensional: some focus on migrants in the host countries who plan to return, others look at return migrants in the country of origin. A number of chapters are multi-sited and look at both the host and 'home' country, including migrants who plan to or actually do re-migrate. Various factors determine the outcomes along a positive–negative continuum, while gender, age and generation make for a nuanced story of return. The policies that encourage or enforce return migration (especially for refugees and irregular immigrants) significantly affect psychosocial wellbeing – both the policies per se as well as their (lack of) consideration of migrants' wellbeing.

The success of the 'return migration project' – be it of an emotional or an economic nature – or the opportunity to elaborate a successful outcome for those experiencing forced return has a significant impact on migrants' psychosocial wellbeing. Structural aspects certainly shape the process of return in this regard, and the transnationality of migrants' experience is an important dimension that informs their perceptions of return, and as a result, their psychosocial wellbeing. Nonetheless, there is a high degree of subjectivity that marks the experience of wellbeing. Subjectivity and the relational nature of migrants' lives appear to be almost completely overlooked in policy-making on return, and consist of an important division between migrants' positioning and policy-making in the field – in both the receiving country and the country of origin. Recent evidence shows that home countries do engage with return migrants, but the issue of psychosocial wellbeing is not top of their policy agendas; even when policies are in place, implementation is often very weak (Vathi *et al.* 2016).

However, the book does not aim to create the impression that all return migrations, at all times and across different locations, are characterised by psychosocial problems, or even poor mental health. By engaging with rich contextual analysis, the various contributions to this volume are successful in highlighting some of the conditions that lead to psychosocial issues, as well as positive outcomes of return. As such, the findings have important policy implications. Psychosocial issues and mental health problems require consideration in policies and committed and continuous investment in social protection systems and health services. Developed countries' policy-makers should stop seeing their interventions in the context of return as instruments to prevent re-migration, whereas those in migrants' countries of origin should be mindful of the impact that returning has on migrants and their families.

References

Barrett, A. and Mosca, I. (2013) Social isolation, loneliness and return migration: evidence from older Irish adults, *Journal of Ethnic and Migration Studies* 39(10): 1659–1677.

Bhugra, D. (2004) Migration and mental health, *Acta Psychiatrica Scandinavica* 109(4): 243–258.

Black, R. and Gent, S. (2004) Defining, measuring and influencing sustainable return: the case of the Balkans. Brighton: University of Sussex, Development Research Centre on Migration, Globalisation and Poverty, Migration Working Paper T7.

Blitz, B., Sales, R. and Marzano, L. (2005) Non-voluntary return? The politics of return to Afghanistan, *Political Studies* 53(1): 182–200.

Boccagni, P. and Baldassar, L. (2015) Emotions on the move: mapping the emergent field of emotion and migration, *Emotion, Space and Society* 16: 73–80.

Cassarino, J.-P. (2004) Theorising return migration: the conceptual approach to return migrants revisited, *International Journal on Multicultural Societies* 6(2): 253–279.

Cassarino, J.-P. (2008) Conditions of modern return migrants, *International Journal on Multicultural Societies* 10(2): 95–105.

Cerase, F.P. (1974) Expectations and reality: a case study of return migration from the United States to Southern Italy, *International Migration Review* 8(2): 245–262.

Christou, A. and King, R. (2014) *Counter-Diaspora: The Greek Second Generation Returns 'Home'*. Cambridge, MA: Harvard University Press.

Connell, J. (2009) Bittersweet home? Return migration and health work in Polynesia, in D. Conway and R.B. Potter (eds) *Return Migration of the Next Generations: 21st Century Transnational Mobility*. Farnham: Ashgate, 139–160.

Conway, D. and Potter, R.B. (eds) (2009) *Return Migration of the Next Generations: 21st Century Transnational Mobility*. Farnham: Ashgate.

Cresswell, T. (2006) *On the Move: Mobility in the Modern Western World*. New York: Routledge.

Davids, T. and van Houte, M. (2008) Remigration, development and mixed embeddedness: an agenda for qualitative research? *International Journal on Multicultural Societies* 10(2): 169–193.

Dodge, R., Daly, A., Huyton, J. and Sanders, L. (2012) The challenge of defining wellbeing, *International Journal of Wellbeing* 2(3): 222–235.

Drotbohm, H. and Hasselberg, I. (2015) Deportation, anxiety, justice: new ethnographic perspectives, *Journal of Ethnic and Migration Studies* 41(4): 551–562.

Elder, G.H. Jr (1994) Time, human agency, and social change: perspective on the life course, *Social Psychology Quarterly* 57(1): 4–15.

Gmelch, G. (1980) Return migration, *Annual Review of Anthropology* 9: 135–159.

Gough, I. and McGregor, J.A. (eds) (2007) *Wellbeing in Developing Countries*. Cambridge: Cambridge University Press.

Gray, B. (2008) Putting emotion and reflexivity to work in researching migration, *Sociology* 42(6): 935–952.

Harper, M. (ed.) (2005) *Emigrant Homecomings: The Return Movement of Emigrants, 1600–2000*. Manchester: Manchester University Press.

Huot, S., Dodson, B. and Rudman, D.L. (2014) Negotiating belonging following migration: exploring the relationship between place and identity in Francophone minority communities, *The Canadian Geographer* 58(3): 329–340.

IOM (2013) *World Migration Report 2013: Migrant Well-Being and Development*. Geneva: IOM.

Janzen, J. (2004) Illusions of home in the story of a Rwandan refugee's return, in L.D. Long and E. Oxfeld (eds) *Homecomings: Refugees, Migrants, and Those Who Stayed Behind*. Philadelphia: University of Pennsylvania Press, 19–33.

Karlsen, S. and Nazroo, J.Y. (2002) Agency and structure: the impact of ethnic identity and racism on the health of ethnic minority people, *Sociology of Health and Illness* 24(1): 1–20.

Koliatis, G., Tsiantis, J. and Madianos, M. (2003) Psychosocial adaptation of immigrant Greek children from the former Soviet Union, *European Child and Adolescent Psychiatry* 12(2): 67–74.

Kulu, H. and Milewski, N. (2007) Family change and migration in the life course: an introduction, *Demographic Research* 17(19): 567–590.

Levitt, P. and Glick Schiller, N. (2004) Conceptualizing simultaneity. A transnational social field perspective on society, *International Migration Review* 38(3): 1002–1039.

Long, L.D. and Oxfeld, E. (eds) (2004) *Coming Home? Refugees, Migrants, and Those Who Stayed Behind*. Philadelphia: University of Pennsylvania Press.

Malkki, L. (1995) Refugees and exile: from 'refugee studies' to the national order of things, *Annual Review of Anthropology* 24: 495–523.

Markowitz, F. and Stefansson, A.H. (eds) (2004) *Homecomings: Unsettling Paths of Return*. Lanham, MD: Lexington Books.

Mirdal, G. (2006) Stress and distress in migration: twenty years after, *International Migration Review* 40(2): 375–389.

Potter, R. and Phillips, J. (2008) 'Mad dogs and transnational migrants'? Bajan-Brit second-generation migrants and accusations of madness, *Annals of the Association of American Geographers* 96(3): 586–600.

Song, C. (2009) Brothers only in name: the alienation and identity formation of Korean Chinese return migrants in South Korea, in T. Tsuda (ed.) *Diasporic Homecomings: Ethnic Return Migration in Comparative Perspective*. Stanford, CA: Stanford University Press, 281–304.

Stefansson, A.H. (2004) Sarajevo suffering: homecoming and the hierarchy of homeland hardship, in F. Markowitz and A.H. Stefansson (eds) *Homecoming: Unsettling Paths of Return*. Lanham MD: Lexington Books, 54–75.

Stevens, G.W.J.M. and Vollebergh, W.A.M. (2008) Mental health in migrant children, *Journal of Child Psychology and Psychiatry* 49(3): 276–294.

Svašek, M. (2010) On the move: emotions and human mobility, *Journal of Ethnic and Migration Studies* 36(6): 865–880.

Svašek, M. (ed.) (2012) *Emotions and Human Mobility: Ethnographies of Movement*. London: Routledge.

Tsuda, T. (2004) When home is not the homeland: the case of Japanese Brazilian ethnic return migration, in F. Markowitz and A.H. Stefansson (eds) *Homecomings: Unsettling Paths of Return*. Lanham MD: Lexington Books, 125–145.

Tsuda, T. (ed.) (2009) *Diasporic Homecomings: Ethnic Return Migration in Comparative Perspective*. Stanford, CA: Stanford University Press.

Urry, J. (2000) *Sociology beyond Societies: Mobilities for the 21st Century*. London: Routledge.

Urry, J. (2007) *Mobilities*. Cambridge: Polity.

Van Hear, N. (1998) *New Diasporas. The Mass Exodus, Dispersal and Regrouping of Migrant Communities*. London: UCL Press.

Vathi, Z. and Duci, V. (2016) Making other dreams: the impact of migration on the psychosocial wellbeing of Albanian-origin children upon their families' return to Albania, *Childhood* 23(1): 53–68.

Vathi, Z., Duci, V. and Dhembo, E. (2016) Homeland (dis)integration: educational experience, children and return migration to Albania, *International Migration*, online 54(3): 159–172.

Wessells, M.G. (1999) Culture, power and community: intercultural approaches to psychosocial assistance and healing, in K. Nader, N. Dubrow and B. Stamm (eds) *Honouring Differences: Cultural Issues in the Treatment of Trauma and Loss*. New York: Taylor and Francis, 276–282.

Wright, K. (2012) Constructing human wellbeing across spatial boundaries: negotiating meanings in transnational migration, *Global Networks* 12(4): 467–484.

Part I

The forced–voluntary continuum in return migration

2 Return to wellbeing?

Irregular migrants and assisted return in Norway

Synnøve Bendixsen and Hilde Lidén

Introduction

After the end of the Cold War, asylum-seekers and irregular migrants became a target group for several state-initiated return programmes. The 1990s have been labelled the 'decade of repatriation': the United Nations High Commissioner for Refugees (UNHCR) at the time considered voluntary repatriation to be the best solution for refugee problems (Black and Koser 1999). Since the mid-2000s, various governments in the European Union have developed different return programmes; they continue to evaluate and restructure these programmes in order to cope with migration generally and irregular migration specifically. The second decade of this century will perhaps be labelled the 'decade of return' in the future.

This chapter discusses the contradictions between the way in which the Norwegian government frames its return policies and migrants' experiences of what return actually means to them. The research questions we ask are twofold. First, what does 'return' mean to different stakeholders? Second, to what extent do considerations of psychosocial wellbeing inform understandings of return from the perspectives of the Norwegian government on the one hand, and of the irregular migrants on the other? Examining return is crucial because there is an underlying presumption that migrants are 'going home' to continue their lives in familiar circumstances when they sign up to assisted return (AR). This starting-point of AR programmes naturalises belonging to a specific country or place. We argue that return has a completely different meaning for most migrants who sign up with AR from that of the government's discourse, which it uses in its return policies. By examining what 'return' means for different actors, and showing how return is related to different expectations of psychosocial wellbeing for migrants and their families, we will illuminate the divergent concerns and prospects of return programmes that the government and the migrants hold. While we argue that a migrant's decision to sign up with an AR programme must be understood in relation to whether (and how) the programme can improve their psychosocial wellbeing, our hypothesis is that the return policies and their implementation do not focus on wellbeing. Comparing migrants' perceptions of return with governmental perceptions will thus expose several important limitations of current AR programmes.

Within its public discussions of refugees, asylum-seekers and economic migrants, the Norwegian government emphasises return 1) to deter those who arrive without documentation, 2) to exercise its sovereignty and the fact that it is in control of the country's borders, and 3) as a measure for reducing the number of irregular migrants who live in its territory. Those who are returning, however, may experience the solution of AR quite differently. Our chapter thus speaks to the need for what Long and Oxfeld state to be an 'ethnography of return migration ... [that would pay] full attention to the diversity, complexity, and instability of return as human experience' (2004: 1–3).

We will first discuss the concepts of wellbeing and return; the second part of the chapter will analyse how the Norwegian government frames AR, as well as the assumptions that these return programmes are based on. The third part then examines return decisions in the case of migrants whose asylum applications have been rejected by the Norwegian authorities. Based on our interviews, we distinguish between three different subjective understandings of 'return': return as foreseeable, return as an uncertainty, and return as continued migration. In the fourth section, we discuss how migrants' understanding of return is tied in with various aspects of their wellbeing. Finally, we make a comparison between the government's framing of return and migrants' understanding of return. We argue that a gap exists between these two understandings of return; this gap has several consequences for the ways in which programmes often malfunction and the possibility of migrants' wellbeing.

Data, methods and concepts

This chapter is based on a research project that included interviews with several migrants who were living in Norway at the time. The data stem from the project 'Comparative Study of Assisted Return', which was a collaborative and comparative research project that studied the return of irregular migrants to Afghanistan, Kosovo, Ethiopia and Iraqi Kurdistan (Brekke 2016; Strand *et al.* 2016). The migrant groups were selected on the basis of the particular return programmes that Norway has set up with the respective governments of Afghanistan (IRRANI), Iraq (IRRINI) and Ethiopia (ARRA), as well as the closure of the equivalent programme with Kosovo (2013).[1] The migrant groups are also representative of the backgrounds of a large percentage of the irregular migrants in Norway.

For the Norwegian portion of the study, we interviewed 17 people who differed in terms of gender (11 men and 6 women), age (from 22 to 64 years of age), time spent in Norway (2 to 20 years) and their status as single people or migrants with families. We interviewed migrants from Afghanistan, Bangladesh, Ethiopia, Iran, Kazakhstan, Kosovo, the Philippines and Russia. In Norway, a majority of those who sign up for AR are former asylum-seekers whose applications for asylum have been rejected in the past. Many migrants live in Norway between two and five years before signing up for AR.

Of the migrants whom we interviewed, some were living in reception centres at the time of the interview, while others had left these centres to live with friends or family; still others had never before lived in a reception centre. All of the migrants had signed up with the International Organization for Migration (IOM) for assisted voluntary return – what the IOM refers to as 'Assisted Voluntary Return and Reintegration' (AVRR). Our data on the ways in which the Norwegian government defines and promotes return draw on 1) different types of documents (interviews in the media, regulations and various information sheets, including the handbook for conversations about return between staff and migrants in reception centres); 2) films that promote AR that are used in reception centres; and 3) interviews with staff of the IOM, the Norwegian Directorate of Immigration (UDI) and different reception centres (Brekke 2016).

Migrants and wellbeing

Various definitions have been proposed for what constitutes psychosocial wellbeing. Much research has focused on the factors associated with a *lack* of wellbeing. Ahearn (2000: 5) states that 'wellness' is 'affected by loss, separation, stress, and trauma (among other things) that are mediated by one's coping ability and social and emotional supports'. The meaning of wellbeing is contextual, situationally specific and subject to change. We approach the term from a subjective standpoint. We consider psychosocial wellbeing to be the individual migrant's subjective assessment of his or her condition and possibility for agency, as well as the social and emotional support he or she might receive in the particular context of being an irregular migrant in Norway. In this category – irregular migrants who have signed up with AR – we have found three particularly relevant factors, which we will discuss further in this chapter: restoring dignity, improving one's 'scope of action' and improving the possibility of fulfilling familial obligations. Because ideas of wellness change with migrants' experiences, psychosocial wellbeing must be understood as a *process*. In this chapter, psychosocial wellbeing is particularly relevant in order to understand the motivations and expectations of a person who enrols in an AR programme.

Migrants arrive in Norway with certain expectations, including that they will achieve asylum, establish a new life and create a different future for their children; they also migrate with the hope of improving their families' living situations through money remittances. During the asylum-application process, this ethos of hopefulness and optimism slowly disappears; some migrants realise that these expectations most likely will not be fulfilled during their time spent in Norway. This expectation gap has a strong influence on their feelings of psychosocial wellbeing – as Vathi and King (2013) also found in their study on asylum-seekers in the UK. Migrants whom we interviewed who had signed up with AR explained to us that their original reasons for migrating included seeking security, basic human rights, sufficient income for maintaining their families, and good health. They had left situations in which these basic components of wellbeing were unattainable, but they now found themselves living in 'irregular' situations in Norway. Because they lived as irregular migrants in Norway, they were unable to fulfil their (or their families') expectations for a better life. This created a strong sense of hopelessness among them; it is in such situations that migrants often prepare for return.

In order to explain how people experience post-return situations differently, several researchers have used the concept of 'preparedness', emphasising the intersection between various factors (both before and after return) as being important for new settlements (Cassarino 2004, 2008; van Meeteren *et al.* 2014). Preparedness includes both a willingness to return and the migrants' readiness to return; the latter refers to any tangible or intangible resources that the migrant can mobilise during the return process. According to van Meeteren *et al.* (2014), positive post-return experiences may be linked to various factors of willingness and readiness to return during the pre-return phase.

In this chapter, we expand on pre-return preparedness by examining the way in which migrants' perceptions of return and their preparedness must be situated in terms of their lack of wellbeing in their current living situations and their expected wellbeing upon their return.

Assisted return

In their book *Return: Nationalizing Transnational Mobility in Asia*, Biao *et al.* emphasise 'return primarily as a policy subject, as an idea, and as a strategic moment when the intersection between nation-states and transnational mobility is particularly visible' (2013: 3). They consider return not as a new type of migration, but as being 'essentially ambiguous' (2013: 3). Return migration is generally defined as 'the movement of emigrants back to their homelands to resettle' (Gmelch 1980: 136). AR assumes as its starting-point that the person does not fulfil the criteria for refugee status as set forth by the United Nations Refugee Convention of 1951. In some countries, for example, only asylum applicants who have been rejected in the past can apply for AR, whereas in others only migrants from specific countries can apply (European Migration Network 2011). Programmes also differ according to which country the migrants are returning to and at which stage in the process the migrants apply (i.e. before or after the rejection of asylum).

In 2002, the Norwegian government initiated a programme titled 'Financial Support Reintegration' for AR that covers the returnees' travel costs and cash for their reintegration. Today, the programme provides participants with financial support of various kinds, including a sum of money that is adjusted according to the participants' country of return, their family status and the period spent in Norway as an irregular migrant; in some cases the sum is adjusted to individual specificities related to vulnerability. A portion of the financial support is made available only on the condition that the migrant will establish a business in his or her country of return; the migrant must apply for the support via a particular system after he or she has returned. Since 2010, more than 7,000 people have returned to their countries of origin through enrolment in these programmes. The main groups include migrants from Iraq, followed by migrants from Russia, Kosovo, Afghanistan and Nepal (Brekke 2016).

A great deal of research has dealt with motivations for return and the sustainability of return for first- and second-generation migrants and irregular migrants (e.g. Black and Gent 2006; Black *et al.* 2004; Cassarino 2004; Fokkema 2011; Hunter 2010; Olesen 2002; Strand *et al.* 2011). Critical, informed research reports have increasingly addressed the difficulty of distinguishing between voluntariness and force when irregular migrants sign up with AR programmes.[2] Scholars have also focused on different post-return experiences (e.g. van Meeteren *et al.* 2014). Still, a gap in our knowledge remains as to what understandings of return are substantiated in government programmes, as well as the question of wellbeing as part of the current politics of return. Thus, it is important to ask: what role does wellbeing play in the government's legitimation of AR programmes and their implementations?

Promoting assisted return: the state actor

In general, according to the Norwegian government, return is viable because the person will *not* face 'being persecuted for reasons of race, religion, nationality, membership of a particular social group or political opinion' (quoting the widely used definition of refugee promoted by the 1951 UN Convention on Refugees). More specifically, we have found five main ways in which the Norwegian government frames return: return as part of the government's interstate policies, return as part of the government's migration policies, return as a humanitarian solution for irregular migrants, return as relocating a person to his or her 'natural' place of living, and return as the re-establishment of the migrant in his or her 'home country'. These frames set the premise and context of the programme, which, in turn, is meant to induce migrants to sign on with AR. And yet, as we will discuss later in this chapter, the frames do not intersect with migrants' own perceptions of their return.

First, a nation-state may create its return programmes as part of an effort to *reaffirm, reconstruct and strengthen its sovereignty*. Return programmes are part of the government's interstate policies and international relations agenda. This is obvious from the agreements that the Norwegian government has pursued with various foreign countries, including Afghanistan, Iraq and Ethiopia; in early 2012, for example, Norway finalised an agreement with the Ethiopian government that facilitated the return of 'irregularised' migrants to Ethiopia; more or less simultaneously, the Norwegian government also created a programme for voluntary return to Ethiopia.[3] Return programmes are part of interstate institutional coalescence; they are part of a nation-state's efforts to increase its control of the mobility of its people through economic incentives. One of the consequences of this system is that the central tension in international migration is no longer between migrants and receiving societies, or between sending and receiving states, but has become one between migrants and alliances of states (Biao *et al.* 2013). Indeed, as Lindquist argues, return has come to function as a form of migrant emplacement that rein-forces particular forms of sovereign power [...] More specifically, return is associated with state attempts to re-establish sovereignty in the face of increasing flows of undocumented migrants – or in some cases anxieties with such flows.

(2013: 125)

Second, we argue that the Norwegian government positions return as a *part of its migration policies*. Government documents, as well as documents from the immigration authorities, discuss 'the plight [of] irregular migrants to return' and state that 'fast return is an important tool [for reducing] the number of asylum applicants without [the] need for protection'.[4]

When explaining the money allowances included in the government's pro-gramme, which it presents as being generous, the government depicts AR as the more affordable option for the public, because it requires fewer resources for the physical movement of migrants compared with forced return (Bendixsen *et al.* 2014). In the media, as well as in discussions with researchers, representatives of the Home Office and the Norwegian government frequently argue that return is important in order for the asylum and migration policy to enjoy legitimacy and for the institution of asylum to be both respected and ongoing.

Third, the government presents AR as a *humanitarian solution*: a way for migrants to 'return with dignity' and as a way to make the future more predict-able for them. The humanitarian solution implied here is that AR is 'a more dignified form of return' when compared with forced return.[5] To the media (and via the government's websites), the government argues that AR pro-grammes provide irregular migrants with the possibility of starting afresh; the government also argues that the possibility of AR helps migrants to act on their own behalf. Although the government presents forced return as the only other viable option for this category of people, it links neither assisted nor forced return to any considerations of restoring the migrants' dignity (and hence well-being) in the country of return. While the notions of dignity and control of one's life were aspects that the migrants discussed when they spoke with us about return, the implications of these notions were quite different between the migrants and the government. We will return to this aspect shortly.

Fourth, the idea of 'return' has become *naturalised*. Malkki has discussed the way in which the homeland or country of origin is generally presented as the normal and even ideal habitat for any person: 'the place where one fits in, lives in peace, and has an unproblematic culture and identity' (1995: 509). The logic of the AR programmes follows from a naturalisation of 'home' and the 'nation-state' as a place of belonging. The government generally presents the return of refugees with the idea that one's nation-state of birth is a natural and neutral place where one belongs. This framing of return as 'going home' lends legitimacy to different governments' return policies (Biao *et al.* 2013). The return discourses that the Norwegian government and the public media project to different types of migrants partly echo one another and collectively naturalise return and home.

This naturalising effect on return must be seen in its historical context. Return, viewed as a natural condition, is enabled by the enactment of various international agreements and the participation of different non-governmental organisations (in Norway, these include IOM in particular), the public media, and business associations. These institutional arrangements that organise mobility (while not actively deterring it) reinforce the dialectics between the national and the transnational. Programmes such as AR are shaped and operationalised by governments' perception of the 'national order of things' (Malkki 1995), or within what Löfgren (1989) has called 'the international cultural grammar of nationhood'. Such argumentations, however, fail to discuss what return means for the migrant, whether or not the migrant still views his or her country of origin as home, and what exactly 'home' means for the migrant; such discussions, if they were held, would link return to questions of improving migrants' future wellbeing. We will discuss these issues in the next section.

Fifth, in terms of how return programmes frame mobility, their implementation follows a specific *politics of rationalities*. The implementation of the programmes and the authorities' expectations of how migrants should respond to these programmes both follow a certain logic – a logic that is tied to the idea of migrants' homelands, planning their next steps and making informed decisions (Bendixsen *et al.* 2014). Mobility, temporality and economic incentives thus become intertwined. The programme is related to a kind of cost–benefit thinking: the idea that people need to make specific, prepared plans for what they will do when they return (in terms of housing and work) in order to, as the government suggests, make 'assisted return and repatriation sustainable and contribute to a durable reestablishment in the home country' (Bendixsen *et al.* 2014).

In summary, return, according to the government, means the implementation of cooperative efforts to control the mobility of people at the nation-state level. As we have seen, 'return' thus means that a migrant should move back to his or her country of nationality, although in some cases the government encounters difficulties in determining which is the migrant's returning state – for example, this may happen when a nation-state denies that a person belongs to its territory.[6] It is important to ask, however, how migrants whose lives are substantially affected and changed by these programmes perceive and approach their impending return. What are the migrants' motivating factors, versus those that the government anticipates? To what extent does the government's approach to return intersect with the way in which the migrants who sign up with AR programmes think about their return?

Assisted return: migrants' perspectives

We are interested here in two main questions. How do migrants who have signed up for AR programmes in Norway view their return? And what role does psychosocial wellbeing have on their perceptions of return and on their motivation to sign up with AR programmes? We found heterogeneous understandings and responses among the migrants during the course of our interviews. These findings cast doubt on the Norwegian government's usage of the term 'return'. One of the most striking outcomes of our interviews was that while wellbeing is only marginally included in the ways in which the Norwegian government presents AR through the idea of 'dignity', the irregular migrants whom we interviewed linked their participation in AR programmes to their expectations of gaining more scope of action, improving their dignity and/or fulfilling family obligations – aspects that we define as a substantial part of their psychosocial wellbeing.

We will first suggest three different ways in which the migrants whom we interviewed understood return: return as foreseeable, return as an uncertainty, and return as continued migration or mobility. These categories are in various ways linked to the expectations of wellbeing that we found. We will then examine how a lack of wellbeing – or hope for improving their future wellbeing – is a motivating factor for signing on with AR programmes in Norway.

Return as foreseeable

The first category consists of respondents who talked about return in a positive manner. For these migrants, their return was close to the way in which the government expected them to go back: namely, to return to their country of origin and to make use of reintegration allowances to start a business or some other productive activity. These migrants were few in number in our study, but sufficient to just about constitute a category. These migrants' decision to return was a direct consequence of their experience that they had completed the tasks that they had set out to do (tasks that may have been modified over time) when they had originally left their country of origin. Their return was an expected part of their migration journey; they expected improved wellbeing mainly because their impending return meant reuniting with family members and was part of their fulfilment of family obligations.

All of these migrants had family waiting for them upon their return; they also felt that their return contexts would be safe ones. They had clear expectations that once they had returned, their living conditions would improve compared with when they had first left (due, above all, to the earnings they had made in Norway); overall, they expected their future social relations with their families to be positive, which would ease their reintegration into society upon their return. One migrant, whose wife and aged parents had remained in his country of origin, told us how he had left home as a child and had travelled through several countries before entering Europe. He planned to live with his aged parents and his wife. To him, the future was open:

> I had problems at home, so I left. I was 13 years old; things were difficult then. There was fighting, so I left for India, Pakistan, Iran, and Turkey. I worked, and then I continued. But after I had lived for several years in Greece, I experienced problems there. And in Norway my asylum application was rejected. My parents are now old, and my wife is having a difficult time, so I have decided to go home. What else can I do?

Another migrant whose wife lived in his country of origin expected that his home society would have changed during the 20 years he had been living in Norway; but, he stressed, his children were now adults and working. He had lived in Norway for a long time, collecting bottles for recycling. Now his task was completed; from his business he had financed his two children's college education at the best universities in their home country. Now he was getting old, and his wife had a job. He thought of potential projects he could initiate once he had returned, but did not yet know what form they would take.

The migrants in this category expected to experience wellbeing when they returned because they had at least achieved some of their migration goals (from the household perspective) by remitting income to their families. For these migrants, returning was an expected outcome of their migration journey, particularly if their families had remained in their return countries. The migrants whom we interviewed who fell into this category had also achieved what could be considered upward mobility by ensuring their children's education in their return countries, or they had obtained new skills in Norway due to their migration; for this reason, they viewed returning as a positive experience. The existence of strong and continued kinship networks in their places of origin encouraged the migrants' return as a long-term strategy, as long as they also perceived their destination to be relatively safe. They did not expect their return to be easy, however, and were still ambivalent about their decision to return. But because they were experiencing multiple and sometimes contradictory obligations towards their families, they all felt that their decision to return was their best option.

Return as an uncertainty

A second category, return as an uncertainty, consisted of those migrants who assessed their return with mixed feelings and whose expected outcomes of their wellbeing upon their return were uncertain. Among this category were migrants who had attempted to acquire an education or build up economic capital before returning, and/or hoped to settle permanently with the hope of a better life abroad. These migrants partly viewed return as the consequence of a failure to achieve their expectations of their migration journeys (cf. Cassarino 2004). One 22-year-old woman told us that she had come to Norway before the age of 18 and had sought to continue her schooling and education in order to become a medical doctor, but she had found that the doors to education (and thus to her future goals) were closed because she was living as an irregular migrant. She now planned to live with her relatives in her country of origin upon her return, while her parents and younger siblings would remain as irregular migrants in Norway. She believed her life would be more normal once she returned; she expected to be able to travel freely, pursue regular youth activities and continue her education. This stood in sharp contrast to her current life in the reception centre, where she experienced a lack of opportunities. For this young woman, her return would improve her wellbeing because it meant taking control of her own life, restoring hope for her future and improving her scope of action.

This category also included migrants whose migration process had been interrupted by life-changing events such as illness or a death in their families back home. One young man told us that his mother had died two years earlier, before he had been able to see her again. Thoughts about his deceased mother, and his life that had passed him by as an irregular migrant who was not allowed to work, had contributed to his decision to return. While he did not make this decision immediately following the death of his mother, her death changed his way of thinking in the longer term. His life in Norway seemed increasingly meaningless to him, and his return to later join his sister in a neighbouring country restored his hope of improving his scope of action; he anticipated working and later getting married with the help of his sister.

Migrants in this category were disappointed about what they viewed to be a lack of human rights in Norway. They expected that their economic situation upon their return would be difficult, and had only vague ideas about how they would manage. Yet, they presented their impending return as a way for them to restore their agency; they expected their families to be a social and economic resource upon their return. They viewed their return as a new starting-point that would transform their current difficult situations.

Return as continued migration

A third category, return as continued migration, consisted of migrants who did not talk about returning as going back to their country of origin but as a next step in their migration journey. Signing up with AR meant continued mobility; it was also a way to escape their position of social 'liminality': several irregular migrants felt that they were trapped in a phase of limbo, in the sense of not being able to move on with their lives. One way to do this would be to transform their social status as a bachelor to that of a married family man, which was their families' social expectation of them. Many of these migrants saw AR as their only viable option. One family whom we spoke with informed us that they would be returning to a place where the man had been threatened by the local mafia; moreover, their whole family in their return nation had rejected them. Nonetheless, the couple felt that returning, as a way to continue their migration to a new region and a new city, was their sole option. In a similar case where the family had rejected the migrants, the only option they saw was to migrate back to Europe. For these families, AR would mean mobility that was spurred on by a lack of any other opportunities; this is an example of how the Norwegian government (via the AR programmes) also produces continued migration.

Return for those in the first two categories described above might well lead to improved social relations, greater possibilities for self-improvement and experiences of happiness, even though they still expected to experience significant hardships in securing their living conditions in future. Like the migrants in the second category, the people in the third category had signed up for AR as a response to a loss of hope and dignity and a way to resume their lives. The difference, however, was that while people in the second category were returning with a vague idea of resettling in their places of origin, people in the third category had no such plans; for them, this seemed to be an impossibility due to various social, economic and/or security reasons. Yet, the way the programme is set up makes the migrants feel the need to frame it as a return to their home countries, even if they plan to continue on to a third country.

Drawing on these categories, in the next section we will discuss in more detail the various factors of wellbeing that the migrants said were motivating factors for signing up with the AR programmes. By so doing, we seek to further investigate what 'return' means for migrants who sign up with AR, and how it ultimately differs from the government's intentions for such programmes.

Expectation gaps and seeking new solutions

Living in Norway as an irregular migrant represents a general lack of wellbeing due to one's illegal status, which involves limited rights and access to healthcare, education and formal work; irregular migrants' housing situations are also difficult. Our interviewees linked their return to their own psychosocial wellbeing, because signing up with AR was a strategy to restore their dignity, gain the possibility of controlling their lives, and fulfil their family obligations, all of which we will discuss further below. This does not mean that they did not also experience continued uncertainty about what would unfold once they returned, or how (or whether) they would be able to achieve better lives for themselves.

Restoring hope and dignity

Hage (2003) stresses that the ability to have hope enables people to invest in their social reality, even when the odds are against their achieving their desires and fear is a constant factor. Similarly, Bourdieu (2000: 221) has argued that hope can be understood as an emotion that creates the possibility for 'people without a future' to act. In contrast, a loss of hope and unfulfilled expectations can make people lose their potential for taking action. Yet, for the migrants whom we interviewed, hope initiated a new range of actions that had not been imaginable to them before; they had considered such actions to be either impossible or undesirable.

Particularly for migrants in categories two (return as an uncertainty) and three (return as continued migration), the conditions they had experienced in Norway were the main incentives for them to sign up with AR. Their experiences that their dignity and human value had been lost and that they were marginalised in Norway made their living conditions hard to bear. As one man told us,

> I die a little bit every day I'm here in Norway; I cannot work, I cannot get healthcare if I need it, I cannot do anything; I'm not treated as a normal human being. What I'm thinking, I will go with IOM – I have to face what happens. I am not a coward. I am not scared to go back. But it is really hard.

By returning, this interviewee hoped that he would be able to restore at least some of his dignity and integrity. Seeing their future hopes and dreams (in particular for their children) slowly being dismantled, and having increased feelings of being stuck – physically, mentally and socially – also made migrants opt for AR.

The migrants for whom return was a continued migration expressed their loss of hope that things would get better. For these migrants, returning became a way of coping both with lost expectations and with the new expectations that had taken shape while they were in the state of asylum application.

Resuming life and scope of action

Their limited rights as irregular migrants in Norway enhanced the shame, marginalisation and precariousness that several migrants experienced due to their illegal status (Bendixsen 2015). As one woman told us,

> I have lived here without rights, without the right to work and have healthcare for four years. It is really hard to live like this for long: without living a decent life, without decency.

Fear of forced return added to this marginalised living condition: some worried that they would be picked up by the police. The migrants experienced an expectation gap between the way in which they expected to be treated as asylum-seekers and their personal experiences as asylum-seekers in the system. For several migrants, signing up for AR meant responding to the need to be able to continue with their lives. Single men, in particular, expressed the necessity of marrying and creating a family. For others, the unpredictability of everyday life as an irregular migrant in Norway was dragging them down; they sought to 'normalise' their lives by attaining legal residency *anywhere*. One person emphasised that it was important for him to obtain valid ID papers and to start life anew. For these people, return is less a matter of moving to another physical space and more a matter of possibly attaining a new social position that would be impossible to obtain in their current place of living.

Fulfilling their familial obligations

Some migrants' inability to fulfil their families' expectations to achieve residency permits, work or to send remittances to their families and relatives made return difficult (Schuster and Majidi 2013, 2015). Returning without having met these social and economic expectations can create a stigma upon their return; this contributes to the fact that their subjective wellbeing is denied. In contrast, for those who had fulfilled their familial obligations and anticipations – and thus had contributed to improving their families' wellbeing – return was strongly linked to the enhancement of their own wellbeing upon their return.

Similarly, the parents whom we interviewed stressed to us how they felt that their obligations as parents were difficult for them to maintain in a satisfactory manner. Their experience was that their children's expectations towards them as parents were impossible to fulfil due to the social, legal and economic circumstances of being irregular migrant parents. A father of six children, for instance, told us how his children had been refused access to school and participation in the school football team when their family had received a second rejection of their asylum application.[7] His experience that his children's education and future possibilities were being hampered – and that their current living conditions were having serious health consequences for both him and his children – induced the father to sign up with AR. Yet, their future after their return remained unknown. They would not settle in the area where they had lived before, but would instead continue on to another district or to another country entirely. Their preparedness for their return was limited, because signing up with AR was their response to a lack of choice: AR did not represent return so much as continued migration. The parents expressed particular concern for their eldest daughter's future.

Return has gender- and generation-specific consequences; different members of one family do not necessarily have the same perception of their return (Cassarino 2008; Erdal and Ezzati 2015). One family whom we interviewed had decided to return due to the negative psychological effects that staying in Norway as an irregular migrant had on the husband. While the family expected improved psychosocial wellbeing for the husband by returning (because it would improve his experience of dignity and his scope of action), the wife believed that return would further diminish her living conditions/wellbeing. As she told us,

> I don't want to [return], and I find no joy in this, but he is my husband and I must follow him. I don't want to go back; I want to be here.

While return for many migrants did not necessarily mean that matters of insecurity had vanished, and they expected difficulties in terms of work, housing and public participation, they also talked about return as a possibility for increasing their scope of action (for example, in terms of achieving an education) and being more in charge of their lives.

The different meanings of return: a brief comparison

Our findings demonstrate that while the notion of 'return' is familiar to migrants, the interventions that both impose and facilitate return (such as AR programmes) frequently conflict with migrants' own perceptions of return (cf. Lindquist 2013). According to the Norwegian government, when someone does not have the right for protection under UN Refugee Convention §28, it means that return 'home' (as a naturalised place) is regarded as safe. Yet, for several of the migrants whom we interviewed, a rejected asylum application did not mean that 'home' represented a secure place. Indeed, for some of these migrants, 'home' no longer existed in their return countries, or it was still in practice an unsafe place to go. The meaning of 'home' is something that changes over time; the migrant may thus have a sense of ambivalence about their 'home' and where they belong (Erdal 2014).

A few migrants, particularly those whom we viewed to be pursuing return as foreseeable (our first category of migrant), returned with AR programmes and followed the reintegration projects more or less in the way in which they were expected to as defined by the programmes (see also Strand *et al.* 2016). We also found that the government's emphasis on 'return with dignity' with AR versus 'return in shame' with forced return had motivated the migrants' decision to sign up with AR. Yet, even if migrants prefer to return via AR rather than via forced return, the question of whether or not their return will signify a life with dignity in the longer run once they return depends – among other things – on their scope of action after their return.

In general, return for migrants is a different experience from that which the Norwegian government presents; the government ties return and the implementation of the programmes to 'going home' in order for the migrants to build a future – a process that the government believes the migrants should plan for before they return. Yet, many migrants who signed up with AR had not visited their return countries for a very long time. In particular, many of the young Afghan migrants whom we interviewed had left Afghanistan for Iran when they were still children. While some had broken their ties with their families, others still had family members in Iran. Their return destination with the AR programme would be Afghanistan, since that was their nationality – even if they had not set foot there since they were children and they had no family or social networks available there to speak of. Indeed, while the government assumes that migrants will have family and social networks in their countries of return, the transnational background of many migrants sometimes means that their social networks exist in different locations than in their countries of return.

In contrast to the government's perception, several migrants physically returned to an unknown place (i.e. internal displacement or to another country) where they had family or would feel safer than they would have in their old 'home' district. Some made use of the AR programmes without the intention of remaining for long in the returning country; instead, they used the AR programmes' financial assistance to facilitate their continued migration journey, as Strand *et al.* (2016) confirmed in a recent study.

Another dimension of migration is the temporality of return. Warner (1994: 171) argues that return, as encapsulated in the dominant discourse, is impossible because of 'the temporal reality of our lives and the changes that take place over time'. Several migrants talked about acquiring new perspectives on society and on the political and social conflicts that they had left behind. For them, return was not a matter of 'going back' to where they had once lived, because of changed family structure or their new perceptions of society and of what 'home' meant to them. This also affected the migrants' ability to prepare during the pre-return stages. Overall, while we may view return to be part of the government's efforts to control migration, in practice one could argue that the government, through its AR programmes, inadvertently produces migration and mobility.

Conclusion

Signing up with AR can be a way for migrants to restore their dignity, to recapture some sense of agency in their lives or to meet family obligations. For many, it is a way to escape the difficult situations they face as irregular migrants in Norway. The fact that they might be able to improve their psychosocial wellbeing in many different ways via AR, however, does not mean that their return will improve their living conditions, that is, their material wellbeing. Return will not mean the same to all migrants: for some migrants, return is a foreseeable part of their migration path; for others, return is an uncertain potentiality; and for still others, return is a next step in their ongoing mobility path.

The way in which they move on (i.e. how they move on, and with what speed) does not only depend on their memories of their past in their 'home' countries; it also depends on the current expectations that they face today. These include expectations from their children (who may not have been to the return country before), from their families and from themselves. For some, a country like Afghanistan is at best a vague childhood memory; their life situations likely will have changed over time (such as due to marriage and childbearing). For some, return is a way to cope with one's past and present losses; for others, however, returning means not losing one's future, thus making their return a life-restoring act.

Overall, migrants' understanding of return is neither heard nor accommodated in the government's return policies – as is the case with its migration policies in general. While the lack of migrant perspectives in policies that concern them and their future lives is not unexpected (given that they are non-citizens of the nation-state that produces these policies), this gap leads to the development of return programmes that risk failing in their intentions, instead producing ongoing mobility. We suggest that future discussions about what 'return' implies need to take into account how psychosocial wellbeing is constituted and experienced and forms part of a migrant's choice of action, and how these are both gender and generation specific.

The state's logic behind AR focuses on the legitimacy of the asylum system, the costs involved compared with forced return, and the idea that assisted return is a more humanitarian solution than forced return. The government envisions its AR programmes as reinforcing and affirming its control over mobility and the nation's sovereignty. We suggest that, rather than reinforcing control, AR programmes actually contribute to producing mobility. In our estimation, one reason for this unintended effect is that the government does not take into account what return means for migrants; we believe that this indicates crucial shortcomings in the AR programmes' conception and implementation.

Policy measures that seek to facilitate AR for migrants must recognise that return can be a part of a migrant's efforts to restore or improve his or her well-being. Return policies (as well as the work of researchers) must distinguish between different ways of understanding return – return as foreseeable, return as an uncertainty and return as continued migration – and what these different forms will mean for migrants' coping strategies and for the sustainability of their return. Among the migrants whom we interviewed for this study, the individuals who felt that they had accomplished their goals as migrants or who felt that they could look forward to opportunities in their countries of origin were more prepared for their return than the migrants in the other two categories. For others, being prepared is a matter of planning, but this may be difficult (if not impossible) for them due to the unpredictability of their circumstances. What this reveals is the necessity of understanding return as a dynamic process that will mean different things to different people.

Notes

1 Country-specific programmes for assisted returns to Afghanistan and Iraq were initiated in Norway in 2003 and include personal advice and economic support for both reintegration and travel costs. In Norway, these programmes are organised by the International Organization for Migration.
2 In Norway, AR was called 'voluntary assisted return' until 2014.
3 In addition, although Norway is not an EU member state, it does cooperate closely with that bloc, particularly in relation to EU immigration policies. Norway has signed the Schengen Agreement (2001), the Dublin Convention (2001) and the Dublin II Regulations (2003). It has also adopted the EU Return Directive. All of these programmes have led to amendments of Norway's immigration laws; see www.globaldetentionproject.org/countries/europe/norway/introduction.html (accessed 31 July 2016).
4 See, for example, the Norwegian government's budget proposal for 2015; see also www.nettavisen.no/nyheter/innenriks/her-settes-asylskeren-pa-flyet-ut-av-norge/502321.html (accessed 31 July 2016).
5 The Home Office representatives have also actively pursued this perspective in meetings with the research team.
6 Norwegian activists have also argued that when people are born in Norway or have lived in Norway for a substantial portion of their lives (in particular children), the question of their 'home' country becomes dubious. While in the last few years the government has opened up to the idea that time spent in Norway should be considered in its assessment of whether or not a person should be allowed to stay (i.e. on humanitarian grounds), it simultaneously emphasises that the migrants themselves, and not the government, are to blame for this period of time.
7 Children in Norway, regardless of their residency status, have a right to primary school, but children in families whose asylum applications have been rejected have no right to attend secondary school; this was the case for the eldest daughter in this particular family.

References

Ahearn, F.L. (2000) *The Psychosocial Wellness of Refugees: Issues in Qualitative and Quantitative Research*. New York: Berghahn.

Bendixsen, S. (2015) Vilkårlige rettigheter? Irregulære migranters tillit, sosiale kapital og kreative taktikker. [Arbitrary rights? Irregular migrants' trust, social capital, and creative tactics.] In *Eksepsjonell velferd? Irregulære migranter i det norske velferdssamfunnet.* [Exceptional welfare? Irregular migrants in the Norwegian welfare state.] Oslo: Gyldendal, 184–202.

Bendixsen, S.K.N., Kjærre, H.A. and Ytre-Arne, B. (2014) *OUT-reach: informasjon om frivillig retur til irregulære migranter utenfor mottak.* [OUT-reach: information on the voluntary return of irregular migrants outside reception.] Bergen: Uni Research, Report 6.

Biao, X., Yeoh, B.S.A. and Toyota, M. (eds.) (2013) *Return: Nationalizing Transnational Mobility in Asia.* Durham NC: Duke University Press.

Black, R. and Gent, S. (2006) Sustainable return in post-conflict contexts. *International Migration* 4(3): 15–38.

Black, R. and Koser, K. (eds) (1999) *The End of the Refugee Cycle? Refugee Repatriation and Reconstruction.* New York: Berghahn.

Black, R., Koser, K., Munk, K., Atfield, G., D'Onofrio, L. and Tiemoko, R. (2004) *Understanding Voluntary Return.* London: UK Home Office.

Bourdieu, P. (2000) *Pascalian Meditations.* San Francisco: Stanford University Press.

Brekke, J.-P. (2016) *Why Go Back? Assisted Return from Norway.* Oslo: Institute for Social Research.

Cassarino, J.P. (2004) Theorising return migration: the conceptual approach to return migrants revisited. *International Journal on Multicultural Societies* 6(2): 253–279.

Cassarino, J.P. (2008) Conditions of modern return migrants. *International Journal on Multicultural Societies* 10(2): 95–105.

Erdal, M.B. (2014) This is my home: Pakistani and Polish migrants' return considerations as articulations about 'home'. *Comparative Migration Studies* 2(3): 361–383.

Erdal, M.B. and Ezzati, R.T. (2015) 'Where are you from' or 'when did you come'? Temporal dimensions in migrants' reflections about settlement and return. *Ethnic and Racial Studies* 38(7): 1202–1217.

European Migration Network (2011) *Programmes and strategies in the EU member states fostering assisted return to and reintegration in third countries.* https://rem.sef.pt/PagesPT/DocsPT/EstudosSinteseEuropeus/programmes_strategies_assisted_return_reintegration.pdf. Accessed 24 November 2016.

Fokkema, T. (2011) 'Return' migration intentions among second-generation Turks in Europe: the effect of integration and transnationalism in a cross-national perspective. *Journal of Mediterranean Studies* 20(2): 365–388.

Gmelch, G. (1980) Return migration. *Annual Review of Anthropology* 9: 135–159.

Hage, G. (2003) *Against Paranoid Nationalism: Searching for Hope in a Shrinking Society.* Annandale, NSW: Pluto Press.

Hunter, A. (2010) Theory and practice of return migration at retirement: the case of migrant worker hostel residents in France. *Population, Space and Place* 17(2): 179–192.

Lindquist, J. (2013) Rescue, return, in place: deportees, 'victims', and the regulation of Indonesian migration. In X. Biao, B.S.A. Yeoh and M. Toyota (eds) *Return: Nationalizing Transnational Mobility in Asia.* Durham, NC: Duke University Press, 122–140.

Löfgren, O. (1989) The nationalization of culture. *Ethnologia Europaea* 19: 5–23.

Long, L.D. and Oxfeld, E. (eds) (2004) *Coming Home? Refugees, Migrants, and Those who Stayed Behind.* Philadelphia, PA: University of Pennsylvania Press.

Malkki, L. (1995) Refugees and exile: from 'refugee studies' to the national order of things. *Annual Review of Anthropology* 24: 495–523.

Olesen, H. (2002) Migration, return, and development: an institutional perspective. *International Migration*, 40(5): 125–150.

Schuster, L. and Majidi, N. (2013) What happens post-deportation? The experience of deported Afghans. *Migration Studies* 1(2): 241–260.

Schuster, L. and Majidi, N. (2015) Deportation stigma and re-migration. *Journal of Ethnic and Migration Studies* 41(4): 635–652.

Strand, A., Bendixsen, S., Lidén, H., Paaske, E. and Aalen, L. (2016) *Programmes for Assisted Return to Afghanistan, Iraqi Kurdistan, Ethiopia and Kosovo: A Comparative Evaluation of Effectiveness and Outcomes*. Bergen: Christian Michelsen Institute, CMI Report 2016/2.

Strand, A., Bendixsen, S., Paasche, E., and Schultz, J. (2011) *Between Two Societies: Review of the Information, Return and Reintegration of Iraq (IRRINI) Programme*. Bergen: Christian Michelsen Institute, CMI Report 2011/4.

van Meeteren, M., Engbersen, G., Snel, E. and Faber, M. (2014) Understanding different post-return experiences: the role of preparedness, return motives and family expectations for returned migrants in Morocco. *Comparative Migration Studies* 2(3): 335–360.

Vathi, Z. and King, R. (2013) 'Have you got the British?': Narratives of migration and settlement of Albanian-origin immigrants in London. *Ethnic and Racial Studies* 36(11): 1829–1848.

Warner, D. (1994) Voluntary repatriation and the meaning of return to home: a critique of liberal mathematics. *Journal of Refugee Studies* 7(2–3): 160–174.

3 Forced to return?

Agency and the role of post-return mobility for psychosocial wellbeing among returnees to Afghanistan, Pakistan and Poland

Marta Bivand Erdal and Ceri Oeppen

Introduction

Experiences of return migrants are shaped by mutually overlapping factors. Be they individual or collective, subjective or objective, legal, political, economic, socio-cultural and/or emotional, all of them can contribute to, or detract from, post-return psychosocial wellbeing. Migration scholars have amply demonstrated that we cannot assume return migration is a simple return to a known society, and that return does not necessarily end the migration cycle (Black and Koser 1999; Long and Oxfeld 2004). Empirical research with returnees demonstrates that return migrants go through processes of (re)adjustment and (re)integration that can be just as challenging as initial migration and integration, sometimes even more so (Gmelch 1980; Muggeridge and Doná 2006). Consequently, the decision to undertake return migration may be as complex as other migration decisions, and, like them, is made under differing degrees of volition.

Investigating this complexity requires a holistic approach. Growing interest in the concept of *wellbeing*, as seen in public policy (see e.g. Dolan *et al.* 2011; IOM 2013), is also reflected in the social sciences, for instance in studies of development (Gough and McGregor 2007) and migration (Wright 2012). This shift is towards more wide-ranging understandings of human activity and experiences that include emotions and subjective viewpoints, alongside traditional indicators of 'quality of life' such as income, literacy and life expectancy. According to Gough and McGregor (2007: 34), 'human wellbeing refers to a state of being with others, where human needs are met, where one can act meaningfully to pursue one's goals and where one enjoys satisfactory quality of life'.

While people migrate for multiple reasons, and some are compelled to, most do so with the aim of improving quality of life, to pursue goals and meet human needs – in other words, to enhance their wellbeing. Wright (2012) shows how wellbeing can be disaggregated into functional wellbeing and psychosocial wellbeing, making the term more operational. Functional wellbeing is shaped by factors such as income, accommodation and employment, which may affect someone's standard of living, whereas psychosocial wellbeing is shaped by individual factors such as values, perceptions and mental health, as well as factors such as family and intimate relationships. However, the two dimensions are clearly interrelated and often interdependent.

Studies of return migration have explored the notions of successful and sustainable return and reintegration (Black and Gent 2006), with 'success' frequently loosely defined or assumed to be implicitly understood. We argue here that an effective way of assessing a return migration's so-called success is by looking at the returnee's wellbeing. Previous studies of return migrants' experiences have identified preparedness and access to social capital support networks as key factors in this regard (Cassarino 2004; King 1986; Rogge 1994). In this chapter, we ask to what extent degree of volition in return affects the lived experiences of returnees, including their post-return psychosocial wellbeing.

To examine this question, we use a subset of qualitative data from the Possibilities and Realities of Return Migration (PREMIG) project (2011–2016). PREMIG studied the experiences of migrants living in the UK and Norway, focusing particularly on how they engaged with the possibility of return and its effects on their lives in Europe.[1] The project also explored the realities of actual return by conducting interviews and focus groups with people who had lived in the UK and Norway and subsequently returned to their countries of origin. This chapter uses data from the fieldwork with Afghans, Pakistanis and Poles, capturing a cross-section of categories of forced or voluntary return experiences. Our comparison incorporates three contexts, categorised according to how degree of volition is often perceived: where almost all return is 'forced' (Europe–Afghanistan); where almost all return is 'voluntary' (Western Europe–Poland); and where most return is 'voluntary' but it is to an insecure political situation sharing some characteristics with Afghanistan (Europe–Pakistan). Our empirical examples question the forced–voluntary distinction by showing how a return labelled as 'voluntary', for example by migration policy-makers, might not be considered as such by those doing the returning.

It might be assumed that forced return results in negative wellbeing outcomes and voluntary return in positive ones. Voluntary returnees may be better prepared for return, both practically and emotionally, and feel they have a sense of agency in their return. Conversely, because those who actively choose to return may have higher expectations, they may be more likely to feel let down by their actual return experience (King and Kılınc 2014; Muggeridge and Doná 2006; Oeppen 2013).

Forced vs voluntary is an oversimplified, albeit highly politicised, distinction. Drawing on our empirical material, we aim to disrupt this sharp dichotomy. We question to what extent return should be labelled 'forced' or 'voluntary' on the basis of bureaucratic distinctions between the two; whether 'voluntary assisted return' is essentially a subset of 'forced' return; and what real impacts the perception of 'forced' and 'voluntary' may have on return migrants' psychosocial wellbeing. In bureaucratic terms, the distinction between forced and voluntary is clear: the latter includes anyone who has consented to return, whether the migrant wanted to or not. This prevailing understanding is influenced by legal and political controls (or lack thereof) on migrants' choice of place of residence. We therefore think more along a spectrum: one that spans forced to voluntary returns but also incorporates sources of relative force, such as family expectations and social norms.

Many factors often associated with 'successful' return, such as accumulation of savings, social capital and other resources (Black and Gent 2006; Cerase 1974; Gmelch 1980), are much likelier to exist in voluntary return – indeed, they may be prerequisites for it. However, preparedness for return does not necessarily mean that return will have a positive effect on wellbeing, as the migrant's post-return experience must also be assessed. We argue that an important factor in shaping return migrants' wellbeing concerns freedom of mobility as an option, even if it is never taken up. In our view, psychosocial wellbeing includes individuals' self-perceptions and experiences, based on their relationships with others and their agency, resilience and ability to gather and use resources (Wright 2009). Our approach hinges primarily on an analysis of our research participants' subjective reflections on their own lived experiences.

The chapter first provides an overview of migration from and return migration to Afghanistan, Pakistan and Poland. Next, we describe our methods and research participants. Vignettes of individuals' experiences are then given to illustrate how we might consider some returns to be more or less forced, even if labelled in strict bureaucratic terms as 'voluntary'. We elaborate on these experiences to evaluate the effects of a) more or less preparedness for return; b) self-perception as a forced returnee or not; and c) connections between return and mobility in their impact on post-return psychosocial wellbeing.

Migration and return in the Afghan, Pakistani and Polish contexts

Afghanistan has a long history of migration and mobility, but after more than 35 years of civil and international conflict, its migration is primarily seen through a forced migration lens. Afghans constitute one of the world's largest refugee populations; there are protracted Afghan refugee situations in both Pakistan and Iran, and an estimated 5 million Afghan-born scattered globally (Oeppen 2010). Alongside international migration, internal displacement in Afghanistan is substantial, as is rural–urban migration (Kuschminder and Dora 2009). Many refugees to Norway and the UK have since gained citizenship there, though as flows from Afghanistan continue, Afghans are found in all stages of the asylum-migration process. Migration for labour and trade continues today, mainly to neighbouring countries and the Arabian Peninsula (Wickramasekara and Baruah 2013).

Return migration to Afghanistan is dominated by return and repatriation of refugees from Pakistan and Iran, with fewer deportations and less 'assisted voluntary return' from farther afield. Afghans who have gained citizenship in Western countries visit Afghanistan for varying lengths of time, their non-Afghan passports serving as an 'insurance policy' against being stuck in

Afghanistan (see Oeppen 2013; Oeppen and Majidi 2015). However, the majority of longer-term returns from the West are removals of rejected asylum-seekers and so-called voluntary returnees. As most do not wish to be in Afghanistan (Oeppen and Majidi 2015; Van Houte 2014), the returns have the potential to produce negative psychosocial outcomes. Even for those who choose to do so, return can be unsettling as returnees confront how both they and Afghanistan have changed in their absence (Oeppen 2013).

Approximately 4 per cent of Pakistan's population are international migrants (Hasan 2010), predominantly in the Gulf States and the Middle East. Other significant hubs include the US, the UK and other European destination countries, including Norway and countries in Southern Europe. Migration in the Pakistani context is also an internal phenomenon, connected with urbanisation as well as internal displacement due to conflict and natural disasters. A 'culture of migration' (Cohen 2004) is significant in particular regional pockets and selectively for populations in urban areas, providing a specific backdrop for how return migration is perceived and experienced (Erdal 2014). Most return to Pakistan is from the Gulf States, where, typically, male migrants receive two-year contracts, frequently extended, before returning to their families in Pakistan. After a spell abroad, though, practical and existential challenges face returning migrants and their families, with implications for psychosocial wellbeing, such as changing gender roles (ul Hassan 2015).

Return migration from Europe, the US and Australia is often tightly intertwined with transnational ties – and transnational living – and contingent on citizenship status in destination countries (Erdal *et al.* 2015). Notably, removals and deportations of Pakistanis occur in Middle Eastern as well as North American and Southern European destination countries (UNODC 2015). Return migration and psychosocial wellbeing in Pakistan are largely distinguished by the places migrants return from and their legal status there, which falls somewhere on a continuum from destination-country citizen to migrant without regular status who has been deported (Koser and Kuschminder 2014).

Emigration is a longstanding trait of Polish society, giving shape to a complex landscape of mobility and belonging that is embedded in constructions of national identity (White 2010). In the nineteenth century, migrants went to the US, with destinations in Europe and beyond increasing over time. Under communism, a steady trickle of Poles sought asylum abroad, and migration persisted throughout the 1990s. Poland's EU accession in 2004 increased opportunities for large-scale emigration, and by 2007, an estimated 2.3 million Poles were living abroad (Kaczmarczyk and Okólski 2008), with figures down to roughly 2.1 million in 2013 (*Economist* 2013), largely due to return migration.

With an established culture of migration – including in popular culture and literature – the question of return in Poland once pivoted around 'the myth of return' (Anwar 1979), nostalgia and national sentiments. Since mass emigration from the mid-2000s onwards, return migration has been put on the agenda by the government, media and civil society. Young Poles' disenchantment, which often feeds discourses of emigration, has been addressed through counter-narratives of return, including government-sponsored return migration schemes providing returnees with information and assistance to settle in Poland. Nevertheless, return migration in the post-accession period has been relatively limited. Given the free intra-European mobility Polish citizenship grants, return migration is not only intertwined with ideas and practices of transnational living, but also with the concept of working abroad but living at home. Therefore, the very notion of 'having returned' can be challenged (Garapich 2009).

Research methods and description of research participants

We draw on data from 54 semi-structured interviews conducted with returnees in Afghanistan, Pakistan and Poland and from seven focus groups of returnees. This is supplemented by two focus groups in each country, during which we spoke with 'locals' without an international migration history residing in the communities where returnees settled.[2] Our analysis is also informed by interviews, focus groups and interactions with Afghan, Pakistani and Polish migrants in Norway and the UK.

Under the auspices of the Possibilities and Realities of Return Migration project (PREMIG), data collection was conducted in collaboration with research assistants and co-researchers, thereby facilitating access, translation and different vantage points for exploring our research questions. Given our positionalities as white female scholars from Europe, working with locals brought balance to the potential that different positionalities have in accessing different kinds of data (see also Erdal *et al.* 2015). Further, we believe that a conscious application of various 'third positions' in migration research (i.e. neither full 'insider' nor full 'outsider') helps overcome the challenges associated with particular power hierarchies, not least in research across North–South wealth and mobility resource divides (Carling *et al.* 2014). In sum, we sought to engage multiple perspectives on volition and the implications of return migration at individual, familial and societal levels for psychosocial wellbeing.

Our use of interview and focus-group guides that were developed jointly within the project permitted comparability across datasets. The interviews and focus groups with returnees dealt with the experience of return migration, including the pre-return phase, the actual movement of coming back, the initial stages after return, and everyday life as a returnee at the time of the interview. Significantly, at the pre-return stage, clear-cut differences appeared between having and not having been involved in making the decisions, as well as degrees of volition and whether decisions were associated with the immigration authorities or a private, family-based setting. The focus groups with locals honed in on their experiences of interaction with returnees and their perceptions of migration and return migration. The focus-group format let us tease out nuances among the participants, illustrating the diverse perspectives of returnees in their countries of origin. In selecting participants, we sought to engage individuals who had been back for at least one year but also had been abroad for at least one year.

In Afghanistan, our sample mainly comprised people who had been deported or had participated in a voluntary assisted return programme; only one returnee had genuinely voluntarily returned. Just one participant was female, reflecting the overall gender profile of returnees from Norway and the UK to Afghanistan. Dimensions of return experiences in terms of psychosocial wellbeing differed among the Afghan returnees, but the fact that most said they had not wanted to return in the first place impacted their post-return wellbeing.

Among the Pakistani participants, most held Norwegian citizenship and some engaged in 'transnational living' between Norway and Pakistan, thus rarely framing their experiences as 'return migration'. With stays in Pakistan lasting one year or more in what might be seen as permanent or quasi-permanent arrangements, experiences of return were associated with particular psychosocial wellbeing outcomes. Tempered by transnational ties, though with clear gendered and generational dimensions, these outcomes differed from the experiences of participants who intended to permanently return and who did not hold European citizenship or any other 'enabling citizenship' giving access to post-return mobilities.

Returnees in Poland showed considerable variation in the framing of their return experiences. Many who had been working abroad for a number of years spoke about temporary international spells for work, rather than emigration and subsequent return. Since they did not see themselves as having 'lived' abroad – they just worked there for a while – their perceptions of return migration experiences and factors related to psychosocial wellbeing were differently framed. Still, questions about societal embeddedness in the context of repeated spells of international mobility point to particular issues regarding psychosocial wellbeing. In other cases, return migration was perceived more distinctively as a return from international migration, perhaps not in permanent terms but clearly with the need to re-establish oneself, with associated challenges of embeddedness.

Through our research with locals without an international migration history, we sought to complement the perspectives of returnees themselves. We examined how return communities perceived return experiences and articulated wellbeing. We also looked at prevailing discourses about return, which revealed expectations towards returnees, and more generalised notions of migration for the psychosocial wellbeing of returnees during different temporal stages of their post-return life.

Differing experiences of forced and voluntary return

In bureaucratic migration management terms, if the returnee returns without assistance from immigration authorities or consents to receiving assistance, then that return is considered voluntary. But whether a return is forced or voluntary is more complicated, even when only considering the bureaucratic forced–voluntary distinction. Migrants may consent to assisted return not because they want to return, but rather, due to lack of feasible alternatives – a case of 'mandatory voluntary return', to use IOM's terminology (IOM 2004).

The question of volition is, however, not solely related to the bureaucracy of migration management. Migrants may want to return, or may not want to return but feel compelled to do so for diverse reasons, such as family wishes or financial issues. Negotiating migration and return migration decision-making at the individual level is tied to family and broader social networks, where normative understandings of individual agency take different forms and socio-cultural and gendered dimensions exist.

Building on approaches finding that volition in return might involve actual or potential force not only by the state, but also by other actors, we view the issue of volition in migration as being on a continuum, rather than in a dichotomy (see Bakewell 2011; Fussell 2012; Koser and Martin 2011). As such, we use the actual lived experiences of forced and voluntary return, in the form of a series of individual vignettes, to unpack the forced–voluntary dichotomy and illustrate the complexity found somewhere in the blurry middle. First, we look at examples of forced and voluntary return that are relatively fixed at the ends of the spectrum. Then we look at examples that challenge the bureaucratic dichotomisation. These examples reveal a more complex lived experience, in which force, or at least coercion, may come from the state and/or a variety of non-state actors.

Forced return

Ahmed (male, thirties) is from eastern Afghanistan.[3] To finance his journey to Europe, his family sold property and borrowed money from extended family. He filed a claim for asylum in the UK, but it was refused; after he appealed the decision, it was refused again and he was given a removal notice. He considered going 'under the radar', but lacking strong support networks in the UK, he could not survive without section 4 support,[4] which required regular reporting to the immigration authorities. Eventually, he was removed by the UK Border Agency, and was living with an uncle in eastern Afghanistan at the time of the interview. Ahmed presents a case that is unequivocally at the forced end of the forced–voluntary spectrum. Ahmed did not want to return to Afghanistan, but immigration authorities forced him to. Although he demonstrated some agency in choosing not to go, as he put it, 'under the radar' in the UK, and thus knowingly exposed himself to possible removal, the decision was made under extreme structural constraints and a lack of viable alternatives.

Saera and Nabeel[5] are a sister and brother of Pakistani origin who were born in Norway and spent their early childhood there with their family. They subsequently moved to Pakistan with their mother and elder brother, while their father stayed in Norway and supported the family by sending remittances. When he died, Saera and Nabeel, then in their early teens, moved back to Norway with their mother. After she died, it emerged that the siblings had received permanent residency and citizenship on false grounds because their mother had omitted to report the exact number of years they had resided in Pakistan. They lost their right to stay in Norway, and were to be deported to Pakistan. After several rounds of appeals, during which a church served as a refuge from the threat of deportation, they won the right to stay on the grounds that their mother's mistake was not something for which they should be held accountable.

Voluntary return

Sofia (female, twenties) came to Norway from Kabul on a scholarship. Once it ended, she returned to Afghanistan out of a sense of duty to apply her education to contribute to Afghanistan's development from within the country. Some family members encouraged her to stay in Europe and apply for asylum, saying that as a woman educated abroad, she would be targeted on her return. But her parents supported her decision to return. Sofia is a rare example of a genuinely voluntary return to Afghanistan by an Afghan in Europe who lacked the insurance policy of a European passport.

Dominik (male, late twenties) is from a small town in Poland. He came to the UK as an Erasmus student, and remained studying and working there for several years, each time extending his stay a little longer. Finally, he decided to move back to Poland to be with his girlfriend and to pursue a PhD at the University of Warsaw. His stay in the UK was never planned as long term, and each extension was due to new opportunities arising. When he did return, it was because he wanted to be with his girlfriend, who was in Poland. The PhD was part of the picture but, in his view, secondary. Holding European citizenship, Dominic was not ruling out future mobility, but he had no concrete plans, and would at any rate describe his past and future mobilities in terms of circulation, rather than migration in any permanent sense.

Not-so-voluntary voluntary returns

Hassan (male, twenties) is Afghan by birth but spent most of his childhood in Pakistan. He applied for asylum in Norway, but his case was rejected. After consulting Afghan friends in Oslo, he realised he lacked enough evidence to support a claim that his life was in danger in Afghanistan. He decided to sign up with the International Organization for Migration (IOM) to return to Afghanistan. He did not want to return, but he knew he was unlikely to regularise his stay – and because he had witnessed the hardships of Afghans without permission to stay in Norway, he decided to rule out staying. Although Hassan 'volunteered' to return, this was not by choice, but rather, due to the lack of viable alternatives.

In debates about just how voluntary assisted return is, many suggest that, at least in the Afghan case, it is the least-worst scenario, rather than an actively chosen option (see Oeppen and Majidi 2015; Van Houte 2014). It is interesting to note that Norway has since dropped the word 'voluntary' from its assisted return programmes, though the British still use it. Nevertheless, while returns like Hassan's might be best labelled 'return with consent', they are still, from a bureaucratic point of view, considered voluntary.

Mobina (female, late forties) lives in Oslo and originates from the Pakistani Punjab. She came to Norway as a teenager, joining her father, who had migrated for work. She married a man who came to live in Norway on a family reunification visa as her spouse. Eventually, his parents in Pakistani Punjab fell ill and his father died, leaving his mother alone. The family decided that Mobina was to 'return' to Pakistan, a country she had never lived in as an adult, in order to be her mother-in-law's live-in caregiver. Mobina had no choice in the matter. She and her three children went to Pakistani Punjab for what turned out to be eight years, while Mobina's husband remained in Norway working. We met her about a year and a half after her return to Norway. No doubt she wished her mother-in-law well, but she had not wanted to live in Pakistan, and certainly not for that long. She was concerned with how the stay would impact her children's prospects in Norwegian society, even though they had kept up with the language. When it came to herself, she was quite resigned, joking about how it was too late for her to get training or a job – her 'ship had sailed'. Still, she was happy to be back in Norway, with her family reunited and the personal freedom to move and interact with different kinds of people.

Jacek (male, forties) returned to Poland after working in construction in Norway on short-term contracts for several years. He comes from a middle-sized town in southern Poland, and was not trained in construction. Working in a male-dominated environment, living in barracks and experiencing problems in his marriage, he started drinking heavily. His relationship with his wife was not helped by his drinking, and she threatened to divorce him if he did not stop. Jacek and his family relied on his Norwegian earnings for everyday expenses and to fund an extension on the house they were building. Yet, despite his emigration's economic rationale, Jacek decided to return to address his alcohol problem and to salvage his marriage. His return was voluntary, though in response to a threat. He saw no alternative but to extract himself from his environment and be physically close to his wife to work on the relationship. Despite Jacek's efforts, their marriage fell apart, and his alcohol addiction lingered. At the time of our interview, he was living across town from his family and interacting with them regularly. Neither he nor his wife was looking for a new partner, keeping him hopeful that there would be another chance for them.

The impact of being prepared to return

Along with the presence and assistance of social networks, one of the most commonly cited factors for a return's success is the returnee's preparedness (Cassarino 2004; Koser 1997). Preparedness is the accumulation of material and financial resources the migrant must invest in return and reintegration, though it could also refer to emotional preparedness and access to and use of relevant information sources. Preparedness thus hinges on wanting to prepare and having the resources and means to do so. It runs parallel to the distinction between capacities and desires in engaging in transnational practices (Al-Ali *et al.* 2001). We find variation between research participants who were deported or returned through so-called voluntary assisted return programmes and those who were not. Although deportees can predict their fate, they often resist the prospect of return, instead pursuing alternative scenarios, including onward migration and post-return re-migration. The notion of preparedness does not necessarily fit into the frames of experience of deportees to Afghanistan. Ahmed felt he had wasted time and effort, including the 'best years of [his] life', on a failed migration project; his mind was set more on maintaining transnational ties and pursuing further migration. He thus invested resources to prepare for that, rather than establish himself back in Afghanistan.

Academic discussions surrounding preparedness to return emphasise material resource accumulation, evidenced by assumptions about remittance-sending and home construction as precursors to return migration (Bauer and Sinning 2009; Dustmann 1997). Both are frequently the objectives of a migration project – and if reached, may lead to return as a next logical step – though mental preparedness is also important. Among our research participants in Pakistan were graduate students who completed degrees in Europe before returning, as planned, to Pakistan. Return migration was anticipated and planned for by the migrants themselves as well as by their families in Pakistan. While pursuing migration in Europe might have been seen as an attractive option, return migration was a set criterion (for instance, due to the time-limited student visa) and therefore an expected outcome. These individuals' experiences and reflections point to significant dimensions of preparedness, connected to expectations concerning the migration project as well as return migration. Participants who had migrated temporarily to Europe to complete a graduate degree did not, upon return to Pakistan, cite onward migration or future international mobility when discussing their goals. Although they did not rule them out, their resources and abilities were geared towards establishing worthwhile professional and private lives in Pakistan, generally with a degree of commitment to helping develop their country. Their preparedness for return – and their attitude towards pursuing a life in Pakistan – is markedly different from, for example, Ahmed's. Perhaps this is mainly due to the context of his migration, from war-torn Afghanistan, with its inherent political and security instability. The contrast may also stem from differing class and socio-economic opportunities among migrants and how their agency and freedom to make choices, even if within set parameters, are experienced in radically divergent ways.

The impact of being perceived as voluntary or forced returnees

In the return migration literature, the question of success or failure is a recurring theme (see Gmelch 1980; King 1986, 2000). Contemporary policy debates link that theme with notions of 'successful sustainable return', which implies return without subsequent re-migration (Black and Gent 2006). However, in canonical accounts of return migration (Cerase 1974; Gmelch 1980), the idea of return as either a success or a failure was more connected to whether migrants achieved something through migration. Did they improve their and their households' lives, or not? Did they worsen their situation in life by migrating? Cerase (1974) showed how the case of 'failed migration' was epitomised by Italian migrants returning from the US empty-handed, in contrast to those who returned to build houses in their communities of origin (cf. Erdal 2012). Yet, evaluations of what is successful and what is not are highly context dependent, and may differ between migrants and non-migrants. Therefore, *perceptions of success or failure* are a useful entry-point to highlight the relative and constructed nature of such evaluations.

Being forced to return by the immigration authorities, as Ahmed was, would indicate to many that the migration was not a success. Not only had Ahmed been unable to stay in the UK, but now the family's investment in his migration to Europe had been 'wasted'. As he put it when asked how others reacted to his return, 'The problem is when you go to your own village, everyone points at you in a mocking manner'. Word spread that he had been sent back from the UK, and he was seen as a failure, or at least he felt he was seen that way. Other research participants in Afghanistan shared how they thought people in Afghanistan assumed they had been sent back for having committed a crime in Europe. Such responses can have a negative effect on reintegration and wellbeing, an observation echoed in other research with Afghan deportees (see Schuster and Majidi 2015). Although people knew Ahmed had been sent back, other returnees in Afghanistan explained how people in Afghanistan saw no difference between those who were removed and those who took up voluntary assisted return. Hassan, for example, said his family thought he was crazy for 'volunteering' to return, but, as he explained, they did not understand the asylum system in Europe.

Although he himself did not stress this, people in Jacek's surroundings observed a man returning to little and low-paid work with a disintegrating relationship and alcohol problems. Neither his migration nor his return would likely be evaluated as particularly successful. Nevertheless, the return to Poland increased Jacek's wellbeing, as he was close to his family, saw his children a lot and had hopes his relationship might work out. He still struggled with alcoholism, but managed to control his drinking to a greater extent than in Norway. He was convinced he would have died as a result of drinking had he stayed in Norway. So, even if evaluated as a failure by bystanders, return to Poland was a great improvement in his self-perceived quality of life. Jacek's story reveals how evaluations of success and failure can differ between the individual level and what is observed from the outside. His story also underscores how the impact of outsiders' perception, itself culturally contingent, is also individually differently received and important to a different extent for an individual's psychosocial wellbeing. For Ahmed, the shame of return was hard to bear; for Jacek, the prospects that not returning held put everything else in perspective.

Cases of so-called voluntary assisted return, and all the more so of actual deportation, are at one end of the migration project spectrum, as perceived in communities of origin. It is worth noting, though, that perceptions vary. In Afghanistan and Pakistan, among migrants not from upper-class families, returning without first securing adequate mobility resources (in the form of European citizenship, so as to be able to migrate again) might elicit questions about the return. Despite Pakistan's culture of migration and the significance of remittances from international migrants, there is an equally strong sense of responsibility to stay and build the country and therefore not to leave: hence the value attached to migrants' returning, particularly when they want to invest and contribute to society's development. Perceptions of return are, therefore, contingent not only on the evaluation of individual migration projects as successes or failures, but also on broader societal conceptions of migration as desirable or not. In all three geographical contexts we are analysing, these are normative questions that intersect with political, security and economic realities for individuals and families. They, in turn, translate into particular mobility choices, often in pursuit of improved psychosocial wellbeing.

The relationship between return and post-return mobility

Dominik, who returned to Poland to be with his girlfriend and pursue his PhD, did not see himself as ever having left. His return migration was a 'natural' move, not signifying a rupture with his mobility to the UK. In cases of transnational mobility, it is useful to examine what implications not seeing oneself as a migrant might have for return and experiences of embeddedness and reintegration in societies of origin. Dominik's strong transnational ties meant that on his return, he could re-enter the social and professional circles with which he had maintained close contact. When intense transnational interactions, personal or professional, are not maintained, or are maintained to a lesser extent, returnees may experience culture shock upon returning. Assumptions about embeddedness remaining the same over time may be challenged due to the lack of preparedness for changes in societies of origin and changes within migrants themselves.

Saera and Nabeel's story shows that bureaucracies are not inclined to acknowledge the importance of wellbeing in transnational living. The siblings' wellbeing in Pakistan, had they had to move back there and stay on indefinitely, would have been severely challenged. They had few networks, had not lived there since childhood, and did not have either parent to help in adjustment processes. Mobina's case of return was voluntary, at least bureaucratically speaking, though it involved force. Her return migration had dramatic effects on her and her children's lives. Mobina emphasised that knowing she could eventually live in Norway again helped her through the eight years in Pakistan. Although her preference would have been to stay in Norway, she subscribed to the value of relatives looking after her elderly mother-in-law, and fulfilling family obligations compensated for the lack of freedom. Overwhelmingly, Mobina's awareness that her return was temporary and that she had the mobility resources and citizenship to move back to

Norway one day was fundamental to her psychosocial wellbeing in Pakistan. Her agency was limited in the decision to return, but the freedom she experienced in knowing she could move again later, as well as in the ways she could shape her life while in Pakistan, underlines the salience of agency, freedom and capabilities.

Among migrants coming to Europe without resources allowing for back-and-forth mobility, acquiring such resources – and remaining in Europe until this has been achieved – is usually the concern that trumps all others. For many Afghan and Pakistani migrants, lack of mobility opportunities is hugely negative for wellbeing, which is why many take the precarious journey to reach Europe, even without legal status. If and when they are returned – whether by deportation or with consent, as in the case of Hassan – their psychosocial wellbeing comes under threat. As with Ahmed, shame may be a factor, but so is the inability to pursue sustainable livelihoods. When opportunities in Afghanistan are experienced as limited, re-migration is often deemed an appropriate response. Energies are thus invested in re-migration, rather than reintegration and local embeddedness. Not all Afghans are international migrants, and those who are have mostly migrated, returned or circulated between Afghanistan, Iran and Pakistan. Most who have migrated to Europe and subsequently returned have migration histories both in neighbouring countries and in Europe. Accordingly, they have weaker links and prospects for, as well as motivation towards, establishing themselves in Afghanistan.

Ahmed and Hassan represent a minority of Afghans who have chosen and been able to migrate to Europe, yet whose return to Afghanistan compromised efforts to improve their wellbeing. On return, they found themselves weakly embedded in society, with constraints on their capability, as well as desire, to achieve embeddedness. The impact on their psychosocial wellbeing was severe, setting back their efforts to establish themselves so as to improve their and their families' quality of life. The force, or at least coercion, in their return transcends actual physical return. The migration controls that limit their re-migration to Europe, as a deportee and an assisted returnee, mean that their psychosocial wellbeing is severely compromised by the constraints on their mobility – especially when they and their families would prefer to be living in Europe. As Hassan said, 'How can a person adjust his life to such conditions? He will soon start feeling crazy from doing nothing all day and will find himself feeling like he's in a cage'. Feeling trapped, or caged, was a sentiment Afghan research participants repeatedly brought up. The feeling appears to reflect Afghanistan's state of insecurity as well as the daunting thought of the challenges that re-migration out of the region would entail.

Conclusion

In this chapter, we identified three factors that were integral to shaping the psychosocial wellbeing of returnees: accumulation of resources, relationships with family members and others, and agency (particularly regarding onward mobility). These strongly resemble factors that migration scholars have identified as being integral to the success, or otherwise, of return. For example, under the category of accumulation of resources, we read 'preparedness'; under relationships, we read 'social capital'; under agency, we read 'degree of volition'.

In contrast to what has been conceptualised by researchers for other contexts (Wright 2012), we see psychosocial wellbeing as affected by both emotional and material aspects of return. We therefore consider psychosocial wellbeing to include individuals' self-perceptions and experiences. These are based on their relationships with others, sense of agency, identity and resilience, though these affective dimensions of wellbeing are strongly related to functional wellbeing, such as ability to gather and use resources (Wright 2009) and to access onward mobility, if desired.

Work on subjective wellbeing in social psychology has linked wellbeing to issues such as identity and social appraisal. Suh's (2002) research on Korean and American students found that social appraisal was a predictor of wellbeing. This could be an interesting avenue for return migration scholars to pursue. Does the return conform to social norms and expectations? How might that affect psychosocial wellbeing? Mobina's return to care for her sick mother-in-law conformed to normative expectations about familial and gendered responsibilities, but she did not perceive her return to Pakistan as positive for her own wellbeing. Ahmed's wellbeing was negatively affected by his inability to conform to normative expectations that he would migrate to Europe and send remittances to support his family. Jacek's return meant he could spend time with his family, but he was not meeting gendered expectations to provide for them due to the difficulty of finding work in Poland compared with Norway. These three examples reveal how complex and context specific are the interactions between norms, psychosocial wellbeing and return migration.

Intuitively, we might expect a forced return to negatively affect post-return wellbeing, while a voluntary return might result in unharmed, if not enhanced, post-return wellbeing outcomes. If preparedness is a key factor for successful return, we might expect voluntary returnees to be better prepared. And if the stigma surrounding forced return is a key factor, we might expect forced returnees to have particularly negative post-return wellbeing outcomes. Empirical research, however, has shown that volition alone does not automatically produce positive post-return outcomes, as expectations among those choosing to return may be very high and therefore liable to disillusionment when faced with the reality of return (King and Kılınc 2014; Muggeridge and Doná 2006; Oeppen 2013).

Overall, as our research shows, post-return wellbeing outcomes vary extensively and cannot be reduced to whether the return is bureaucratically labelled 'forced' or 'voluntary'. We argue that an agency-centred approach, rather than simply maintaining bureaucratic forced–voluntary distinctions, provides a more nuanced understanding of how return affects post-return wellbeing. That said, we also acknowledge how these bureaucratic distinctions constrain or enable return migrants' agency, particularly in relation to post-return mobility.

These findings should be kept in mind by actors seeking to influence return migration decision-making or to manage or facilitate return, and who support migrants and mobile populations more broadly. Considerations about psychosocial wellbeing are crucial to successful policies and planning. The main challenge lies in the realisation that the scope of agency is significant for psychosocial wellbeing – migrants' choices may be at odds with policy aims. Arguably, the insight that agency really does matter may enable more effective policy-making, from the state perspective, while still ensuring decent and humane approaches to the individuals targeted by interventions.

Finally, we find that preparedness, practically as well as emotionally, is strongly tied to a sense of agency (or a self-perceived lack thereof), which could be helpful in understanding the negative wellbeing outcomes of forced return. Mobility resources and opportunities for post-return mobility seem essential, though on balance, so is the agency of migrants. At the individual level, we also find that while states are the primary source of coerced return, family and social norms are additional sources, which are likely to have significant impacts on post-return psychosocial wellbeing. The relative roles of agency and post-return mobility opportunities are thus key to understanding the varied outcomes of psychosocial wellbeing for returnees to Afghanistan, Pakistan, Poland and possibly many places elsewhere.

Notes

1 'Possibility of return' is meant in its broadest sense: even those who said they never want to return still entertained the idea as a possibility, while those who were actively planning to return could well never put those plans into action. Both scenarios still required thinking about a possible return.
2 For Afghanistan, this criterion was broadened to include people with no migration history beyond Asia, as finding participants with no international migration history at all (i.e. not even to Pakistan and Iran) proved too difficult.
3 All names are pseudonyms, and where necessary other identifying details are altered.
4 Section 4 is minimal social welfare given to rejected asylum-seekers in the UK who can prove they would be destitute without that support.
5 Widely known in Norway due to media coverage and advocacy efforts, this case was mentioned by several informants. In this exceptional case, we did not conduct interviews with the individuals involved.

References

Al-Ali, N., Black, R. and Koser, K. (2001) The limits to 'transnationalism': Bosnian and Eritrean refugees in Europe as emerging transnational communities, *Ethnic and Racial Studies* 24(4): 578–600.

Anwar, M. (1979) *The Myth of Return: Pakistanis in Britain*. London: Heinemann.

Bakewell, O. (2011) Conceptualising displacement and migration: processes, conditions, and categories, in Koser, K. and Martin, S. (eds) *The Migration-Displacement Nexus: Patterns, Processes, and Policies*. Oxford: Berghahn Books, 14–28.

Bauer, T.K. and Sinning, M.G. (2009) The purpose of remittances: evidence from Germany, *Jahrebucher fur Nationalokonomie und Statistik* 229(6): 730–742.

Black, R. and Gent, S. (2006) Sustainable return in post-conflict contexts, *International Migration* 44(3): 15–38.

Black, R. and Koser, K. (eds) (1999) *The End of the Refugee Cycle? Refugee Repatriation and Reconstruction.* Oxford: Berghahn Books.

Carling, J., Erdal, M.B. and Ezzati, R. (2014) Beyond the insider-outsider divide in migration research, *Migration Studies* 2(1): 36–54.

Cassarino, J.-P. (2004) Theorising return migration: the conceptual approach to return migrants revisited, *International Journal on Multicultural Studies* 6(2): 253–279.

Cerase, F.P. (1974) Expectations and reality: a case study of return migration from the United States to southern Italy, *International Migration Review* 8(2): 245–262.

Cohen, J.H. (2004). *The Culture of Migration in Southern Mexico.* Austin, TX: University of Texas Press.

Dolan, P., Layard, R. and Metcalfe, R. (2011) *Measuring Subjective Well-being for Public Policy.* Newport: Office for National Statistics.

Dustmann, C. (1997) Return migration, uncertainty and precautionary savings, *Journal of Development Economics* 52(2): 295–316.

Economist (2013) Poland's emigration headache. *The Economist*, 5 November. www.economist.com/blogs/easternapproaches/2013/11/poland-and-eu. Accessed 10 July 2015.

Erdal, M.B. (2012) 'A place to stay in Pakistan': why migrants build houses in their country of origin, *Population, Space and Place* 18(5): 629–641.

Erdal, M.B. (2014) The social dynamics of remittance-receiving in Pakistan: agency and opportunity among non-migrants in a transnational social field, in Rahman, M., Yong, T. and Ullah, A. (eds) *Migrant Remittances in South Asia: Social, Economic and Political Implications.* London: Palgrave Macmillan, 115–134.

Erdal, M.B., Amjad, A., Bodla, Q.Z. and Rubab, A. (2016) Going back to Pakistan for education? The interplay of return mobilities, education, and transnational living, *Population, Space and Place* 22(8): 836–848.

Fussell, E. (2012) Space, time, and volition: dimensions of migration theory, in Rosenblum, M.R. and Tichenor, D.J. (eds) *The Oxford Handbook of the Politics of International Migration.* Oxford: Oxford University Press, 25–52.

Garapich, M.P. (2009) 'Wyjechalem ot, tak… i nie jestem emigrantem': Polski dominujacy dyskurs migracyjny i jego kontestacje na przykladzie Wielkiej Brytanii ['I have left just like that… and I am not an emigrant': Polish dominant migration discourse and its contestations based on the example of the UK], *Studia Migracyjne-Przeglad Polonijny* 4(35): 41–65.

Gmelch, G. (1980) Return migration, *Annual Review of Anthropology* 9: 135–159.

Gough, I. and McGregor, J.A. (eds) (2007) *Wellbeing in Developing Countries.* Cambridge: Cambridge University Press.

Hasan, A. (2010) Migration, small towns and social transformations in Pakistan, *Environment and Urbanization* 22(1): 33–50.

IOM (2004) *Essentials of Migration Management, Vol. 3: Return Migration.* Geneva: IOM.

IOM (2013) *World Migration Report 2013: Migrant Well-Being and Development.* Geneva: IOM.

Kaczmarczyk, P. and Okólski, M. (2008) Demographic and economic impacts of migration on Poland, *Oxford Review of Economic Policy* 24(3): 600–625.

King, R. (ed.) (1986) *Return Migration and Regional Economic Problems.* London: Croom Helm.

King, R. (2000) Generalizations from the history of return migration, in Ghosh, B. (ed.) *Return Migration: Journey of Hope or Despair?* Geneva: International Organization for Migration 7–55.

King, R. and Kılınc, N. (2014) Routes to roots: second-generation Turks from Germany 'return' to Turkey, *Nordic Journal of Migration Research* 4(3): 126–133.

Koser, K. (1997) Information and repatriation: the case of Mozambican refugees in Malawi, *Journal of Refugee Studies* 10(1): 1–17.

Koser, K. and Kuschminder, K. (2014) *Comparative Research on the Assisted Voluntary Return and Reintegration of Migrants*. Geneva: IOM.

Koser, K. and Martin, S. (2011) The migration-displacement nexus, in Koser, K. and Martin, S. (eds) *The Migration-Displacement Nexus: Patterns, Processes, and Policies*. Oxford: Berghahn Books, 1–13.

Kuschminder, K. and Dora, N. (2009) *Migration in Afghanistan: History, Current Trends and Future Prospects*. Maastricht: Maastricht Graduate School of Governance, Migration and Development Country Profiles.

Long, L.D. and Oxfeld, E. (eds) (2004) *Coming Home? Refugees, Migrants, and Those Who Stayed Behind*. Philadelphia: University of Pennsylvania Press.

Muggeridge, H. and Doná, G. (2006) Back home? Refugees' experiences of their first visit back to their country of origin, *Journal of Refugee Studies* 19(4): 415–432.

Oeppen, C. (2010) The Afghan diaspora and its involvement in the reconstruction of Afghanistan, in Oeppen, C. and Schlenkhoff, A. (eds) *Beyond the 'Wild Tribes': Understanding Modern Afghanistan and its Diaspora*. London: Hurst, 141–156.

Oeppen, C. (2013) A stranger at 'home': interactions between transnational return visits and integration for Afghan-American professionals. *Global Networks* 13(2): 261–278.

Oeppen, C. and Majidi, N. (2015) Can Afghans reintegrate after assisted return from Europe? Oslo: PRIO, Policy Brief 7.

Rogge, J. (1994) Repatriation of refugees: a not so simple 'optimum' solution, in Allen, T. and Morsink, H. (eds) *When Refugees Go Home*. London: James Currey, 14–49.

Schuster, L. and Majidi, N. (2015) Deportation stigma and re-migration, *Journal of Ethnic and Migration Studies* 41(4): 635–652.

Suh, E.M. (2002) Culture, identity consistency, and subjective well-being, *Journal of Personality and Social Psychology* 83(6): 1378–1391.

ul Hassan, S.M. (2015) Pakistani migration to the Gulf and development in the Miranzai valley in Pakistan, in Rahman, M. and Yong, T. (eds) *International Migration and Development in South Asia*. London: Routledge, 203–217.

UNODC (2015) *The Socio-Economic Impact of Human Trafficking and Migrant Smuggling in Pakistan*. United Nations Office on Drugs and Crime. www.unodc.org/documents/pakistan/The_Socio-economic_impact_of_human_trafficking_and_migrant_smuggling_in_Pakistan_19_Feb_2015.pdf. Accessed 23 June 2015.

Van Houte, M. (2014) Moving Back or Moving Forward? Return Migration after Conflict. Maastricht: PhD thesis, University of Maastricht.

White, A. (2010) Young people and migration from contemporary Poland, *Journal of Youth Studies* 13(5): 565–580.

Wickramasekara, P. and Baruah, N. (2013) *Labour Migration for Decent Work in Afghanistan: Issues and Challenges*. Bangkok: International Labour Organization Regional Office for Asia and the Pacific.

Wright, K. (2009) Review essay: well-being, poverty and social policy, *Global Social Policy* 9(1): 135–140.

Wright, K. (2012) *International Migration, Development and Human Wellbeing*. Basingstoke: Palgrave Macmillan.

4 Between 'voluntary' return programs and soft deportation

Sending vulnerable migrants in Spain back 'home'

Barak Kalir

Introduction

On the prelim to the informative pamphlet in which the Young Men's Christian Association (YMCA) specifies the requirements and conditions for applying to its assisted voluntary return programmes there are colour photos of Machu Picchu, Isla de Pascua and a colourful carnival, an eagle's eye view of Rio de Janeiro, and a shot of a person in a traditional calabash gourd against a scenic Patagonian background. The caption above the collage of attractive photos leaves you wanting: 'If you are thinking of returning …' To prevent you from thinking that you are browsing a brochure of a travel agency for your dream vacation to Latin America, the purpose of the pamphlet is stated in bold letters: 'Voluntary Return Programs'. Upon opening the pamphlet, a beautiful photo of an airplane flying into the orange sky at sunset accompanies detailed information about the different programmes: the benefits that each of them offers, and the requisites for applying to each modality. On the back cover of the pamphlet, an artistic photo of piled-up suitcases adorns a short poetic text about the concept of 'Return …':

> Leaving the land, the home, the family … is never easy. But often necessary … When today we consider returning to the country that we left, different sentiments are provoked in us … The yearning to return to the home that we left, to unite again with families and friends ….

This chapter, although focusing empirically mostly on the case of YMCA in Spain,[1] draws attention to two cunning elements that are characteristic of programmes of assisted voluntary return (AVR) across Europe: first, the very classification of these programmes as being based on the voluntarism of the migrants; second, the implicit formulation with respect to a return of migrants to their 'home' (country). In the first instance, the chapter demonstrates that these two guileful elements are problematic in their claims and manipulative in their formulation. Yet, the greater goal of the chapter is to argue that the couching of migrants' assisted return in the language of voluntarism, patterned on positive notions of 'home', reveals the deeper neoliberal ideological underpinnings of such programmes as part of the 'migration apparatus' (Feldman 2012). Accordingly, I contend that so-called 'voluntary return programmes' are based on the exact same logic that champions state sovereignty in justifying forced removals and violent deportations. I thus coin the term 'soft deportation' as a more appropriate way of referring to such programmes, which are, de facto, an integral part of the overall biopolitical scheme that absolves the territorial removal of illegalised subjects under state sovereignty.

As it appears from the websites and pamphlets of organisations that operate AVR, as well as in my interviews with non-governmental organisation (NGO) workers who interact with migrants, the prime target of these programmes in Spain is vulnerable people with a migratory background. At the frontline of implementing AVR are NGO workers who engage in face-to-face interactions with potential returnees. While all migrants who comply with the basic requisites for AVR are included, particular attention and top priority are given to people who suffer from poverty, economic and social marginalisation, or psychosocial malaise. The system is thus geared towards returning precisely those individuals and families who are most in need of urgent social, economic and psychological assistance. Yet, the assistance that is on offer for these vulnerable people is in the form of returning them 'voluntarily' to their 'home'.

AVR programmes, in their function as soft deportation, should therefore be seen as part and parcel of states' immigration regimes, aiming at the incorporation of healthy, fully employed and self-sustaining migrants, while rejecting and repatriating 'failing' migrants. AVR programmes render the psychosocial wellbeing of migrants a crucial criterion for assessing their 'success' or 'failure' as potential members of the host society.

Let me be clear from the outset that my intention here is not to accuse NGO workers who facilitate AVR of misleading migrants or luring them into the decision to return. On the contrary, most of the NGO workers whom I interviewed and observed in their interaction with migrants demonstrated a high level of professionalism, empathy towards the migrants, and a genuine intention, in my opinion, to help migrants to come to the best decision regarding their future, even when this meant declining the services of AVR.

It is, nevertheless, precisely because NGO workers are clearly not behind any ill-intended or anti-migration policy that I argue that the ideological groundworks that legitimise AVR have been perfected. A critical interrogation of AVR reveals how hegemonic ideas about free choice, state sovereignty and territoriality, which are invested in notions of 'voluntarism' and 'home', eloquently succeed in concealing the violence that is implied in using them for promoting AVR, instead of looking for solutions that do not involve the territorial removal of people with a migration background who are found in dire situations. AVR programmes are embedded in and plastered with a dominant morality that not only justifies the repatriation of psychosocially affected people by the sovereign state, but also renders it a benevolent act of caring for those who failed to manage their life in the destination country. As the number of people who return each year via AVR is limited (mostly by budget allocation), it can be argued that the instrumentality of these programmes is to be found not only in the repatriation of vulnerable people, but also in the fashioning of a morality that legitimises states' immigration regimes, which include coercive practices of forced removal and violent deportations.

The chapter continues with a short note on the European scheme for AVR and the manner in which I methodologically examined it in Spain. It is then followed by two sections, which critically dissect the major notions that frame AVR, namely 'voluntarism' and 'home'. The chapter concludes by reflecting on the ways in which NGO workers are swayed to become part of the migration/ deportation nexus. I dwell on the dilemmas and rationalisations of NGO workers as they expose the construction of a morality that legitimises soft deportation and reinforces states' immigration regimes that exclude vulnerable people, instead of attending to their psychosocial wellbeing in Spain.

Voluntary return programmes in Spain

Spain, like many other countries across Europe, has been facilitating in recent years AVR for migrants, either with or without a legal status, who are in a vulnerable situation, suffering severely from economic and/or social exclusion (Koch 2014; Ruben *et al.* 2009; Webber 2011). In the period from 2008 to 2013, the European Return Fund allocated, as part of its programme 'Solidarity and Management of Migration Flows', a sum of €676 million towards AVR to be operated in different EU member states. In Spain, it is the Interior Ministry that was tasked to manage this fund, issuing a tender for organisations to present their bid for receiving a slice of the overall budget. Among those organisations in Spain that have been receiving funding to operate AVR are an inter-governmental organisation (IOM) and a number of NGOs: some international (Red Cross, YMCA) and some local (ACCEM, CEPAIM). The European Return Fund provides up to 75 per cent of the budget for each approved voluntary return programme. In Spain, the Ministry of Health, Social Services and Equality is the main body that provides the other 25 per cent of the budget for the organisations that operate these programmes.

AVR is basically offered to all migrants and asylum-seekers, with legal or illegalised status, who 1) do not hold Spanish nationality; 2) do not have any legal prohibition on leaving the country; and 3) are ready to sign a contract that impedes them from coming back to Spain for any work-related activity for a minimum period of three years. While different organisations offer different variants of AVR, most offer some sort of pre-return assistance (legal, psychological, medical, as well as the practical arrangements of flight tickets, transport to the airport and so on), and monetary assistance in the form of a one-time bonus (usually €300 to €1,300 per person; in the case of a family, the total sum can thus be up to a few thousand euros). In addition, certain organisations also offer returnees some sort of capacity-building: training in the setting up of a small business or in acquiring a certified qualification, such as a kindergarten teacher or a chef. Certain organisations go even further and work together with returnees on a plan for reintegration, which may include assistance in their country of origin with setting up the business or seeking employment and/or education.

This chapter is based on 18 months of non-consecutive and ongoing field-work in Spain, which I have been conducting since April 2014. The study of the implementation of AVR is part of a larger research project that aims to explore the social life of states' deportation regimes. I conducted 12 interviews with managers and workers in different NGOs that facilitate AVR programmes in Catalonia and Madrid. In the immigration department of Catalonia as well as at the municipal level in Barcelona, I met with high-ranked civil servants who are involved in implementing voluntary and forced removals. At the YMCA facility in Barcelona, I was allowed to attend four meetings with individuals and families who sought AVR. I also held numerous informal conversations with workers in the YMCA and made on-site observations. In addition, I have talked to 14 people who have been subjected to policies of territorial removal in Spain.

Voluntarism

During my first interview in the municipality of Barcelona with the head of the 'Service of Attention to Immigrants, Foreigners and Refugees' (SAIER), the civil servant who is in charge of AVR, the latter began her introduction of SAIER's work by resolutely stating: 'One important thing before we start, here at SAIER when we discuss voluntary return, we do not make any link with the theme of deportation. Here the people who are interested in having information are coming *only* and *whenever* they want to come'. The words 'only' and 'whenever' were particularly stressed by her. At a later moment in the interview, she pointed to the entrance door that automatically opens to a busy street next to Plaza España: 'If they walk through this door we welcome them. If you come here, we listen to you and we serve you. For us it does not matter whether you are a regular or an irregular migrant'. Those working at SAIER emphatically stress the voluntarism of people who seek their services. Disregarding on purpose the il/legal status of people underscores, in the eyes of SAIER staff, their moral stance and humanitarian approach in helping those in need.

According to those who design and implement AVR, the voluntarism of these programmes is based on the alleged free choice of migrants to seek out these programmes and to return to their home country of their own free will. One need not evoke the old debates around agency vs structure, idealism vs determinism, or existentialism vs structuralism in order to point out the feeble grounds on which AVR programmes proclaim the element of voluntarism. It suffices, in fact, to listen to those who facilitate AVR in order to note the incongruous usage of 'voluntarism' in this context. The head of SAIER passionately explained to me the reason behind the decision to launch in 2014 a new service for migrants who seek to return 'home':

We did a lot of thinking before we proposed this change in SAIER [to offer comprehensive information about and support to AVR]. We realised that there were many migrants who ended up, because of the crisis or because of psychological issues, in a horrible situation, with no job, no income, sometimes even living in the street. So if these people decide that they want to return to their country of origin, then it is our task to help them.

Similarly, the manager of YMCA in Barcelona told me about their internal deliberations before deciding to facilitate AVR:

When we started thinking about it we didn't feel comfortable. Return programmes are not part of our work at YMCA. We work on the integration of children, youth and families in difficult conditions of vulnerability. So when we considered incorporating voluntary return programmes, we felt a bit difficult with it. But then we said that we would pay close attention to the manner in which we accompany these people, to whom will we offer this help, and in what situations are the people who decide to leave. And what we saw was that people are in a very difficult situation. The truth is that it is not so voluntary. But at the end people return happily. Well, not happily, but there is not a complete breakdown (because of the return) as we were afraid there might be.

It is clear that the idea of those who are involved in facilitating AVR is that the motor behind these schemes is people's desperation, lack of hope, and the harsh situation in which they find themselves. The part of the story usually omitted is that these people are not offered any institutional assistance in Spain to haul them out of their predicament. The 'return preparedness' (Cassarino 2014) of many who seek AVR is thus reduced to negative motivations, stemming from their vulnerability, and not from aspiring ideas and/or enabling resources that may render return an attractive life strategy. In this case, when the most vulnerable people are selected to become AVR 'clients', there are few prospects for them to enjoy an improved life upon return, let alone to contribute to the development of their country of origin.

With the economic crisis in Spain, many families with a migration background are now fully dependent on soup kitchens and on basic assistance that they receive each month from charity organisations and NGOs. Under the hegemonic neoliberal ideology, 'failing' migrants should not become dependent on the welfare state. They should, instead, either be sustained by the 'humanitarian sector' or be removed from the territory of developed nation-states. As many people who decide to seek AVR suffer from severe psychosocial and/or mental health conditions, and are left to their own devices by the state, to what extent can anyone genuinely frame such decisions as voluntary? The notion of voluntarism under such circumstances is a double euphemism, standing de facto for an exclusionary state structure that benevolently 'offers' certain people to 'take a decision' when no other options are available.

One is reminded here of the classic scene in Elia Kazan's film (1954) *On the Waterfront*, where the poor dockworkers have to gather each morning at the port and fight to get hired as day labourers for what would be a 16-hour hard working day for a miserable wage. Of course, they all come to the port each morning out of choice, and if they are lucky to get hired, they work of their own free will. Clearly, one can only talk here about the voluntarism of the dock-workers, or call their exploitative employment a 'voluntary subsistence pro-gramme', by powerfully ignoring the structural conditions of non-unionised labourers, the powerful capitalist company, the non-interventionist state (or intervening only on behalf of the employers' interest), and the overall despair of people living in extreme poverty, in bad health and with no certainty about their future income. Can anyone seriously refer to the decision of dockworkers to get hired in this constellation of circumstances a case of voluntarism? Indeed, although the film celebrates the agency of the oppressed dockworkers, it never-theless grimly shows that attempts to reject exploitative employment, or to stand up against the structural injustices of the system, result in violent destitution.[2]

Recent academic literature on AVR has made a compelling argument about the misleading element of voluntarism that is implied in return programmes. In a polemical manner, Frances Webber (2011) has questioned 'How voluntary are voluntary returns?' By systematically matching the explicit goals of these pro-grammes with the results they achieve, and by pointing to the practices of inter-national, national and local agencies that are involved in the implementation of such programmes, Webber unequivocally concluded that 'Virtually none of the schemes currently operating as "voluntary return programmes" from Europe meet the criteria for voluntariness'. Webber then continues to make the charge that 'Voluntary return is instead offered as a less painful alternative to continued destitution followed by (inevitable) compulsory return' (2011: 103). Scrutinis-ing AVR in Britain as applied to migrants and asylum-seekers from Afghanistan, Blitz *et al.* (2005: 182) conclude that 'Afghans are being urged to return by means of financial inducements, and sometimes under the threat of repatriation. In this context, we can discern a new category of "non-voluntary" returns where individual choice has little real meaning'.

In Spain, I talked to a few migrants whose return has been assisted by YMCA. Most of them were very content with the support they received and were grateful to the workers at YMCA for their attention and careful handling of the entire process. Some migrants mentioned that they were happy to leave Spain, but mostly because their life there had become impossible. Others appeared to be worried and defeated. At any rate, the point I am pressing here is that our critical and ethical analysis of the manner in which AVR operates within the larger nexus of migration/deportation management by states should not be confused with the experiences and judgement of 'voluntarily' returned people. These emic judgements are already shaped by, and should be seen as the outcome of, a state-led migration apparatus that (im)poses the option of voluntary return solely against the option of an illegalised life and/or a marginal existence and painful exclusion from social benefits. As an experienced worker at YMCA explained to me,

> We have two main profiles of people who ask for voluntary return programmes. One kind is of those who realise that their life in Spain is not going to be so good as it was and they prefer to leave, or those who came here to complete a certain goal – have enough money for buying a house, or sending their children to university, or putting up a business – and once their goal is completed they go back home happily. The other kind is people in really bad situations, extreme poverty, living in the street, mental pathologies. These people have a horrible life here; for them it is ... well, it is voluntary return in quotation marks. It is just that they have no other option.

Almost all the people I talked to were unequivocal about considering or accepting AVR as a last resort. It was the severe psychosocial issues that led them to an engagement with AVR. Importantly, in Spain, migrants who have gained residency and have been settled for many years in the country can lose their legal status and become deportable when they fall into a period of unemployment. As explained by Garcés-Mascareñas (2013: 12),

> Immigrants [who are] unable to demonstrate their integration as workers during the first five years of residence run the risk of losing their legal status and, in most cases, fall back into illegality. This loss of legality has been far from infrequent due to the extremely high numbers of temporary immigrant workers and the instability that characterises the Spanish job market.

This is a clear case whereby the state eclipses its citizenship regime under the market logic. On the one hand, healthy, employed and self-sustaining migrants, preferably highly skilled, are welcome to stay and can achieve a legal status; on the other hand, ill, vulnerable, dependent migrants, suffering from psychosocial issues, are rejected by the Spanish state and designated for 'rehabilitation' back in their home country. The Spanish state, in a deep and perverse sense, induces the flexibilisation of certain people's sense of belonging to a country where they have been settled for years, and where they have invested their productive (labour) and reproductive (raising families) energies (cf. Kalir 2010).

Some migrants in dire situations, who approached YMCA for a first interview, explained that they still had some hope of getting a new employment contract that might secure them some income and the possibility of maintaining their status as residents or for legalising their undocumented status. It was only if that contract did not materialise, they explained, that they would continue with the AVR because they were otherwise afraid for their (family's) sustainability, health and, as some mentioned, their sanity.

This is why I am interested here in understanding the logic that sways NGO workers in Spain to go along with and facilitate AVR, while understanding that these are state-led impositions that, in the lack of any alternative, should be regarded, at best, as pseudo-voluntary return and, at worst, as a form of 'soft deportation'. One clue for answering this intriguing question may be found in the ostentatious deployment of the notion of 'home' in the formulation and implementation of AVR.

Home

'*Thinking of return? Thinking of home?*' – this slogan adorns the IOM page where information can be downloaded and a telephone number is publicised for bringing interested migrants up to speed with information on AVR. '*Thinking of home? Voluntary return brings you back home*' is the banner on posters that have been recently used in Belgium for promoting a campaign for AVR administrated by the Federal Agency for the Reception of Asylum Seekers (Fedasil). In Spain, '*Back Home! Voluntary return programs*' is the catchphrase chosen by *Rumiñahui*, a voluntary association established in 1997 dedicated to defending the rights of migrants, facilitating their integration and improving their quality of life *in Spain*.

This is a random sample of organisations that emphatically profile AVR as a return to one's 'home'. It is characteristic of organisations that facilitate AVR to deliberately deploy the notion of 'home' as a signifier for a desired place to which migrants are to be returned. The idea of 'home' in this context is clearly meant to index positive notions such as safety, familiarity, comfort and so on. After all, in popular culture, as in traditions across the world, 'home' is where everyone wants to be. In their alluring deployment of 'home', campaigns for AVR completely ignore other possible meanings that are carried by the concept for the people they target (see King and Christou 2010). For example, 'home' can be an exclusionary space and a potentially violent environment (Price 2002), or the hallmark of patriarchal configurations that place the responsibility for taking care of one's family on individualised parents, mostly through the depreciated labour of women (Ahmed 1999; Brun and Fábos 2015; Young 1997).

One need only consider the experience of millions of people around the world who suffer from domestic violence. Often they are unable to physically challenge their abusive spouse, and their 'home' becomes a hell on earth. Under a hegemonic patriarchal system, attempting to stop the violence, by an appeal to legal means or a close circle of family and friends, often results in adding insult to injury, as a harsh stigma is placed precisely on those who protest against the violence that is enshrined by their 'home'. For the victims of domestic violence who end up in a hospital or in a shelter, a return 'home' often spells out the next horror. It is interesting to note that violence suffered in the private sphere, as in the case of domestic violence, is not recognised by the 1951 Convention relating to the Status of Refugees as grounds for seeking asylum in another country. Only state violence, or violence perpetrated on collective grounds, as in racial, ethnic and religious persecution, is included in the 1951 Convention.

Private violence, according to this international convention, is a matter to be resolved in one's own 'home' (country).

Consider here also the experience of millions of people who have suffered from ethnic or religious persecution in their 'home' land. Scores of Jews, who managed to escape Nazi Germany during the Second World War, were eventually returned 'home' only to face extermination. Those who survived the horror often refused to ever set foot on German 'home' ground for the rest of their lives. Writing on more recent experiences of refugees' repatriation in Europe, Black (2002: 136) contends that the political geography of return to Bosnia and Kosovo 'involves much more than the ethnic geography of where people used to live, and can now live. It involves a series of interconnections and dynamic political, economic and social changes that call into question our very notion of what "home" is'.

In its territorial dimension, 'home' is, in fact, an inherently exclusionary notion. It implies borders and ownership that fervently demarcate the insiders from the outsiders. In the name of homeland security, democratic countries around the world violate their citizens' most basic human rights (see, for instance, the Patriot Act in the US), launch pre-emptive wars that kill scores of innocent civilians (witness the acts of the 'Coalition Forces' against Afghanistan), and invest billions in fortifying borders – from the US–Mexico border to the incarcerated Gaza strip, and from the Spanish enclaves of Ceuta and Melilla in Africa to the Evros region on the border between Greece and Turkey.

It is, therefore, my contention that the positive notion of 'home' as deployed by those who propagate AVR is not only highly incomplete, but also one that ideologically reflects the position of the sovereign, patriarchal state. In this sense, deploying the notion of 'home' as a protective and desired place should be seen as a cynical discursive exercise that ignores and negates the experience of many subordinated, destitute and mobile subjects. At YMCA, one of those working on AVR told me that she saw the return to one's home as an integral part of the migratory process: 'I believe that normally everyone wants to return to their home. I don't believe that there are many people who stay forever in another country'.

In Spain, many of those who solicit AVR are long-term settled individuals and entire families with a migratory background. These are people who have been living and working in Spain for many years, but more recently lost their jobs, like many other Spaniards, due to the economic crisis. Instead of there being an institutional programme of assistance to all those who are hit by long-term unemployment in this time of crisis, the state of Spain, and the many organisations that work with it on AVR, press those people with migratory background to leave the country and return to their 'home'. A return 'home' is then framed as a solution to their predicament of unemployment, poverty and exclusion. The perverse proposition that a return to one's 'home' is the best way to deal with difficult situations is found in the fact that, almost without exception, all the organisations that facilitate AVR mention that priority is given to those who appear to be in the worst of situations. Here is a typical phrasing of this priority, by the Red Cross in Spain:

> This service, at no cost to participants, is aimed at offering social assistance and facilitation of voluntary return to countries of origin to people from extra-communitarian [non-EU] states in an irregular administrative situation, with special priority for those who are at risk of social exclusion, have acute health concerns and/or belong to groups with high degree of vulnerability like female victims of gender-based violence, minors, victims of human trafficking or torture, etc.

It is unclear on what grounds it is suggested by states and organisations that a return 'home' to a place which people tried so hard to leave, or where they have been tortured, would constitute a solution to their predicaments. Not even in the case of those suffering from unemployment and economic marginality is it clear why a return, usually to a much poorer country than Spain, will assist in any form their way out of poverty. It is, therefore, precisely here that the positive deployment of the notion of 'home' is meant to perform emotional work – through nostalgia and romantic ideas – in convincing people in despair to leave Spain. At the same time, the positive idea of sending people to their 'home' morally persuades those who implement AVR to believe that what they do is not contributing to 'cleansing' society of debilitated migrants, but is, instead, benevolent and in the best interests of the people they service.

At YMCA, the workers who facilitate AVR made it clear to me that they evaluate carefully and attend to the request for assisted return of every person who comes to their office, but they first offer AVR to those in situations of extreme poverty or homelessness. In fact, their preferred population comprised those who were referred to the YMCA for voluntary return by social workers. These people were clearly already known to the local and/or national authorities as being in a dire situation and with little hope of getting any meaningful assistance in Spain. Tellingly, an evaluation of the psychosocial wellbeing of returnees is not part of the contract of NGOs that facilitate AVR programmes. Nevertheless, some NGO workers told me that they occasionally stayed in touch with returnees. This was either because returnees contacted NGO workers to express their gratitude (via phone calls, emails and letters) or because NGO workers were worried about the safety and overall wellbeing of returnees, and wanted to hear from them a 'sign of life'.

The swaying of NGO workers to implement AVR

For many critics of AVR, it is predominantly the IOM that is seen as using notions like humanitarianism and dignity in assisting states to conceal the repressive elements of their migration policies. Ashutosh and Mountz (2011: 34), interrogating the role of the IOM in managing return programmes in Australia, conclude that 'the IOM functions as a state apparatus in supranational guise …

the IOM transforms the state through the language of international humanitarianism, giving the appearance of state subjection to global protocols that would otherwise signal the limits of the nation-state'. Webber (2011: 105) also singles out the IOM as a major culprit in permitting states to hide behind the idea of voluntarism, while in fact 'for the IOM, the lack of real choice is seen as a key ingredient to the success of the "voluntary" return programmes they offer. [...] Acceptance of the AVR option rests on there being no other choice'.

In Spain, the number of deportations from 2010 to 2014 stood at 26,291, the highest in Europe in comparison with all other states.[3] In the very same period, AVR has been made extensively available in Spain through the European Return Fund and the Spanish government. This non-coincidental concurrence of state instruments in 'migration management'[4] confirms the working idea of the IOM, as well as of state officials and some NGOs. AVR is only effective when the alternative is an expected forced deportation.

While the IOM has historically been the major organisation to facilitate AVR across the world, it is important to note that, more recently, numerous NGOs, on international, national and local levels, have entered this expanding niche. The IOM is explicitly committed to working with states in managing migration flows, and it is for this reason that such involvement with AVR is in line with its mission statement. The situation is different in the case of many NGOs whose prime mission is to support the integration of marginalised migrants into the local society where they reside. It is this missing link that I attempt to highlight and analyse here: what motivates NGOs such as the YMCA to work with states in implementing so-called voluntary return programmes whose aim is almost opposite to theirs, namely, to de-integrate and repatriate marginalised people to their so-called 'home'?

There is an immediate pragmatic answer to this question: running AVR is a profit-making activity for civil-society organisations that often struggle to secure budgets for their activities. This is, in fact, what the manager of YMCA Cataluña openly admitted, albeit with evident discomfort:

> At the time that you are not dependent on your own funds but on a certain funder, then it is ... well, it is complicated. This [AVR] is one such case. You need to understand that as NGOs we are not governmental, we are dependent either on our own financing, like from membership fees, or on donors, including the state. We see the commercial part, the one in which we engage in more business-like activities, as the means through which we can then support the social activities that we offer. It is a sort of survival strategy. To help out a family in a difficult situation can take one or two years, even three. We need to be able to say, 'we are going to be by your side helping you in the coming three years'. This is our responsibility. We must take care of the financial side of our organisation. There are many marginalised families that if we don't help them they will disappear [from our reach] and will end up in a very bad situation, precisely at the moment that they need us most. So it is inconvenient to situate ourselves in this way,

but if we want to help certain families, we sometimes must take decisions that are not so pleasant [like AVR]. It is our responsibility.

The manager went on to say that she could clearly see the problematic ethical issue in having YMCA facilitating AVR. She recounted her hesitation at first over YMCA implementing such programmes. Since it has been decided in favour of implementing AVR, she claims to understand perfectly whenever certain employees at YMCA do not wish to be involved in this activity.

Although the ethical issue of facilitating AVR by the YMCA has been thrown open, and workers can take a personal position on it, it appears that a unanimous idea prevails about the moral good that is underlining the work on these programmes. Here is how one YMCA employee who is in charge of the implementation of AVR saw it:

> I maintain that we are helping people. To be honest, I don't think much more than that. I have a person in front of me who is requesting assistance and I am going to try to help this person. It is true that sometimes I'm thinking, 'with this kind of budget what would I do? Integration, capacitation …' But at the end, there is a person who demands it [AVR] and is suffering, and has a goal [to return] … so, here I am [to help].

The idea of voluntarism as in 'voluntary return' springs from the trope of neoliberalism, which champions rational and free choice as it ideologically forms and bureaucratically treats members in society as autonomous individuals who are able and expected to conduct themselves responsibly (Povinelli 2011; Rose 1999). Voluntarism thus has a double task here in morally justifying the otherwise ethically problematic implementation of AVR by NGOs like YMCA. First, it puts all the responsibility for the decision to return on migrants.[5] Second, it ignores all the structural injustices, discrimination and exclusion that have produced the marginality and vulnerability of migrants who are now pushed to demand a 'voluntary return'.

Let me repeat here that what I suggest is not that NGO workers are adopting blindly the logic that is promoted by the state in dealing with vulnerable subjects with a migration background. From my interviews and observations of workers at YMCA, there can be little doubt that they are mostly driven by a deep intention to assist to the best of their ability people who are seen to be in need of help. Many of the workers at YMCA are deeply committed to the values of social work and the humanistic treatment of vulnerable individuals and groups. They establish close relationships with those they assist, and they often invest much more time and effort than is formally required by their job in making sure that returnees receive the best treatment that they possibly can. As one worker at YMCA told me, 'We get to know some of them very closely. We visit them at home and we know their children. It becomes almost like a family. Then when they leave we often hug them and cry with them. It can get very emotional'.

The emotional labour involved in implementing AVR programmes undoubtedly buttresses the conviction of NGO workers regarding the ethics of humanitarianism and benevolent morality that underpin their work. Yet, the manner in which ideology works to sway civil-society actors is a much more sophisticated and indirect one. In the case of development aid, Chipkin (2003: 73) defined the notion of 'assistance' as the 'process whereby the state tries to capture [individuals] into a host of relationships ... to compel them to act according to what it defines as functional/social/ethical behaviour'. While Chipkin points to the way in which the state brings into its ideological circle those individuals who are being helped, I highlight the fact that a similar incorporation into the state logic and its neoliberal ideology is at work with respect to those, like YMCA workers, who are entrusted with facilitating assistance to the subjects of aid/development/voluntary return.

Many neoliberal Western states have been rolling back the welfare state (Wacquant 2010) while simultaneously engineering a space for civil-society and charity organisations to do the work of managing and assisting certain populations (Junge 2012; Navaro-Yashin 2002). In order for this political configuration to function effectively, civil-society organisations have been made financially dependent on the state (and/or other private funders) and ideologically incorporated into the hegemonic neoliberal thinking that lowers the threshold for a moral and ethical questioning of the very logic of managing populations in a particular fashion. I thus fully agree with Chipkin (2003: 73): 'We can say that such assistance is not simply about helping residents exercise their rights as citizens. It is about producing them as citizens in the first place!' In this vein, AVR programmes have two interrelated consequences: first, they shape the ethics of NGO workers who assist vulnerable populations with a migratory background; second, these programmes are not simply about helping migrants to go back 'home', but rather, about reproducing or even reinventing vulnerable subjects as migrants who are not in their 'home' and should thus seek protection and help for their predicaments elsewhere. Rejecting a solution for these predicaments within the Spanish territory is thus made ethically unproblematic, and helping vulnerable subjects to leave Spain and return 'home' becomes a moral act.

Epilogue

At the international airport of Barcelona, in May 2015, I meet up with Gaia[6] from YMCA. She is in charge on that day of seeing off a few of those who leave Spain via AVR. Gaia needs to provide each of the returnees with the promised €400 cheque, and have them sign some final documents before they depart. It is clear that all the returnees are on good terms with Gaia. She knows them each by their personal name, including the children and babies. Some want to have a last photo with Gaia before going through passport control. After he checked in to his flight to Guayaquil, I talk with Vicente, who lived for 15 years in Spain and is now returning to Ecuador. 'I tried everything I could that this moment would not come', he tells me laconically. Having accepted his inevitable return, he muses, 'I had a very good life in Spain. I now return to nothing in Ecuador'. I ask Vicente about the treatment he received at YMCA. 'They are doing a wonderful work there. I am thankful for everything they did for me'. Vicente still has two hours before his plane will take off. He sits down and stares at the check-in counter. Gaia, who just helped a family of four to check in for their flight to Honduras, comes to ask if I will join her for a coffee at the automatic machine nearby. 'After the check-in I usually let them be. There is not so much more to say and I also feel exhausted', she explains as we throw our coins into the coffee machine.

'What if Vicente or any of them will now decide to go back to Barcelona instead of boarding the flight?' – this thought occurred to me and I voiced it to Gaia. 'They can do it if they want. There is nothing I can do. I am not the state', she replies. 'So it is not very effective …' I began saying, but Gaia quickly cut me off: 'If you ask me, it is not effective at all. They can also return tomorrow to Spain and work again without documents. They only sign a paper saying they are not able to return for formal work or business related purposes. But many of them worked here anyway without documents, so for them there is no difference. This voluntary return is clearly just to get them out of the country and to check a box'.

In this chapter I have argued that NGO workers choose to overlook the fact that many of the people who seek AVR have been excluded and forced into a condition of vulnerability by a lack of state provisions and by disputed regulations. By not fighting this institutional marginalisation, and by facilitating a humane implementation of AVR, NGOs contribute to the depoliticisation and, indirectly, to the legitimisation of state policies that very often exacerbate the fragile psychosocial condition of vulnerable people (cf. Kalir 2015; Kalir and Wissink 2016).

As I demonstrated, those at YMCA who implement AVR are not doing it blindly. Indeed, on the contrary, most of them evaluate these programmes as ineffective in guaranteeing a sustainable return. Some are also critical about the potential adverse effects for people who suffer from severe psychosocial problems that should be resolved here and now, and not by returning them to their 'home' country.

In Spain, as in many other countries that promote AVR, the wide implementation of these programmes by critical managers and workers in civil-society organisations illustrates the triumph of the neoliberal state in creating a financial and ideological configuration under which repressive policies are executed by do-gooders. In such a constellation, hegemonic ideas inform structures and practices that determine the treatment of some of the most vulnerable subjects in our societies, whose migration background can be easily reactivated for setting them apart and for treating them as objects of 'voluntary' removal to their 'home'.

Notes

1 I would like to thank all my informants for kindly and candidly interacting with me during my research in Barcelona and Madrid. I also thank Russell King and Zana Vathi for useful comments while working on this chapter. A special thanks to Kipod, who is still looking for a 'home' out there. This research was supported by the European Research Council, Starting Grant 336319, *The Social Life of State Deportation Regimes: A Comparative Study of the Implementation Interface.*
2 For an interesting take on the striking similarities between the situation of nineteenth-century dockworkers and immigrant day labourers in the US today, see Skerry (2008).
3 See cadenaser.com/ser/2015/04/03/sociedad/1428012211_939510.html (accessed 5 May 2015).
4 The commonly used term 'migration management', introduced in 1993 by the Commission of the United Nations to improve the governmental regulation of migration, only further depoliticises the political project behind the extreme measures taken by states to secure their borders (Geiger and Pécoud 2010).
5 The tendency to attribute ample agency to mobile subjects, while ignoring structural and cultural conditions that shape such agency, is typical of much of the literature on migration theories (on circumventing this tendency, see Kalir 2005; Kalir and Sur 2012).
6 All names in this chapter are pseudonyms.

References

Ahmed, S. (1999) Home and away narratives of migration and estrangement, *International Journal of Cultural Studies* 2(3): 329–347.

Ashutosh, I. and Mountz, A. (2011) Managing migration for the benefit of whom? Interrogating the work of the International Organization for Migration. *Citizenship Studies* 15(1): 21–38.

Black, R. (2002) Conceptions of 'home' and the political geography of refugee repatriation: between assumption and contested reality in Bosnia-Herzegovina, *Applied Geography* 22(2): 123–138.

Blitz, B.K., Sales, R. and Marzano, L. (2005) Non-voluntary return? The politics of return to Afghanistan, *Political Studies* 53(1): 182–200.

Brun, C. and Fábos, A.H. (2015) Making homes in limbo? A conceptual framework, *Refuge* 31(1): 5–17.

Cassarino, J.P. (2014) A case for return preparedness, in Battistella, G. (ed.) *Global and Asian Perspectives on International Migration*. Cham: Springer, 153–165.

Chipkin, I. (2003) 'Functional' and 'dysfunctional' communities: the making of national citizens, *Journal of Southern African Studies* 29(1): 63–82.

Feldman, G. (2012) *The Migration Apparatus*. Stanford: Stanford University Press.

Garcés-Mascareñas, B. (2013) Reconsidering the 'policy gap': policy implementation and outcomes in Spain. Barcelona: GRITIM UPF Working Paper Series 18.

Geiger, M. and Pécoud, A. (2010) *The Politics of International Migration Management*. Basingstoke: Palgrave Macmillan.

Junge, B. (2012) NGOs as shadow pseudopublics: grassroots community leaders' perceptions of change and continuity in Porto Alegre, Brazil, *American Ethnologist* 39(2): 407–424.

Kalir, B. (2005) The development of a migratory disposition: explaining a 'new emigration', *International Migration* 43(4): 167–196.

Kalir, B. (2010) *Latino Migrants in the Jewish State: Undocumented Lives in Israel*. Bloomington: Indiana University Press.

Kalir, B. (2015) The Jewish state of anxiety: between moral obligation and fearism in the treatment of African asylum seekers in Israel, *Journal of Ethnic and Migration Studies* 41(4): 580–598.

Kalir, B. and Sur, M. (2012) *Transnational Flows and Permissive Polities: Ethnographies of Human Mobilities in Asia*. Amsterdam: Amsterdam University Press.

Kalir, B. and Wissink, L. (2016) The deportation continuum: convergences between state agents and NGO workers in the Dutch deportation field, *Citizenship Studies* 20(1): 34–49.

King, R. and Christou, A. (2010) Cultural geographies of counter-diasporic migration: perspectives from the study of second-generation 'returnees' to Greece, *Population, Space and Place* 16(2): 103–119.

Koch, A. (2014) The politics and discourse of migrant return: the role of UNHCR and IOM in the governance of return, *Journal of Ethnic and Migration Studies* 40(6): 905–923.

Navaro-Yashin, Y. (2002) *Faces of the State: Secularism and Public Life in Turkey*. Princeton, NJ: Princeton University Press.

Povinelli, E. (2011) *Economies of Abandonment: Social Belonging and Endurance in Late Liberalism*. Durham, NC: Duke University Press.

Price, J. (2002) The apotheosis of home and the maintenance of space of violence, *Hypatia* 17(4): 39–70.

Rose, N. (1999) *Powers of Freedom: Reframing Political Thought*. Cambridge: Cambridge University Press.

Ruben, R., van Houte, M. and Tine, D. (2009) What determines the embeddedness of forced-return migrants? Rethinking the role of pre- and post-return assistance, *International Migration Review* 43(4): 908–937.

Skerry, P. (2008) Day laborers and dock workers: casual labor markets and immigration policy, *Society* 45(1): 46–52.

Wacquant, L. (2010) Crafting the neoliberal state: workfare, prisonfare and social insecurity, *Sociological Forum* 25(2): 197–220.

Webber, F. (2011) How voluntary are voluntary returns? *Race and Class* 52: 98–107.

Young, I.M. (1997) House and home: feminist variations on a theme, in I. Young (ed.) *Intersecting Voices: Dilemmas of Gender, Political Philosophy, and Policy*. Princeton, NJ: Princeton University Press, 134–164.

Part II

Ancestral returns, adaptation and re-migration

5 Roots migration to the ancestral homeland and psychosocial wellbeing

Young Polish diasporic students

Marcin Gońda

Introduction

One consequence of the recent turbulent history of Poland is a large Polish diaspora. After the collapse of communism in 1989, some of its members began to return to their ancestors' country. Among these 'returnees' is a group of young people of Polish descent from the former Soviet Union who undertake or have undertaken university studies in Poland. Since return possibilities are limited, migration for educational reasons often remains the only attainable way of moving there (Lesińska 2010: 4–5).

This chapter explores the experience of Polish diasporic students from the post-Soviet states who are studying in the ancestral homeland. They are mainly the descendants of Poles who remained in exile as a result of resettlements into the Soviet territory during the Second World War and the post-war shifts of Poland's borders westwards. For the purpose of this study, Susanne Wessendorf's concept of 'roots migration' (2007) will be utilised, as it best justifies these young adults' complex situation. In fact, the students are not 'returning' to Poland, since they actually never left it (Nowicka 2000: 8). The 'return' term is mostly used to analyse the counter-diasporic move of first-generation migrants to their native homeland. It might seem, therefore, that it would be more accurate to define the investigated group as 'second- or subsequent-generation returnees' (King and Christou 2008: 1–4) or, perhaps, 'ethnic return migrants' (Tsuda 2009: 2). Both these notions denote the 'return' of the descendants of diaspora members to the ethnic homeland after a long period of living abroad. These conceptualisations, however, are not wholly satisfactory either. Despite maintaining transnational contacts, and even having experience of short stays in the homeland, later-generation migrants often refuse to perceive their transfer there as a return. Similarly, they do not exclusively feel a sense of full belonging to any given national community, as they might be of multi-ethnic background. Existing studies on returns do not provide precise terms to describe migrants of mixed ethnicity relocating to a seemingly known place from which only some of their family stem. The 'roots migration' concept seems to answer these conceptual challenges, as it refers to 'the migration to a place where members of the second generation originate from, but where they have never lived' (Wessendorf

2007: 1084). It acknowledges migrants' intergenerational and ethnic affinity features but does not necessarily explore the ontology of return itself (Gońda 2015: 70).

There is a small but scattered literature on the phenomenon of diasporic youth studying in the ancestral homeland. Whereas there are several studies on the situation of foreign students in host countries (e.g. Asmar 2005) and their subsequent return to their countries of origin (e.g. Bijwaard and Wang 2013), the reverse problem of educational mobility as a means of return migration seems to be a rather Polish specificity (Dzwonkowski *et al.* 2002; Mucha 2003; Wyszyński 2005). When it comes to the general problem of students' psycho-social situation upon migration, the papers of Poyrazli *et al.* (2010) and Desa *et al.* (2012) are worth mentioning. Such studies are, however, mostly limited to quantitative investigations by cross-cultural psychologists on students' accultura-tive stress. There is also a more general lack of research on the psychosocial dimension of students' and children's return migration (Vathi and Duci 2016). My contribution, therefore, brings new findings to the issue of return migration undertaken through the higher education channel.

The chapter's aims are twofold. First, it analyses the strategies of roots migra-tion to the predecessors' country and examines how the notions of 'nation', 'home(land)' and 'belonging' are experienced and constructed by students when in the countries of birth and upon arrival in Poland. Consequently, the article tackles the problem of mutual perceptions of members of the same national community – diaspora in the post-Soviet countries and Poles in Poland. The aim is to determine the consequences of existing ethnic images on the interviewees' national identity and adaptation within Polish society.

Second, the chapter focuses on the impact of roots migration on students' psychosocial wellbeing. Hereinafter, the term 'psychosocial wellbeing' is under-stood with respect to various emotional, social and cultural dimensions of potential migration outcomes (Wessells 1999). In contrast to the broader and externally determined concept of 'human wellbeing', which essentially concen-trates on the relation of being with others (Gough and McGregor 2007), my approach addresses a multiplicity of factors influencing one's migration, creating a deep insight into an individual's internal and subjective perception of the chal-lenges implicated in the process of migration and beyond. Consequently, I try to reconstruct students' coping practices in the ancestral homeland. Migration researchers often consider the 'homecoming' as psychosocially 'safe' as it consti-tutes the 'natural' closure of the migration circle (cf. Boccagni 2011). This pre-sumption mostly refers, however, to first- or second-generation adult returnees who usually have maintained linkages with their country of origin. Many studies show that other returnees are more vulnerable to the unfavourable effects of this kind of mobility. For instance, Vathi and Duci (2016) note that returnee chil-dren's psychosocial condition can be negatively affected not only by their young age (and, thus, exclusion from the decision-making process) and the socio-spatial context (place of relocation), but also by their lack of prior diasporic belongingness.

These conceptual doubts raise the following questions, which frame my study. How does it work out for teenagers who come alone (without their families) to the ancestral country (often without prior experience of visiting it, and with a strongly mythologised image of it) from which only part of their family stems (as they often come from multi-ethnic families)? How do they adapt to these allegedly 'known' (but in fact, often rather 'unknown') surroundings? How does their roots migration affect their psychosocial condition? Does it bring a sense of psychological security, or rather, psychological disturbance? What resources and coping strategies do they employ to counteract the adaptation challenges they face and to protect their psychosocial wellbeing? What impact does roots migration have on their further life arrangements? Finally, how do the psychosocial processes that accompany cross-border mobility shape their sense of belonging?

Methodology

In order to reconstruct students' roots migration, Fritz Schütze's biographical method of data collection and analysis was used (1983). The empirical basis of the study is 60 biographical narrative interviews carried out between 2010 and 2014 in several Polish academic centres.[1] The interviewees were recruited via a snowballing technique, which deliberately aimed at a broad and diversified sample in socio-demographic terms. The interlocutors were between 19 and 40 years old and arrived in Poland between 1992 and 2013. There were 32 female and 28 male interviewees. The largest groups came from Ukraine (18 interviewees) and Belarus (16), with smaller numbers from a range of other post-Soviet territories including, in the examples quoted here, Russia, Moldova and Lithuania. Among the interviewees there were both 30 current students and 30 graduates, so that insights into both initial and further stages of adaptation to Polish society could be provided. The interviews lasted from 45 minutes to 4 hours.

The selection of this research method is based on the conviction that migration should not be considered as a decontextualised activity but, rather, as a consequence of individualised decisions and the socio-cultural, economic and political conditions in both sending and receiving countries. Moreover, since migration is undertaken at different stages of one's life cycle, it needs to be analysed as continuous throughout life rather than completed at a definitive moment (Ley and Kobayashi 2005: 111). It has important consequences for the entire course of a migrant's life, especially when it is undertaken at an early age, as in the case study presented here. The biographical orientation answers this challenge, as it enables the researcher to trace migration pathways within complex and shifting social, cultural, political and economic contexts. Given the fact that analysis of narrative interviews reconstructs social events from the individual's perspective, it seems to be an appropriate tool to get an insight into the emotional and subjective dimensions embedded in the process of migration and beyond, irrespective of the number of cases being reviewed (Gońda 2015: 71).

Polish diaspora in the post-Soviet countries

Various estimates indicate that there are up to 20 million people of Polish origin living outside Poland, making that diaspora one of the world's largest. However, its diversified structure and wide geographic distribution hinder calculations of its actual size. It includes both migrants in recent years to other EU states and people born outside Poland, that is, descendants of Poles who left the country (voluntarily or involuntarily) in the nineteenth and twentieth centuries, whose ties with the ancestral country may now be very weak. The Poles in Western Europe or North America are mainly voluntary labour migrants (or their children). The reasons for the presence of a diaspora of over 1 million of Polish origin in the former USSR are more complex. They are mostly the descendant generations of ethnic Poles who remained abroad as a result of deportations to the Asian territories of Tsarist Russia and later the Soviet Union during the nineteenth century and the Second World War, as well as resulting from the post-war changes of Poland's borders. These groups are considered as victims of the Soviet regime and, thus, the Polish authorities have a moral obligation to compensate their time in exile (MSZ 2014: 5).

Between 1944 and 1959, there were two repatriation waves covering about 2 million Poles from the USSR who had been Polish citizens in the interwar period (1918–1939). The return of other Poles, who inhabited or were resettled there before 1918, was blocked for political reasons. The Polish minority in the East became an issue of public discourse after the collapse of communism in 1989. However, due to Poland's precarious economic condition during its transition to a market economy, bringing them back was not possible, and thus the state's support was limited to ad hoc aid, namely, preserving Polish culture and language and improving their living conditions (Hut 2014: 9–13). Furthermore, despite a number of preferential admission solutions for returnees having been introduced later, in fact, they do not encourage return migration (Lesińska 2010: 4–5). Still today, the repatriation system remains inefficient and prospective returnees have to overcome lengthy procedures to get Polish citizenship. Regional governing bodies are obliged to cover returnees' reception costs, but they are hesitant to fulfil these duties. In consequence, between 1997 and 2014 only 7,036 people benefited from the repatriation programme (GUS 2015: 469).

Currently, diasporic Poles from the post-Soviet area return via one of three 'paths': institutional, individual and educational (Grzymała-Kazłowska and Grzymała-Moszczyńska 2014: 601–603). The first of these covers returns within the state's repatriation system. Despite numerous Poles living in Lithuania, Belarus and Ukraine, the Repatriation Act of 2000 promotes arrivals from Asian territories of the former USSR. Limitations in this respect result from the authorities' wish to compensate diaspora members who could not take advantage of the post-war repatriation. Difficult living conditions are an additional argument for repatriation from those areas in the first place.

Returns from the East are important for Poland's interests, both for historical reasons and in the context of its progressive depopulation. It is hard to imagine foreigners who could potentially adapt more easily to Polish society. Meanwhile, existing economic and organisational conditions do not allow all interested Poles to return. Therefore, some diaspora members undertake, like other labour migrants, individual migration to Poland without institutional help – the second return path.

Consequently, due to weak effectiveness of the official repatriation programme and the lack of wider support for individual returns, educational migration – the third pathway – often remains the only attainable way of moving to Poland. It is estimated that in 2014 young people of Polish descent represented one-fifth of the 46,000 'foreign' students in Poland (GUS 2015: 467). This can be attributed to special enrolment programmes, including scholarships for young diaspora members. The basic aim of these initiatives is to strengthen the Polish diaspora by facilitating their higher education in Poland and then working for the Polish communities in the East. They are entitled to simplified entry and admission procedures as well as free access to the health service and the right to work or run business without permits. In practice, it is also easy for them to extend their stay permits and to receive Polish citizenship.

Expectations on roots migration

The traditional meaning of the Greek term 'diaspora' refers to a population of shared ethnic and cultural identity scattered as a result of traumatic events, such as resettlement, persecution or genocide (Cohen 1995: 5). Memory of this 'catastrophe' is the identity binder of both diaspora members and co-ethnics in the homeland. Their collective identity and distinctiveness from other groups are defined by constantly sustained transnational contacts and identification with the ancestral country. This becomes their 'true home' and the subject of their collective nostalgia and longing. At the same time, the memory of the homeland, being one of the pillars of diasporic identity, is mythologised through narratives delivered by older community members (Safran 1991: 83–99). Idealised images of the ancestral country that are maintained by successive diasporic generations are accompanied by concrete, although often contradictory, ideas and expectations upon arrival there.

Analysis of the interviews that I collected reveals that roots migration is the result of a complex decision-making process. It is the manifestation of a typical second- or later-generation return pattern, when an individual makes an emotional and existential journey to the source of his or her self-identity and reunites with the ideological homeland. The predecessors' country is perceived as the 'true' place of belonging, where one feels he/she most belongs (King and Christou 2008: 17). Return is principally an autonomous decision based on one's desire to reunite with co-ethnics who share the same cultural and historical origins and narratives. However, since a returnee's origin creates a binding relation with the homeland, return can also be considered as an obligation towards older diaspora members (Gońda 2015: 74). As the original, first-generation migrants and displaced persons often cannot relocate back to the homeland themselves, due to their age, failing health, financial circumstances or personal obligations, the dream of homecoming is projected onto the next diasporic generations (Datta 2013: 97–98). This was the case with Agata (29 years old, born in Lithuania) who fulfilled her parents' dream of return to Poland: 'Dad often mentioned that he had dreamt of moving to Poland, but probably he would not be able to adapt there at his age'. Another interviewee, Bartek (25, Russia), treated his migration to Poland as a tribute to his late father:

> Surely my father greatly appreciated Poland, he wanted to come back here … I sometimes tell myself that my father did not come back but I came back … He left Poland but I returned here …

Furthermore, roots migration could be a result of individual (re)discovery of ethnic roots and the consequent desire to rebuild a partially lost identity, to restore the 'natural order of things' after decades of separation by deepening the connection to the land of the ancestors (Boccagni 2011: 471). The 'return' becomes, in the words of King and Christou, a 'cathartic mission to reclaim [the homeland's] sacred sites and to re-enter its mythic space and time' (2008: 17). The roots migrant's plan is to relocate the dislocated self and to achieve stability and coherence of past times and places. As Darek (29, Belarus) explains,

> I can't think otherwise, this is the way I was brought up … From the first moment I was thinking of my national belonging, when they explained me what the nation is, and it was said I was Polish, there was no other possibility: 'You're Polish, your homeland is Poland, your capital is Warsaw.'

In the case of another interviewee, Lena (37, Belarus), her roots migration was an escape to validate her Polish identity, which she had previously perceived as inferior and backward as compared with the still-dominant Soviet identification:

> I perceived my Polishness as a disadvantage, I was a bit ashamed I was Polish … But at the same time I had a feeling that I couldn't get away from that because I had a Polish father and a large family in Poland, even my mother's name was Kowalska so she too was probably Polish but registered as Belarusian … I felt this was something I couldn't escape from, so I felt I should move to Poland as well.

On the other hand, beside the symbolic and ideological importance of the ancestral homeland for roots migrants, one can observe the weight of instrumental and pragmatic motives related to the possibility of studying abroad and further economic advancement or other living opportunities (Gońda 2015: 82). It is often accompanied by romanticised images of 'mountains of gold' or 'land flowing with milk and honey', which are collectively transmitted to subsequent generations by the diasporic community (Głowacka-Grajper 2007: 335).

Interestingly, the mythologisation of Poland as 'paradise' or the 'promised land' mainly appeals to people who have never visited that country before going there to study (Dzwonkowski *et al.* 2002: 70). For instance for Maria (26, Belarus), Poland appeared to be 'such an idealistic country ... It was something remote, entirely modern, a place where everything was different, was better ...'

Homecoming becomes above all an opportunity for personal empowerment and self-development that is hard to reach in the post-Soviet countries due to either personal or institutional constraints. Therefore, limited access to reputable university studies and the poor state of the job market in Ukraine encouraged Julek (22, Ukraine) to enrol for his studies in Poland:

> I came to the conclusion that I needed to go to Poland, because in Poland at least I would have a chance to achieve something by myself, thanks to my work, my brain ... I would not have to pay someone, I would not have to make it up in the wrong way, right? All you have to do is just to study hard, pass exams and then you get a scholarship ...

However, despite Poland being perceived in the East as an area of relative prosperity, democratic standards, well-mannered inhabitants and a generally higher civilisational order, it still remains a transit migration country *en route* to the 'genuine' Western Europe (Gońda 2015: 76). This attitude also applies to students of Polish descent: 'You know, the closer to the West, the better it is ...' (Nadia, 24, Ukraine); or 'If I had to choose between coming to Poland and Germany, of course I would choose Germany because they are simply better' (Tatiana, 26, Moldova).

In many respects, then, students' roots migration is quite different from the typical return model and rather more like the general phenomenon of international student migration. It achieves its primary goal when it is performed in order to gain educational or professional qualifications and, in parallel, to launch individualisation and emancipation processes (Gońda 2015: 81–82). It is an emotionally neutral area of greater opportunities. This was the case with Paweł (21, Belarus), whose arrival was not ideologically driven but resulted from his ambitions for professional development:

> It doesn't mean that if the grandmother is Polish, because her ID says that she is Polish, her grandson has to attend the Polish Club meetings. No, it was not motivated by any such national factor. It was just, frankly speaking ..., I'm sure it was not because of our nationality, but for other reasons. It was not even perceived at first as an opportunity, but simply a chance for a youngster to develop smoothly.

Roots migration, therefore, may not necessarily be an attempt simply to restore the links with one's homeland. Young people of Polish origin from the East, who were born and raised abroad, whose families stay in exile for generations and are often of multi-ethnic background, do not exclusively perceive

Poland as their 'homeland' and other Poles as their 'fellow-countrymen' (Wessendorf 2007: 1087). While the desire to return is embedded in the definition of diaspora, roots migration can be initiated, like labour migration, because of economic considerations. Thus, it should not be considered as an expression of an ideological desire to unite with the nation, but, rather, as an expression of individualistic and instrumental motivation to improve one's immediate and long-term socio-economic situation (Tsuda 2009: 2).

Adaptation challenges

Irrespective of different expectations underlying students' relocation, the arrival itself has substantial influence on their psychosocial condition and, thus, their ongoing residence in Poland. It is predominantly related to the process of acculturation – the cultural changes arising from contact between people of two distinct cultures and exhibiting different behaviours. One of its negative outcomes is the stress experienced during adjustment to a new culture. According to Berry *et al.* (1987), this can be manifested in a deterioration in general health status, including changes in somatic, psychological and social conditions due to the adaptation required to, among other things, food, weather, physical environment, housing conditions, interactional styles, symbolic systems, or norms and values in a new milieu. The level of acculturative stress depends on a number of conditions, including a migrant's personal characteristics (amount of exposure to a new culture, education, sex, age, psychological make-up, etc.), the host society's political and social attitudes towards immigrants and the resources available for their integration, as well as similarities between the host culture and that of the newcomers. Thus, the more closed and different the host culture is for a migrant, the more acculturative stress he/she will face (Desa *et al.* 2012: 365).

Although the people I interviewed did not face major acculturation problems, due to their relative cultural similarity to Polish society, they nevertheless confronted some adaptation challenges that are typical for educational migrants. During their first months at their Polish universities, they experienced 'normal' academic-related stressors such as problems with following lecturers' instructions, participating in class discussions, and constant worries over their academic achievements. Adjusting to the new requirements of higher education is stressful for any students, but these challenges are multiplied for international students (Poyrazli *et al.* 2010). Unlike their domestic counterparts, foreign students usually have fewer resources to cope with these problems. Confronting traditional academic challenges requires more effort than for their local peers. In consequence, in a situation of lack of social and psychological support, this can lead to feelings of alienation, meaninglessness and social estrangement (Desa *et al.* 2012: 365–366; cf. Pedersen 1991).

Other stress factors make students' psychosocial condition vulnerable. Feelings of being confused, lost and isolated often transform into more serious symptoms of anxiety and depression, especially in the early months. An additional explanation for lack of psychological comfort is the age of students at the time of arrival in Poland. Most people finish secondary school in the post-Soviet republics at the age of 16–18, so when they come to Poland they are younger than their Polish peers, who usually finish secondary school at 19. Furthermore, moving to Poland is usually their first experience of living alone, with all the obligations and challenges that entails.

Disrupted family and friendship ties also make their stay in the new socio-spatial environment a serious challenge (cf. Vathi and Duci 2016). Homesickness, loneliness and helplessness are often reported by the interviewees. The first day in Poland as the moment of entering adulthood is memorably described by Darek (29, Belarus) as follows:

> The first period in Poland was incredibly tough in psychological terms ... The first day when I arrived at night by bus, we entered the students' residence and of course nobody helped us as it was 3 a.m. ... So I entered my room and it was totally empty, bare walls, empty furniture, no bed sheet ... We had to survive somehow until the morning ... At 5 or 6 a.m. it was getting brighter and I looked out of the window and I saw this grey city ... I was alone in my room, there were cockroaches there ... And my first instinct was to buy a return ticket and go home ... It was because I had lived with my parents, they had provided me with everything, and all of a sudden you're alone. And you have to do everything, meals, laundry, passing exams.

These experiences are in contrast with preceding idealised visits to Poland. Before arriving to study at university, teenagers of Polish origin often take part in trips, short educational courses or pupil exchanges in Poland. These short visits offer an opportunity to familiarise themselves with the language, culture and historical sites, but they are not enough to give an in-depth view of the 'real' Poland. As a result, the initial experiences of living there often destroy the students' prior image of the ancestral homeland (King and Christou 2008: 18–20). Tatiana (26, Moldova) recollects her first affective reactions to the surprisingly unpleasant urban environment in Poland:

> When I arrived in Poland I noticed that, like in every other country, there are both nice and ugly places and it is the same here, it is nice but poor, it is ugly because it is dirty, there are many poor people ... In Moldova there are also poor and wealthy people, there is a middle class, but there are not so many homeless people and drunkards ... And it frightened me a lot ... And these grey buildings, as if there is no other colour ... And this weather, autumn ... I was always cold, much colder than in Moldova ...

Although students generally have the cultural competencies to live in this supposedly known country, they often cannot fully adapt to the new reality. This is especially true for students with a strong 'Polish identity', for whom the arrival in the ancestral country had strong emotional value (Dzwonkowski *et al.* 2002: 80).

It does not necessarily refer to university standards, economic conditions or the institutional and legal sphere, as these domains are generally more satisfying than in their countries of birth. It applies, rather, to the host-society Poles, who are experienced as different from what the students imagined or were told about in the diaspora.

Strangers in the ancestral homeland

The key to adapting to a new country is the relationship with the host society. It is worth mentioning in this context Simmel's well-known dual concept of the 'familiar' and 'the stranger' (cf. Simmel 1950). This division is one of the fundamental forms of categorising the social world, particularly important in a situation of contact between different cultural groups. It reflects both the objective differences between sending and receiving countries, and subjective terms such as beliefs and opinions about the scale and nature of these variances and mutual attitudes. Migrants may be perceived as strangers by the host society, and, *vice versa*, they may perceive this society in the same way. Cultural distances between those two groups, which are built on mutual perceptions, stereotypes and prejudices, may diminish or, on the contrary, increase (Nowicka 2000).

A wide cultural distance can also apply to members of the same national community who, due to various circumstances such as migration, deportation or border shifts, were kept apart but then come back into contact. The young people of Polish descent face antipathy from part of Polish society. The latter sustain negative stereotypes of the Soviet people, with which the Polish minority in the East is identified. The most common symptoms of this are the use of the derogative terms '*Ruski*' or '*kacap*' and unpleasant treatment in public situations (Głowacka-Grajper 2007: 335–336). Although students do not usually face other, more overt acts of discrimination, this lack of acceptance has a substantial influence on their psychosocial wellbeing. Julek (22, Ukraine) notes:

> One's Eastern origins are enough to be harassed. It is very simple: 'You are Ruski' and that's it. But no one knows I'm studying here, no one knows I'm working here, maybe I am here on a trip, they don't know that ... Ruski and that's it ... Every Russian-speaking person has these problems, these stereotypes and xenophobia.

An important marker that affects students' wellbeing is their Eastern Slavic accent. Since they are not able to easily 'get rid' of it, they isolate themselves in Russian-speaking groups, which, in turn, further impedes their adaptation. Since language remains one of the major criteria of belonging to the Polish nation, lack of full expertise in this area excludes the resettlers from the community (Nowicka 2000). The Poles also swagger over the 'poor *Ruskis*' and try to demonstrate their alleged civilisational and moral superiority over Russia and the USSR. This denigration is expressed mainly by the elderly, who remember the Second World War and the communist regime imposed later by the Soviets.

Interestingly, strong feelings of alienation are caused not only by the unfavourable reception by the host society but also by the students' self-aware cultural distinctiveness and the feeling of sharing the same Soviet heritage. Many narratives reveal a sense of cultural inferiority of their countries towards Poland as a representative of the West. However, the post-Soviet republics' difficult historical experiences, common cultural references and interactional styles foster students' deep identification with that area. Maria (26, Belarus) comments on that shared past as follows:

> I felt a bit different ... I felt that I had grown up in a different culture ... It is not only about the Belarusian culture, but it is about the culture of people affected by socialism and the Soviet Union because all these countries have one thing in common ... And despite it's been 20 years now you can still feel that this whole system is still present in these countries and it is a part of the mentality of the people ... At least the mentality of my generation, because when I was born the USSR still existed.

These negative attitudes towards incoming foreigners of Polish descent are often accompanied by public ignorance about the East, including the Poles living there. This is a result both of the deliberate policy of disinformation run by communists before 1989, which was aimed at erasing deportations into the USSR from the collective memory, and of the limited reference to the Polish diaspora in the contemporary public discourse (Nowicka 2000: 7). Often this ignorance and exclusion becomes an instrument in undermining students' Polishness and, consequently, their right to the state's financial support. Julek (22, Ukraine) bitterly comments on this issue:

> I had problems usually with people of the lower social classes, these stereotypes are popular on a terrible scale among them, this xenophobia is widespread. I don't know why ... All we know, it is a result of their low intellectual level, like, for them the whole of Ukraine is part of Russia, for them anyone who is from the East is Russian, never mind that he is Ukrainian or Polish, they do not accept that it may happen that a Pole can be born outside Poland. And yet every second one of them goes to England to work.

The informants employ different coping strategies to overcome the stress of acculturation and to counter discrimination. Schmitt *et al.* (2003) note that the likelihood that international students will identify with other international students or co-ethnics rather than with host nationals rises with an increase in perceived prejudice. And indeed, some of the interviewees feel distant and tend to reduce their relationships with the 'local' Polish students. They often associate more with student groups from their countries of birth or simply Russian-speaking groups. Their cultural distinctiveness, common social and political references, as well as shared norms and values compensate for the lack of acceptance by the hosts.

Nevertheless, some interviewees make an effort to overcome stereotypes and educate the locals about the history of Poles abroad (or the East in general). Agata (29, Lithuania) told of the following episode:

> Once in a student dorm I had a big quarrel because one student told me, there were some sport games, maybe it was at a party, football or something … and someone came up to me, drinking beer and told me: 'Well, you probably support only the Kazakhs?' … and I said: 'But why?' … and a very strange discussion started because he said: 'Because you're Ruska, since you're from the East, it's natural that you have to support them, all foreign students from the East here support them so I don't understand why you're different' … I was amazed, I had to give him a lecture for the next half an hour about what it means to be a Pole in the East …

They also attempt to diminish the impact of other stress factors. Frequent (real or virtual) contacts with their family back in the East are the main palliatives for stress-related symptoms. Students also try to improve their Polish language and cultural competencies as well as establish social networks with the locals (cf. Vathi and Duci 2016). These strategies are important, since the similarity between an individual's native culture and the host culture is hardly enough for successful adaptation. It is also strongly determined by one's general positive attitudes to establishing relationships with local groups as well as personal features such as openness, extroversion and good communication skills (cf. Poyrazli *et al.* 2010).

Consequences for national identity

Poland's inhabitants, on the whole, are not sympathetic to the arrival of immigrants and those of different ethnic origin, and this opposition seems also to include those who belong to the same national community but represent different patterns of Polishness. Interestingly, according to my informants' statements, neither do the Poles in Poland fulfil the pattern of the Polish patriotism that is transmitted in diaspora. This is often understood by them in primordial terms – as love of the country, importance of ethnic kinship, preserving ethnic traditions and language, or knowledge of the country's history and geography. When they arrive in Poland they expect to experience that same approach and knowledge among compatriots. It appears, however, once again that the ancestral country's reality does not meet their hopes. Maria (26, Belarus) discovers that Polish citizens are highly ignorant and chauvinistic, and their patriotic declarations are not reflected in their real actions:

> I came here and I noticed that most of it is just … words. I always emphasise that I am a Pole … But I increasingly began to see the difference between the Poles living in the country and those outside of the country … I'm not talking about the Poles in Belarus, I'm talking in general about the Polish community outside the country … This is a completely different

mode of Polishness ... People who live abroad can only be recognised as 100 per cent true Poles ... Those who live in Poland, they have always this syndrome of resentfulness; most of them are people who not only have prejudices towards other nations but primarily have prejudices towards their own nation, they are nationalists in most cases ...

In parallel to the Poles questioning the Polishness of the incoming students, some students consider their Polishness to be completely different and call into question Polish citizens' means of participation in the nation's life. The discrepancy between expected and actual attitudes again intensifies students' feeling of strangeness in the homeland. Their experience brings to mind Alfred Schütz's classic concept of 'the homecomer' – an individual coming back home after a long absence who 'expects to return to an environment of which he always had and – so he thinks – still has intimate knowledge and which he has just to take for granted in order to find his bearings within it' (1945: 369). The homecomer's knowledge and cultural competences create a sense of security and confidence in relation to his/her country. However, during separation from the homeland, the intimate bond that links the homecomer with his/her compatriots markedly fades. Consequently, the return turns out to be a deep disappointment. The homecomer is no longer expected to come back home, and those who stayed are no longer regarded as the people he/she had previously left and then recalled. As in many students' cases, the homecomer finally becomes a stranger in their own home (Waniek 2008: 47–48).

This redefinition of national community is reflected in the continuation of Maria's narrative when, in contrast to the observed attitudes of Polish citizens, she defines the category of the 'true Poles' and attributes it to the Poles in the East, including her community in Belarus. Whereas 'true Polishness' is represented by the Poles living in the diaspora, 'traditional Polishness' is associated with the parochialism, backwardness and nationalism of the present citizens of Poland. The 'true Poles' maintain a common memory of the homeland and cultivate its heritage:

> The Poles who live outside Poland can be called patriots, they are the people who know the history of the country, the tradition, culture etc., because their parents teach them that ... and the people who have this every day are not aware in fact of their ignorance ... And when I came in Poland I often faced such situations, people didn't know about all these basic traditions like Christmas Eve dishes, they didn't know about the basic historical facts, about geography.

Interestingly, Agata (29, Lithuania) points out that it is easier to be a 'true Pole' abroad, where an idealised image of the homeland is passed to succeeding generations and the longing for the country preserves that positive attitude, rather than in Poland itself, where daily experiences foster more critical attitudes towards the state or the national community:

I always tried to defend that Polish identity, I didn't let others criticise it ... I didn't let others do that because I simply believe in it ... Too much energy was put by Poles in Lithuania into maintaining this Polish identity, to protect it, to have these Polish schools and so on ... I discuss it often with my friends from Poland and I tell them that I'm more patriotic because I appreciate it more, because you had it all time and we had to fight for it ... And consequently people become more respectful towards me ...

To sum up, although roots migration is usually the consequence of a complex but still individual decision-making process of a person who hopes to renew relationships and to live among people who share the same social, cultural and historical narratives, his/her arrival can be highly disappointing (King and Christou 2008: 18–20). While in the case of emigration to a foreign country one can expect loneliness and integration problems, in the situation of a return to the ancestral homeland, one usually hopes for an easy adaptation. However, this process may turn out to be unexpectedly difficult. The absence of common understanding leads to an individual's alienation in a seemingly known environment (Schütz 1945). Paradoxically, it often then leads to a similar sense of loneliness and alienation as is the case for regular (first-generation) migrants in new countries (Datta 2013: 97).

The narrators' families suffered from ethnic persecution in Soviet times, and still in their countries of birth often experience ongoing ethnic tensions (e.g. in Ukraine, Russia, Lithuania and Kazakhstan). Although they expected to study in Poland free of these problems, it appears that they cannot rid themselves of this ethnic fate. As Aleksandra (29, Belarus) commented, 'In Kazakhstan we were Poles, later in Belarus we were Poles, here we are Russians'. Tatiana (26, Moldova) explains it further:

The Poles somehow treat me better as a Moldovan than a Russian, so it is easier for me to be a Moldovan ... but in Moldova I've never been a Moldovan ... I was there, so to say, a Pole ... but here I've never been and I will never be a Pole and I'm here a foreigner with Moldovan citizenship ... And who do I feel? ... I feel like myself ... no I'm not able to clearly answer, I'm not a Pole for sure, nor Moldovan either.

As a result, moving to and remaining in the ancestral country often results in the hybridisation of students' national identification. Several affiliation combinations are possible, including single identification (Polish), double identification (e.g. Polish-Ukrainian or Polish-Lithuanian), identification with the dominant nationality of the country of birth, identification only with the Poles in the East or other forms of more cosmopolitan affiliation (Dzwonkowski *et al.* 2002: 133–140).

Conclusions

Although the Polish diaspora in the former USSR benefits from the Polish state's specific policy towards 'welcoming' them back to the ancestral homeland, the system of support for them remains highly inefficient. The most accessible return path is educational migration. Foreign youth of Polish descent arrive in Poland with high expectations, related either to the renewal of their linkages with the ancestral homeland or to opportunities for economic advancement and personal development. However, when in Poland, they are faced with a lack of acceptance on the part of the host society, which transmits a generalised negative stereotype of the Soviet people onto the incoming co-ethnics. They also meet with typical academic-related problems and other institutional barriers during the first months in the new environment. Irrespective of students' prior migration motives, these unexpected problems lead to identity tensions and sometimes acute psychological disturbances, including acculturative stress, feelings of confusion, alienation or homesickness that, for some students, may result in symptoms of depression (Pedersen 1991; Vathi and Duci 2016). Despite several coping strategies undertaken to counter these negative experiences, students' young age, lack of direct parental assistance and minimal social support mean that they continue to suffer psychosocially (Poyrazli *et al.* 2010).

It appears that roots migration is not a simple matter of 'returning' 'home' for later-generation migrants, since they experience significant uncertainty as to where they really belong (Gońda 2015: 73). Their conceptualisations of home are often multi-sited or unclearly stated: is it the ancestral country itself or, rather, a mythologised imaginative construction (King *et al.* 2011: 485)? Lack of confidence in this respect is especially vivid at the time of transnational homing experiences of migrants who perceive the home as simultaneously stable and fluid, lived and imagined, localised and transnational (Walsh 2006: 123). This also applies to those of a strong Polish identification, who received from their families a highly idealised image of the homeland. Roots migration leads, then, to a clash of different patterns of Polishness that are carried by two separate groups of Poles, those in Poland and those in the diaspora. It results in mutual questioning of the ways of belonging and participation in the life of the Polish nation and, thus, psychosocial discontent.

The students' sense of alienation is also compounded by the distinctiveness of their post-Soviet culture. The common fate of the former USSR's inhabitants becomes the foundation of their group identity. This lack of understanding, or unsatisfactory conditions after arrival, may result in their leaving the ancestral country and launching a renewed negotiation process regarding other places of positive identification (Boccagni 2011: 470). It is further facilitated by growing transnational tendencies that dismantle the previous attachments to a given place and make cross-border mobility continuous rather than completed (Ley and Kobayashi 2005: 111–113).

The biographical data collected by this research prove that roots migration is an open process with a scarcely definable beginning and end. In contrast to both common-sense considerations and many research findings, which identify return as the closure of one's migration circle, roots migration does not necessarily lead to the completion that the migrant expects. It does not bring much sense of psychosocial stability and safety either. It should be understood, rather, as one of potentially many steps in a migrant's cross-border mobility. Taking into account the interviewees' young age and the mobility possibilities due to Poland's membership in the EU, their further migration is highly likely. Roots migration also has crucial impacts on the entire course of migrants' lives, even though it does not affect single biographies in the same way or at the same stage of mobility. Like any other migration, it is shaped by 'crisis' experiences of different intensity (Breckner 2007: 140), which, however, not only result from the initial acculturation problems but also reflect strong feelings of strangeness in supposedly known surroundings.

Note

1 The interviews were conducted for the purpose of the author's PhD project in the Faculty of Economics and Sociology, University of Łódź, entitled 'The Students of Polish Descent from the Post-Soviet Successor States: Cultural Experiences and Identity Transformations'. The research was co-financed by the Polish National Science Centre, grant no: UMO-2012/07/N/HS6/01457.

References

Asmar, C. (2005) Internationalizing students: reassessing diasporic and local student difference, *Studies in Higher Education* 30(3): 291–309.

Berry, J.W., Kim, U., Minde, T. and Mok, D. (1987) Comparative studies of acculturative stress, *International Migration Review* 21(3): 491–511.

Bijwaard, G. and Wang, Q. (2013), Return migration of foreign students, *Norface Discussion Paper Series*, no. 2013–05. www.norface-migration.org. Accessed 5 October 2015.

Boccagni, P. (2011) The framing of return from above and below in Ecuadorian migration: a project, a myth, or a political device? *Global Networks* 11(4): 461–480.

Breckner, R. (2007) Case-oriented comparative approaches: the biographical perspective as opportunity and challenge in migration research, in Schittenhelm, K. (ed.) *Concepts and Methods in Migration Research. Conference Reader*: 113–152. www.cultural-capital.net. Accessed 5 October 2015.

Cohen, R. (1995) Rethinking 'Babylon': iconoclastic conceptions of the diaspora experience, *New Community* 21(1): 5–18.

Datta, A. (2013) Diaspora and transnationalism in urban studies, in A. Quayson and G. Daswani (eds) *A Companion to Diaspora and Transnationalism*. Oxford: Blackwell, 88–105.

Desa, A., Fatimah, Y. and Abd Kadir, N.B. (2012) Acculturative stress among international postgraduate students at UKM, *Procedia – Social and Behavioral Sciences* 59: 364–369.

Dzwonkowski, R., Gorbaniuk, O. and Gorbaniuk, J. (2002) *Świadomość narodowa młodzieży polskiego pochodzenia z byłego ZSRR studiującej w Polsce*. Lublin: Towarzystwo Naukowe Katolickiego Uniwersytetu Lubelskiego.

Głowacka-Grajper, M. (2007) Rodacy–cudzoziemcy. Młodzi Polacy z Litwy, Białorusi i Ukrainy na studiach w Polsce, in E. Nowicka and S. Łodziński (eds) *Kulturowe wymiary imigracji do Polski. Studia socjologiczne.* Warszawa: Wydawnictwo ProLog, 329–358.

Gońda, M. (2015) Biographical pathways of roots migration: the case of students of Polish ancestry from the post-Soviet area, *Polish Sociological Review* 189(1): 69–84.

Gough, I. and McGregor, J.A. (eds) (2007) *Wellbeing in Developing Countries.* Cambridge: Cambridge University Press.

Grzymała-Kazłowska, A. and Grzymała-Moszczyńska, H. (2014) The anguish of repatriation: immigration to Poland and integration of Polish descendants from Kazakhstan, *East European Politics and Societies and Cultures* 28(3): 593–613.

GUS (Główny Urząd Statystyczny) (2015) *Rocznik demograficzny 2015.* Warszawa.

Hut, P. (2014) *Polska wobec Polaków w przestrzeni poradzieckiej. Od solidaryzmu etnicznego do obowiązku administracyjnego.* Warszawa: Oficyna Wydawnicza ASPRA.

King, R. and Christou, A. (2008) Cultural geographies of counter-diasporic migration: the second generation returns 'home'. Brighton: University of Sussex, Sussex Migration Working Paper 45. www.sussex.ac.uk. Accessed 5 October 2015.

King, R., Christou, A. and Ahrens, J. (2011) 'Diverse mobilities': second-generation Greek-Germans engage with the homeland as children and as adults, *Mobilities* 4(6): 483–501.

Lesińska, M. (ed.) (2010) Polityka państwa wobec migracji powrotnych własnych obywateli. Teoria i praktyka. Warsaw: University of Warsaw, Center of Migration Research Working Papers, no. 44/102. www.migracje.uw.edu.pl. Accessed 1 October 2015.

Ley, D. and Kobayashi, A. (2005) Back to Hong Kong: return migration or transnational sojourn? *Global Networks* 5(2): 111–127.

MSZ (Ministerstwo Spraw Zagranicznych) (2014) *Rządowy program współpracy z polską diasporą w latach 2015–2020.* www.msz.gov.pl. Accessed 5 October 2015.

Mucha, J. (2003) Ethnic Polish students from the Former Soviet Union in the homeland of their forefathers. An empirical study, *East European Quarterly* 37(2): 167–194.

Nowicka, E. (2000) *Polacy czy cudzoziemcy? Polacy za wschodnią granicą.* Kraków: Zakład Wydawniczy 'Nomos'.

Pedersen, P.B. (1991) Counseling international students, *The Counseling Psychologist* 19: 10–58.

Poyrazli, S., Thukral, R.K. and Duru, E. (2010) International students' race-ethnicity, personality and acculturative stress, *Journal of Psychology and Counseling* 2(8): 25–32.

Safran, W. (1991) Diasporas in modern societies: myths of homeland and return, *Diaspora* 1(1): 83–99.

Schmitt, M.T., Spears, R. and Branscombe, N.R. (2003) Constructing a minority group identity out of shared rejection: the case of international students, *European Journal of Social Psychology* 33(1): 1–12.

Schütz, A. (1945) The homecomer, *American Journal of Sociology* 50(5): 369–376.

Schütze, F. (1983) Biographieforschung und narratives Interview, *Neue Praxis* 3: 283–293.

Simmel, G. (1950) The stranger, in K. Wolff *The Sociology of Georg Simmel.* New York: The Free Press, 402–408 (originally written 1908).

Tsuda, T. (ed.) (2009) *Diasporic Homecomings: Ethnic Return Migration in Comparative Perspective.* Palo Alto: Stanford University Press.

Vathi, Z. and Duci, V. (2016) Making other dreams: the impact of migration on the psychosocial wellbeing of Albanian-origin children and young people upon their families' return to Albania, *Childhood* 23(1): 53–68.

Walsh, K. (2006) British expatriate belongings: mobile homes and transnational homing, *Home Cultures* 3(2): 123–144.

Waniek, K. (2008) Homecomer: some biographical implications of immigrants visiting their former homes, *Przegląd Socjologiczny* 57(2): 45–66.

Wessells, M.G. (1999) Culture, power and community: intercultural approaches to psychosocial assistance and healing, in K. Nader, N. Dubrow and B. Stamm (eds) *Honouring Differences: Cultural Issues in the Treatment of Trauma and Loss*. New York: Routledge, 276–282.

Wessendorf, S. (2007) 'Roots migrants': transnationalism and 'return' among second-generation Italians in Switzerland, *Journal of Ethnic and Migration Studies* 33(7): 1083–1102.

Wyszyński, R. (ed.) (2005) *Mniejszość polska na rozdrożu. Studenci i absolwenci uczelni polskich pochodzący z Litwy, Białorusi i Ukrainy*. Warszawa: Instytut Socjologii Uniwersytetu Warszawskiego.

6 'This country plays tricks on you'

Portuguese migrant descendant returnees narrate economic crisis-influenced 'returns'

João Sardinha and David Cairns

Introduction

Prior to the financial crisis of 2008, Portugal had been undergoing a process of significant development in regard to its economy and society. Inclusion in the European Union brought some tangible benefits to the country, including the modernisation of the public and private sectors, especially infrastructure, aided by EU financial transfers. Major international events also gave the country unprecedented visibility: most notably the World Exposition of 1998 (EXPO 98) and the EURO 2004 football tournament. Drawn by the new apparent prosperity, Portugal witnessed a significant inflow of return of its former emigrants, not only first-generation leavers but also their 'second-generation' offspring, some of whom had left Portugal as young children, others having been born in the country of their parents' emigration. This chapter focuses on this second generation of migrants, who, having 'returned' to Portugal at a time of relative economic growth, are now experiencing a different social and economic reality, with the prospect of staying in the 'home' country and of returning to their previous place of residence both endangered by the spread of austerity, unemployment and job precariousness in the wake of the crisis (Cairns *et al.* 2016).[1]

Statistically speaking, the years 2013 and 2014 saw an estimated 110,000 Portuguese depart for other shores in each year (Pires *et al.* 2015). At a personal level, the human costs associated with this mobility cannot be ignored, especially with psychosocial effects on the individuals concerned caused by economic downturn and instability in the national labour market, as well as migration at an unpredictable time. Psychosocial wellbeing is generally thought to be determined by factors that allow an individual, along with his/her immediate family, to accomplish what they consider to be the best quality of life. Accomplishing psychosocial wellbeing, therefore, can be perceived as a path whose ultimate goal is life's contentment and all that it might entail (see Wright 2009). Within a return migration setting, it may be the return itself that defines one's contentment – to be in the place where one's psychosocial wellbeing is realised. For migrant descendant returnees, their sense of contentment and completeness may thus be found in the land of ancestry. Such completeness, however, may be challenged if the resources and conditions needed to accomplish the sought-after quality of life are not provided, or are there at the beginning but then disappear. Under this scenario, one's psychosocial wellbeing may be impacted, leading to a process of self-negotiation. Central to such mediations is the question: what is the best option in order to accomplish the best life one can have? For a migrant returnee, the outcome of such a negotiation may ultimately lead to a 're-return' (i.e. a return to the country one had earlier moved from) or maybe migration to a third country.

Of course, prospective re-return migrants will usually possess one resource that provides a means of escape: their prior citizenship of the other country. In this sense, engaging in re-return processes can be linked to (re)securing wellbeing, not only in respect to counteracting the negative impact of the crisis upon personal stability but also in providing a source of relative comfort. This chapter sets out to examine this process, focusing on two potential 're-return' countries: Canada and France. Through narrative analysis, we first observe the expectations, encounters and conflicts experienced by returnees when they first arrived in Portugal in the 1980s and 1990s. We then examine re-returns and onward migrations to 'third' countries during the current economic downturn in Portugal, paying particular attention to the impacts of the economic crisis and mobility on psychosocial wellbeing.

Methodological considerations and interviewee typologies

The data presented in this chapter draws on fieldwork with Portuguese-Canadian and Portuguese-French migrant descendant returnees to Portugal, derived from two separate research phases: the first carried out from 2008 to 2012 as part of the research project *The Return of the Portuguese Second-Generation to Portugal: Identity, Belonging and Transnational Lives,* and a second phase from 2013 to 2015 and the research project *REPOR – Luso-Descendant 'Returnees' in Portugal: Identity, Belonging and Transnationalism.*[2] We used in-depth interviewing as the primary form of data collection, allied to ethnographic observation of respondents, with a central aim of unveiling meanings and emotions encoded in the act of return during times of economic crisis. We highlight the imperatives confronting these individuals, paying particular attention to what drives 'return' processes, thus making a link between shifts in the economic fortunes of a society and the effect this has on people in terms of their everyday lives.

In carrying out the fieldwork, the first phase took place when all interviewees resided in Portugal, and all interviews were face-to-face. In the second phase, face-to-face interviewing was also the preferred method; however, given that some participants had by now 're-returned' to France and Canada, some were conducted online. The first-phase interview schedule focused on (1) (re)integration issues, (2) identity and belonging, and (3) local and transnational networks, while the second round of interviews included questions on the impact of the economic crisis in Portugal and its influence on current and future mobility plans, as well as the social, professional and emotional impacts.

A total of 42 interviews were conducted – 22 with Portuguese-Canadians and 20 with Portuguese-French. Case selection was guided by the following variables: age upon return (ten years of age or over), minimum length of stay in Canada or France (at least ten years), gender balance (13 Portuguese-Canadian males and 7 females; 9 Portuguese-French males and 13 females), age span (participants were born between 1964 and 1988, with 1976 as the mean year), education level (a broad mix ranging from secondary school to graduate and postgraduate degree), and territorial distribution of return in continental Portugal (15 resided in the district of Lisbon, with the remainder scattered across various other towns and cities). Beyond these variables, we also point out that, of the 42 interviewees, 28 returned to Portugal unaccompanied, while the other 14 returned with family (nine as offspring of the family unit; five as a parent within a new family unit). All participants' parents were Portuguese nationals. Concerning further mobility after returning to Portugal, since 2010, five of the Portuguese-Canadians had 're-returned' to Canada, while another two had moved to a third country. Of the Portuguese-French participants, four had returned to France.

Theorising migrant descendant returns

That there should be an explicit link between socio-economic context and the decision to migrate, or in our case return to the ancestral homeland, seems obvious. Structural factors such as prevailing labour market conditions, access to welfare provision, including health and education, and general political stability are important considerations for all citizens, migrants or otherwise, in making life plans, as are less readily quantified issues such as hopes for the future and feelings of personal wellbeing. The basic position can be summarised as: the better things are, the more likely people are to stay; while on the flip side, the worse conditions become, the greater the risk of an exit. Introducing this reductionist logic into our research context of contemporary Portugal would therefore lead us to assume that an event such as the ongoing economic crisis, with its potential to destabilise social, economic, political and ontological security, must surely stimulate a rise in outward migration among those wishing to escape growing hardship and declining life chances.

In regard to return migrants, this might mean that societal change in the post-return environment corrupts the idyll of pre-return expectations. Whether or not this is the case is open to question and is an issue explored in the empirical discussion. But, alongside the obvious 'crisis = migration' assumption, we should consider a number of factors that may confound our expectations of interviewees' expectations and realities. First, as in other countries subject to bail-outs administered by the troika of the International Monetary Fund, the European Central Bank and the European Commission, the impact of austerity has not necessarily been general but, rather, concentrated among certain sections of the population, at least in regard to labour market marginalisation. In the case in Portugal, young people have disproportionately suffered, as they have in many other crisis-affected countries.[3] This implies that, in regard to economic position, older respondents within our study may not necessarily be part of the 'crisis cohort'. Nevertheless, within the everyday impact of a rising cost of living and general anxiety about the future, one's psychosocial wellbeing may be hard to ignore, even for older, more economically insulated citizens.

A second consideration concerns how (return) migration decisions are made. For example, our prior understanding of transnationalism stresses the importance of social relationships and cultural attachments as much as, or more than, economic imperatives (Levitt and Glick Schiller 2004). Therefore, even where there are diminished job prospects or a strong risk of unemployment, evident financial risks may not be sufficient to out-pull the gravity of homeward ties. Other ancillary factors include dependency upon the resources embedded in family and peer networks. While this issue has been explored in relation to mobility decisions of young people (see Cairns 2014a, 2014b), for the mobility of migrant descendants (Sardinha 2011a), reliance upon and obligations towards significant others such as parents, children and spouses will inevitably impact upon the decision to stay or leave. In the case of our migrant descendant returnees, some found partners in Portugal and started families of their own; some returned with their parents or had their mother and/or father join them after their initial move; others took up residence in Portugal with an already established family. In this sense, we can observe the confounding effect of everyday life upon the making of migration decisions, stretching beyond human-capital considerations and testing the limits of transnationalism. Nor is the potential returnee free from more concrete mobility obstacles: citizenship can be a drawback to free movement, as not possessing full citizenship of a country – as may be the case with family members born in Portugal when it comes to a re-return – reduces mobility choices.[4]

Looking towards the psychological dimension of return, we should also acknowledge that factors unrelated to social and economic conditions may have a disruptive influence upon settlement, or conversely, help a return migrant cope with a disrupted civil sphere. In the context of childhood migration, Vathi and Duci (2016: 55) have argued that there is a need to use the term 'psychosocial wellbeing', rather than concepts associated with clinical psychology, as a means of assessing the emotional, social and cultural aspects of 'potential outcomes from migration' (see also Wessells 1999). Such considerations also mean that we can anticipate a multiplicity of (return) migration responses to the challenges inherent in the contemporary Portuguese context, creating new research questions in the process. Fortunately, the diversity of our empirical material allows us to illustrate different scenarios, including moving towards an understanding of the interaction between dramatic social and economic change and return migration, and the effects such an interaction may have on the opposing 'should I stay or should I go' scenarios at a time of economic crisis.

Returned to Portugal during 'the good times' – expectations, encounters and conflicts

It is common for homeland return projects to involve plans for enhancing an individual's socio-economic status. Some studies on second-generation return to the country of ancestry have argued that socio-professional opportunities are perceived to be better in the ancestral homeland, as well as uncovering the desire and motivation to invest in regional and community development – notable in this regard are several studies of the Caribbean context (Conway and Potter 2006; Lee-Cunin 2005; Rodman and Conway 2005). In the case of Portugal, research on Portuguese migrant descendant return (cf. Afonso 1997; Sardinha 2011a, 2011b) at a time when the nation was experiencing relative economic prosperity has revealed that migrant offspring return was not only driven by wanting to 'return' to roots (Wessendorf 2007) or the desire 'to be Portuguese in Portugal', but also a need to work and grow professionally in the country their parents had departed from.

In carrying out their moves, returnees in our study noted various types of professional or personal development opportunities. The return to the ancestral homeland was frequently made thinking that their know-how and educational capital would permit labour-market entry in Portugal. Many interviews referred to their knowledge of other languages, and having been educated in what they perceived as superior education systems. Still others, opting to return to the ancestral village their parents had departed from, and where they had often spent their days when holidaying in Portugal, were aware of the realities of rural life in terms of opportunities and infrastructure (e.g. Roca and Martins 1999). A third group came with the intent of pursuing their education in Portugal, having as their primary goal earning a university degree as preparation for the job market there (Sardinha 2011b). In all these scenarios, pragmatic considerations were accompanied by a more emotional connection to Portugal: whatever the motivation, there was a sense that there would be a personal benefit to be gained from a return through becoming connected to the 'homeland' and finding one's self socially, culturally, psychologically and spiritually more 'complete'.

The return itself is seldom carried out blindly. On the contrary, migrating to the ancestral homeland is long pondered and carefully calculated, and family connections often loom large in these calculations. Various studies (Cassarino 2004; Fog Olwig 2007; Gmelch 1992; Potter 2005; Reynolds 2008) highlight that strong family ties to the homeland provide the primary reason for return over and above economic, social and political considerations. Potter, for example, notes (2005: 14): 'return migrants are best viewed as people endowed with social capital, potential and realized'. Similarly, King and Christou (2008) outline three key challenges to be overcome if the 'return of social realism' is to be successful: finding a place to live (a real sense of home in the homeland); economic security (a job); and a circle of friends. Beyond being an important factor in accessing resources or gaining knowledge of them, family and social networks frequently serve to ease any initial shock of adaptation, providing a buffer against what may often be unknown or seem strange. These connections, however, generally become less relevant as one becomes a part of the daily routines of the returned-to country.

The time dimension should, therefore, imply increased adaptation and higher levels of wellbeing as one becomes ensconced in community and family life in the homeland. But is that necessarily the case? King and Christou (2008: 18–19) stress that second-generation homecomings are 'myth-laden missions'. Upon facing the realities of everyday life in the ancestral homeland, returnees soon come to realise that preconceived notions of the mythical and historic homeland, which may have been the catalyst of their return, diverge from the realities of everyday life (Markowitz and Stefansson 2004). In the narratives collected from our participants, disappointment and anger, often leading to stress and mental health issues, were emphasised in relation to dealings at both personal and institutional levels. These reactions were brought about by what can be termed 'socio-cultural shocks' driven by the discovery of previously unknown characteristics of Portugal and of the Portuguese. Societal and organisational 'let-downs' deriving from encounters with the 'inner workings' of Portuguese society and state institutions – such as the excessive bureaucracy, the lethargy of Portuguese public services, widespread corruption, and the lack of a sense of service and friendliness in shops and businesses – were outlined as distorting wellbeing. Statements such as the following were common among the respondents, stressing negative interactions with institutions and a different service culture:

> Sometimes I regret having moved to Portugal when I start thinking about how in France I could quickly get a doctor's appointment, and accomplish other practical things like that … the hospitals, the health centres, the financial services … things that facilitate our lives.
>
> (Jacqueline, 47, Portuguese-French)

> Taking care of certain matters here will drive anyone to depression. It is common to be attended to by someone who hates their job, who doesn't want to be bothered or simply can't be bothered to do things right. There's no coordination when it comes to public services. I've gone through things that were a living hell here.
>
> (Roberto, 39, Portuguese-Canadian)

This latter quotation is a particularly strong illustration of the impact relatively quotidian matters have on wellbeing: the 'living hell' of having to deal with inefficient public services. Such experiences obviously shatter the bucolic myth of Portugal as a sun-drenched or rustic paradise, and it is only through acceptance of such institutionalised inefficiencies that an adjustment can be made: reminding oneself that the person who hates their job may be perfectly justified in doing so due to their own difficult working conditions.

The confrontations and disillusionments described by the above quotes also relate to misguided perceptions of what was expected upon returning. As stated by another participant, Afonso (Portuguese-Canadian, 36 years old), 'I moved [to Portugal] because I loved the place, and I still do. But the more time I spent here, the more I realised I didn't really know the place'. For the offspring of Portuguese migrants, accomplishing the 'homecoming' was seen initially as a superlative happening, including not only the fulfilment of 'ethnic completeness' (Christou 2006), but also the accomplishment of one's personal and professional development. But then, real-life experience demolishes the gentle façade of pre-return idealisations, themselves often based on 'carnivalised' holiday experiences (Afonso 1997; dos Santos 2005). The vision of Portugal as a laid-back, easy-going nation, of 'constant fun in the sun', where one believed one could accomplish all one dreamed of at the time of return, evaporates. In the words of Carla (42, Portuguese-Canadian), 'To me, there were no wrongs in Portugal. [...] It was a better life than in Canada ... at least I was led to believe that. [...] When I got here, I was proven wrong'. Similarly, Pedro (43, Portuguese-French-Canadian) talked about what he saw and perceived as his ancestral homeland when he'd come to Portugal on holidays:

> In the 80s and 90s I'd come here with my parents and we'd see these new highways, big shopping malls, big events like EXPO 98 and how modern things were getting. I remember my dad saying once: 'Even construction workers are playing golf in this country these days'. It seems like everyone was doing well. It really made no sense to be an emigrant when people here were living better lives. Of course we know now that the country and basically everybody was living beyond their means and that the governments and the banks encouraged and supported it all. I saw what I thought were the fantastic lives people were living here at the time and of course I wanted it too. Now, we think about it, and we come to the conclusion that it was all a big farce.

Given the longitudinal nature of our study, our fieldwork has taken on the objective of comparing the time when our participants returned with the current crisis-dominated period. Having experienced both realities, the research participants talked about the 'misguided perceptions' of Portugal that served to lure them to the country. Most described having been clueless about the true nature of the Portuguese socio-economic and political environment upon returning, due to their knowledge being restricted to familial memories, cultural stereotypes of the 'good life' and socially unrepresentative short holiday visits. One area highlighted by the respondents was that of the Portuguese job market. Some of the returnees thought their know-how and educational capital would permit labour-market advancement, only to be confronted with a different reality. Sergio (36, Portuguese-Canadian), for example, expresses his difficulties in entering the Portuguese labour market, making it clear that knowing other languages, having been educated and brought up in Canada, actually does not help:

> I think having a different way of thinking or a different way of being is prejudicial to us. There is still this tendency of wanting a homogeneous way of thinking here when it comes to employing people, and not accepting alternative ways of being. Speaking various languages or having a degree from a North American university is not an advantage like a lot of people like to think it is. The reality is that it's not easy to find the right job here and it takes a few years to make the right contacts. Those from here know the systems, they know how things work. It's not only the '*cunha*' factor [who you know etc.] though. We know that's how things work around here, but beyond that you have to know how to play the game, who to talk to, what to say and what not to say. The people here have a certain baggage and the tools that fit the Portuguese system and we don't. Their parents know people, our parents don't live here. We need time to learn and to make contacts; we need to gather our own social capital.

Thus, a general consensus among respondents is that those born and raised in Portugal are at an advantage when it comes to the job market, for they have accumulated social/human capital and know the systems of the country. It is felt, therefore, that they have an inside track. The often-referred '*cunha* system' is seen as a point of distinction between Portugal and Canada/France, with respondents stressing that in Canada and France, it is often the other way around – 'it's what you know and what you can contribute, and not who you know, that can provide you with an inside track'.

Upon returning, a large number of migrant descendants chose to study or search out employment in an area that enabled them to use their languages, especially in multinational companies, the tourist industry and language teaching. These employment sectors in some cases contributed to the segregation of returnees by enabling them to continue to indulge in a French or Anglophone lifestyle, having other French or Canadian individuals as classmates or work colleagues, and, of course, speaking French or English. Outside the work environment, this can equally transpose to the family environment, as was the case with Isabel (41, Portuguese-French), who reflected on her home and professional interactions:

> I'm a French professor at a French Studies Department where many of my colleagues are French professors. The truth is I don't get many opportunities to practice my Portuguese since we all speak French to each other. [...] Almost all my friends are Portuguese-French. With my children and my husband, who is also a Portuguese descendant, I speak French with them. [...] You take the good with the bad ... French is what I know, more than anyone here. I make a point of being French here. I even make a point of shopping for food at the French supermarket chains here.

Isabel brings to light how her world is very much a French world, which, in turn, has led to a process of auto-segregation from the local population. The extent to which her desire to maintain a French lifestyle in Portugal is beneficial is a question worth analysing. In his study on the perceptions of Portuguese nationals towards Portuguese emigrants, Gonçalves (1996) explains that, upon returning, Portuguese emigrants often suffer the brunt of stereotypes held by Portuguese society towards them. This, the author explains, is due to such factors as an obsessive utilisation of 'foreignisms' (e.g. vocabulary, architecture, tastes, etc.) as a way of 'showing off'; negatively perceived factors that are carried over to the offspring, often affecting their psychosocial wellbeing more than that of their parents.

Thus, driven by sentiments of alienation and differentiation, it becomes common for returned descendants to search out others in the same predicament (dos Santos 2005). Such individuals share not only similar integration experiences and difficulties, but also the same references of identification, defined by their biculturality, as well as common languages. Alienation and rupture thus put a check on their search for belonging, especially at a changed historical moment when Portugal was beset by a severe economic downturn.

'Should I pack yet again?' – negotiating crisis-influenced re-return or migration to a third country

We have seen that processes of integration are not always easy for the descendant returnees. With the passing of time, and as they find their own way in Portuguese society, it is common that major life shifts take place, influenced by the return itself and by other events in the country, including the loss of economic stability. Needless to say, as opposed to those who have never lived outside of Portugal, for the returnee, there is always the 'safety-net country' to consider: an escape facilitated by having dual citizenship and transnational connections. In the second phase of our research, participants were asked to discuss the impact of the economic crisis in Portugal on their lives, and whether it had affected them to the point of motivating a return to Canada or France, or moving on to another country. While the majority felt affected economically by the crisis in some way or another, it was those from Canada who expressed a desire to leave Portugal, more so than individuals from France.

Of those already outside Portugal, the general sentiment is that they were driven out by the economic crisis, with the majority stating that it had not been their choice to pursue further mobility; instead, they were driven by insecurity and discomfort, as in the following examples:

> I remember when I moved to Portugal, being nervous and excited at the same time. There was this sense of adventure. Going back [to Canada] was nerve-racking as well, but it was so sad for me. I remember packing my bags and crying. Things were getting worse with the economic situation

here and things weren't going to get better in the near future, so I figured it was time to go back, not that I wanted to go.

(Marcia, 36, Portuguese-Canadian)

I blame Portugal for forcing me to leave; all the 'rottens' of this country – the government, the corruption – all the things and the people that flushed Portugal down the toilet. And don't tell me we're all responsible because I don't believe that! The people who don't know how to govern the country and those who stole from the country, they're the ones responsible, not only for me, but for the hundreds of thousands that are leaving.

(Fernando, 45, Portuguese-French)

Reading these narratives, we see that beyond the sentiment of *having* to leave as opposed to *wanting* to leave, these respondents express anger and sadness, leading to inner tension and conflict at being driven by circumstances and not their own choice. At the heart of this renewed mobility are the pressures of providing an economically stable life for themselves and their families. Financial imperatives are thus at the heart of the emotionally packed decision to leave (Brooks and Simpson 2013).

Of the 30 individuals in the sample who were still residing in Portugal, there is no agreement around the vexed issue of staying or leaving. Of those intending to go, it was often the case that the possibility of further mobility was always an integral part of their plans or way of life – a strategy to be 'held in their back pockets' if desperate times called for its activation. For others, the facilitation of a re-return was related to the form and intensity of ongoing transnational relations with the country of their parents' immigration and of their own earlier lives – especially the ways in which their remaining family, friends and colleagues in these 'new transnational spaces' linking Portugal to France and Canada could help them with their resettlement there (Pries 1999, 2001; Sardinha 2014). Yet, hesitation seemed the most common reaction to the question posed about re-return.

I'm clinging on until the last minute. See if things improve and if the job market improves. Once I've exhausted all possibilities, I'll go ... I'll have no other option. I could go back right now and re-start my life; but then I think, is this something I want to do? I don't feel the rope tightening around my neck just yet, but when it does, I'll escape at the last minute.

(Sara, 34, Portuguese-French)

I'm trying to find work from here first. I'm not limiting my search to France though, although going back to France would make more sense. The thing is I don't want to be a burden on anyone, nor go anywhere blindly.

(Victor, 37, Portuguese-French)

We talk about going and we try to idealise what it would be like for all of us [the family] living in Canada, but in the end, there's that bit of fright. Change is a scary thing and it's not only me anymore like it was when I moved here.

(Telmo, 38, Portuguese-Canadian)

While many possess the desire and motivation to go back to Canada or France, or to migrate elsewhere, the above citations let us know that factors such as hoping for economic improvement in Portugal, not wanting to leave without guarantees of being able to sustain one's self where one is going, as well as the insecurities associated with further mobility, hold these individuals back. The next three quotes raise other issues that hold the returnees back from making their U-turn – sentiments of belonging (now stronger in Portugal than in the country of their upbringing); where other family members are now located; and understandable feelings of inertia.

My life is here – my work, my family, my friends. Moving out would mean starting over again. My parents are retired now and they're here in Portugal. I couldn't leave them. I couldn't take their grandchildren from them for example. It's just not an option. We're here for the good or for the bad now.

(Dina, 34, Portuguese-French)

This is where I feel most at home. When I go back to Canada, although it's fun to see my old friends again, it's no longer the way it was. It feels weird to go back to my old town, to be honest. If someday I have nothing else here and if a job were to come up there, I'd go, but that would be a last resort thing.

(Jorge, 44, Portuguese-Canadian)

There are good and bad things ... We have good food, climate, we have our soccer. We have all these distractions. Not everything is to be decided around the crisis or because of the crisis. Let's not think about those things. If you let the negatives control you, you will die sooner. I take it one day at a time and keep life simple, doing the things I like. I don't plan on going anywhere.

(Tiago, 36, Portuguese-Canadian)

Sentiments of belonging, and having a stable network one can rely on and does not wish to be parted from, are central reasons for staying. Portuguese culture and staying close to family – paying particular attention to children's agency in the decision-making process (Tyrell 2011) – is a way of safeguarding the psychosocial wellbeing of all parties involved, for leaving Portugal might bring (more) trauma and distress. Intergenerational ties and the emotional cost of re-migrating are thus factors that keep these individuals in Portugal. Gender also plays a role in decision-making, for it is more often than not women who safeguard the larger family unit. This is exemplified in Dina's quote above, connecting grandparents and grandchildren, making it known that family togetherness is valued above all. Moreover, in the third quote, by Tiago, we also see how it is preferable to stay in Portugal because of the creature comforts. Food, climate and football are just a few things that enhance health and wellbeing for this interviewee.

One key factor for not wanting to leave that is not mentioned above, however, is having secure employment. As simply put by Salvador (38, Portuguese-Canadian), 'I have a job and it's one I won't be losing anytime soon, so I have no reason for wanting to leave Portugal'. By contrast, those who have left Portugal did so because they had no work and no way to sustain themselves. Additionally, the majority of those who desire or possess a plan to re-return or to go to a third country are either unemployed, very poorly paid, in precarious jobs or close to losing their job. Asked if he would have the same desire not to leave Portugal if he were to lose his job, Salvador responded:

> Well, if you have Canadian citizenship, all you need to do is buy a plane ticket. You ask any returnee that question and I'm sure they'll all give you a similar answer to this: if things are bleak here and I have free access to a place where things are better, of course I'm going to mull things over and see what's best.

Conclusion

The objectives of this chapter have been twofold: to observe the return to Portugal of Portuguese migrant descendants from Canada and France at a time of economic prosperity, and then to analyse migration processes and considerations after the economic crisis. With the shift from economic prosperity to economic crisis, returnees were left to rethink their presence in Portugal. The initial act of return to Portugal served to find an ancestral home and improve wellbeing at a relatively good time in the country's history. Yet, in the midst of this return, transnational links were maintained, facilitated by dual citizenships and transnational family and friendship networks. Such resources have since been reactivated by some who have felt the brunt of austerity, who left Portugal in order to find work and to build better conditions for themselves and their families.

Processes of negotiation during times of economic crisis, as we have seen, can be quite straightforward. Within the context of contemporary Portugal, the ongoing economic crisis has destabilised socio-economic and even ontological, identificational security in the lives of our participants. As a result, new trends of 're-return' and onward migration have been observed. However, the financial downturn has not stimulated much outward migration or greatly increased a desire to do so. The reason for this goes hand-in-hand with the arguments of Levitt and Glick Schiller (2004) and the manner in which existing and developing social relationships and cultural attachments weigh heavily upon further mobility decisions; sometimes more so than purely economic considerations. Evidence of this comes from the fact that, despite unemployment rising and businesses failing, the financial squeeze caused by these economic trends may not be reason enough for further mobility to be actualised. Strong family and peer networks *in loco* become influencing factors in the (im)mobility decision-making process. While there are many disappointments and frustrations among second-generation returnees resettling in Portugal, and sometimes these can lead to thoughts and plans to re-return or re-emigrate, there are also powerful psychosocial wellbeing factors resulting from being in Portugal, related to family and personal relationships, lifestyle, climate and other cultural attachments. A 're-return' process involves starting over again, and this option is generally rejected unless the circumstances of staying in Portugal become dire.

Our participants may not experience the same levels of psychosocial trauma as other individuals suffering war, pestilence or detention, or other types of politically forced migration/return. For our interviewees, further mobility seems to become a more viable option only when it is perceived that their lives are 'reaching rock-bottom' from an economic survival standpoint. Abandoning Portugal for this reason may bring anguish and trauma, yet such strong feelings will often end up as secondary when survival is on the line. Therefore, mobility as an option and mobility as an actual practice bring different psychosocial impacts for the returnees.

Notes

1 We use the term 'return' to signify moving to the parental/ancestral homeland, even though, for those born in the migrant host country, this is not a 'true' statistical return. For further discussion on this point see King and Christou (2008).
2 The first project was João Sardinha's postdoctoral fellowship at the University of Coimbra and his central research project at the Portuguese Open University, while the REPOR project was funded by the FCT (Portuguese Foundation for Science and Technology), grant no. PTDC/ATP-GED/4567/2012.
3 See, for instance, Aassve *et al.* (2013); Bell and Blanchflower (2011); Cairns (2014a); Cairns *et al.* (2014); Dietrich (2013).
4 It should be noted that mobility rights take on different contours when citizenship is a factor at play. In relation to France, given that there is free movement between Schengen countries, which include both Portugal and France, the lack of French citizenship does not become an obstacle. In the case of Canada, on the other hand, only the children of returnee descendants born in Canada can have their parent(s) request Canadian citizenship for them as well. Spouses or partners, on the other hand, have to be sponsored. In the case of returnees possessing Canadian citizenship but not born in Canada, these individuals will need to apply to sponsor their spouse or partner and children.

References

Aassve, A. Cottini, E. and Vitali, A. (2013) Youth prospects in a time of economic recession, *Demographic Research* 39(36): 949–962.

Afonso, S. (1997) A Segunda Geração e o Regresso. A Geografia do Actor de Fronteira. Coimbra: Master's dissertation in Sociology, Faculty of Economics, University of Coimbra.

Bell, D.N.F. and Blanchflower, D.G. (2011) Young people and the great recession, *Oxford Review of Economic Policy* 27(2): 241–267.

Brooks, A. and Simpson, R. (2013) *Emotions in Transmigration: Transformation, Movement and Identity*. New York: Palgrave.

Cairns, D. (2014a) 'I wouldn't want to stay here': economic crisis and youth mobility in Ireland, *International Migration* 52(3): 236–249.

Cairns, D. (2014b). *Youth Transitions, International Student Mobility and Spatial Reflexivity: Being Mobile?* Basingstoke: Palgrave Macmillan.

Cairns, D., Alves, N. de A., Alexandre, A. and Correia, A. (2016) *Youth Unemployment and Job Precariousness: Political Participation in the Austerity Era*. Basingstoke: Palgrave Macmillan.

Cairns, D., Growiec, K. and Alves, N. de A. (2014) Another missing middle? The marginalised majority of tertiary educated youth in Portugal during the economic crisis, *Journal of Youth Studies* 17(8): 1046–1060.

Cassarino, J.-P. (2004) Theorising return migration: the conceptual approach to return migrants revisited, *International Journal on Multicultural Studies* 6(2): 253–279.

Christou, A. (2006). *Narratives of Place, Culture and Identity: Second-Generation Greek-Americans Return 'Home'*. Amsterdam: Amsterdam University Press.

Conway, D. and Potter, R.B. (2006) Caribbean transnational return migrants as agents of change, *Geography Compass* 1(1): 25–45.

Dietrich, H. (2013) Youth unemployment in the period 2001–2010 and the European crisis – looking at the empirical evidence, *Transfer: European Review of Labour and Research*, 19(3): 305–324.

dos Santos, I. (2005) Being a part of several 'worlds': sense of belonging and wedding rites among Franco-Portuguese youth, *Narodna umjetnost. Croatian Journal of Ethnology and Folklore Research* 42(1): 25–45.

Fog Olwig, K. (2007) *Caribbean Journeys: an Ethnography of Migration and Home in Three Family Networks*. Durham, NC: Duke University Press.

Gmelch, G. (1992) *Double Passage: the Lives of Caribbean Migrants Abroad and Back Home*. Ann Arbor: University of Michigan Press.

Gonçalves, A. (1996) *Imagens e Clivagens: Os Residentes Face aos Emigrantes*. Porto: Afrontamento.

King, R. and Christou, A. (2008) Cultural geographies of counter-diasporic migration: the second generation returns 'home'. Brighton: University of Sussex, Sussex Centre for Migration Research, Working Paper 45.

Lee-Cunin, M. (2005) My motherland or my mother's land? Return migration and the experience of young British-Trinidadians, in R.B. Potter, D. Conway and J. Phillips (eds) *The Experience of Return Migration: Caribbean Perspectives*. Aldershot: Ashgate, 109–134.

Levitt, P. and Glick Schiller, N. (2004) Conceptualizing simultaneity: a transnational social field perspective on society, *International Migration Review* 38(3): 1002–1039.

Markowitz, F. and Stefansson, A.D. (eds) (2004) *Homecomings: Unsettling Paths of Return*. Lanham, MD: Lexington Books.

Pires, R.P., Pereira, C., Azevedo, J., Espírito Santo, I., Vidigal I. and Ribeiro, A.C. (2015) *Emigração Portuguesa. Relatório Estatístico 2015*. Lisbon: Observatório da Emigração.

Potter, R.B. (2005) The socio-demographic characteristics of second-generation return migrants to St Lucia and Barbados, in R.B. Potter, D. Conway and J. Phillips (eds) *The Experience of Return Migration: Caribbean Perspectives.* Aldershot: Ashgate, 27–47.

Pries, L. (1999) New migration in transnational spaces, in L. Pries (ed.) *Migration and Transnational Social Spaces.* Aldershot: Ashgate, 1–35.

Pries, L. (2001) The approach of transnational social spaces: responding to new configurations of the social and the spatial, in L. Pries (ed.) *New Transnational Social Spaces: International Migration and Transnational Companies.* London: Routledge, 3–33.

Reynolds, T. (2008) Ties that bind: families, social capital and Caribbean second-generation return. Brighton: University of Sussex, Sussex Centre for Migration Research, Working Paper 46.

Roca, M.N. and Martins, E. (1999) Emigração, regresso e desenvolvimento no Alto Minho, in *Regiões e Cidades na União Europeia: Que Futuro? Actas do VI Econtro Nacional da APOR.* Coimbra: APOR, vol. II, 977–990.

Rodman, J. and Conway, D. (2005) Young returnees in Grenada: adaptation experiences, in R.B. Potter, D. Conway and J. Phillips (eds) *The Experience of Return Migration: Caribbean Perspectives.* Aldershot: Ashgate, 89–108.

Sardinha, J. (2011a) 'Returning' second-generation Portuguese-Canadians and Portuguese-French: motivations and senses of belonging, *Journal of Mediterranean Studies* 20(2): 231–254.

Sardinha, J. (2011b) Neither here nor there: identity constructions, conceptions of 'home' and the transnational lives of second-generation Luso-Canadians and Luso-French in Portugal, in I.M. Blayer, F.C. Fagundes, T. Alves and T. Cid (eds) *Storytelling the Portuguese Diaspora: Piecing Things Together.* New York: Peter Lang, 153–174.

Sardinha, J. (2014) Securing networks or networks of security? Portuguese emigrant descendant returnees negotiate transnational positioning, *Interdisciplinary Journal of Portuguese Diaspora Studies* 3(2): 413–432.

Tyrell, N. (2011) Children's agency in family migration decision making in Britain, in C. Coe, R.R. Reynolds, D.A. Boehm, J.M. Hess and H. Rae-Espinoza (eds) *Everyday Ruptures: Children, Youth, and Migration in Global Perspective.* Nashville, TN: Vanderbilt University Press, 23–38.

Vathi, Z. and Duci, V. (2016) Making other dreams: The impact of migration on the psychosocial wellbeing of Albanian-origin children and young people upon their families' return to Albania, *Childhood* 23(1): 53–68.

Wessells, M.G. (1999) Culture, power and community: intercultural approaches to psychosocial assistance and healing. In K. Nader, N. Dubrow and B. Staum (eds) *Honouring Differences: Cultural Issues in the Treatment of Trauma and Loss.* New York: Taylor and Francis, 276–282.

Wessendorf, S. (2007) 'Roots-migrants': transnationalism and 'return' among second-generation Italians in Switzerland, *Journal of Ethnic and Migration Studies* 33(7): 1083–1102.

Wright, K. (2009) Well-being, poverty and social policy, *Global Social Policy* 9(1): 135–140.

7 'Invisible' returns of Bosnian refugees and their psychosocial wellbeing

Selma Porobić

Introduction

Among the most noteworthy aspects of the 1990s war in Bosnia and Herzegovina (hereafter BiH) was the scale of displacement that it produced through the systematic persecution and expulsion of civilians on ethnic grounds. It resulted in the creation of homogeneous ethnic territories and unprecedented socio-demographic transformations in that country. When the war ended in December 1995, 1.2 million Bosnian refugees were dispersed in 157 different countries across the globe, including 350,000 in Germany alone, closely followed by a group of neighbouring countries, Croatia, Serbia, Slovenia, Austria and Switzerland, as well as Sweden and, later, the US, Canada, Australia and other recipient countries.

Formerly one of Yugoslavia's six federal units, BiH achieved independent status following the 1992–1995 war, which was brought to an end by the Dayton Peace Accords (DPA), signed in 1995 in Dayton, Ohio. The war had devastating consequences, with over 100,000 dead and around 2.2 million displaced (over half the country's total population). The Dayton Accords divided BiH into three parts: the Federation of Bosnia and Herzegovina (FBiH), the Republika Srpska (RS) and the Brcko District. The accords also created the Office of the High Representative (OHR) to oversee the implementation of the civilian aspects of the peace agreement on behalf of the international community, thereby making BiH function as an 'international protectorate'.

The right to return for displaced Bosnians became enshrined in the Annex VII of the Dayton Accords, stating that 'All refugees and displaced persons have the right freely to return to their homes of origin. They shall have the right to have restored to them property of which they were deprived in the course of hostilities since 1991 and to be compensated for any property that cannot be restored to them'. Following the designation from the UN Secretary-General, the UNHCR was entrusted with the role of coordinating among all agencies assisting with the repatriation and relief of refugees and displaced persons. Formal recording of the return started from 1997, when refugees and internally displaced persons (IDPs) registered with the Commission for Real Property Claims of Displaced Persons and Refugees, which was responsible for the processing of property claims. At the same time, between 1997 and 1999, the German authorities pursued a rigorous policy of repatriation, regardless of the structural unpreparedness of BiH to receive back refugees. Especially crucial was the poor security situation, impacting both the refugees' ability to return to their home areas and their willingness to do so. However, following the decisive and strict repatriation politics, the German authorities returned hundreds of thousands of Bosnians with a combination of coercion and extensive pay-to-go schemes.[1] Other countries, such as Sweden, Austria, the Netherlands and the US, had different approaches, such as collective repatriation schemes, pre-return assistance and look-and-see tours, accompanied by various forms of support after return to BiH. In addition, the authorities in the Scandinavian countries, Germany, the Netherlands and Switzerland offered pay-to-go incentives to the returning refugee families, which were equivalent to an annual family income in BiH at that time (Valenta and Strabac 2013). Incentives were offered not only to potential returnees, but also to local municipalities that received and accommodated them.

As the incentives for return increased, along with a gradual diminishing of local hostilities, accompanied by the international community's enforcement of the Property Law Implementation Programme, the returns of refugees and IDPs grew in number.[2] By 2006, the UNHCR office affirmed that over 1 million people displaced by conflict and ethnic cleansing, of whom half were refugees, could reclaim their property and return to their original residences. These achievements are unquestionably a product of the substantial international investment in the Bosnian peace process that incorporated reparations for those displaced by war in the form of a rights-based return (Fagan 2003, 2009).

On the other hand, an extensive body of literature, including studies on the return of displaced Bosnians (de Andrade and Delaney 2001; Fagan 2011; Ito 2001; Jansen and Löfving 2008; Philpott 2005; Phuong 2000; Stefansson 2006), points to clear disparities between the return policies and returnees' post-return realities, in most part due to the unfavourable political and socio-economic situations faced upon return. In these studies, researchers frequently argue that return policies were not properly adjusted in order to match the needs of IDPs and refugees in achieving long-term and sustainable return, and that many of the registered returnees after property repossession moved elsewhere – either to other areas in the country, where their ethnic group is the majority, and hence for reasons of security, or abroad due to better life opportunities, thus re-emigrating and leaving the country once again.

In addition, the continuous trend of post-war emigration, with the accent on skilled, highly educated and young people, resulting in a substantial brain drain, has been alarmingly high (around one-third of the total population), and this problem remains to the present day. The high rate of emigration puts BiH in the first place in Europe and seventh in the world for the number of emigrants and diaspora compared with the total number of inhabitants living in the country.[3] Furthermore, research and reports by human rights monitoring agencies[4] have demonstrated that a substantial number of returnees today, 20 years after the war and enormous international return efforts, still remain in a fragile situation, lacking dignified conditions, and requiring additional support and assistance to access basic human rights and minimal living standards in their home areas.

In terms of qualitative research, anthropologists have also contributed a number of studies of return and home (re)making in BiH, most of which were carried out in the early 2000s, a peak period in the return process.[5] On the other hand, the literature on settlement and integration of Bosnian refugees in the asylum countries is even richer; this literature demonstrates high levels of integration and little motivation and incentives for return to post-Dayton BiH (Kostić 2013; Porobić 2012; Valenta and Ramet 2011; Valenta and Strabac 2013). According to these researchers, while most Bosnian refugees 'dream of returning home' (Valenta and Ramet 2011: 5), the large majority do not actually return. Instead of leaving and reintegrating, they embark on a back-and-forth process, leading over time to the development of transnational lives (Eastmond 2006).

For Bosnian refugees, reintegration upon return has been particularly difficult due to a number of factors, among which divisive ethnic homogenisation politics and corruption stand out as important impediments (Huttunen 2010; Toal and Dahlman 2011). To summarise, both the economic and the political 'pull factors' for achieving a long-lasting return have been particularly weak in the Bosnian case, and in spite of the comprehensive return assistance by the international community and the substantial funds invested in return, it remains a highly contested matter.

In contrast to the vast body of literature on internationally managed return and its sustainability, the research presented in this chapter centres around the impact of 'voluntary' and self-organised return on the returnees' wellbeing in the more recent post-return context. It draws on qualitative data in describing the 'social realities from the perspective of the subject' (Chadwick et al. 1984: 207), and affirms that the psychosocial wellbeing of returned migrants is interlinked with return being a social process within a specific situational context, in which returnees are reconstituting their social worlds.

As is abundantly evident throughout this book, the concept of wellbeing is elusive and complex. My understanding of wellbeing links closely with the social narratives that permeate migration processes, since they are constructed in different settings, including the settlement and return context, which contribute both to shaping migrants' ideas of 'being well' and to related aspirations for wellbeing (Wright 2012). The question that figured most prominently in my research was 'How did the decision of return and the experience of it impact on the migrants' psychosocial wellbeing?' I looked at the psychosocial wellbeing of the migrants as being closely interlinked with or embedded in the broader socio-economic adjustment processes, and in relation to the structural environmental stresses faced (Black and Gent 2006).

Narrative study of migrants' life return projects

The study is based on an extensive narrative data collection, conducted over the period from November 2014 to March 2015, which focused on the migrants' *life return projects*. The term 'life return projects' was coined for the purpose of immersive in-depth study of the migrants' return reality. The research aimed to conceptualise return as a holistic *lifelong project* by prioritising the collection and analysis of migrants' experiences and practices, that is, their motivations, strategies and actions in pursuing their return projects and the consequent effects on their wellbeing.

This study acknowledged *temporal differentiations* between three significant waves of refugee returnees in BiH, namely (i) early repatriation, assisted and non-assisted, from 1997 to 1999 (mainly from Germany, Croatia and Serbia), (ii) voluntary assisted return, following property restitution, from 1999 to 2002 (from EU and other Western countries, plus Serbia and Croatia), and (iii) recent and self-organised return of refugee diasporans (after 2005, from Scandinavia, the US and other EU countries). These temporal differentiations are further linked to the status of refugees in recipient countries, the nature of their return and subsequent socio-economic differences in reintegration. Thus, we can clearly demarcate refugee returnees in the early years of return, who returned from the refugee camps in Croatia and Serbia, from those who received returnee incentives from Western countries prior to return, and the latest returnees, who benefit from naturalisation and longer-term socio-economic integration in the settlement countries. In between these, there are mixed categories that should also be considered. However, this research purposefully targeted the last category of returnees, those who benefit from citizenship and integration in the settlement countries of Western Europe, as they have not been researched before.

The fieldwork comprised four years of observations and numerous informal talks, finally leading to 27 in-depth interviews (60–90 minutes long), primarily putting in focus this 'statistically invisible' yet now-present voluntary return population consisting of former refugees who acquired citizenship in the Western settlement countries.[6] These returning migrants are first-generation refugees who have returned in the last five to ten years. However, they are not registered as returnees but as foreign citizens and/or as BiH citizens today, provided that they hold a dual citizenship (as is the case, for example, with all Bosnian refugees settled in Sweden, who have had the opportunity to obtain a dual citizenship).[7] Especially poignant for these returning migrants is that they are naturalised and have spent ten years (the temporal average in the sample) living abroad and fully integrated in a socio-economic sense. The countries that they returned from are Norway, Sweden, the UK, Germany, Austria, Switzerland, Italy, the US and Canada. The majority of our informants (18) are female; 9 are male. This is the result of the snowball technique used for recruiting informants for interview. Only three of them are single, while the remaining majority are married with children born both in BiH and in settlement countries, who returned with them to BiH. The average age among informants is 35, with the oldest interviewed person being 47 and the youngest 29.

Half of the informants are self-employed and entrepreneurs, who either brought their businesses from the settlement countries to BiH or manage their companies abroad from BiH, and/or have started their businesses upon return to BiH (with the help of savings or company investments that they initiated). Of the informants who are not private entrepreneurs, most work in the settlement countries' state and private agencies represented in BiH (embassies, development agencies, international schools) or for various international and non-governmental organisations. None of them works in the public sector. All hold university diplomas from the settlement countries, the majority of which are in engineering and social sciences (economics, business management, law, languages, human rights, political sciences).

The research locations chosen for interviewing were big urban centres, where the majority of the interviewees from previous observations and informal talks were most easily found and where most work opportunities are found in BiH. They included Sarajevo, Mostar, Tuzla and Banja Luka.

I now present the empirical findings from the research in two different sections corresponding to the overarching themes that emerged from the narrative data analysis: first, the motivations and expectations of return, and second, the impact of post-return experiences on the psychosocial wellbeing of the returnees.

Motivations and expectations of return

'I always felt like waiting for something in a waiting room' (Amila, female, age 41, returned to Mostar in 2010, after 17 years in Norway). From the accounts of informants in this study, it became clear that their involuntary leaving of the country due to the war situation, and the numerous losses (material, social and cultural) that forced migration brought about, have impacted on their motivations and decision-making to return. For the majority, the return to BiH is described as an important life goal, since the experience of being forcibly uprooted lingered on in their lives abroad. This sort of experience was regularly linked with deep emotions, referred to as a 'sense of nostalgia' that could be 'healed' only if the desired goal of return became realised in practice. Zetter (1999) notes that refugees think of the past, from which they derive their identity, in a highly romanticised way. This is how Nejra, who lived in Germany during 1993–1998, and later moved to the US, where she lived till 2007, when she returned to Sarajevo, described it:

> There was never a feeling of being unaccepted by them, but it was more a feeling of nostalgia within us. We had always big plans about return and we kept the contact with the family left behind and our friends ... We wanted our two sons to get to know where their parents came from ... We had regular contacts with people in Bosnia and Bosnians in Germany ... We had

that sense of belonging in US ... We had a lot of things there, but you always think about the place you originate from and always feel drawn to it ... There is a void in you, like a feeling that life was halted, left there, because we had to leave the country ... Everything that happened seems a bit like a dream to you, and not reality.

Other returnees were also very explicit and said that 'nostalgia' made them return, but they also emphasised their free choice in returning:

> total nostalgia ... we returned for good ... No one believed us but I really felt like a stranger and for years dreamt about return and homecoming to Sarajevo. I am very emotional person.
>
> (Nina)

> ... my answer is nostalgia. I have US citizenship and can choose to live where I prefer, and I chose to live here.
>
> (Amir)

Among things that returnees very often mentioned as a key influence on their decision to return was the factor of dissimilarity in the lifestyles of the home country and the settlement country. All spoke vividly about the problems encountered with social life, very often remarking on their inability to bond with the locals, not because they did not want to or had not tried hard, but because they felt rejected, ignored or not understood. Parallels are drawn between the current post-return social life, encompassing enriching and intimate social ties, often expressed as 'normal social ties', and their previously poor social lives in the settlement countries, oftentimes without 'real friends or friendships' or with only 'shallow' and 'interest-oriented relations'. These contrasts, between unsatisfactory social lives abroad and satisfying ones lived now, are particularly strong among the informants from Sweden, Norway, Canada and the US. Amila, a mother of a boy and a girl, aged six and nine, and a returnee from Norway to her hometown Mostar, noted:

> I didn't fit in. Over there, they are much colder, we are warmer and live a family life ... I was very unhappy with my social life there ... We couldn't see ourselves there, especially when kids arrived ... I didn't like how they treat kids, the elderly, and all that would affect our kids too ...

In another study of Bosnian war refugees in Sweden, one of the important reasons for returning to Bosnia, as discussed by 20 informants, was the social gain and expectations of major relief on the emotional and identity levels, including feeling 'less of an alien', freed from exclusion as an immigrant or foreigner, and expectations of returning to previous relationships and feeling that they 'belonged again'. All of these were seen as having an impact on their future overall wellbeing (Porobić 2012: 154).

Besides dissatisfaction with their social lives, those who returned from the US also remarked on the lack of time to socialise due to the stress of career-minded lifestyles and constant competition in the workplace – which they longed to leave by returning to BiH. Emil, who returned as a single man from the US in 2005, after 11 years of life there, noted:

> The life rhythm is very fast and this precisely is the reason for my return. You work enormously, then arrive home alone and wonder, why does a man work at all? ... To have a family, house, work, car? ... And so I said to myself, 'I can have all those things in Bosnia too'. Indeed, since I came back I have 'nested' much more than during my whole stay in America.

Similar findings relating to Bosnian values that involve a richer family-centred social life, in which the core family has quality time together every day, a situation not achieved in the settlement country, were observed by Handlos *et al.* (2015) researching elderly return migration from Denmark to Bosnia. Moreover, in her research on Bosnian refugees' psychosocial wellbeing in Sweden, Eastmond (2000) discussed distress at the personal, familial, societal and political levels. She pointed to the recovery of a 'normal' social and economic functioning of family life, social exchange and work as crucial factors for Bosnians in Sweden that somewhat cushioned the stress of displacement and promoted better all-round health. Indeed, as a person's support system is a crucial factor in psychosocial adjustment, the family and community have become relevant foci for research on forced migrants' wellbeing (Ahearn 2000).

In a similar way, informants in this study, although representing a relatively young average age of 35 years old, often referred to their longing for the 'everyday culture' in BiH, which in their own words involved '*rahatluk*' (a laid-back life), '*merhamet*' (kindness and generosity with a sharing spirit between people), a family and friends-focused life, humour in the workplace, and a general sense of a relaxed lifestyle. These cultural values, encompassing everyday social practices, were difficult to attain in the settlement countries. Adnan, a returnee from Switzerland to Tuzla (although his hometown is Kozarac in Republika Srpska) after 15 years abroad, explained how he had a lot of friends in Switzerland but they could not match the 'warmness between people' and genuine socialising practices that he hoped to find again upon return to Bosnia:

> There isn't any of that Bosnian warmness and '*merhamet*', and all that between people, there is none. There is only work and money, but it's specific. Around 8 p.m. it's all empty in the streets.

In addition, 7 out of the 27 informants explained how patriotism and feelings of obligation to help develop the post-war home country were essential bases of their motivation to return, and that these still prevail as relevant factors of coping with everyday stresses in BiH. Clearly, from their life stories, the career goals and education profiles in the settlement country were chosen in accordance with the aspirations to return and engage in reconstruction and development work. Niva, a woman who returned in 2006 from Sweden after 13 years there, wanted to contribute to transitional justice work in BiH:

> I was an idealist at first, but I really felt that a lot of people like me could contribute towards state-building.... I didn't return out of patriotism, I simply could not deny the fact that my state existed with all its problems, and I felt a need to return ... ever since I worked within the field of transitional justice ... that was my way back....

Silove (1999) notes that participation in the restoration of society's heritage and culture and the development of new structures that foster justice and communal participation can be useful in restoring a sense of community for forced migrants, which in itself has the potential to contribute to the improved mental health of individuals and communities in post-conflict societies.

Besides altruism, more individualistic approaches to return were found, as in the case of Samir, a male returnee from Norway to Sarajevo:

> I was preparing for return quite a long time, talking to myself and all, worked on myself psychologically ... In short I am an idealist and resolved with myself that upon return I will not watch TV and read newspapers, because then I would not remain positive and aim to change things ... I am trying to create a better world for myself ... of course I am bothered because of injustice around me ... One day it will be better.

On the other hand, difficulties in adjusting to the settlement country's employment and economic conditions, and the more practical and 'cheaper' dimensions of life in BiH, were mentioned by Emir, a 43-year-old man who returned from the US to Sarajevo (although his hometown is Sipovo in Republika Srpska) after 11 years of life abroad:

> I wasn't really relaxed regarding the economic situation in America and when you start ageing you realise that life is cheaper in Bosnia, and in that sense it is easier to live in Bosnia than America. I also started thinking about ageing, children not being with me, if my wife will have retirement and other things.

Another returnee from the US, Amir, apart from economic stresses, spoke at length on his perceived discrimination as a motivational factor in his case for returning to BiH.

> I had hit a glass ceiling in America, and realised that you can only view things through glass to the other side of the wall, and you can never reach that level. When you see what immigrants are faced with, then you are on your knees. You are seeing huge discrimination. It's crazy.

A male returnee, Idriz, who returned to his hometown, Mostar, twice from Norway, talked about feelings of 'otherness' and alienation, describing his position in Norwegian society as being 'unheard':

> We both worked but were silent … we didn't like that … somehow like you never quite express yourself fully … We started planning for return, especially when kids came.

The youngest returnee interviewed – a 29-year-old woman who had been in Germany and the US – returned in 2009 for studies in Europe, first engaging in university education in Hungary and then returning to Bosnia. Previously, she had regularly visited for vacations with her family from the US. She said that she came back to learn about Bosnia and create a personal link with a home country: 'I wanted to create my own opinions about my home country, learn and experience the food, the language'.

The motivation to return was already present during the early integration phase into the host societies. Hence, it was not a sudden decision but gradual, and more informed by experiences of life in the settlement country than the structural relations in BiH (Cassarino 2004). Moreover, all participants mentioned how they actively kept ties with families, relatives and friends, and visited regularly, thus maintaining their presence and informing themselves about the current situation in BiH. A female returnee from Germany and the US, who returned with her family after six years of life in the US (in 2007), gave an example of how a gradual process of return in a self-managed manner often takes place after a number of summer and vacation visits to BiH:

> We came back visiting little by little and started doing small-scale projects in Bosnia, first as an artist, both me and my husband. Gradually this led to returning permanently.

In addition, as Amila, a returnee from Norway, explained, a staged and well-planned economic return is crucial for the realisation of return projects among this returnee population:

> I did not leave willingly but was forced to leave my home … Already in 2007 I said to my husband to go back but he stopped me and we waited till 2010, when we had established our business more firmly … We left the company there but returned for good here… it's not easy to earn a living here.

Evidently, the overall motivations for return stem from the initial trauma of involuntary displacement, nostalgia, alienation, lack of quality time, poor social life in the settlement country, and longing for specific cultural aspects of everyday life in BiH. These deprivations were compensated for by short visits prior to return, as well as a willingness to help reconstruct the post-war society.

Some differences across gender and socio-economic backgrounds could be observed. Women holding university degrees more explicitly indicated their motivation as being development work in the home country, as well as wanting their children to learn about the culture and background of their parents, while men said that they were more drawn to the richer social life, business investments and cheaper cost of living in BiH when compared with the settlement countries.

Impact of return on migrants' wellbeing

> We don't belong anywhere anymore, life here isn't good and we are keeping our options open.
>
> (Ana, UK returnee to Sarajevo)

The positive tone of informants shifts very quickly to a negative one when they stop talking about their reasons to return and start narrating about how they experience their life since return. The quote above comes from a female returnee from the UK in 2000, as she made known all the downsides of family life in Sarajevo and explained how her family keeps thinking of re-emigrating again.

Based on her research on Bosnian refugees in Great Britain and the Netherlands, Al-Ali (2002) observed that, rather than living a 'double life', Bosnian refugees found themselves in an unclear situation, positioned between two realities – not feeling 'at home' in these host countries or in the country of origin. Likewise, I found in an earlier study that the feelings of ambivalence regarding the socio-cultural belonging of settled Bosnian war refugees were produced by the changed social and political conditions in BiH, and by the structural treatment that they experience in the resettlement society, which restricts their subjectively desired integration and emplacement opportunities. To quote at length from my earlier study:

> Within the receiving society, they are, in the best case recognized as Bosnians or Bosnian refugees and immigrants, though they themselves often feel like individuals – something they are never recognized for. In such circumstances, they begin to identify themselves with their feeling of inner 'homelessness', 'non-belonging' and 'in-between realities' which they by now have integrated into their self-image and their personal identity, at the same time opposing a dominant approach to their identity construction as a fixed category.
>
> (Porobić 2012: 157)

All returnees underline how their citizenship gives them great flexibility to move back to the settlement country at any time if they need or wish to do so. They keep their options open all the time and mainly link this kind of readiness and flexibility in being mobile to the unstable socio-political situation in BiH, above all the chronically high unemployment and the generally poor future outlook. Family life being under threat, in that the children's future is endangered, comes first on the priority list. The possibility of re-emigration is mostly related to greater possibilities in the settlement country, including better prospects for children's education, access to a better quality and range of communal services, and their own professional and career development. To quote from two return-ees from Norway:

> We have the feeling that we are here for good but also as if we sit on two seats at the same time ... Because of the kids, the reasons to go back to Norway are stronger ...
>
> (Idriz)

> I always have this readiness that, 'if something happens', to get my family out, like in the 90s ... because it's not so much better here except for the shooting, we are spared from that at least ... it's horrible in Mostar ...
>
> (Emil)

It is apparent that returnees' openness to flexible mobility patterns is conditioned by their previous war experiences and their current children-oriented lives. They have an awareness both of the security risks (unstable political situation) and of the economic and educational disadvantages in the home country. For this reason, they have adopted a predominantly 'open-ended return' as their coping option and future hope, due to having legal access to the settlement countries' social services and stronger economy and the privilege of citizenship – all enabling easy mobility (see Stefansson 2006). They all have access to 'enabling citizenship' and residence rights in the settlement country, and frequently use these as an asset while undertaking the return and re-emigration projects. One could say that they return and establish their lives despite numerous instabilities. Precisely for that reason, they keep the awareness of challenges, obstacles and disadvantages of life in BiH alive, and contrast them with the realities they left for return to BiH, which are always available in the settlement countries.

In addition, being met with a negative attitude for having chosen to return presents an additional challenge. This is now a prevalent local attitude towards these recent returns from abroad, since emigration is more salient to Bosnians today. The interviewees' experience of return therefore also reflects this negative reception attitude and the reactions of the locals who stayed. For these locals, the return is deemed a poor choice, 'a mistake' that the returnees repeatedly need to explain and justify. Of course, this attitude impacts on their wellbeing and is a rather central part of informants' stories, in that they feel a bit frustrated by such perceptions:

> Whenever I say I returned, people here tell me that I am out of my mind, but there are many like me here ... everyone has their own path in life and

it's difficult to share that with people here who all want to leave the country
and go to Norway and Sweden ...

(Idriz, male returnee from Norway)

However, their determination to rebuff the negative attitudes attached to the
choice of return is rather high. Adnan, a returnee to Tuzla from Switzerland,
uses patriotism as both a motivational factor and a source of his resilience in the
post-return reality whenever his return is brought into question:

> No one ever said to me that it was a smart move to return here, only that I
> am abnormal for coming back ... My key reason was patriotism, pure love
> towards my country and a wish to give something back from what I've
> learned. So I don't see how damaged the infrastructure is, like everyone
> else, I don't see the garbage on the streets, but concentrate on what is
> positive ... Returnees can change things around in BiH for the better: I
> always think that returnees can do much more than those who have stayed.

Additionally, there are several negative factors in the BiH's post-war society
that informants describe as real obstacles to their long-term stay, as they directly
impact on their wellbeing and quality of life. Dissatisfaction with the standard of
education, persisting ethnic divisions, and slow socio-economic progress in the
country are factors typically mentioned as impacting negatively on the wellbeing
of families who returned. The future of the children is a major concern, due to
these structural negativities. Children have thus been motivators both for return
and for contemplating re-emigration among the informants. Different coping
strategies have been presented for overcoming the educational obstacles impacting on the children's future. For example, issues pertaining to poor education
and the difficulties of adaptation are resolved by having children attend classes
in the language of the settlement countries – especially English – in order for
them to continue to study abroad at some future time.

> We want them to have an option to go to the US and study there.... We
> brought some positive educational practices and put these in use here
> because of the local ones that dominate ...

(Mila, returnee from US)

Finally, the centrality of the war experiences and dealing with the traumatic
past were seen by several informants as highly relevant to their persistence in
pursuing the right to return and restoring their lost life and hopes for the future
in BiH today:

> It took twenty years for me to grow up and become aware, to return and
> then realise that I am welcome only if I am silent here. They have forgotten
> the children from the war. I haven't seen any documentaries on this topic,
> perhaps one book only.... it's never too late but we need to understand

what happened here ... and how people survived ... Today here in BiH many think if you left in 1992 you haven't seen the war because bigger towns continued to be destroyed till 1995 ... people think the more you stayed, the greater your suffering ... I remember for example my father who needed a year to recover from not being able to help his country and my mum losing 17 pounds, my dad becoming grey-haired overnight ... All we fought for during our long years in Germany was to recover our dignity, we lived through sleepless nights, many ... and even more nights to regain a belief in the future again ... that's my scream of truth, my return.

(Adis, returnee from US and Germany)

In Adis's quote there are clear interlinkages between trauma, remembrance and return motivations and experiences. It is instructive to compare these psychological categories, both motivating return and also framing the many stresses encountered upon return, with my earlier findings among settled Bosnian refugees in Sweden (Porobić 2012). In the earlier study, I found that resilience (including religiosity) was geared towards dealing with the symptoms and realities of 'in-betweenness' that Bosnian war refugees faced in Sweden, impacting their psychosocial wellbeing, social identity and integration. Return, imagined as both a 'project' and its subsequent realisation, was seen on the one hand as a means of relieving the stresses of displacement (uprootedness, non-belonging, homesickness etc.) but on the other hand also as the potential cause of renewed suffering, because return amounts to yet another new start. For many, there was a time difference of around 20 years since leaving the country, resulting in difficulty in grasping the fundamental changes occurring in Bosnian society in the meantime. These had to be confronted upon return, along with the multiple and varied individual experiences of war, displacement and trauma faced by themselves, other returnees and the 'locals', who all had their own narratives of war and post-war life.

Discussion

An important aspect of the findings in the present study clearly points to the fact that, for the majority of Bosnians settled in the Western recipient countries, the motivation to return was already present during the early phase of integration into these host societies. Hence, it is not a sudden decision, but is gradual and informed more by experiences of life in the settlement country than by the structural relations in BiH. The decision-making process of return has strong temporal and experiential dimensions and is formed on the basis of strong pro-return emotions, intertwined with other motivational drivers, related to the quality and experiences of social life in the countries of settlement, and their expectations related to return, based on their previously internalised social and cultural values as well as the more psychological emotions of war-displacement and nostalgia. In addition, return plans and decisions are informed through the transnational ties that these migrants maintain with the country of origin, particularly the return visits. As a result, experiences of life upon return and the stresses and strains faced due to the structural issues typical of post-conflict societies have a 'surprising' effect on the returnees and tend to be dealt with ad hoc. Imagining and preparing the children for a possible re-emigration to the settlement country seems to be the prevalent method of coping with these stresses encountered in the post-return context – in much the same way that imagining and actualising return from the receiving countries was their coping mechanism in an earlier phase of their lives.

These results clearly point to practices of 'home-making' being conditioned by the specific and contrasting socio-economic, political and cultural contexts of both the home country and the settlement country that Bosnian refugees seek to integrate and reconcile in their return-life projects. The main principle of such integration seems to evolve around a set of social practices that reveal return as a gradual, lifelong project, being negotiated and undertaken in different places at the same time, thereby reducing risks and maximising opportunities where these are limited. Such practices are also seen to be transgenerational, as they involve the whole family's flexible mobility patterns, back and forth between the home country and the settlement country.

These findings have also shown that, for these returnees, wellbeing is conceived not so much as an individual-scale entity, but instead is positioned within the family and the broader social relations of the community, where decision-making, planning, integration and self-actualisation are all taking place (Porobić 2016). Indeed, kinship and friendship established and preserved through social networks are deemed 'fundamental adaptive devices' (Hajdukowski-Ahmed *et al.* 2009) that help people adapt to a new environment and conditions. In this way, this study has revealed that approaching forced migrants' return practices means studying longitudinal life-projects embedded in broader societal contexts that have inevitable effects on overall psychosocial wellbeing. These are intertwined with broader socio-economic questions, particularly of educational relevance, healthcare provision and neighbourly relations. They also indicate open-ended returns and greater transnational mobility within each household as a necessary coping device for achieving satisfactory life conditions while practising return to BiH. Using Eastmond's (2006) phrase, one can see that these voluntary returnees engage in 'social reconstruction processes of (re)creating, in new circumstances, the social relations, identities and cultural meanings through which people in a post-war setting (re)connect to a particular place and community as "home"'.

Conclusion and policy implications

Under ideal conditions, the notion of voluntary return should encompass the concept of agency and decision-making based on individual motivation. In this context, the decision to return may be motivated by the accommodation of important psychosocial needs, including the relief from trauma, a sense of belonging, a secure identity, and emotional and patriotic attachments that are often difficult to establish in a foreign environment. In practice, however, migrants, and especially refugees, are rarely able to make individual divisions free of external influence, including pressures from sending and receiving governments and international politics as well as trends in protection and assistance to war-displaced populations.

In contrast to individualistic accounts of return, the concept of return is also linked with post-conflict stabilisation based on macro-political considerations. Human rights monitoring agencies such as the Organisation for Security Cooperation in Europe (OSCE), in addition to refugee protection agencies such as UNHCR, have been contracted to further the return project by developing, implementing, coordinating and monitoring specific programmes (Koser 2000). These have been mainly focused on the effectiveness of acute humanitarian assistance and provision of services, and less on addressing the long-term engagement in much-needed comprehensive reintegration programmes focusing on the self-sufficiency of the returnees, and in particular making the returnee environments more receptive to the voluntary returnees in a long-term perspective beyond the immediate post-conflict period.

This qualitative research clearly unveils the paradoxes of the narrow rights-based and sedentarist arguments for return within a peace-building framework, enshrined in the Dayton Peace Accords, by pointing to the psychosocial realities and structural reintegration struggles, but also the resourceful transnational mobility patterns employed by displaced persons and returnees in pursuing their entitled returnee and (re)integration rights within the challenging political, socio-economic and cultural context of the post-Dayton BiH. It illustrates that the return, falsely and simplistically conceptualised as the 'end of the migration cycle' and of refugee suffering, and further legitimised within the widely accepted policy and practice of a 'durable solution', is highly problematic from the standpoint of the psychosocial wellbeing of the displaced persons and families (Porobić 2015). This is especially poignant when focusing on the psychosocial aspects of 'renormalisation' of the war-shattered lives of displaced populations in a community context and in a long-term perspective.

Finally, these results provide useful policy-oriented information and recommendations regarding the too-often overlooked 'agency' factor in the conceptualisation of refugee return. They thus reopens the criticism of assisted return as carried out by the so-called competent and relevant national and international actors (involved in supporting and facilitating this option as one of the durable solutions for the forcibly displaced), as opposed to a successful and meaningful return grounded in the social agency of forced migrants and the gradual building of return projects (Porobić 2016). In these projects, social support and broader psychosocial wellbeing should be afforded more research and practical attention. Social integration involves a behavioural component evidenced by engagement in a wide range of socially affirming activities or relationships, as well as a cognitive component that involves a sense of community and identification with one's social roles (Cohen 2004). Such an integration, supported by programmes targeting return, could ameliorate the manifold stresses encountered in this research. Policies should, therefore, offer instrumental support (material assistance), informative support (advice and guidance) and emotional support (caring and trust, ventilating emotions) in the processes of reintegration that inevitably take a long time in post-conflict societies.

Notes

1 Compilation of information available in the Global IDP Database of the Norwegian Refugee Council, www.ecoi.net/file_upload/dh1359_01694bih.pdf (accessed 31 July 2016).
2 The main boosts to minority returns came after 1998, when the Office of the High Representative (OHR) more aggressively detained local warlords for criminal activities. In 1999, the High Representative pushed through stronger security, measures and property laws intended to support return to minority areas. Consequently, over 90 per cent of the claims filed for the restitution of property under these laws were addressed.
3 Bosnia and Herzegovina's Migration Profile for 2014, Ministry for Security, Sector for Immigration, Sarajevo, May 2015, http://msb.gov.ba/PDF/MIGRATION%20 PROFILE_2014_ENG.pdf (accessed 31 July 2016).
4 There are several reports, mostly on the early phases of the return process, by policy researchers (e.g. Belloni 2005; D'Onofrio 2004; Ito 2001) as well as NGOs and international organisations such as Human Rights Watch, International Crisis Group, IOM and UNHCR.
5 The majority concern Bosniak IDP returnees in Republika Srpska in Krajina (e.g. Huttunen 2010) and in North-East BiH (Jansen 2011). Some studies also take into account returnees' relationships with stayees and displaced persons who settled nearby (Stefansson 2006), others encompass movements across the Inter-Entity Boundary Line in both directions (Jansen 2006, 2008), and some work deals with relations between stayees and newcomers of the same nationality in Sarajevo (Stefansson 2004).
6 I would like to acknowledge that 14 of these interviews were conducted by Dragana Kovacevic, University of Oslo, during her Visiting Fellowship at the Centre for Refugee and IDP Studies, University of Sarajevo. Her fieldwork was extended by my own research – both of which were initially intended to contribute to a joint study of return from Western European countries.
7 In 2013, after years of political dispute and in connection with the first national census held after the war (the last having been conducted in 1991 in Yugoslavia), a state-level law was passed that allows Bosnian citizens settled abroad with foreign citizenship to keep Bosnian citizenship. In practice, this means that regardless of where you settled during the war and obtained citizenship, you are still not erased from the national register of citizens in BiH and can retain all identification documents including Bosnian citizenship if needed. This makes the registration of returnees difficult to trace in the national statistics.

References

Ahearn, F.L. (2000) Psychosocial wellness: methodological approaches to the study of refugees, in F.L. Ahearn (ed.) *Psychosocial Wellness of Refugees: Issues in Qualitative and Quantitative Research.* New York: Berghahn, 63–80.
Al-Ali, N. (2002) Loss of status or new opportunities? Gender relations and transnational ties among Bosnian refugees, in D. Bryceson and U. Vuorela (eds) *The Transnational Family: New European Frontiers and Global Networks.* Oxford: Berg, 83–102.

Belloni, R. (2005) Peacebuilding at the local level: refugee return to Prijedor, *International Peacekeeping* 12(3): 434–447.

Black, R. and Gent, S. (2006) Sustainable return in post-conflict contexts, *International Migration* 44(3): 15–38.

Cassarino, J.P. (2004) Theorising return migration: the conceptual approach to return migrants revisited, *International Journal on Multicultural Societies* 6(2): 253–279.

Chadwick, B.A., Bahr, H.M. and Albrecht, S.L. (1984) *Social Sciences Research Methods*. New Jersey: Prentice-Hall.

Cohen, S. (2004) Social relationships and health, *American Psychologist* 59(8): 676–684.

D'Onofrio, L. (2004) Welcome home? Minority return in south-east Republika Srpska. Brighton: University of Sussex, Sussex Migration Working Paper 19.

de Andrade, J.H.F. and Delaney, N.B. (2001) Minority return to South-Eastern Bosnia and Herzegovina: a review of the 2000 return season, *Journal of Refugee Studies* 14(3): 315–330.

Eastmond, M. (2000) Refugees and health: ethnographic approaches, in F.L. Ahearn (ed.) *Psychosocial Wellness of Refugees: Issues in Qualitative and Quantitative Research*. New York: Berghahn, 33–40.

Eastmond, M. (2006) Transnational returns and reconstruction in a post-war Bosnia and Herzegovina, *International Migration* 44(3): 141–166.

Fagan, P.W. (2003) Post-conflict reintegration and reconstruction: doing it right takes a while, in N. Steiner, M. Gibney and G. Loescher (eds) *Problems of Protection: The UNHCR, Refugees and Human Rights*. New York: Routledge, 213–217.

Fagan, P.W. (2009) Peace processes and IDP solutions, *Refugee Survey Quarterly* 28(1): 31–58.

Fagan, P.W. (2011) *Refugees and IDPs after Conflict: Why They Do Not Go Home. Special Report*. New York: United States Institute of Peace.

Hajdukowski-Ahmed, M., Khanlou, N. and Moussa, H. (eds) (2009) *Not Born a Refugee Woman: Contesting Identities, Rethinking Practices*. New York: Berghahn (first edition 2008).

Handlos, L.N., Olwig, K.F., Bygbjerg, I.C., Kristiansen, M. and Norredam, M.L. (2015) Return migration among elderly, chronically ill Bosnian refugees: does health matter? *International Journal of Environmental Research and Public Health* 12(10): 12643–12661.

Huttunen, L. (2010) Sedentary policies and transnational relations: a 'non-sustainable' case of return to Bosnia, *Journal of Refugee Studies* 23(1): 41–61.

Ito, A. (2001) Politicisation of minority return in Bosnia-Herzegovina – the first five years examined, *International Journal of Refugee Law* 13(1–2): 98–122.

Jansen, S. (2006) The privatisation of home and hope: return, reforms and the foreign intervention in Bosnia-Herzegovina, *Dialectical Anthropology* 30(3–4): 177–199.

Jansen, S. (2008) Troubled locations: return, the life course, and transformations of 'home' in Bosnia-Herzegovina, *Focaal* 49: 15–30.

Jansen, S. (2011) Refuchess: locating Bosniac repatriates after the war in Bosnia-Herzegovina, *Population, Space and Place* 17(1): 140–152.

Jansen, S. and Löfving, S. (2008) *Struggles for Home: Violence, Hope and the Movement of People*. Oxford: Berghahn.

Koser, K. (2000) Return, readmission and reintegration: changing agendas, policy frameworks and operations programmes, in B. Ghosh (ed.) *Return Migration: Journey of Hope or Despair?* Geneva: International Organization for Migration, 57–99.

Kostić, R. (2013) Exploring trends in transnational practices of conflict-generated migrants: Bosnians in Sweden and their activities towards Bosnia and Herzegovina, in M. Hadžihafizović (ed.) *Migration from Bosnia and Herzegovina*. Sarajevo: Faculty of Political Science, University of Sarajevo, 35–45.

Philpott, C. (2005) Though the dog is dead, the pig must be killed: finishing with property restitution to Bosnia-Herzegovina's IDPs and refugees, *Journal of Refugee Studies* 18(1): 1–24.

Phuong, C. (2000) Freely to return: reversing ethnic cleansing in Bosnia-Herzegovina, *Journal of Refugee Studies* 13(2): 165–183.

Porobić, S. (2012) *Resilience and Religion in a Forced Migration Context: A Narrative Study of Religiousness as a Resilience Factor in Dealing with Refugee Experiences from a Post-Migration Perspective of Bosnian Refugees in Sweden*. Lund: Lund University.

Porobić, S. (2015) Asking the right questions in research on psychosocial well-being research, *Forced Migration Review* 50: 24–25.

Porobić, S. (2016) Bosnian 'returnee voices' communicating experiences of successful reintegration: the social capital and sustainable return nexus in Bosnia and Herzegovina, migration, values, networks, wellbeing, *Sudesteuropa* 64(1): 5–26.

Silove, D. (1999) The psychosocial effects of torture, mass human rights violation and refugee trauma: towards an integrated conceptual framework, *The Journal of Nervous and Mental Disease* 187: 200–207.

Stefansson, A. (2004) Refugee return to Sarajevo and the challenge to contemporary narratives of mobility, in L.D. Long and E. Oxfeld (eds) *Coming Home? Refugees, Migrants, and Those Who Stayed Behind*. Philadelphia: Pennsylvania University Press, 170–186.

Stefansson, A. (2006) Homes in the making: property restitution, refugee return, and senses of belonging in a post-war Bosnian town, *International Migration* 44(3): 115–139.

Toal, G. and Dahlman, C.T. (2011) *Bosnia Remade: Ethnic Cleansing and Its Reversal*. Oxford: Oxford University Press.

Valenta, M. and Ramet, S.P. (2011) Bosnian migrants: an introduction, in M. Valenta and S.P. Ramet (eds) *The Bosnian Diaspora: Integration in Transnational Communities*. Farnham: Ashgate, 1–23.

Valenta, M. and Strabac, Z. (2013) The dynamics of Bosnian refugee migrations in the 1990s, current migration trends and future prospects, *Refugee Survey Quarterly* 32(3): 1–22.

Wright, K. (2012) Constructing human wellbeing across spatial boundaries: negotiating meanings in transnational migration, *Global Networks* 12(4): 467–484.

Zetter, R. (1999) Reconceptualizing the myth of return: continuity and transition amongst the Greek-Cypriot refugees of 1974, *Journal of Refugee Studies* 12(1): 1–22.

Part III

Asylum systems, assisted returns and post-return mobilities

8 'Burning without fire' in Sweden

The paradox of the state's attempt to safeguard deportees' psychosocial wellbeing

Daniela DeBono

Introduction

This chapter critically analyses the official discourse of protection of migrants' psychosocial wellbeing by drawing on first-hand experiences of migrants who are living through the forced return migration process in Sweden.[1] Forced migrants resist their return decision in various ways. For the authorities, they have become 'police cases'; therefore, they are people who need to be removed from the territory by force. Sweden is a developed welfare state, which has earned an international reputation as a country where human rights are respected (Grimheden 2006). It also fares well with respect to migrants' rights and entitlements in both the legal and welfare systems (MIPEX 2014). However, little is known about the psychosocial wellbeing of migrants who are living with the imminent risk of deportation and how they, themselves, perceive and are influenced by it.

The start of the deportation process is when a person who has been given a 'decision to leave' refuses to comply or to collaborate with the Swedish Migration Agency. At this point, the case is handed over to the police, with the understanding that some element of force might be needed to implement the return decision. Forced returnees can be asylum-seekers whose applications are turned down, or people who for various reasons have lost their permit to stay, or never obtained one. They are all people whose dreams of establishing themselves in Sweden have been rendered grim. More critically, they are people coming to terms with the prospect that they may be returned to their official country of origin or to a third country. For asylum-seekers, this is often the same country from which they fled, and have spent years building a case for not being returned there; or, if they have spent their lives in another country, it is a country they do not know. For migrants, this period in their lives is imbued with fear, uncertainty and an ebbing, but still present, hope that their situation might change.

In spite of their irregular status, the Swedish state has an obligation to ensure that the basic human rights of these migrants are safeguarded. In the area of returns, this obligation is reflected in law. The European Return Directive, transposed into the Swedish Aliens Act in 2012, puts an obligation on EU member states to ensure that all returns, including forced returns and detention, are conducted in accordance with 'fundamental human rights' and in a 'humane and dignified' manner.[2] This chapter deals with human rights in a broad manner, looking at the underlying principles rather than the specific human rights laws. Nonetheless, since my focus is primarily on psychosocial wellbeing, it is good to keep in mind the fundamental rights to life and health found in all the major human rights treaties.

From the point of view of psychosocial wellbeing, there are two characteristics of Sweden's international image that condition migrants' experiences of living as deportables. The first is derived from the excellent reputation that Sweden has built as a country where humanitarian activity is valued together with human and children's rights. What emerges from observation in the field is that this reputation is accompanied by high expectations of sympathy and compassion. Following this is an appreciation of the highly regulated and non-corrupt Swedish migration and asylum system, fuelling further expectations of fairness, justice and non-discrimination. Reminiscent of Graeber's ideas on the 'utopia of rules', Sweden offers the utopian promise of fairness brought about by an impersonal, impartial bureaucracy, as opposed to structures built on family connections, patrimonial power and wealth, which are seen to lend themselves to nepotism and corruption (Graeber 2015). But the transparent bureaucracy 'bites back' when its rules are broken, with the threat, or actual exercise, of force. Indeed, when migrants receive the return decision, the disappointment is accentuated by both raised expectations and the harsh reality of sanctions should they fail to obey the rules. These are contradictions to which the system is 'blind', but which emerge powerfully from the 'everyday' narratives shared by the migrants. The shadow that is cast on their wellbeing is penetratingly dark. This is powerfully and vividly encapsulated in this quote:

> Most of the immigrants are coming here because they want to live in paradise, but which kind of paradise is this which is burning you without fire yeah. You're burning without fire in Sweden.
>
> (Kader, Afghanistan, 21, male)

Migrants at risk of deportation live a life of exclusion. The degree of exclusion varies according to the situation and status of the migrant. Being deportable in Sweden is characterised by dependency on the system, powerlessness to change, an inability to plan for the future, and overall, the fear of being sent back to the country of origin. The gravity of the impact of the return decision, which, in the absence of collaboration, can be executed by force, is conditioned by several factors. The feelings of rejection, exclusion and fear of being returned are not new to a deportee. For many, there is a gradual increase of these sentiments brought about by the sequence of unsuccessful applications for asylum and ensuing civil and judicial appeals. These feelings are confirmed on a daily basis by the severe limitations on their lives and the 'limbo' state that they find themselves in. Participation in community activities is curtailed: their living conditions can make this better or worse, as does their legal status. If they are in hiding, their activities are further limited, and finally, detention is the crowning stage of exclusion. The return decision – 'the negative' – starts a downward spiral that has a grave impact on their wellbeing:

> I have gotten psychological problems after they give me the negative. My situation has become worse day by day.
>
> (Ismat, Afghanistan, 29, male)

This chapter approaches this discussion through the migrants' own subjective experiences of the deportation process, with a focus on aspects of their psychosocial wellbeing and health. It contributes to the few publications and studies on detention and deportation in Sweden, most recently by DeBono *et al.* (2015), Khosravi (2009), Puthoopparambil *et al.* (2015) and Sager (2011). It is also an attempt to contribute to the broader discussion of what could constitute 'humane and dignified' treatment in the deportation process. This is done by producing knowledge through original empirical material of how migrants subjectively experience the deportation process, and in particular how they present issues pertaining to their own psychosocial wellbeing.

My analysis of these experiences yields some clear patterns and trends. The ethnographic research for this paper, conducted during 2014 and 2015, includes 26 in-depth interviews, one to five hours in duration, with migrants of different ages, genders and nationalities, most of whom were living in Sweden and were deportable. Standard procedures of interviewing vulnerable people were adhered to during the in-depth interviews: the interviewers explained the nature of the research, that there could be no direct benefit to their case, and that they could stop the interview at any point, and care was taken to ensure that only the issues brought up by the migrants themselves were discussed.[3] Most migrants indulged in long conversations during the interviews, often sharing information that went beyond the scope of the interview. This indicates that the interview was not perceived as part of the system, as official or as intruding. Other interviews were held with state officials in order to contextualise the data.

Psychosocial wellbeing and its consonance with human rights

In recent years, in a clear move away from the medical model whereby wellbeing had been reduced to the medicalised definitions of psychological states, the term 'psychosocial wellbeing' is used to refer to the close connection between psychological aspects of human experience and the wider social experience. Various migration bodies, such as the International Organization for Migration (IOM) and the United Nations High Commissioner for Refugees (UNHCR), refer to the importance of migrants' psychosocial health and wellbeing, and have built development programmes and services around this concept and the understanding that both psychological and social aspects are necessary to migrants' wellbeing (IOM 2013).

The concept of psychosocial wellbeing denotes a comprehensive person-centred approach to mental wellbeing, which values social interactions, networks and connectedness. It follows that psychosocial wellbeing is culturally specific. Factors that can nurture psychosocial wellbeing include agency, autonomy and control; participation and involvement; social relationships and networks; and personal and community safety (Caplan 2002; Correa-Velez *et al.* 2010; Egan *et al.* 2008; Kohli and Mather 2003; Martikainen *et al.* 2002).

Psychosocial wellbeing and access to quality mental health care are recognised by the UN and human rights organisations as key requirements of human rights and social justice (UN 2011). The World Health Organization (WHO) includes mental health as a crucial factor in overall health (WHO 2010). The Society for the Psychological Study of Social Issues (2014: 1–2), in a statement presented to the international community in 2014, recommends that governments and all stakeholders:

- include psychosocial wellbeing as a contributor and an outcome of sustainable development;
- make quality mental healthcare accessible to all sectors of society, as a requirement of human rights and social justice;
- implement the Social Protection Floor Initiative, including access to mental healthcare within primary healthcare, taking care of basic human needs of all vulnerable groups;
- provide mental health counsellors and social workers, trained in culturally specific methodology and techniques, to train and work with local communities in recognising mental health problems;
- ensure that all services are implemented according to ethical principles that affirm the dignity of everyone.

The relationship between psychosocial health and human rights, increasingly presented as self-evident by international organisations, has, however, been critically assessed. Grove *et al.* (2006) claim that this relationship does not have deep roots, but is superficial and incidental; at best, they are 'fair weather friends'. They trace the convergence of the two to a period when health professionals and psychologists had been exploring human rights dimensions to their work. The emergence of this relationship became apparent with the tsunami of 26 December 2004, which affected 12 countries, 8 of which experienced significant tragedy (Grove *et al.* 2006).

In spite of this theoretical critique, the concept of psychosocial wellbeing serves as a good theoretical concept to analyse migrants' subjective experiences of the deportation system. It is an approach that allows us to deal with the difficult question of whether the impact on migrants' wellbeing is proportionate to the state's obligations to manage migration and its borders. It also allows us to look at these issues intersectionally, where migration, human rights and considerations of psychosocial wellbeing meet, rather than treating them as isolated matters. Ultimately, it helps to answer the critical question: is the proclaimed protection of migrants' psychosocial wellbeing by the state a paradox in the deportation process?

The Swedish returns system

Sweden has developed broad immigration and asylum policies, which have been refined over the years. The first deportation act was passed in 1914, whereas the first comprehensive immigration act was enacted in 1927. Significant reforms were introduced in the 1960s Aliens Act, and in 2012, amendments were made in order to complete the transposition of the European Return Directive. All aspects of immigration are administered by an autonomous agency called the Swedish Migration Agency, set up to ensure consistency and coherency in the migration policy. The vision of the Migration Agency is 'Sweden – a nation open for the possibilities of global migration'. On their official website, this is explained thus: 'At the Migration Agency we see migration as a positive force, something that contributes to making our country richer, both financially and culturally' (Swedish Migration Agency 2015). The government's goal for the Swedish Migration Agency is

> to ensure a long-term, sustainable migration policy that safeguards asylum rights and, within the framework of regulated immigration, facilitates mobility across borders and promotes a needs-driven labour immigration, while utilising and considering the development effects of migration, and furthering European and international cooperation.
>
> (Swedish Migration Agency 2015)

It is noteworthy that asylum is placed at the very top of the agenda, and as a result, the asylum system is sophisticated and highly regulated. It is difficult to say whether the Swedish asylum system, or any other asylum system for that matter, has achieved the necessary standards of justice and fairness. However, the Swedish system, in the words of the Commissioner for Human Rights, 'ensures respect for due process requirements and provides for a fair hearing and proper appeal procedures' (Council of Europe Commissioner for Human Rights 2007: III (24)). Returns, both 'voluntary' and 'forced' as defined in bureaucratic terms, are also the responsibility of the Migration Agency. The Migration Agency endorses a policy of encouraging voluntary returns. The ratio of voluntary returns to forced returns is high, reaching 76:24 in 2014 (these figures also include Dublin returnees). As other research has shown, the terminology does not really do justice to this case – 'voluntary' means cooperation with the authorities, and is often still imbued with unwillingness to return from the migrants' perspective. This is the official language of the state: harsh, bureaucratic and divorced from the migrants' experiences. And this is how Graeber's conceptualisation of 'structural violence' can transform into physical harm:

forms of pervasive social inequality that are ultimately backed up by the threat of physical harm invariably tend to create the kinds of willful blindness we normally associate with bureaucratic procedures.

(Graeber 2006: 112).

Hence, structural violence can quickly translate into physical violence when returnees transgress, or speak out against the official rules: suffice it to mention police, security officers and different sanctions imposed by the state. The physical and spatial displacement from one country to another, one culture to another, one community to another, is violence of the most existential kind.

The Swedish Migration Agency is responsible for managing the five migrant detention centres (*förvar*) in the country, which operate primarily as pre-removal centres. In the implementation of forced returns, the police are entrusted with cases where migrants have resisted the decision or absconded. Transportation is administered by the Swedish Prison and Probation Service (*Kriminalvården*). Sweden, most notably, has refrained from outsourcing the transportation or running of detention centres to multinational profit-making companies, which can have calamitous, even lethal, effects on the migrants (Gammeltoft-Hansen 2013).

There is as yet no expansive human rights critique of the Swedish migration, asylum and deportation system. Current critique generally deals with the tightening of structural or policy issues and the administrative slackening of standards (Council of Europe Commissioner for Human Rights 2007). The authorities tend to respond and address issues within a few years. The internal human rights critique is more vigorous, focusing on the conditions in detention (Swedish Red Cross, *Förvar under lupp*) and respect for the *non-refoulement* principle.

What 'burning without fire' means: living as deportables in Sweden

The return process, fraught with anxiety as it is, can become overwhelming for migrants who resist the decision. This section explores the overarching fear of return frequently reiterated by irregular migrants themselves. Migrants at risk of deportation may be living in the Swedish Migration Agency's accommodation, or in the community with their whereabouts known to the authorities; they may have absconded and be living in hiding; or they may be in detention. Some issues are common irrespective of their situation: for example, migrants mention mental health problems such as insomnia, paranoia, anxiety, physical manifestations of distress and a general sense of weariness often referred to as 'ageing more rapidly'. There are also issues that are particular to their situation. Detention, for example, creates acute mental health problems and a total sense of powerlessness over their situation. This is supported by the study conducted by Puthoopparambil *et al.* (2015), who argue that migrants' lack of control over their own lives in detention centres is key to understanding the detrimental effect of detention on migrants' health.

Deportability in this study is broadly understood as constructing not only positions in the labour market (De Genova 2002) but, following Sager (2011: 162), also 'positions in family life, in the streets and in relation to subjective experiences of the body, the self and the future'. Deportability, and the accompanying fear it provokes, has a profound effect on an individual's life; it 'organises a range of aspects relating to everyday life in clandestinity' (Sager 2011: 162), and it has an effect on emotional wellbeing by creating a constant feeling of vulnerability and surveillance.

Fear of being sent back home

The fear of being sent to their official country of origin (which, for migrants who have lived in other countries, does not necessarily denote their 'home') emerged from most of the interviews as an all-consuming fear. Many participants emphatically explained that their life was in danger, or that they would be detained, if they were sent back to their country of origin. This fear conditioned their lives and the choices they made. It serves to explain some of the more drastic choices, such as the decision to go into hiding and live underground, an experience that is particularly difficult in Sweden. Fear is a feeling that is difficult to conceptualise, rationalise or understand. Most found it severely debilitating. The fear of return can be difficult to understand or to convey to another person. For most of the migrants, the countries they were at risk of being sent to were in conflict or post-conflict situations. There is an uncanny certainty in their fear, which is very difficult to dismiss. Notice the similarities in the following three quotes, as well as the fear and the conviction in the migrants' articulations:

> If they find my husband they would kill him, and me; after that they would cut off my head, cut off the heads of my children.
>
> (Bahara, Afghanistan, 27, female)

> If I go to Afghanistan, I have to do something for myself. If I stay at home someone will kill me because I have problems there. At that time I have to choose one of two ways, either wait for the guy to kill me or else I should take a gun to start fighting, I have to join a warlord.
>
> (Kader, Afghanistan, 21, male)

> In Kuwait, of course they are going to put me in jail because I am against Kuwait and because I am stateless.
>
> (Mohammad, Kuwait, 28, male)

This fear also translates into fear of the Swedish authorities, who have the responsibility for returning them. Particularly those who are living underground speak of a fear of the police. This is derived from the fact that although the Migration Agency retains responsibility for the implementation of the return decision, the apprehension is delegated to the police. Those who are in hiding have greater reason to be scared, because the police are actively searching for irregular migrants without a permit to stay. Rashid explains how this fear restrained his movements:

> I was afraid that if I go out the police will come and find me, arrest me. The problem is that I couldn't even go outside so I was confined to my home.
>
> (Rashid, Afghanistan, 20, male)

During autumn 2014, the Swedish police took part in a European project called Operation Mos Maiorum. The aim of this two-week project was to detect, detain and possibly deport irregular migrants in the 25 participating EU countries. Bahara relates how this increased their fear and restricted their movements to their apartment:

> You know for two weeks the police searched [referring to Mos Maiorum]. We don't go outside, and we don't have any food during those two weeks because we cannot buy it. It was a high risk to go outside. We were just eating things we had at home.
>
> (Bahara, Afghanistan, 27, female)

Paranoia is not limited to the authorities; migrants are scared that other people could turn them in. This fear does not only limit their movements, but critically, it also limits their access to different services. For example, with the enactment in 2008 of the Health and Medical Care for Asylum Seekers and Others Act, irregular migrants (without a *personnummer*) have access to emergency care and 'care that cannot be deferred'. However, when Mahdi (Afghanistan, 20, male) fell ill at school, where he had not told anyone about his new status, he was reluctant to visit the hospital. Miranda uneasily attends open daycare (*öppen förskola*), but is paranoid when she hears people speaking Swedish around her:

> Since I don't speak Swedish, quite often I feel afraid that someone is going to call the police and say that it is someone here who doesn't speak Swedish.
>
> (Miranda, Albania, 23, female)

Only a handful of informants did not mention their fear either of being returned back or of the Swedish authorities. Salah is one of the exceptions. He had been living a rather ordinary life until he was apprehended and detained. Salah said that he had been working and had an apartment and claimed that he was not afraid of the authorities:

> I was never, never afraid. I told them whatever you need, I'm here. I have given them the address, I live here [street name]. I have told them 'welcome, no problem, no problem'.
>
> (Salah, Algeria, mid-thirties, male)

This scenario is not improbable. Indeed, there are people, the so-called 'unde-portable deportables', who do not enjoy a right to stay in Sweden and have been given a decision to return, but the authorities for some reason or another are unable to deport them (Leerkes and Broeders 2010: 831). This inability to deport, when migrants are aware of it, appeases their fear.

'I am below zero': powerlessness and lack of control over their future

Migrants decry the lack of control over their lives and their future. This is a classic 'in limbo' situation, characterised by powerlessness, dependency and de-personalisation (cf. Vathi and King 2013). It is also brought about by what Sager (2011) correctly describes as a spiral of decreasing social rights, meant as a series of coercive measures to encourage migrants to leave the country voluntar-ily. Yousef puts it across very powerfully: 'I am minus zero. Zero has meaning, I am below zero' (Yousef, Kuwait, 39, male). Migrants, as Emmanuel (Nigeria, 30, male) put it, are 'just waiting for what they're going to say next'. It is a humiliating situation; the future for many is a black hole. They have no idea what it holds for them, they are unable to take any decisions and, overall, there is a foreboding sense that the future is 'very dark'. This is a big source of stress for many. Mahdi is tired and explains it thus:

> Before I thought a lot about my future, what I wanted to become and things like that. But now when I lost my hope, I don't think so much, I don't have the energy right now ...
>
> (Mahdi, Afghanistan, 20, male)

Ana expresses indignation over her lack of decision-making power in similar terms. Unlike most of the others, she points out the irony and unfairness of her future being in the hands of people who do not know her, that is, the Migration Agency officers:

> I think it is the person who is making the decision, the one woman and one man, I have the names here [...] these two persons have my life in their hands. These two persons make the decision, am I okay or not? Two persons that I have not met. I don't know who they are; they have never seen my face ... All my life somebody else has told me how to live. Some-body who doesn't know me, somebody who has never seen me, who has never eaten with me, talked with me, drank with me. They are making deci-sions on how I should live.
>
> (Ana, Serbia, around 40, female)

Particularly interesting is the parallel that Ana draws to the oppression she experienced in the past – 'all my life somebody else has told me how to live' – and the parallels she draws with the Swedish migrant authorities. Indeed, the migrants' expressions of feelings and emotions are rarely neatly categorised geo-graphically or temporally. When speaking about experiences, migrants connect and draw parallels with other, even if totally unrelated, experiences they have had in the past, testifying to the complexity of the upheaval they experience as a result of their status in Sweden.

Dependency on 'the system' and participation in the community

The increasing dependency on the Swedish asylum and deportation system is frustrating and disempowering for migrants. It eats away at their sense of self-worth. Vlad's quote below includes a mention of the metaphor of the 'animal' as the non-human – this resonates strongly with other studies (DeBono 2013) of migrants who are either in detention or do not have control over the deci-sions being taken regarding their own lives.

> I want to get the opportunity to take care of myself. I am not an animal, I am also a person. [...] But I don't need the help that they give me. Give me a chance to work and I'll take care of myself.
>
> (Vlad, Russia, 21, male)

For migrants at risk of deportation who are living in the community, the lack of activities brought about by their situation, as well as the accompanying stress, cements the feeling that they are wasting their lives. Typically, Salim says: 'all we do is eat and sleep' (Salim, stateless Palestinian, early 40s, male); Yousef says his life has 'no meaning' and Omar (stateless Palestinian, around 30, male) says that the lack of meaningful activity makes him 'feel like an animal'. These kinds of comments belie a deeper sense of sadness and lethargy. They are an indication of the profound loss of wellbeing, and the lack of initiative or possible oppor-tunities for getting out of the situation.

Many have taken considerable risks and they feel there is no return on their investment. Most are young, healthy individuals. Planning for the future is an important part of their lives. They describe how, if they are forced to leave Sweden one day, they will be leaving without any new skills. In three years, Teka (Ethiopia, 27, male) says, he did not even get to learn and use the Swedish language. Finally, there is a sense of weariness and fatigue, often expressed as a feeling of 'becoming old' or feeling 'older than one's years', brought about by their experience in Sweden: 'When I came here I was fresh like a 14-year-old boy and now my hair has become white' (Wali, Afghanistan, 27, male).

Housing provided by the Migration Agency and its implications

The Swedish Migration Agency provides accommodation for asylum-seekers, including migrants at risk of deportation. In 2014, two-thirds of the persons received by the Migration Agency were living in Migration Agency housing; the rest were living in their own housing, often with family and friends.[4] Some of them still had their cases being processed by the Migration Agency; others had had their cases transferred to the police. The Migration Agency prefers to rent its own apartments to asylum-seekers, but when that is not possible, they temporarily use privately owned apartments. The Migration Agency is unable to plan the location of these housing units due to rules of public procurement. The outcome is that this housing is spread across the country, with some being located far away from a Migration Agency office.

Contact with other residents at the Migration Agency centres is often limited. This is due to many factors, including the brevity of some of the residents' stays, the lack of a common language and the distrust that characterises people in these situations. Wali describes how newly arrived migrants avoid him because they do not want to listen to the difficulties he has faced: 'they do not want to hear about problems [...] that is why they do not want contact' (Wali, Afghanistan, 27, male).

It is not only the location of the centres that is isolating; it is also the migrants' constrained financial situation. All asylum-seekers, including returnees and forced returnees, have social rights. These state benefits change – and generally decrease – according to the various statuses the migrants hold. Their isolation does not help to ameliorate the migrants' wellbeing, in particular for those who are at risk of deportation. Wali, who at the time of the interview lived in a transit centre outside of a small town, describes:

> We do not have any money for the bus to go outside of here, we are far away from any bigger cities. When you go there it is about 150 kronor for one family, just for one-way. We cannot go outside of this small place ... When you are in a small town like this you do not have any contact with another person and that will be boring for you.
>
> (Wali, Afghanistan, 27, male)

Living in the shadows: hiding and impermanence

Unlike those who live in housing provided by the Migration Agency, those in hiding are trying to conceal their whereabouts from the authorities. The interviewees in this situation are living in different types of housing, but common to all of them is that they have contacts in Sweden who are assisting them. A common source of stress for those in hiding is their housing situation, which is often temporary. The migrants who are hiding describe how they are always looking for housing, and at certain points they have been forced to sleep outside in parks, or in train stations. In addition to the pressure of finding housing, persons living in hiding are often very worried about being detected by police or other authorities.

Migrants who do not have good contacts often have a hard time remaining in hiding even if they would like to. Swedish organisations and personal networks are a source of assistance, information and resources, without which it is almost impossible for a person to live underground. Ana, for example, had been in Sweden for a very short time. Her case was fast-tracked, and although she had the right to appeal, she claimed that her flight was booked before the two to three weeks within which she could appeal. She had no contacts with any Swedish organisations or persons outside of the Migration Agency and therefore did not have the means to move into hiding or protest her decision.

Irregular migrants have a right to social welfare benefits; however, access varies across municipalities. In some municipalities, to avoid disclosing their own address, migrants have provided the address of the organisation helping them when applying for social welfare. Some do not pick up their social welfare benefit and rely solely on the financial support of their networks. Others manage to access their social welfare but need the financial support of their networks to make ends meet. Storai (Afghanistan, 23, female), who has children, categorically states: 'if the organisation wasn't here, we would be hungry by the end of the month'.

Parents who are not in hiding tend to present the situation for their children in Sweden as one which is overall an improvement compared with their country of origin; but parents who are in hiding are worried about the effects of their current situation on their children's development, wellbeing and opportunities. Intergenerational transmission in migrant families is permeated by stress in the case of families who are deportable. For example, Aamir believes his children's speech development has been delayed:

> My children are three years old and they cannot speak. I don't think this situation is good for the children. My stress and tension is not good for my sons. We are both stressed and tense all the time. We can't play with the children now; my babies are feeling that we are not happy.
>
> (Aamir, Afghanistan, 30, male)

Of high concern is the unintentional projection of parents' fears onto their children. Aamir and Bahara describe how their children, just like them, are scared of the police:

AAMIR: We talk about the police, that we don't want the police to see us; we don't want to go with the police. We often talk about the police and my children are scared of the police.
BAHARA: For example, last night our son woke up in the middle of the night, at 3 o'clock, and cried. We asked him why; he just said 'police, police, police'.
AAMIR: I think he was dreaming about the police coming.
> (Aamir and Bahara, Afghanistan, 30, male and 27, female)

Parents lament not having access to child daycare services where their children could interact with other children and adults. They feel that this has a negative impact on their children's development and wellbeing. Access to daycare services for children whose families are at risk of deportation differs between different municipalities. Ismat describes how being able to attend daycare has improved his daughter's situation:

> My daughter had psychological problems … All the time she was asking about the house that we had before that was very big … She asked me for that house. 'Why don't we go back there to our home?' But when she has been to the '*dagis*' [daycare], she is feeling better.

(Ismat, Afghanistan, 29, male)

More shockingly, and echoing a recurring theme, some parents explain how, in spite of the poor conditions they have in Sweden, the situation for their children is still an improvement on what they faced in their country of origin. A good example of this is Arjana (Albania, 35, female) and her family, who were living in hiding in Albania due to a blood feud. Her children were not able to go outdoors in Albania. In Sweden, they are staying at the Migration Agency's transit centre, and their activities are much less restricted. Arjana says: 'The children can go outside and run, play ball and such things … They like it here'. Bahara relates a similar experience: 'My children have friends here … They're going to swimming. We don't have stress from attacks. It's relaxed' (Bahara, Afghanistan, 27, female).

In spite of the challenges brought about by hiding and the fear of going outside, most migrants explained why it was still worth staying in this miserable situation rather than being deported. Even so, a few change their minds and decide to go back. Emmanuel lived underground in Sweden for three years. He got so weary and stressed out by the situation that he wrote to the police in a desperate attempt to legalise his situation. The police did not respond to his request. He was subsequently detained after being caught with an invalid bus card. He describes how he did not try to run away when the bus company called the police since he was so sick of his situation, which, he claimed, was no improvement on the situation he had experienced in his country of origin. Emmanuel speaks of his weariness and despair: 'I ran from the time that they wanted to deport me in 2011 until now. I was out there, living a life that is kind of no hope, no future, nothing' (Emmanuel, Nigeria, 30, male).

Detention and wellbeing: waiting for the inevitable

Detention is by far the most restrictive situation and produces extreme life conditions for people at risk of deportation. Detention has an obvious highly negative impact on the migrants' wellbeing. This is documented in many studies in Sweden (Puthoopparambil *et al.* 2015) and in other countries (JRS-Europe 2010; Robjant *et al.* 2009). Migrants' fears of being returned to their country of origin are sky-high at this point: they present high levels of stress, anger at being locked in, and evident signs of apathy and resignation. Vlad puts it thus:

> You feel like an animal. You cannot decide anything for yourself, you can only listen to what they tell you to do and then do it. It's like you are … you know a slave.
>
> (Vlad, Russia, 21, male)

The Swedish Migration Agency is responsible for the migrant detention centres. The centres are run by civil staff and are not run as high-security units. There is a steady routine inside detention, primarily set by meal times. Migrants can take part in several, albeit limited, activities. Detention centres differ on access to the courtyard outdoors, but on the whole they share basic facilities such as internet access and access to a games room, they are allowed to keep their mobile phones (without a camera), and they all receive daily pocket money. This money is used to buy products from the vending machines, to charge their phones or to pay relatives or friends to purchase products from outside. Migrants can receive visitors during visiting hours.

International independent observers have highlighted the overall good conditions inside migrant detention centres in Sweden. The Council of Europe's Committee for the Prevention of Torture highlighted that material conditions, space, food and staff were of a high standard in the two detention centres they visited (Council of Europe 2009: 41–45). These comments are confirmed by the migrants, some of whom were in a position to compare these migrant detention centres either with other forms of confinement in Sweden, such as prison and police arrest, or with other prisons and migrant detention centres in other countries (within and outside Europe). The same report, however, criticised the authorities over additional safeguards for people detained under the Aliens Act, such as access to lawyers, the possibility of informing a relative or a friend, and others. More pertinently, the report criticised healthcare: psychiatric and psychological support was lacking, and 'access to health-care staff was controlled by custodial staff who questioned inmates about the reasons why they wished to see a doctor/nurse' (Council of Europe 2009: 44).

Just as with other deportees, impermanence and a sense of continuous movement are what characterises the detained deportees' everyday life. Contact between detainees is often superficial, and support is derived mainly from friends and organisations. This is partly due to the negative effects of arbitrary detention, but can also be explained by the generally short duration of stay in detention, which in 2014 was an average of seven days (Swedish Migration Agency 2015). Vlad's description of the coping strategies and interactions between the detainees gives the sense that this solidarity stems more out of need than out of choice:

> We have fun sometimes together. And sometimes everybody has problems. Everybody there has their problems, they think a lot. But sometimes we play on the Internet so that the thoughts do not eat us up.
>
> (Vlad, Russia, 21, male)

Migrants complain of lack of sleep, of the torturous waiting for the inevitable to happen. It is common that this combination of detention, stress and uncertainty disrupts their natural diurnal rhythm. At night, when it goes quiet inside the detention centre, detainees' anxiety rises and disrupts their sleep; conversely, detainees find it easier to relax and sleep during the day when there are activities and sounds. The next two quotes communicate this:

> You cannot sleep here, it is not possible to sleep here. Maybe because of stress? I cannot describe it. Maybe we have too much energy because you're always inside, no activity.
>
> (Vlad, Russia, 21, male)

> I'm not sleeping so much. [...] I wait for the day they'll take me. I'm just waiting for that now because I know they didn't understand [me] so I wait for that. [...] I don't know the day.
>
> (Teka, Ethiopia, 27, male)

These echo findings of a JRS-Europe study with 685 detainees in 23 EU member-states. Detention, they found, significantly harms the health of migrant detainees both physically and mentally (JRS-Europe 2010). The diminished health is attributed to the cramped living conditions and the psychological stress produced by detention and confinement. This contributes to increasing feelings of anger, which compounds the situation. Another conclusion from this study was a clear indication that the health of migrant detainees progressively worsens with the period of time spent in detention (JRS-Europe 2010: 13).

The physical and mental health of migrants at risk of deportation

During the interviews, some migrants were close to tears. Their anger and distress were evident, alongside symptoms of extreme hopelessness. All these symptoms are generally associated with depressive episodes or traumatic incidents. In a study on people seeking asylum in Sweden, Brekke (2004) argues that these symptoms are only partly brought about by the waiting time. He observes a tension between the wishes of the asylum-seeker to obtain a residence permit and the authorities' confusing duality of both encouraging integration (in case the migrant is granted asylum) and remaining open to return and deportation (in the case of an unsuccessful outcome). In our case, the conflicting tension between the wishes of the asylum-seeker and the diametrically opposed decision of the state to remove the migrant from Swedish territory is clear, and serves to augment the symptoms brought about by waiting. These augmented effects are discernible in the migrants' articulations of their mental and physical health.

Many migrants refer directly to physical and mental problems brought about by the high level of stress and constant worry. Common symptoms are intense anxiety, fatigue and depression. Yousef (Kuwait, 39, male) has a plausible explanation: 'I'm sleeping poorly because of my brain is working constantly'. Wali, on being informed by the police that the deportation of him and his family was imminent, was totally overwhelmed:

> The police told us, we will send you on Tuesday to Afghanistan. We do not have appetite for eating anything, I have not slept for three nights.
>
> (Wali, Afghanistan, 27, male)

Fatma, a young Kuwaiti migrant, feels that all her thinking and worrying have made her both physically and mentally ill. Mohammad also describes how his health has deteriorated since he was denied asylum; he has visited the doctor multiple times for different conditions:

> When I came here I have gone to the doctor maybe like 100 times. I get sick every time because they [the Migration Agency] give me negative, negative.
>
> (Mohammad, Kuwait, 28, male)

Aamir also has concerns regarding his physical health:

> I have a big 'push' over my heart, lots of stress. And I think about what if my heart stops, what will happen to my future, my daughter's future? I talk to my wife about my death because I have too much stress. I'm a human, I'm not a machine; I'm human, same as you. Six years of stress will come to me … I have lived for six years with high stress. Two years here. I'm human, I cannot … [live with all this stress].
>
> (Aamir, Afghanistan, 30, male)

Many of the interviewees themselves diagnose their mental health problems as rooted in depression. Some of them have thoughts of, or even attempt, suicide. This is not uncommon in migrant detention centres, as Robjant *et al.* (2009) show in their analysis of different research projects spanning the US, Australia and the UK, which all look into the effects of detention on migrants. Kader portrays the complete desperation he felt after he received his third negative decision. He also ended up homeless when he absconded and left the Migration Agency's housing to avoid being caught. He felt completely lost and overwhelmed, as though there was no way out of his misery. Sweden would not allow him to stay, going back to Afghanistan was too dangerous an option, and the Dublin regulation made it impossible for him to apply for asylum in other European countries. Kader recalls this desperation:

> The only solution you have is to finish yourself. Yeah I tried lots of times to kill myself but fortunately I failed.
>
> (Kader, Afghanistan, 21, male)

Migrants mentioned coping strategies but rarely elaborated on them. Our participants might have had a tendency to overstress the negative aspects in interviews as a clear indication of the precarity of their situation. However, it is also clear that the migrants felt the need to speak out about their ordeal, indicating that they did not have many avenues for externalising this. Coping strategies included relying on the support of their community, friends, activist groups and networks; but it is also common in such situations to avoid speaking about the issue. In some cases, this was because they were surrounded by people who had their own serious problems to grapple with; in other cases, their fear of being apprehended by the police made them generally distrustful. However 'strong' and 'determined' they presented themselves, migrants at risk of deportation appeared to have little space and time to invest in coping strategies, or to take care of themselves.

Conclusions

The metaphorical expression 'burning without fire' is a powerfully evocative rendering of the experience of forced removal for deportees and migrants at risk of deportation in Sweden. This chapter has shown how deportable migrants in Sweden are enduring hardships that, in their different ways, they experience as 'burning' – as extreme, painful, agonising – in spite of the relatively good structures in place, or rather, the well-regulated, sophisticated bureaucratic structures in place. It conveys the paradoxical situation of, on the one hand, having an immigration, asylum and returns system that has deservedly in some areas (less in others) gained a reputation for being a good and fair system. On the other hand, there is the momentous impact of the return decision on the migrants, and the ensuing hardships once they become migrants at risk of deportation, and eventually deportees. The hardships, in Graeberian terms, could be explained as a necessary feature of modern bureaucracies, which operate through the constant threat of violence and harm in the case of transgression or resistance. Migrant narratives of their deteriorating mental health show the embodiment and consequence of this violence.

'Burning without fire' is also an adequate allegory for another key tension that can be found in migrants' narratives: this is the trade-off that migrants make, preferring to remain in the miserable situation of deportables in Sweden rather than to be sent back to their country of origin. This chapter has shown that migrants' psychosocial wellbeing is severely compromised, to different degrees depending on the different situations that a deportable migrant can be in. The trade-off that many of these people are consciously making, by choosing to remain as irregular deportables in Sweden and not return, involves putting their own health at risk. This chilling realisation serves as an indicator of the gravity that a possible return constitutes for the migrants. As can be seen from Bahara's sombre and resolute quote, she 'accepts' living with the problems in Sweden rather than go back. And Rashid, Miranda and others live in misery and fear of the Swedish police, rather than go back. Therefore, the 'burning without fire' metaphor also denotes, for lack of a better word, the paradoxical 'choice' that the migrants deliberately make. A choice that they are forced into by their personal and structural circumstances. A choice that no one should have to make. This is a 'forced choice' that brings to the fore the sheer absurdity of trying to discuss a deportee's psychosocial wellbeing and health. A forced choice that does not remove the state's responsibility to minimise the harm done. A choice that forces people to live in such dire situations puts an obligation on all political actors – state, non-state, global and local – to discuss this situation and search for alternatives.

Notes

1　The author acknowledges the work of Karin Magnusson and Sofia Rönnqvist, collaborators in the original project (DeBono *et al.* 2015). Furthermore, I thank Rachael Scicluna, Zana Vathi and Russell King for feedback on draft versions.
2　Return Directive 2009, Preamble and Article 8(4).
3　Pseudonyms are used throughout this chapter to protect the interviewees' identities. For more detail on the project and its methodology, see DeBono *et al.* (2015).
4　Data from Swedish Migration Agency, *Arsredovisning 2014* (Annual Budget Report). Norrkoping: Migration Agency, 2015. www.migrationsverket.se/download/18.39a9c d9514a346077212ead/1424702424160/%C3%85rsredovisning+2014.pdf. Accessed 25 September 2015.

References

Brekke, J. (2004) *While We Are Waiting: Uncertainty and Empowerment among Asylum-Seekers in Sweden*. Oslo: Institute for Social Research.

Caplan, S.E. (2002) Problematic Internet use and psychosocial well-being: development of a theory-based cognitive–behavioral measurement instrument, *Computers in Human Behavior* 18(5): 553–575.

Correa-Velez, I., Gifford, S.M. and Barnett, A.G. (2010) Longing to belong: social inclusion and wellbeing among youth with refugee backgrounds in the first three years in Melbourne, Australia, *Social Science and Medicine* 71(8): 1399–1408.

Council of Europe (2009) *Report to the Swedish Government on the Visit to Sweden Carried out by the Council of Europe Committee for the Prevention of Torture and Inhuman or Degrading Treatment or Punishment (CPT) from 9 to 18 June 2009*, CPT/ Inf (2009) 34. Strasbourg: Council of Europe.

Council of Europe Commissioner for Human Rights (2007) *Memorandum to the Swedish Government: Assessment of the Progress Made in Implementing the 2004 Recommendations of the Council of Europe Commissioner for Human Rights*, CommDH(2007)10, Strasbourg, 16 May 2007.

DeBono, D. (2013) 'Less than human': the detention of irregular immigrants in Malta, *Race and Class* 55(2): 60–81.

DeBono, D., Ronnqvist, S. and Magnusson, K. (2015) *Humane and Dignified? Migrants' Experiences of Living in a 'State of Deportability' in Sweden*. Malmö: Malmö University, Malmö Institute for Studies of Migration, Diversity and Welfare.

De Genova, N. (2002) Migrant 'illegality' and deportability in everyday life, *Annual Review of Anthropology* 31: 419–447.

Egan, M., Tannahill, C., Petticrew, M. and Sian, T. (2008) Psychosocial risk factors in home and community settings and their associations with population health and health inequalities: a systematic meta-review, *BMC Public Health* 8(1): 239.

Gammeltoft-Hansen, T. (2013) The rise of the private border guard: accountability and responsibility in the migration control industry, in T. Gammeltoft-Hansen and N. Nyberg Sørensen (eds) *The Migration Industry and the Commercialization of International Migration*. London: Routledge, 128–151.

Graeber, D. (2006) Dead zones of the imagination: on violence, bureaucracy, and interpretive labor: The 2006 Malinowski Memorial Lecture, *Journal of Ethnographic Theory* 2(2): 105–128.

Graeber, D. (2015) *The Utopia of Rules: on Technology, Stupidity, and the Secret Joys of Bureaucracy*. Brooklyn NY: Melville House.

Grimheden, J. (2006) The self-reflective human rights promoter, in J. Grimheden and R. Ring (eds) *Human Rights Law: from Dissemination to Application: Essays in Honour of Göran Melander*. The Hague: Brill,

Grove, N.J., Zwi, A.B., Silove, D. and Tarantola, D. (2006) Psychosocial health and human rights: fair weather friends? Examining post-tsunami interventions in conflict-affected areas, *Australian Journal of Human Rights* 11(2): 71–94.

IOM (2013) *World Migration Report 2013: Migrant Well-Being and Development*. Geneva: IOM.

JRS-Europe (2010) *Becoming Vulnerable in Detention: Civil Society Report on the Detention of Vulnerable Asylum Seekers and Irregular Migrants in the European Union (The DEVAS Project)*. Belgium: Jesuit Refugee Service.

Khosravi, S. (2009) Sweden: detention and deportation of asylum seekers, *Race and Class* 50: 38–56.

Kohli, R. and Mather, R. (2003) Promoting psychosocial well-being in unaccompanied asylum-seeking young people in the United Kingdom, *Child and Family Social Work* 8(3): 201–212.

Leerkes, A. and Broeders, D. (2010) A case of mixed motives? Formal and informal functions of administrative immigration detention, *British Journal of Criminology* 50(5): 830–850.

Martikainen, P., Bartley, M. and Lahelma, E. (2002) Psychosocial determinants of health in social epidemiology, *International Journal of Epidemiology* 31(6): 1091–1093.

MIPEX (2014) *Migrant Integration Policy Index 2015: Sweden*. www.mipex.eu/sweden. Accessed 25 September 2015.

Puthoopparambil, S., Ahlberg, B.M. and Bjerneld, M. (2015) A prison with extra flavours: experiences of immigrants in Swedish immigration detention centres, *International Journal of Migration, Health and Social Care* 11(2): 73–85.

Robjant, K., Hassan, R. and Kataona, C. (2009) Mental health implications of detaining asylum seekers: systematic review, *The British Journal of Psychiatry* 194(4): 306–312.

Sager, M. (2011) *Everyday Clandestinity: Experiences on the Margins of Citizenship and Migration Policies*. Lund: Lund Universitet.

Swedish Migration Agency (2015) The Mission of the Migration Agency [online]. Last updated 8 April 2015. www.migrationsverket.se/English/About-the-Migration-Agency/Our-mission.html. Accessed 18 September 2015.

The Society for the Psychological Study of Social Issues (2014) Statement submitted by the Society for the Psychological Study of Social Issues and co-sponsored by the International Association of Applied Psychology, the International Council of Psychologists, the World Council for Psychotherapy, the American Psychological Association and other accredited members of the Psychology Coalition at the UN Statement in support of the Assessment of the Status of Implementation of the Programme of Action of the 1994 International Conference on Population and Development. New York: UN, 7–11 April 2014.

UN (2011) *Report of the Secretary-General to the Commission for Social Development on the Priority Theme of Poverty Eradication.* New York: UN.

Vathi, Z. and King, R. (2013). 'Have you got the *British?*' Narratives of migration and settlement of Albanian-origin immigrants in London, *Ethnic and Racial Studies* 36(11): 1829–1848.

WHO (2010) *Mental Health and Development.* Geneva: WHO.

9 The return of refugees from Kenya to Somalia

Gender and psychosocial wellbeing

Nassim Majidi

Introduction

In his now seminal paper on reconceptualising return migration, Jean-Pierre Cassarino writes (2004: 271): 'The propensity of migrants to become actors of change and development at home depends on the extent to which they have provided for the preparation of their return'. Cassarino's work theorises return migration as a process that requires resource mobilisation and preparedness in order to lead to sustainable and positive outcomes. When forced circumstances lead refugee populations to live in protracted situations in camp settings, their level of resource mobilisation and preparedness is often hampered. Refugee return and repatriation programmes can help address these gaps by providing assistance to return. Yet, most of the focus of repatriation programmes has been either on the male head of household or on vulnerable female-headed households, rather than on women as central social and economic actors in return. Individual biographies, and especially women's biographies of return migration, have been missed.

Exceptions exist in the literature. The work of Christou highlights the fact that Greek-American women returnees see themselves as 'good mothers, good wives, good sisters but also honourable and obedient daughters' (2003: 71). Education, work and careers also figured prominently in the discourse: 'they were all central for them as female returnees' (2003: 71). My research yields similar findings on Somali refugee returns from Kenya to Somalia, with women's aspirations in return being multifold, multiscalar and relational: they strive for a return that can fulfil their own expectations, as well as those of their children, their families and their husbands. They seek emotional, social and cultural outcomes from their migration. Beyond human or material wellbeing, they strive for psychosocial wellbeing. Documenting the process of achieving such wellbeing, in contexts of protracted displacement and return, is key to informing better policies and programmes that can support returnees and their reintegration process.

The current data available on returns from Kenya to Somalia, from 2014, shows that returnees' psychosocial wellbeing is hampered by three key factors: planning for the logistics of return, the recurrence of split families, and the inability to work or negotiate post-return roles in a new environment. This leaves the door open for repatriation programmes and policies to fill the psycho-social gap by ensuring smoother transitions in return, and better-informed return decisions by women.

This chapter considers the return process of Somali refugees from Kenya through the prism of women's experiences before departure and upon return. The transition to 'home' is analysed through expectations and outcomes for psychosocial wellbeing. Do women *act* return, *choose* return or *endure* return, or all of the above? What are the consequences of returns for women's psychosocial wellbeing, and what are the policy implications? These research questions were raised through an inductive approach and in-depth fieldwork. The initial project from which this chapter stems started with a broader outlook on the spon-taneous return of refugees – from Kenya to Somalia. While in the field, the research team identified the role of women as standing out in the return process. This chapter delves into these findings, challenging the view of return as male dominated and highlighting the important role played by women – as mothers, wives, next of kin and workers.

Methodology

Fieldwork in northern Kenya shows a 'stepwise' or 'staged' migration (Hondagneu-Sotelo 1992), with men leaving first, their wives and children second. This fits with historical migration patterns of the male head of house-hold leaving first, establishing a home for himself and waiting for the right timing – and financial endowment – to ask for his nuclear family to join him. In the case of returns to Somalia, the 'right time for return' or 'financial tipping point' has been, for some families, the 'Pilot Project of Voluntary Return of Somali Refugees' launched by the United Nations Refugee Agency with non-governmental organisation (NGO) partners in December 2014: an opportunity for refugees to return to Somalia and for families separated across the border to reunite.

Qualitative data collected in late 2014[1] provide a sample of refugee and returnee experiences and voices. The methodology is multi-sited and trans-national in design to track the continuum in the migration-return corridor involving two developing countries from the Global South, an addition to the literature on returns, which has mainly focused on the North–South dynamics of migration control.

The decision-making process and its link with psychosocial wellbeing are ana-lysed through a comparative perspective using data collected across the border in Kenya and in Somalia from camp-based and urban Somali refugees and returnees. This cross-border research includes 60 case studies and 12 focus group discussions in four locations: Eastleigh and Dadaab (Kenya) and Kismayo and Mogadishu (Somalia). A third of these interviews were conducted with women. The research did not aim at interviewing children – yet children's voices were captured in interviews with their parents, acknowledging their role in migration processes and the impact their wellbeing can have, in turn, on their parents' psychosocial wellbeing. The two are seen as intrinsically linked in this research: parent wellbeing being connected to children's wellbeing. When the latter voice their discontent in front of their parents, it reinforces the finding that psychosocial wellbeing is a complex process in return.

For the Kenyan field locations, urban refugees were interviewed in Eastleigh, Nairobi, and camp refugees in five camps in Dadaab. In-depth information was collected on refugees' lives and living conditions in Kenya, their intention to stay or return, decision-making processes, access to livelihood and employment, protection issues in Kenya and their expectation of life in Somalia.

In Somalia – in Mogadishu (for urban returns) and Kismayo (the main area of refugee origin) – in-depth interviews and focus-group discussions were held to explore the challenges faced during the journey and upon return, protection issues and priorities upon return, decision-making processes, levels of information, and differences between expectations and reality of return.

Women in return migration

The transition back home for returning migrants is rarely analysed from the angle of children and women. Although research shows that children are, or can be, involved in family migration decisions (e.g. Bushin 2009), most papers on return to (post-)conflict settings have taken adult men's voices about their forced or voluntary return experiences and have looked at economic and development issues (Schuster and Majidi 2013, 2015). In this contribution, women are not seen just as the main carers for their children, but as having multiple roles and relations that affect their decisions about return, which in turn affect their own and their children's psychosocial wellbeing. Returns – whether in the literature or in assistance programmes – have been gendered and have generally focused, either explicitly or implicitly, on male returnees (see, for instance, the various contributions in King 1986). The case of returns to Somalia supports the need to adopt both a gender-sensitive outlook on returns and a psychosocial understanding of returns beyond the material dimensions of the return phenomenon.

Most migration policies have been 'gender-blind' (Ghosh 1999). Academic research has, in the past 30 years, raised the profile of women in migration, illustrating the distinct behaviour and practices that women adopt to negotiate their migration and their economic roles within households. From a psychosocial perspective, one of the first studies of the readjustment process of women returnees was by Gmelch and Gmelch (1995) in an ambitious comparative study of returns to Ireland, Newfoundland and Barbados. Meanwhile, El-Bushra and Sahl (2005) discuss the impact of war and conflict on gendered roles, illustrating 'a tendency for migrant women to take on more and different roles as providers and protectors of families, to draw confidence and determination from these experiences, and to develop their political consciousness and agency' (El-Bushra 2000: 5). Yet, such new roles can come with unintended consequences for the overall wellbeing of families, since women are frequently unable to leverage their transition to new roles effectively (Brun 2000; Turner 2000). The gendered task-sharing among return migrants (cf. Sakka *et al.* 1999) focuses women's role on the process of return – that is, the logistics of return – rather than on post-return outcomes.

Vathi and Duci (2016) highlight the invisibility of children in the literature on return migration. Similar conclusions can be reached on the place and role of women in return migration. From an assistance perspective, the notions of vulnerability and protection supersede considerations of agency and women's participation in return. The wellbeing of women is viewed through a protection lens focusing on gender-based violence, rather than recognising the agency of women and their role in the household before, during and after return. This tends to reinforce patriarchal systems and undermine the role of women and children – rendering them secondary actors in return migration: actors in terms of logistics but not as decision-makers. In the literature and in practice, gender issues have been understood from a vulnerability standpoint, focusing on gender-based violence against refugees, recognised as a crime in UN Security Council resolutions.[2] The tendency to adopt a gender-based view has stigmatised women as passive actors and victims, without fully addressing their contribution to the collective migration enterprise.

The marginalisation of gender in return migration scholarship (Mahler and Pessar 2006; Meares 2007) has limited researchers' understanding of the decisions affecting post-return outcomes, of family dynamics and of the social construction of women, men and children post return. The lack of evidence on the role of women in return migration processes has meant a failure to build evidence-based policies that can allow women to fulfil their role, and to build their resilience, even in the most conservative societies.

Even less has been written about the psychosocial issues in the context of return. Psychological health and stress factors testify to different levels of insecurity experienced by women, men and their children in return (Suarez-Orozco and Qin 2006). This is particularly the case for women in situations of split returns. Women suffer from separation as they live the burden of a broken family, both materially and morally, adversely impacting their psychosocial equilibrium: their psychological and social worlds conflict (D'Angelo and Pasos Marciacq 2002; Piper 2005). Family separations and transnational dynamics impact children differently depending on the lengths of separation and the people from whom they are separated – leading at times to depressive symptoms (Suarez-Orozco *et al.* 2002). While such studies have focused on the impact of stepwise migration in immigrant homes, this chapter analyses the repercussions for children upon 'return' to their motherland in Somalia,[3] and furthermore assesses a knowledge gap regarding the children left behind in refugee camps while their families return to their motherland.

Previous studies have shown that a lack of belongingness and harsh socioeconomic conditions in return contexts negatively impact children's psychosocial wellbeing in migratory contexts (Vathi and Duci 2016). Building on such research, the impact of the lack of belongingness is here addressed as a concept with socio-spatial roots (Yeoh and Lam 2006). In the case of refugee and returnee children, there are two components: the family and friends (the social component of belonging to a group) and the location of habitus (the spatial component). Modifying either of these two elements can have psychosocial impacts that negatively impact children, with immediate or staged reactions. Previous research has revealed the costs of (im)mobility, both for children left behind and for those who migrate with a parent to 'high-risk' settings and countries like Somalia (Yeoh and Lam 2006). In this study, the question of 'home' is questioned (Ahmed 1999; Brah 1996): it commonly refers to refugees' location of origin, but should not be applied to children by mere association with their parents. Instead, for children who have grown up in refugee camps or urban settings in Kenya, the family's country of origin may be the 'strange land' (Ahmed 1999; Ahmed *et al.* 2003).

The logistics of return: women as actors

For Somali refugees in Kenya, the decision to stay or return is driven by necessity. For male heads of households, it is the need to work, and to care for elders in the country of origin. For women, it is the need to reunite with their relatives, the search for support, or the necessity of finalising the decision to return of the head of household: women are central in turning the return decision into a reality.

Women play a key role notably in 'split returns' or the 'stepwise return migration': families are split across the border, men having returned to Somalia to find work, check on the security situation, reconnect with family care for their parents and elders in an emergency, or simply to establish a base ahead of the return of the family. Alternatively, during over two decades of protracted exile, the birth family and the in-law family may have been split. Generations or spouses live across borders contemplating the timing of their reunification. Husbands leave to set up a base – or in reaction to an emergency need – and ask their wives to take the responsibility for bringing over the rest of their family. In these cases, Somali refugee women are left with the burden of planning return for themselves, their children and perhaps other family members. Some showed signs of concern, anxiety and fatigue, lacking trust in the answers obtained and seeking verification for these. The uncertainty women are left in becomes their problem to cope with. This puts more pressure on women's shoulders as logistical actors – while men are remote actors.

Men are seen as the head of the family and the sole authority on decision-making – as expressed by one of the respondents in Mogadishu: 'As a Somali community, the father is the head for all decisions so I suggested that idea to my wife and she agreed with me'. In these situations, women's voices are still heard in the implementation of the men's decisions; they are involved in the process – although not from the outset. They are the ones who turn the decision into reality for the family, taking care of practical considerations in preparation for return.

Many interviewees spoke of a 'wait and see' strategy: male heads of household first travel on their own to Somalia to assess the feasibility of setting up a family base before a collective return is enacted. The timing and process of return depend on the male heads of household, who give the ultimate 'go ahead' to return. As a result, women's preparedness is hampered because, in this process, they react to the men's decision to return: women may lead the return process, but they rarely start the decision-making process.

Female respondents interviewed were looking forward to being reunited with their husbands, as they felt vulnerable on their own in the camps in Dadaab; similarly, women wanted to reconnect with their fathers and brothers, and elderly women with their sons. Some women are forced to leave not out of choice but rather, out of necessity, as they are unable to cope with life alone in the camps. Their experiences of stress and anxiety reflect a closed, claustrophobic environment that oppresses them. Hence, going back to Somalia is a return that they equate with expectations of higher emotional wellbeing. Although they understand that they may not benefit from the same level of food aid, they also value, for their emotional wellbeing, the freedom to move, to reunite with family and to be 'free'. Thus, return is desirable and is expected to enhance their psychosocial wellbeing.

The logistics of return, then, fall on the women: as refugees, the first step is to speak with representatives of United Nations High Commissioner for Refugees (UNHCR) and the implementing partners in the main field offices. Women stand in line from early morning to seek information from translators, project managers and whoever else may be in a position to provide information. They triangulate and crosscheck information, sometimes returning multiple times to assess the same information. All of our interviews were a two-way process: as much as we asked questions on returns, women asked us similar questions on the return process, to ensure they were well prepared. Taking third-party actors such as researchers on board brings reassurance and diminishes the fears and anxieties of return. Knowledge is a key to reassuring women and a first step in the logistical process. Yet, their knowledge-building focuses only on the process of return – getting from point A to point B; no questions are asked about what happens once they have arrived and are reunited with their families. The second step in the logistical process is, then, to prepare the children to return. The third step, packing the limited belongings, is usually the least stressful part of the ordeal for women. The next section will focus extensively on the interactions with children and women's interactions with them in framing, shaping and planning for returns.

Split returns

Here is better because I am living with my husband. I do not have any stress of what will happen in his absence. We can know each other's situation. My son and my husband had left a year before me, and were communicating with me. They persuaded me to join them. So I left with our other three children and I feel happier now that I am back with them.

(Mumina, 50)

Most refugee returnees from Kenya interviewed in Kismayo returned at a turning-point in their life, in reaction to a situation of emotional insecurity. Relationality drives returns: family issues of a variety of types, whether family violence, family illness, elderly parents or the need to reunite after facing the hardships of being separated from close relatives. In these cases, women are responding to a crisis or a shock: the primary motivation remains safeguarding and protecting the family:

> My main reason of moving from Kenya to Somalia was that some of my family members, like my brothers and cousins who were here in Somalia, were not willing to come back to Kenya, so I decided to join them and live with them. I made the decision and everyone in my family agreed with me.
>
> (Fatumo, 34)

Women take on an active role in shaping their children's choices and understandings of return, often by advising them on whether to stay or return. They take the conscious step of protecting their children, even if this means separating them from their parents, thereby contributing to continued split families. Interviewed in Kenya, before departure, and in Somalia, upon return, women raised concerns for their children that caused them, as mothers, high levels of stress and anxiety. Their biggest fear for their children was on the transport back to Somalia, considering it to be inadvisable in physical security terms for women with children to travel across the border, a journey that men made often but that was not considered safe enough for children. As a result, split families were split further: husbands left first, then women left second, leaving all or some of their children behind with relatives in the camps. This was the case for younger women, in their thirties, who did not have the strength or confidence to take their children with them to Somalia. For those whose children were older, or those whose children did not attend school, the decision to travel back was easier. Those who left children behind left them because of the dual presence of relatives and of schooling opportunities in Kenya, which remain insufficient in Somalia.

Women repeatedly spoke of making decisions, but not wanting to impose any decision on their children. Depending on their age, and more so for children who were in their teenage years, women gave a choice to their children: return with them or stay behind. The research outlined an intergenerational dimension of return through a link between gender and education as determinants of return: repeatedly in interviews, girls chose to stay if they could, if they were given an option, while boys preferred to 'return' to Somalia. Girls were scared of the implications of their return for the timing of their marriage, which they perceived as bound to happen earlier than if they stayed in the camps, where girls were given more time to settle into a new family – they went to school, did chores around the house and so on.

> I know that as I am going as a young woman, I will be forced to get married. Even if I refuse, I will be forced into it. Since my tribe is there, they will feel shame if I am not married; they will insist.
>
> (Shukri, 20)

Somali women who had returned agreed that it was an inevitable choice for girls to make. The following quote is from a divorced mother of four who left before the UNHCR repatriation package in 2013:

> I decided myself. As for my children, some agreed and others stayed behind. Those who did not agree were my two daughters. They had no choice other than to stay in Kenya as they still go to school. I do not recommend them to come back to Somalia. They should stay in Kenya and, if they are lucky enough, they should look for resettlement abroad.
>
> (Elmi, 55)

What are the actual outcomes for children in the return process? In interviews with parents, they voiced an understanding that return for them, as adults, is one process, whereas returning their children would have other implications, potentially negative for their upbringing. Return for a parent does not necessarily equate to 'return' for the children – that is, to a place they were not born into and where they might not enjoy the same quality of life. Pragmatic considerations can lead parents to leave their children behind in the refugee camps in Kenya. Lack of educational provisions is the biggest obstacle hindering returnee families with children, sometimes leading to conflict and splits within a family, or to children being left behind – a key child protection concern raised in the study of spontaneous returns and cross-border flows between Kenya and Somalia.

In fact, education was often one of the contributing drivers to leaving Somalia in the first place, as this father interviewed in Dadaab confirmed:

> I decided to leave Somalia so that I could give a better education to my children. It is very important to me that they receive a good education. I have made all my choices with that priority in mind. I knew that education would be better in Dadaab than in Somalia.
>
> (Faisal, 35)

Prioritising education may lead families to split, even within Kenya. Children and youth leave Dadaab's camps for Nairobi, but not to Somalia. Departure from the camps, in such cases, does not equate to return. On the contrary, refugees seek better opportunities in Nairobi – whether better education or better healthcare. As the same interviewee continued, 'There is in general a much better education offered to people in urban areas. In settlements it's not good'.

As a driver for exile, education remains the main obstacle to return for most families. Hence, if adverse shocks require adults to return, they may leave their children behind, as noted above. The sample surveyed showed a prevalence of split families and protection issues affecting women and children left behind in Kenya following their husbands' and fathers' departure to Somalia for family circumstances or livelihood opportunities. Split families are a concern for children. Children separated from their families are left behind with their uncles and grandparents, or more distant relatives, in order to pursue their education while their parents leave for Somalia. Splits among the siblings are also common, whereby the younger children go with their families and the older ones stay behind. Hence, the split occurs on multiple levels: split from their fathers, then split from their mothers, and perhaps too from their siblings. This leads to a renegotiated sense of family and place belonging. Oftentimes, grandparents, uncles or aunts stay with the children, bringing them up in their own families as the primary caretaker. In these cases, shocks are minimised, yet belongingness has to be renegotiated in a new family. They may keep the same walls and the same rooms, and hence they remain very much located in the same space; but the fact that they no longer have their parents to turn to isolates children. Their hearts, minds, and emotional and physical presence become stretched across time and space.

In the worst cases, the plans for children to stay behind and attend school are derailed due to basic financial considerations. Parents are not able to send money back from Somalia 'as planned', because they did not know how difficult it would be for them to resume their livelihoods in the homeland. Freedom of movement does not translate into the freedom to work, in a context where opportunities are extremely limited or simply do not exist. Being unable to send money back or to bring their children across, those who have relocated to Somalia are unable to function as the economic mainstay of their families. Meantime, those children who are left behind find themselves not only separated from their parents but also detached from their old life in other ways: no longer going to school, and hence, no longer interacting with their friends in the same way.

> I left five of my children with my brother in Kenya. I could not afford their upkeep, so my brother suggested that they should stay with him. He works as a casual labourer. But my children in Kenya do not go to school because my brother cannot afford to pay for their school fees; he pays only for their most important basic needs.
>
> (Mother, 46, Mogadishu)

Other mothers decided to take their children back with them, regardless of the educational gap. They named specific problems related to food security and nutritional intake as potentially harming their children's development in the longer run in the camps. Regarding food security, mothers complained of a lack of variety in the food distributions affecting their children's development: a common complaint given that only grains are distributed as the main staple instead of meat and milk. Women related their children's school drop-out to their inability to concentrate. Reportedly, refugees receiving remittances from the diaspora or those involved in trade and business activities are able to supplement their diet, while the poorest are fully dependent on aid.

Dignity is a concept that contains elements of choice, redress and restitution. Dignity is an important conceptual element of human and psychosocial wellbeing, but it has particular nuances in a refugee context. Redress is a cornerstone of dignity (Bradley 2007): through this process, inequalities are recognised, and refugees seek pathways to resolve them. Not being dependent on aid or on networks in Somalia, refugee returnees are left to fend for themselves. This endows them with a degree of agency, but often in very tough circumstances. Although still in difficult living conditions, lacking the most basic protection standards, returnees can be empowered by return if they are properly supported and enabled. Youth want to have a future in Somalia, women want to be actors in the reintegration process, and children are already working if they are not going to school. Yet, although it is a step forward for adults, children often do not understand why they had to return and ask when they will be going back to the camps.

In conversations held with children upon return, in the presence of their grandparents, girls were more vocal about return than boys. Age and gender were factors that impeded the ability to 'integrate' in schools or in city life in Mogadishu. Girls had a difficult time reuniting with distant relatives, with new homes and with their schools. They were not able to find a comfortable space of integration and psychosocial wellbeing in the family, housing or educational aspects. In two interviews, parents explicitly complained of threats to their daughters' safety during the return process – blaming such threats to their physical safety, through attempted rapes, as being the main concern in their 'reintegration'. In the words of a refugee, the 'untold story' is the story of rapes on the journey back to Somalia. Beyond the violence that women may experience is the fear of the violence itself. Girls listened to their parents telling these stories in interviews and were visibly uncomfortable. Yet, they would not speak. Not having a voice in the decision to return to a place they did not know, but that sounded frightening, invariably led them to have bad dreams at night, with girls reportedly not sleeping well upon return.

> I am not happy at all in Somalia; I had the dream of one day going abroad with my family in the refugee camps, it's like they shut down my dreams. While in Kenya I was a schoolgirl though sometimes I also worked as a house-help to support the family's income. But it was better than here. I am not intending currently to stay in Somalia.

> (Anab, 23, female, single)

What happens next? Negotiating post-return roles

'The international refugee regime [...] is predicated on the assumption that refugees will not re-migrate after return' (Iaria 2014: 43). In the case of Somali refugees returning from Kenya and interviewed in 2014, large gaps in post-return knowledge and information persist that destabilise this sedentary view of return. They range from information about road conditions to livelihood opportunities and local market dynamics in Somalia, as well as the level of assistance and institutional support upon return. These information gaps threaten the sustainability of wellbeing upon return. Women want to work, but lack the network and the capital to do so. Women's opinions on their livelihoods are in one sense promising: they want to contribute upon return, but do not know how or where to start. These aspirations turn into frustrations, as most women are unable to work. This, in turn, negatively impacts women's sense of belongingness, generating a cycle that undermines the sustainability of return. In Kenya, male refugees learned mainly casual labour in the form of brick-making, low-skilled construction work, transporting firewood, and in some cases, driving. For those living in urban areas with the right to work, some men operated as mechanics or tailors, or were students. Women interviewed mentioned selling snacks and tea and working as house-helps while in exile. But, in reality, what are women's skills? What can women do if they want to work upon return? These questions are introduced to them for the first time late in the return process, indicating limited 'preparedness' (cf. Cassarino 2004) for the return and what happens after.

> Yes, I am an able person who has the ability to work, I can be a housemaid, or I can own my own business if I am given some investment for a start capital. For now I am not working: I did not learn any skill in Kenya. Unless I start a business, which I do not have the capital for, it is difficult to get a job in Somalia.
>
> (Woman, 40, Mogadishu)

Women's experience of exile in Kenya was marked by the lack of freedom to move or to work, both being sought upon return to Somalia; or they were allowed to work and do business in Kenya, notably in Nairobi's Eastleigh neighbourhood, but are not given such opportunities in Somalia. In the words of one of the returnee women interviewed in Mogadishu,

> I was a hawker, I used to do business selling tea on the shopping streets of Eastleigh. But here in Somalia, there are no such opportunities for me. I had an income [in Kenya] but here I am unemployed. I am hopeful that I will get employed in the near future.

Women find it difficult to access work, and find that they have no support in this process – whether from their families or from external actors. Two women, interviewed in the same district of Mogadishu, explained that they were given assistance not as female returnees, but as 'vulnerable people who could not help themselves' – they were given food vouchers. They matched these with domestic work, baby-sitting and cooking for other homes. Yet, this did not provide them with sufficient financial means to put their children into school, because their income remained too low and unpredictable.

While men may have access to the support systems of relatives or external aid, women lack both. As an example, at the time of this research, most programmes on food security and livelihoods targeted women-headed households or men involved in farming and vocational skills training. Training programmes and labour market integration often take these two approaches – not targeting women at large, but only vulnerable women. Programmes are gendered in a way that considers women as social rather than economic actors. Aid dependency and the lack of legal recourse to work means that many refugees never actually worked while in exile. For others, the challenge was finding skills in a new Kenyan environment. For Somalis from Kismayo, most were pastoralists and farmers before their displacement. Upon return, women are not able to achieve what they hoped to achieve. They self-reference cooking, tailoring and farming in interviews as potentially productive skills and the basis of much of their hopes after return. Women go as far as asking for capital to start up their own business in Somalia. They are willing to work as domestic workers, and in small businesses – such as cafés or selling snacks.

Experiences of return require adjustment to a society. In Somalia, returnees face compromise over basic services, access to clean water, free education, and above all free food – but they enjoy free movement and being home. Yet, their coping mechanisms are too weak to handle life back in Somalia. They will certainly develop coping strategies with time, to better adapt to their new circumstances, but the initial transition is a shock to them. 'I have not been able to cope with the challenges' or 'I used to just manage by skipping breakfast, lunch or supper', but that is no longer enough. There are gaps in assistance and in the presence of NGOs in Kismayo and Mogadishu, and insecurity in Mogadishu, gaps that returnees did not expect – at least, not to such an extent. This can be mitigated when family networks work, yet generally, networks remain weak. Whether through split families keeping one foot in Somalia and one foot in Kenya, or through supportive and resourceful families upon return, transnational support systems in split families or links to the diaspora are essential for returnees to be able to experience a positive return process. Alternatively, they may intend to go back to Kenya, but realise they may not be able to do so. A common coping mechanism is to leave the refugee ration card behind in the camp with a trusted neighbour or a relative, as a safety mechanism to ensure a possible reintegration into refugee life, if the reintegration upon return to Somalia fails.

> I was a special case in Dadaab, but not here. All humanitarians were supportive in the camps, people in the camps were divided in two special cases, just like me, I was a divorcee – that is why they helped me several times.

But here all people are victims, no one is safe. In the refugee camps where I was recognised as a divorcee, I could get some privileges but here all the IDPs are all vulnerable to the same circumstances of having poor basic requirements.

(Sitey, 33, divorced with four children)

Among those interviewed in Mogadishu, some women worked in domestic jobs – washing clothes, caring for babies or cooking for others. Men worked in quarrying, construction sites or selling snacks in the street (as some had done in Kenya). Returnee men expressed interest in working in the transportation sector: some have experience as drivers of big trucks but have not found opportunities in that sector. Women are willing to work upon return but are excluded from possible jobs – notably in the booming construction sector in Mogadishu, for instance. The lack of preparation of women, before they return, on the possibilities of work and conditions of work available to them in Somalia leads to a gap that makes them feel out of place: this is not the return they had expected. When, on top of that, they are facing separation from their children or other relatives, there is a low point in their return process that threatens their reintegration prospects. Some of the women interviewed voiced that they wanted to return to Kenya. For them, 'return' no longer means Somalia; rather, 'return' means going back to Kenya and a better sense of belonging in the refugee camps. They feel lost in Somalia and have no sense of purpose any more. The burden of planning for the logistics of return, splitting families and not being able to negotiate an active life upon return all contribute to a demoralised state, one that conveys clear signs of psychosocial stress.

Conclusion and policy implications

This research has shown that psychosocial wellbeing is both an ongoing process and a relational state of being with others. In the case of Somali refugee women returning from exile to their homeland, their relational state includes their relation to their partner, their children and their next of kin. It also includes the pursuit of their own goals, their freedom to express themselves, to move, to work – rights that were limited in exile. Expectations are, therefore, that return will increase psychosocial wellbeing. Instead, this case study of Somali refugee returnees from Kenya to Somalia reveals an overall negative impact of return decisions on women's psychosocial wellbeing in three ways.

First, women are relied upon to facilitate the move from the country of exile to the country of origin: they lead the logistical process of return and of family reunification. Their focus on getting from point A to point B, the stress of the cross-border journey, and the feeling of solitude and of a stepwise return all weigh on their wellbeing.

Second, women make choices and decisions in the best interest of their children. But the long-term impact on both them and their children may be, on balance, negative. They opt for split returns, leaving behind some or all of their children in the camps in Kenya, where education is better than in Somalia. Education was a key consideration for exile in the first place, and it remains a key consideration upon return. Leaving children behind means another split in the family, with consequences for the emotional wellbeing of all concerned. Children go through a double process of adaptation: in Somalia, they go through a process of reunification with family and reintegration that can be complex to negotiate (Suarez-Orozco *et al.* 2002); in Kenya, they have to adapt to a new family set-up and the prospect of a family reunification that may be in the distant future. This places a burden on children, who find themselves either negotiating a new family life or negotiating a new future – in both cases, the role of education in refugee and returnee households is at the centre, and children's adaptation to new settings poses a psychosocial challenge that can lead, as my data show, to stress and solitude. Either way, whether through splits or through return, children's difficulties impact their parents' wellbeing.

Third and last, women face a difficult transition from refugee to returnee status, being unable to find the freedom to work that they expected. Their expectations of their role upon return, as people who can be economically active, are not met by the reality on the ground. Certainly, any more positive transition will require more time. But the satisfaction about the return is overshadowed by a strong disappointment over the outcomes, which makes them question the validity of their decision to return, and its sustainability. They begin talking about possibly returning, this time, to Kenya. As a result, for many of the Somali refugees and returnee families interviewed, return is not the 'end of the refugee cycle'.

The policy implications of these findings highlight the role that return programmes and repatriation assistance can play. My recommendations aim at three levels of psychosocial wellbeing – emotional, socio-economic and cultural – giving women a sense of belonging and an identity that matches their own perception of their agency.

First, then, there should be a protection policy targeting women and their children. Discussion with women about the challenges that face their children upon return, or if they are left behind, reveals the need for establishing the conditions to allow them to make better-informed decisions. The impact of split families can be better managed through a stronger programming focus on the psychosocial risks in split family decisions and stepwise migration.

Second, there should be explicit planning for women's skills and linkages to the labour market post return, in order to allow them to leverage their transition from 'refugees' to 'returnees' effectively. At present, women's willingness to work is not matched by their ability to work, as opportunities are lacking and livelihoods programmes are ill-adapted to their profiles. Women want to be key actors in the return process, from planning to resuming livelihoods upon return. Yet, that spectrum is difficult to achieve, and their expectations do not match the reality of return.

Third, there is an urgent need to create 'safe spaces' for women in Somalia. To restore dignity, 'safe spaces' are needed in Somalia – spaces for youth to learn skills and work, spaces for women to have access to a future livelihood, and spaces for children to go to school and for girls to spend time together, outside of school and outside of domestic work, to share stories, dreams and leisure time. They need to be offered something that they cannot get in the camps: a viable connection to their motherland.

Notes

1 The data in this paper stem from a research project conducted by the author and a team of researchers at Samuel Hall (www.samuelhall.org) in a research endeavour commissioned by UNHCR Somalia.
2 See Security Council Resolutions 1325 (2000) and 1820 (2008).
3 I put 'return' in quote-marks here because many Somalian refugee children have never been to Somalia.

References

Ahmed, S. (1999) Home and away: narratives of migration and estrangement, *International Journal of Cultural Studies* 2(3): 329–347.

Ahmed, S., Castañeda, C., Fortier, A.M. and Scheller, M. (eds) (2003) *Uprootings/Regroundings. Questions of Home and Migration*. Oxford: Berg.

Bradley, M.C. (2007) Return in Dignity: a neglected protection challenge. www.rsc.ox.ac.uk/files/publications/working-paper-series/wp40-return-in-dignity-2007.pdf. Accessed 31 July 2016.

Brah, A. (1996) *Cartographies of Diaspora: Contesting Identities*. London: Routledge.

Brun, C. (2000) Making young displaced men visible, *Forced Migration Review* 9: 10–12.

Bushin, N. (2009) Researching family migration decision-making: a children-in-families approach, *Population Space and Place* 15(5): 429–443.

Cassarino, J-P. (2004) Theorising return migration: the conceptual approach to return migrants revisited. *International Journal on Multicultural Societies* 6(2): 253–279.

Christou, A. (2003) Migrating gender: feminist geographies in women's biographies of return migration, *Michigan Feminist Studies* 17: 71–103.

D'Angelo, A. and Pasos Marciacq, M. (2002) Nicaragua: protecting female labour migrants from exploitative working conditions and trafficking. Geneva: ILO GENPROM Working Paper 6.

El-Bushra, J. (2000). Gender and forced migration: editorial. *Forced Migration Review* 9: 1–7.

El-Bushra, J. and Sahl, I. (2005) *Cycles of Violence: Gender Relations and Armed Conflict*. London: ACORD.

Ghosh, J. (2009) Migration and gender empowerment: recent trends and emerging issues. Human Development Research Paper 2009/04. www.atria.nl/epublications/2009/Migration_and_gender_empowerment.pdf. Accessed 31 July 2016.

Gmelch, G. and Gmelch, S. (1995) Gender and migration: the readjustment of women migrants in Barbados, Ireland, and Newfoundland. *Human Organization* 54(4): 470–473.

Hondagneu-Sotelo, P. (1992) Overcoming patriarchal constraints: the reconstruction of gender relations among Mexican immigrant women and men, *Gender and Society* 6(3): 393–415.

Iaria, V. (2014) Post-return transnationalism and the Iraqi displacement in Syria and Jordan, *International Migration* 52(6): 43–56.

King, R. (ed.) (1986) *Return Migration and Regional Economic Problems*. London: Croom Helm.

Mahler, S.J. and Pessar, P.R. (2006) Gender matters: ethnographers bring gender from the periphery to the core of migration studies, *International Migration Review* 40(1): 27–63.

Meares, C. (2007) From the Rainbow Nation to the Land of the Long White Cloud: Migration, gender and biography. PhD thesis in Sociology, Massey University, New Zealand. http://muir.massey.ac.nz/bitstream/handle/10179/625/02whole.pdf?sequence=1. Accessed 31 July 2016.

Piper, N. (2005) *Gender and migration*, Global Commission on International Migration, background paper. http://incedes.org.gt/Master/pipersesentacuatro.pdf. Accessed 31 July 2016.

Sakka, D., Dikaiou, M. and Kiosseoglou, G. (1999) Return migration: changing roles of men and women, *International Migration* 37(4): 741–764.

Schuster, L. and Majidi, N. (2013) What happens post-deportation? The experience of deported Afghans, *Migration Studies* 1(2): 221–240.

Schuster, L. and Majidi, N. (2015) Deportation stigma and re-migration, *Journal of Ethnic and Migration Studies* 41(4): 635–652.

Suarez-Orozco, C. and Qin, D.B. (2006) Psychological perspectives on migration and gender, *International Migration Review* 40(1): 165–199.

Suarez-Orozco, C., Todorova, I. and Louie, J. (2002) Making up for lost time: the experiences of separation and reunification among immigrant families, *Family Process* 41(4): 625–643.

Turner, S. (2000) Vindicating masculinity: the fate of promoting gender equality, *Forced Migration Review* 9: 8–9.

Vathi, Z. and Duci, V. (2016) Making other dreams: the impact of migration on the psychosocial wellbeing of Albanian-origin children and young people upon their families' return to Albania, *Childhood* 23(1): 53–68.

Yeoh, B. and Lam, T. (2006) *The Costs of (Im)mobility: Children Left Behind and Children Who Migrate with a Parent*. Bangkok: UNESCAP.

10 Time heals?

A multi-sited, longitudinal case study on the lived experiences of returnees in Armenia

Ine Lietaert, Eric Broekaert and Ilse Derluyn

Introduction

In recent decades, return migration has received increased attention in migration policy and research (Black and Gent 2006; Cassarino 2004; Matrix Insight 2012). Despite previous approaches to return migration as an 'easy', 'natural' or 'unproblematic' homecoming, it is now well recognised that return migration is a multi-phased, multi-layered, long-lasting and complex process and experience, which is sometimes even experienced as more difficult than the initial migration (Black *et al.* 2004; Ghanem 2003; Markowitz and Stefansson 2004).

Migrants' post-return experiences are influenced by different elements. Cassarino (2004, 2008) has proposed that differences in post-return experiences can be explained by migrants' 'return preparedness', composed of two elements: first, the free choice of migrants to return, or their *willingness* to return; and second, their *readiness* to return, above all their abilities to collect those resources that are needed to return. Both elements are, according to Cassarino, strongly influenced by circumstances in both the host and the home country.

With respect to the first element, the 'willingness' of migrants to return, it is widely recognised that the voluntary or forced nature of migration (in general, not only related to return migration) may influence migrants' psychosocial wellbeing (Bhugra 2004). With regard to return migration in particular, different authors have stressed the importance and centrality of migrants' motives to return, and their agency in the process of deciding whether to return or not – thus, their 'voluntariness' to return, since this may influence returnees' range of options and their rate of success after return (Cassarino 2004), their possibilities of embedding themselves in the society of the country of origin (Ruben *et al.* 2009), and their possibilities of creating feelings of belonging post return (De Bree *et al.* 2010). Yet, researchers have also indicated that there is no strict distinction between forced and voluntary migration; the decision to migrate, or to return, is often 'mixed', and a response to a complex set of factors of both compulsion and choice (Turton 2003; Van Hear *et al.* 2009). Therefore, it is a false assumption that voluntary migration would be a 'safe' form of migration in terms of its consequences for migrants' psychosocial wellbeing (Vathi and Duci 2016).

The second element in Cassarino's model, migrants' 'readiness to return', is said to be dependent on migrants' ability to collect, or their possession of, capital and resources to support this return process. This factor has received support in different studies as being influential in returnees' evaluation of the return experiences and migrants' living conditions after return (Bhugra 2004; Van Meeteren *et al.* 2014).

Next to this focus on returnees' pre-return situation as elaborated by Cassarino, other scholars have looked at the impact of the entire migration experience on how returnees experience their return, since migrants' evaluation of this return experience may depend on their initial migration motives (Constant and Massey 2002). As Van Houte and Davids (2008) indicate, understanding migrants' post-return experiences demands a holistic approach whereby the experiences and living conditions during previous migration phases are considered. Similarly, Gualda and Escriva (2014) stress that previous experiences affect returnees' post-return possibilities, resources, and perceptions and evaluations of their living situation.

Third, returnees' experiences of their return are also influenced by how they manage to reintegrate or readjust in different life domains (Ruben *et al.* 2009). Yet, this reintegration process is strongly influenced by the specific context in the country of origin, and migrants' personal capital and access to resources (Pedersen 2003; Van Meeteren *et al.* 2014). Various interrelated and dynamic impacting factors may be identified here, whereby individual returnees evaluate these factors differently (Gualda and Escriva 2014; Pedersen 2003). First, the ability to establish a secure material base for living is considered a central element in the return experience (Pedersen 2003). Second, migrants' social networks and their reintegration therein may be important resources for receiving emotional support and help to solve problems in the return process, and for an overall greater wellbeing (Ruben *et al.* 2009). However, the supportive effect of social networks seems to be higher for migrants from privileged socio-economic backgrounds (Pedersen 2003), and the inability to meet familial expectations related to the migration process may also hinder a positive return experience (Van Meeteren *et al.* 2014). Finally, returnees' sense of belonging to, or, in contrast, their sense of disconnection with, the country of origin may affect their return experience and wellbeing (Pedersen 2003; Vathi and Duci 2016).

While there seems to be quite extensive knowledge of possible factors impacting returnees' post-return living, most studies use a cross-sectional approach, studying this group at a particular moment in their return process. There are very few longitudinal studies on returnees' living situations. Further, next to the paucity of studies incorporating the dynamic character of return migration, there are few studies that try to capture the complexity of these migration processes (Wright 2011), since most focus on only one or a couple of impact factors. Third, most studies look at returnees' living situations in terms of their economic situation; less attention is paid to returnees' subjective experiences of their return situation and their entire migration process (King *et al.* 2014; Wright 2011).

Looking at the return process as a 'situated concept' framed in particular spaces, events and experiences, we use this contextualised approach to examine returning migrants' wellbeing from a longitudinal perspective. Through an in-depth longitudinal follow-up of the return migration trajectories of four return-ees, we aim at capturing the complex interplay between different material, perceptual and relational dimensions of return processes, and at getting insight into returnees' lived realities and their subjective experiences of wellbeing throughout the return process. We put particular emphasis on including a diversity of grades of 'voluntariness' in people's return decisions in our study, given the emphasis this has gained in previous studies (e.g. Long and Oxfeld 2004; Markowitz and Stefansson 2004).

Methods

Study participants

In order to explore how migrants experience their return trajectories and how their wellbeing is shaped throughout the return migration process, this study examined the first two years in the return process of four migrants who were returning from Belgium to Armenia.[1] The respondents were selected out of a larger study, in which we conducted a longitudinal follow-up of 65 migrants who were returning to Georgia and Armenia with support from the Belgian assisted voluntary return and reintegration (AVRR) programme as provided by the non-governmental organisation (NGO) Caritas International. For this study, we chose to select a homogeneous group in terms of their country of origin (Armenia), in order to reduce the heterogeneity in terms of the returning country context.

Armenia is characterised by high emigration rates (Gevorkyan *et al.* 2006), due to, among other reasons, natural disasters, armed conflicts and the socio-political crisis after the collapse of the Soviet Union. Currently, the country is still recovering from the hard years following its independence, and is confronted with a poor socio-economic situation, high poverty levels, unaffordable or unavailable healthcare and unstable political conditions, which are all still important causes of emigration, mainly to Russia, but also to Western Europe and elsewhere (Bakhshinyan 2014; Falkingham 2005). For most migrants, migration to Russia is mainly temporary, while migration to Europe is intended to be permanent. Upon migration to Europe, Armenian emigrants often take their family with them, and the majority ask for asylum. However, asylum recognition rates are very low, and most are not officially allowed to stay permanently (Bakhshinyan 2014).

We purposefully selected four cases that provided a rich account of the return experience and differed widely in their 'willingness to return'. This latter element was identified through looking at returnees' motives to return and whether they perceived their return mainly as compulsion or as choice. Although we acknowledge that the return of migrants with AVRR support is seldom truly voluntary (Webber 2011), we found important differences in how people themselves labelled their decision to return as a 'voluntary' or a 'forced' decision. The study sample consisted of one single returnee, one couple and two families (two parents with minor children). All of our respondents applied for asylum, but received a negative decision. Given that our research focused on their lived experiences related to their return process, we did not ask for more information about the background of their asylum application. Yet, we talked about their motives to migrate: two respondents migrated to work and to improve their living conditions, one interviewee migrated to get medical treatment that was not available in Armenia, and one respondent left Armenia out of fear for his own and his family's safety due to a conflict with a powerful individual. Pseudonyms are used throughout the study to preserve the anonymity of the participants.

Data collection and analysis

In this study, we interviewed the participants three times: before they returned, so while they were still in Belgium, but had already decided to return; once during the first year after their return to Armenia; and then again during the second year after return. The interviews before return took place in a separate room in the office of Caritas International, after the migrant had signed up for the AVRR programme. Research aims and conditions of anonymity, confidentiality and informed consent were clarified at the beginning of each interview. After the interview, the respondents were asked to reconfirm their willingness to continue their participation and be interviewed again within the first and second years after return. The interviews after return were held at a location chosen by the respondents (once, the interview took place at the office of the local NGO supporting the returnee, twice at the returnee's business place, and five times at the returnee's home). Three interviews were conducted without an interpreter (in French) and the other nine interviews with the support of an Armenian (n=5) or Russian (n=4) interpreter. Although two families with children were part of our sample, we only interviewed adults; in the case of a couple/family, both adults were interviewed together, though each time one person predominantly answered the questions. In the case of the families, this was the father; in the case of the couple, it was the woman. On the rare occasions when differences in perspective emerged between the partners, this will be referred to explicitly. In these semi-structured interviews, we used open-ended questions to ask returnees about their lived experiences regarding their living conditions, wellbeing, migration trajectories and return processes.

All interviews were recorded, literally transcribed and analysed with the Interpretative Phenomenological Analysis (IPA) method, a qualitative research approach for exploratory and detailed examination of how people make sense of life experiences (Smith *et al.* 2009). The IPA method emphasises the detailed analysis of particular cases, with each case as an entity on its own; IPA, therefore, is conducted with small, but purposively homogeneous, samples, so that convergence and divergence can be examined in detail. Following Smith *et al.* (2009), at first we executed a case-by-case analysis. We started with an interpretative reading of the transcribed interviews of the first case, followed by an initial coding process, whereby all text fragments that seemed important to our central research questions were marked and annotated in the text. In a subsequent reading, we noted the general theme to which the text fragment related, which resulted in a thematic grouping of the fragments. Next, we looked for temporal evolutions within the themes and interactions between the different themes. This process was repeated for each respondent, and memos about evolutions and interactions were kept during the case-by-case analysis, to facilitate further comparison. As the final step, we looked for patterns of evolutions and interactions across cases, on which we will elaborate in the discussion section.

Our findings need to be interpreted in the light of some study limitations. First, given its focus on an in-depth exploration of a situated return experience, the country-specific approach and the small research group (n=4), the study sample limits the generalisability of our findings (Van Meeteren *et al.* 2014). Second, the selection of other case studies, even returning with the same support programme to the same country of origin, could have revealed additional or different results. Third, although the involvement of an interpreter was often essential to overcome language barriers, the interpreter–respondent interaction could have impacted respondents' answers (Edwards 1998), and the translations limit the possibilities of making linguistic comments and interpretations during the IPA analysis (Smith *et al.* 2009).

In the next section, we first present respondents' return motives and their plans upon return, which provide insights into their attitudes and feelings about the return, and into their general wellbeing before their departure to the country of origin. Second, we present data from the interviews after migrants' return to Armenia for each respondent separately, as a case study in its own right, in order to do justice to the dynamism of the return experience and the rich data obtained for each participant (Smith *et al.* 2009). In a third section, we look at patterns of evolutions and interactions across cases.

Initiating the return process

At the time of the first interview in Belgium, the respondents had already made the decision to return to Armenia within the framework of the AVRR programme. During these interviews, it became clear that all respondents were confronted with a gradual deterioration of their overall quality of life in the course of their stay in Belgium, in particular a deteriorating housing and financial situation. They were living with acquaintances or had to leave the asylum centre, were not working and no longer received any financial support.

While Grigor (male, 42 years) found his living situation in Belgium manageable, because he occasionally earned money and could stay with friends, he chose to return because his personal problems in Armenia were solved and he missed his wife and children. In this respect, Grigor's case differed from the other three cases, all of whom had migrated together with their nuclear family. Additionally, due to his previous working experiences in Armenia, Grigor had a clear view on how he wanted to use the reintegration budget he was allocated, and this made him enthusiastic about the return, and gave him a clear perspective for his future life.

> I have experience because I also had an internet café in Armenia before I came to Belgium. I want to open a new one. I am a specialist. I know it will work, it is a good business. [...] It is important, I have to start business, because I have two children, you know.

Davit's (male, 28 years) motivation to return was a combination of many factors and thus rather mixed. The living circumstances in the host country forced him to return: he and his family could no longer stay with his Belgian friend, who had already hosted them for several months, he could not find a job, and his family had no money any more. Yet, he really wanted to return too, since an Armenian friend told him that it was safe to return, and his wife and children felt very unhappy in Belgium, because they missed their wider family and had experienced the life in the asylum centre as very stressful and threatening. His wife's depression, caused by their living situation in Belgium, was a clear push factor to return, though the return decision was framed as a positive choice, because Davit believed that returning would be better for the overall wellbeing of his family. Like Grigor, he had a clear view on his plans after return (cattle breeding), and really hoped he could reclaim his place as a professional sports trainer. During this interview, he stressed that he wanted his return to be a voluntary return.

Narek and Lilit, the remaining two cases, seemed only to be motivated to return because of their living conditions in Belgium. Narek (male, 27 years) and his family applied for asylum several times, and when their lawyer informed them that they had run out of all possible options and had to leave the asylum centre, they decided to return. Once the decision was made, Narek was convinced that buying a car with the reintegration budget was the best option, and would provide the family with an income. The only thing he kept doubting was whether the promised reintegration assistance would indeed be given to him.

Also for Lilit (female, 33 years) and her husband, the financial support they received stopped when their asylum application was rejected. They could no longer pay their rent, and so moved to the house of some friends. However, when they were asked to leave the house, they saw no other option than to return. They were deeply anxious about the return. They had no idea where to live, since they had sold their house before migrating, or how to use their reintegration budget to gain an income. These elements created nervousness and fear of the insecure future they would face after return. These participants thus experienced the return process, and particularly the period between the application and the announcement of the return date, as highly stressful, which further impacted their wellbeing. This was also the case for Davit: his difficulties with the Armenian embassy in obtaining all the necessary documents prolonged the waiting time before he could return, which made him feel powerless and depressed. Both Lilit and Davit expressed feelings of great relief when the moment of their departure arrived.

Longitudinal perspectives on respondents' lived experiences of return

Before the actual return, the respondents were confronted with quite similar living contexts in Belgium, with overall rather limited readiness to return (cf. Cassarino 2004), but still quite divergent outlooks towards their upcoming return. The interviews carried out after their return to the country of origin revealed that respondents' perspectives on the return process differed from their initial views before their return, and continued to change over time. We now present these changes in respondents' lived experiences for the four different case studies.

Declining wellbeing – changing evaluations

Grigor, who was eager to return and had a clear view on what to expect and what to do after his return to Armenia, expressed in the second interview, seven months after his return, that he felt very happy. He had bought six computers and joined a friend's internet café; he was pleased with the way the business was going, and felt very proud to announce that he had found a location for his own business, which he would start in a month. He felt that the return process went smoothly, and he expressed strong feelings of belonging and satisfaction with Armenian cultural habits, such as family, food and festivities.

> Everything was normal, I adapted immediately, I was born here you know. I love my country, because this is my country.

Grigor said that he was 'very, very pleased' with the decision to return, and he even regretted his initial migration to Belgium, mainly because of the separation from his family:

> I strongly regret that I went there, I would not do it again, I lost two years because of that. It was my big mistake to go there without my family, I should have taken them with me [...] I am happy here, I can live well and I am with my wife and children, so everything is good, everything is normal.

He did not miss Belgium at all, though he was a bit nostalgic about the time he had stayed in Sweden, where he lived with his family for seven years, pointing to elements in the Swedish society that he felt were better than in Belgium.

However, in the third interview, one year and five months after he had returned from Belgium to Armenia, his wellbeing had drastically changed:

Grigor now regretted his return, and thought about moving to Sweden. This re-evaluation was mainly due to drastic changes in his personal situation: he had split up with his wife and they now lived separately. Although he still enjoyed running his business, he expressed frustration towards the situation in Armenia, with rising prices, hard work for an insufficient income, and little possibility of improving his standard of living:

> I have no house. Even if I work 100 years, I will not be able to buy myself a house here. If I work the same in Europe, I think I can manage.

His previous migration experience influenced him now in a different manner:

> [My stay in other countries] has affected me, and I don't want to stay here. I want to leave.

Although he also stated he would always miss his country, the lack of perspectives, and probably also the loss of belonging to a family, made him want to re-migrate to Sweden, where he intended to reapply for asylum. Despite his claim having already been rejected twice (in Sweden and in Belgium), he believed that 'maybe this time, it will be different', as he knew stories from people in a similar situation who did get residence documents.

Return as relief and struggle – ambivalence in the return experience

Davit's return motives before the actual return were rather mixed, and his view on his post-return wellbeing was also quite nuanced. Eight months after his return, he had built a shed and had bought cows, which he considered as a profitable income-generating activity in his particular village, though he was confronted with rising forage prices, making it uncertain whether his investment would bring his family any profit. Further, he experienced difficulties in re-entering his professional sports career, because of clientelism and because he did not have the 'right' political connections.

Yet, despite the rather difficult adaptation process during the first weeks after having been abroad for five years, and the harsh financial situation, Davit was quite positive regarding his situation. His wife and children were pleased that they were back in their home country, and they felt much more free now, compared with living in the asylum centre or being reliant on friends. This feeling of freedom strongly enhanced their wellbeing.

> My son asked me: 'Mum, we do not go to Belgium anymore, do we? Because there, we always have to sit inside the house and we cannot play'.
>
> (Davit's wife)

Despite being happy to be back in his homeland, Davit saw little long-term future for him and his family, due to the country's difficult socio-economic situation, the lack of jobs and the corruption and clientelism, which made it hard to reach a normal living standard or any possibility of 'building up' something in life. Also, his perspective on the migration experience was rather ambivalent: on the one hand, he regretted the migration because he considered it a failure, and because he was confronted now with the difficulty of restarting life and regaining a place in his profession. At the same time, he mentioned that he did not regret the migration, 'because I have made good friends, I did sports and was appreciated'. The following quote points to these contradictory experiences regarding his stay abroad:

> I lived in extremes there. I saw very good things, but also experienced very bad things, periods when we were really hungry. So my opinion about my stay is very dispersed. Fortunately, I found people there who really helped me.

He still expressed frustration towards 'the Belgian system' that had denied him a residence permit despite his following all the rules. Yet, these personal experiences that evoked a negative perception of his living situation in Belgium before departure were now, after his return, distinct from the overall image he held of Belgium, which he now described as a good and fair country, where he would have liked to stay. Still, the overall evaluation of his migration experience led to the conclusion he would never want to live there again.

During the third interview, a year and a half after his return, his financial situation and general wellbeing had declined, because, despite his continuous efforts, the cattle breeding failed and he still had not regained his professional status as a sports trainer.

> Look ... It is just too difficult to live here. I don't even mean to live 'normal', I mean, it is difficult to live 'a little bit normal'. There is corruption everywhere ...

But although his situation had evolved negatively, his perspective towards his migration and return experience had not changed:

DAVIT: I see everybody leaving from Armenia [...]
INTERVIEWER: You would like to go to another country as well?
DAVIT: Me? No, no! For me, it is finished leaving, 'fini partir'! I left, then I came back here, and then after two or three months leave again? No, no, I'll stay here. Where would I go? Papers [residence permit] are a big problem for me, I would not be able to work.

He still felt that he had been influenced by the migration experience, as it had changed certain attitudes (being more punctual, for instance), yet this only evoked frustration and irritation in the daily confrontation with the 'non-European' Armenian approach to daily life, and particularly the way services and (equal) treatment were (not) provided to people.

An unexpected appreciation of life in the home country

Narek and his family returned when all possible options to prolong their stay in Belgium were exhausted. Yet, once the decision to return was made, Narek had a clear view on what to do after return. Immediately after return, he bought a car and restarted his work in the distribution of goods to shops. At the same time, he renovated one floor of his father's house, in which they lived, yet he kept on dreaming of buying land and building his own house in the future. Although Narek had expressed limited willingness to return, he described their return as 'coming home'. After his return, he felt that during his stay abroad, he had missed things that had happened in his family, and thus felt happy being back. Moreover, as Davit also did, Narek expressed how he regained the possibility of living a social and active life, and he liked the comfortable feeling of being in his own country: 'The return was the right solution for us, if you stay in your own country, it is worth millions', in contrast with 'feeling stressed as foreigner abroad'. This image of his return and his home country largely differed from how he described both elements in the interview before his departure. Furthermore, these positive feelings had an explicitly positive impact on his wife's mental health as well:

> It was awfully difficult in Belgium. My wife lost two babies there. This was because of the stress, she had nothing to do there all the time, she could not do anything. Now she is back, and we are not going to the doctor, she hasn't got these problems anymore.

The difficult migration experience and positive return experience influenced Narek's overall view about migration: he regretted his migration, the loss of time with his family, and the loss of money that he could have used much better in Armenia. He therefore stated that he would never go abroad again:

> Sincerely not. Even if I would know there was a job in Russia or in some European country and I would be paid 5,000 euro, I would not go. God knows. It is right that you are in your country with your family and you have to work as hard as you can and not run after the money.

One year later, Narek had made steps in extending his activities, improved his income and renovated his living place. Realising this (albeit limited) progress resulted in increased feelings of wellbeing and an unchanged evaluation of his return and migration experience: 'It changes slowly, but it does improve. I just have to be patient and work hard'.

Improving wellbeing – changing evaluations

Finally, also for Lilit and her husband the return decision was made because of external push factors, and before their departure, they had no idea how to manage life once they returned. During the second interview, Lilit was really nervous and depressed, and expressed deep desperation with their living situation. The couple had solved their housing problem through moving in with Lilit's mother (who had not migrated and still lived in her house in a village), but the quality of the house was very bad (no sanitation or kitchen). Further, Lilit explained how she was confronted with inaccessible and unaffordable healthcare, while both her husband and mother were sick, and the impossibility of finding a job. She described their return as 'their only choice' at that moment, though she now largely regretted this decision:

> In Belgium, we were advised to go to other countries, but we could not, we had no money, the only option for us was to return. But now we have returned, and we are very, very disappointed, because there is no law, and our state, our government, is just making a massacre, a genocide. It is a nowadays genocide. Now I have returned, and I face a lot of problems here, to whom can I address myself? I will ask the president, what can you do for me? How can I take care of my sick mother, sick husband? Ok, let's say that Belgium has provided 500 euro for medical support, it is finished. What will I do afterwards? Whose toilet to clean in order to earn a little money? I have an education but how can I earn money in order to take care of them and to come out of the situation?

Her image of Belgium remained very positive, and she mainly stressed the huge difference between the two countries in how both doctors and officials treat you.

During the third interview, the couple's wellbeing had increased remarkably. Seeing no prospects in the village where they were living, they moved to Armenia's capital, and although they were still confronted with a difficult financial situation, Lilit was working. Although the job was temporary, being able to work strongly improved her wellbeing, made her feel proud, and gave her feelings of agency to change her situation. With regard to the decision to return, the opinions of the couple differed: Lilit's husband said he would like to migrate again, since it was so difficult to find work in Armenia, and given that he had lived half of his life abroad, he felt unfamiliar with the Armenian context. He considered it to have been his wife's decision to return to Armenia. Lilit, on the contrary, still considered their return as the only possible option at that moment:

> When people are surprised that we returned after eight years, I explain it was impossible to stay there, because it was not legal, that's all. They often ask: Couldn't you go to live in another European country? But no, never. I am tired of it, you have to change your whole life, and then restart in another country.

Like Grigor and Davit, they still felt the huge impact of their migration experience in their current lives; yet, in contrast, they described it as something positive:

By our nature, we are very honest people, so while living in Belgium, no matter how bad it was or how difficult the living conditions were, we always followed the rules. It was like this in Belgium, and now we are continuing in the same way here in Armenia.

Again, the difference between Armenia and Belgium was stressed, though they also noticed a certain adjustment to the Armenian context:

Here in Armenia, there is a lot of 'mal-education'. Bus and taxi drivers for example use very bad language. In the beginning, I was really stressed by that, but now I am used to it again [laughs].

Cross-cutting themes in changing perspectives

Across the different cases, the evolutions and changes found in the post-return situations of the respondents stressed the dynamic character of the return migration and reintegration processes, confirming that return is not only a stage within a possible ongoing migration cycle, but an ongoing process in itself. The return process and respondents' post-return situations clearly influenced their evaluation of their overall wellbeing. Throughout these four stories, both deterioration and improvement in returnees' wellbeing could be found at different times, as well as rather ambivalent evaluations of their wellbeing, since the return to the country of origin often entailed elements of both hardship and satisfaction. Clearly, migrants' perspectives on their return decisions and experiences also evolved over time – illustrated by the stories of Narek, Lilit and Grigor. In each of these cases, the changes in perspective on the return experiences were strongly linked to changes in their post-return situations and overall wellbeing, whether it was an improvement of their psychosocial wellbeing (Narek: between the situation before return and one year after return; Lilit: between the first and the second year after return) or a decline (Grigor: between the first and the second year after return). This supports Pedersen's (2003) statement that the everyday life-situations and the meanings that returnees themselves attribute to their situation strongly affect how migrants experience their return, illustrating that past experiences are always remembered and interpreted in light of the present (Eastmond 2007).

In accordance with these changes in perspective on the return experience, the respondents' stories also exposed the importance of the broader migration experience within the return process (Gualda and Escriva 2014; Van Houte and Davids 2008), and how their perspectives on, and the impact of, these migration experiences differ for each individual, even within the same family (cf. Lilit and her husband). The experiences of Narek and Davit convinced both that they would never migrate again, evoking the feeling that their return was the 'right' decision for them; yet Narek regretted the migration, while Davit did not, and Davit's story illustrated how a migration process can be experienced as very ambiguous (Cornish *et al.* 1999; Ghanem 2003; King and Christou 2010).

Their migration experiences also influenced their perception of the home country: for Narek, his experiences in Belgium led to a higher appreciation of his life in Armenia; for Davit, they created a more nuanced view on life in Europe – as being positive, though unreachable without a residence permit. In contrast, Grigor's story showed how his previous migration experience in Sweden, in combination with declining current wellbeing, made him long to migrate again. Even so, during the first interview after return, his view on his migration experience was countered by a strong feeling of belonging to his country of origin. These evolutions illustrate how the meaning of places can change over time (Levitt and Rajaram 2013) and under the influence of migration experiences and changes in post-return living situations. The stories also illustrated that locality matters, given the fact that the place to which people return influences their options (cf. Davit) or how the change in place of living, from the village to the city, opens new perspectives (cf. Lilit).

Further, the stories of Lilit and Davit showed that they recalled a positive image of the host country, despite their personal difficulties and harsh experiences in Belgium (Kubal 2015). This shows that returnees' views on the migration process can become detached from personal experiences, and can lead to an 'idealisation' of the migration experience and how well everything functioned abroad (Pedersen 2003). This is analogous to how researchers describe an idealisation of the home country on the part of migrants abroad (Cornish *et al.* 1999; Markowitz and Stefansson 2004; Warner 1994). Our respondents described how their attitudes changed under the influence of their migration experiences, and their view on 'how things are done in Belgium' became a 'moral touchstone', a 'frame of reference', contrasting with the difficulties and injustices they were confronted with in their country of origin (Levitt and Rajaram 2013; Pedersen 2003). Lilit described this as something positive, making her a better person; though for Davit, it led to frustration when confronted with the disjuncture between both places and the clash between his changed mentality and the post-return reality (Pedersen 2003).

Finally, the stories were less consistent about the continuing influences of the migration experiences. While, on the one hand, the experience seemed to have a continued importance for and understanding of life in the home country (Pedersen 2003; Storti 2001), Lilit, on the other hand, pointed to its decreasing influence and the fact that she gradually 'became Armenian again'.

Conclusion

This study explored the dynamics of migrants' return experiences in a multi-sited, longitudinal research project on returnees' lived experiences of their return from Belgium to Armenia in the framework of a governmental assisted voluntary return and reintegration programme. We hereby captured the meaning these returnees attach to their return experiences and the dynamic interplay between the different dimensions in the return trajectories, in particular in relation to their pre-departure living situation and views.

Based on a detailed reading of these cases, four concluding points can be made. First, the findings confirmed the value of Cassarino's (2004) theory of return preparedness, in particular the importance of migrants' willingness and readiness to return. It appeared that when returnees had a clear view of their likely post-return living situation while they were still in the host country, the return process went more easily. It provided returnees with a sort of 'orientation' immediately after return, which positively influenced their wellbeing in the first year after the relocation. These ideas about the possible direction in life after returning depended on the specific work experience of the returnee or his/her locality of return (e.g. cattle breeding as the only possibility for making investments in a village).

However, throughout these returnees' stories, some nuances about the influence of returnees' willingness can also be seen. As time passed, the opportunities or obstacles created by the specific living context in the country of origin became more prevalent. The respondents' stories indicated that their evaluation of the return experience depended more on their post-return situation and wellbeing than on the initial degree of willingness to return, a hypothesis that, given the specific and limited group of returnees and the relatively small variation in their initial willingness to return, needs further exploration. The respondents' willingness to return did influence their perception of the return process, though this changed over time and in relation to the fluctuations in their post-return situations. This observation adds to the argument that more willingness to return will not automatically simplify the return and reintegration process. This, in turn, reinforces the need to avoid the false dichotomy between forced and voluntary return (Turton 2003; Van Hear *et al.* 2009; Vathi and Duci 2016). The renegotiation of return experiences in the light of post-return living situations and previous migration experiences shows how migrants' views of their return experiences can be seen as performative acts (Butler 1993), through which decisions, belonging and the meaning of places and experiences can be reinterpreted and relocated into personal biographies (King and Christou 2010) in order to rationalise and cope with apparent contradictions and make sense of the return experience (Cornish *et al.* 1999; Eastmond 2007).

Second, and related to the first element, our findings stress how the different factors described in the literature as impacting returnees' post-return living situations and their wellbeing post return are indeed important, but they strongly interact and influence each other. This supports the need for a holistic approach when analysing how returnees experience their return (Ghanem 2003; Gualda and Escriva 2014; Van Houte and Davids 2008).

Third, the study illustrates how return migration can influence returned migrants' wellbeing, though in a very diversified way, as the stories showed how return improves as well as decreases returnees' wellbeing. Migrants' wellbeing also played a role in people's decisions to return, as explicitly shown in Davit's story; and, as illustrated in all four stories, the respondents' post-return wellbeing impacted their views of their return and the entire migration experience. Yet, this association between wellbeing and return migration is often also mediated by other factors, such as the returnee's evaluation of his/her return experience or returnees' resilience, individual values and priorities.

Finally, the multiple changes in the lived experiences of the returnees suggest the necessity of incorporating a temporal dimension into the study of return experiences (Levitt and Rajaram 2013). These four case studies were not exceptional in the wider study sample of 65 returnees, and their stories relate to the stories and perspectives of many others. Yet, the multiple factors that influence return experiences, and their strong interaction, highlight the necessity to be cautious with generalisations about returnees (Ackermann 2003; Gualda and Escriva 2014). Therefore, returnees' complex subjectivities entail a valuable analytic power (Lawson 2000), and qualitative and longitudinal approaches are necessary to enable understanding of the multiplicity of return experiences and returnees' wellbeing.

These conclusions, based on returnees' lived experiences, carry important policy implications for AVRR programmes supporting the return process of these migrants. First, the results indicate the importance of support during the return process, both before leaving the host country and after returning to the country of origin. Guidance given before the return may help returnees to reflect upon their readiness and willingness to return, and might give them a clearer orientation about what to do immediately after return. Both elements may help to bridge the often difficult initial period immediately after the return and may also positively influence their wellbeing once they have returned. Even so, the dynamic character of return migration, reintegration processes and returnees' post-return situations indicates that support for returnees needs to be available over a longer period of time, if needed and asked for by the returnee and/or his or her family.

Second, AVRR programmes are generally designed with the overall aim of facilitating 'sustainable return', mostly defined as the definite stay of returnees in their home country and, thus, the absence of re-migration (Cassarino 2008; Matrix Insight 2012). Yet, the strong influence of the living contexts in the country of origin after return, and the fact that AVRR programmes only focus on short-term support for individual returnees, without targeting the broader contexts in which they are implemented (Schuster and Majidi 2005), render this focus on the 'sustainability' of return an unrealistic goal. We thus need to rethink these AVRR programmes' goals, and therefore argue for more flexible and less stringent programmes that can be more closely aligned to returnees' specific needs and desires and to the particular contexts in which they are implemented.

Note

1 The data collection for this case study and for the larger longitudinal follow-up study was conducted by the first author as part of her PhD (see Lietaert 2016).

References

Ackermann, L. (2003) Violence, Exile and Recovery: Reintegration of Guatemalan Refugees in the 1990s – A Biographical Approach. Oxford: PhD thesis, University of Oxford.

Bakhshinyan, E. (2014) *Assessment of Health Related Factors Affecting Reintegration of Migrants in Armenia.* Yerevan: IOM.

Bhugra, D. (2004) Migration and mental health, *Acta Psychiatrica Scandinavica* 109(4): 243–258.

Black, R. and Gent, S. (2006) Sustainable return in post-conflict contexts, *International Migration* 44(3):15–38.

Black, R., Koser, K., Munk, K., Atfield, G., D'Onofrio, L. and Tiemoko, R. (2004) *Understanding Voluntary Return.* Brighton: University of Sussex, Centre for Migration Research.

Butler, J. (1993) *Bodies That Matter. On the Discursive Limits of Sex.* London and New York: Routledge.

Cassarino, J.-P. (2004) Theorising return migration: the conceptual approach to return migrants revisited, *International Journal on Multicultural Societies* 6(2): 253–279.

Cassarino, J.-P. (2008) Conditions of modern return migrants, *International Journal on Multicultural Societies* 10(2): 95–105.

Constant, A. and Massey, D.S. (2002) Return migration by German guestworkers: neo-classical versus new economic theories, *International Migration* 40(4): 5–38.

Cornish, F., Peltzer, K. and MacLachlan, M. (1999) Returning strangers: the children of Malawian refugees come 'home'? *Journal of Refugee Studies* 12(3): 264–283.

De Bree, J., Davids, T. and De Haas, H. (2010) Post-return experiences and transnational belonging of return migrants: a Dutch-Moroccan case study, *Global Networks* 10(4): 489–509.

Eastmond, M. (2007) Stories as lived experience: narratives in forced migration research, *Journal of Refugee Studies* 20(2): 248–264.

Edwards, R. (1998) A critical examination of the use of interpreters in the qualitative research process, *Journal of Ethnic and Migration Studies* 24(1): 197–208.

Falkingham, J. (2005) The end of the rollercoaster? Growth, inequality and poverty in Central Asia and the Caucasus, *Social Policy and Administration* 39(4): 340–360.

Gevorkyan, A., Marshuryan, K. and Gevorkyan, A. (2006) Economics of labor migration from Armenia: a conceptual study. Washington: Armenian International Policy Research Group, Working Paper 06/05.

Ghanem, T. (2003) When forced migrants return 'home': the psychosocial difficulties returnees encounter in the reintegration process. Oxford: Refugee Studies Centre, Working Paper 16.

Gualda, E. and Escriva, A. (2014) Diversity in return migration and its impact on old age: the expectations and experiences of returnees in Huelva (Spain), *International Migration* 52(5): 178–190.

King, R. and Christou, A. (2010) Cultural geographies of counter-diasporic migration: perspectives from the study of second-generation 'returnees' to Greece, *Population, Space and Place* 16(2): 103–119.

King, R., Cela, E., Fokkema, T. and Vullnetari, J. (2014) The migration and well-being of the zero generation: transgenerational care, grandparenting, and loneliness amongst Albanian older people, *Population, Space and Place* 20(8): 728–738.

Kubal, A. (2015) Legal consciousness as a form of social remittance? Studying return migrants' everyday practices of legality in Ukraine, *Migration Studies* 3(1): 68–88.

Lawson, V.A. (2000) Arguments within geographies of movement: the theoretical potential of migrants' stories, *Progress in Human Geography* 24(2): 173–189.

Levitt, P. and Rajaram, N. (2013) The migration–development nexus and organizational time, *International Migration Review* 47(3): 483–507.

Lietaert, I. (2016) Perspectives on Return Migration: a Multi-Sited, Longitudinal Study on the Return Processes of Armenian and Georgian Migrants. Ghent: PhD dissertation, Ghent University.

Long, L.D. and Oxfeld, E. (eds) (2004) *Coming Home? Refugees, Migrants, and Those Who Stayed Behind*. Philadelphia: University of Pennsylvania Press.

Markowitz, F. and Stefansson, A.H. (eds) (2004) *Homecomings: Unsettling Paths of Return*. Oxford: Lexington Books.

Matrix Insight (2012) *Comparative Study on Best Practice to Interlink Pre-Departure Reintegration Measures Carried Out in Member States with Short- and Long-Term Reintegration Measures in the Countries of Return*. Brussels: European Commission Directorate-General Home Affairs.

Pedersen, M. (2003) Between homes: post-war return, emplacement and the negotiation of belonging in Lebanon. Geneva: UNHCR, New Issues in Refugee Research Working Paper 79.

Ruben, R., Van Houte, M. and Davids, T. (2009) What determines the embeddedness of forced-return migrants? Rethinking the role of pre-and post-return assistance, *International Migration Review* 43(4): 908–937.

Schuster, L. and Majidi, N. (2013) What happens post-deportation? The experience of deported Afghans, *Migration Studies* 1(2): 221–240.

Smith, J. A., Flowers, P. and Larkin, M. (2009) *Interpretative Phenomenological Analysis*. London: Sage.

Storti, C. (2001) *The Art of Coming Home*. London: Intercultural Press.

Turton, D. (2003) Conceptualising forced migration. Oxford: Refugees Studies Centre, Working Paper 12.

Van Hear, N., Brubaker, R. and Bessa, T. (2009) Managing mobility for human development: the growing salience of mixed migration. Oxford: UNDP, Human Development Research Paper 2009/20.

Van Houte, M. and Davids, T. (2008) Development and return migration: from policy panacea to migrant perspective sustainability, *Third World Quarterly* 29(7): 1411–1429.

Van Meeteren, M., Engbersen, G., Snel, E. and Faber, M. (2014) Understanding different post-return experiences, *Comparative Migration Studies* 2(3): 335–360.

Vathi, Z. and Duci, V. (2016) Making other dreams: the impact of migration on the psychosocial wellbeing of Albanian-origin children and young people upon their families' return to Albania, *Childhood* 23(1): 53–68.

Warner, D. (1994) Voluntary repatriation and the meaning of return to home: a critique of liberal mathematics, *Journal of Refugee Studies* 7(2–3): 160–174.

Webber, F. (2011) How voluntary are voluntary returns? *Race and Class* 52(4): 98–107.

Wright, K. (2011) Constructing migrant wellbeing: an exploration of life satisfaction amongst Peruvian migrants in London, *Journal of Ethnic and Migration Studies* 37(9): 1459–1475.

Part IV
Life course, family and health

11 The need to belong

Latvian youth returns as dialogic work

Aija Lulle

Introduction

I propose to look closely at the notion of *internal dialogue* as a crucial resource, which is used by individuals in order to understand their need to belong to places and people (Mellor *et al.* 2008). Before going deeper into relationships between belonging, return migration and agency among young people, I set out the following necessary propositions. First, there are various returns, all of them altering the unidirectional, 'naturalised' understanding of a permanent return to one's homeland. Second, an inner dialogue of return experiences is polyvocal, drawing on and incorporating various temporalities and spatial references as well as corporeal and sensory experiences beyond discursive representation. And third, a dialogic narrative allows young people to deconstruct and understand their own constrained agency when they were engaged in various migration trajectories, not necessarily as a result of their own free will.

Several historical storylines related to migration are especially powerful in Latvia, and these continuously feature in the background of youth return narratives. One of these is exile: during the Second World War, escaping Nazi German and Soviet occupations as well the as threat of deportation to Siberia, many Latvians went into exile. Before the re-establishment of the independent state in the early 1990s, at least 150,000 Latvians lived outside Latvia's territory (Ministry of Foreign Affairs 2013). Many of these exiles were members of the intelligentsia and the owners of businesses. The idea of return to an independent Latvia someday, either for themselves or for their children and grandchildren, was the most powerful driving force for these exiles over many decades. Latvia was idealised as the only place in the world where Latvians could really be at home and fully express their identity. Moreover, return from exile was a fundamental idea already in the late nineteenth and early twentieth centuries, when the possibility of establishing an independent nation-state was spreading internationally. In the meantime, exile is also related to feelings of loss, threat and anxiety, which often become internalised individually, as famously stated by Edward Said (2001). This powerful historical narrative of exile is continuously picked up and transformed in contemporary individualised contexts by those who currently reside outside Latvia and aspire to return to their own or their ancestors' homeland.

More recently, Latvia, with a population nowadays of barely 2 million inhabitants, has experienced one of the largest emigration rates from Eastern Europe over the past decade and more. According to Latvian statistics, at least 230,000 have left Latvia since 2001, mainly to the UK, Ireland and, increasingly, also to the Nordic countries and Germany (Central Statistical Bureau 2014). Most of these recent migrants either have children, plan to establish families soon, or are relocating their entire families abroad in the hope of providing a more stable future for their offspring (Hazans 2011).

A recent émigré, open to the new possibilities in the European labour market and with a pronounced wish to return to the homeland, has become one of the most characteristic social figures, with a particular narrative line in contemporary Latvia (Lulle 2014). Yet, the return has a stronger dimension in being imagined than actually executed. Hazans (2011) estimates that during the economic boom in 2005–2007, around 30–40 per cent of Latvian emigrants returned after a short time abroad. Many of them, however, left again when the severe economic crisis hit the country in late 2008.

Finally, which is less well known and politicised, various kinds of cosmopolitan mobilities actually exist in Latvian society. The capital city Riga has for centuries been a place where several cultures and languages co-exist. Therefore, I will be attentive to the narrative line whereby the young Latvians whom I interviewed developed a dialogue of 'situated cosmopolitan belonging' through a range of temporal and spatial references. These references will be traced methodologically in what Mikhail Bakhtin called *dialogical work*, which I will present in the next section. Understanding of 'otherness' upon migrants' return to their 'home' country and culture becomes visible through this dialogical work, both for me as a researcher and for my informants who generously entrusted their return migration stories to me. Also, through references across both time and space, it becomes possible to forge a cosmopolitan belonging to the parental homeland, as I will demonstrate in the case of one of the main protagonists of this chapter.

Dialogical work: a note on methodology

There have been recent calls for study across various disciplines to recognise the importance of children's wellbeing and agency, and to develop methodological approaches in order to better understand this migratory category (see e.g. Ní Laoire *et al.* 2011; Piperno 2011; Vathi and Duci 2016). Interest in children's agency goes hand-in-hand with a demand for innovative methodological guidance (e.g. Nabors 2013; Saracho 2014; Tisdall *et al.* 2009). However, Eastern European contexts have largely remained understudied within this field.

I aim to understand return experiences as a dialogic exchange – continuous interaction with one another's thoughts and a speaker's orientation towards active understanding (Bakhtin 1986). A narrative is embedded in long-existing, sometimes forgotten and revived discourses and ideas, but it is also addressed to someone and anticipates future responses. Narrative interviews are not only stories but an ongoing dialogue with self, which was presented to me, a Latvian researcher. On most occasions, the interviewee inferred that I understood and could relate to certain discourses in Latvian society with respect to belonging and return. Therefore, I will analyse the modalities of individual temperament-related psychosocial needs of belonging in a broader context of corporeality in time and space. A narrative is necessarily polyphonic: it includes many references, arguments and discourses of return, some or many of which do not belong solely to the speaker, because they are borrowed or incorporated from the discourses and arguments of others, or play into broader metanarratives that circulate in the public sphere.

I draw on 12 narrative interviews with adolescents and young people with various experiences of return to Latvia. The interviews took place at various times during 2012–2014 and were recorded under explicit signed consent from the individuals concerned, and from their parents in the case of informants under 18 years of age.[1] All names are pseudonyms, and some other personal details have been changed in order to ensure the anonymity of informants. Before I present and discuss key themes from the youth narratives, I will briefly describe the conceptual ideas that frame return migration experiences as dialogic work.

Many returns: relational and dialogic

The conceptual approach used in this chapter is grounded in the understanding that there are various returns, which are represented in polyvocal narratives by young people. Return is imagined often during migration, and 'return mobilities' (King and Christou 2011) include various kinds of home visits, temporary stays and more permanent returns. Moreover, for some, that is, children who were born in a different country and were taken back to their parents' homeland, the parental return becomes immigration for them. It is also important to highlight that most of the informants experienced migration when they were under age and therefore were legally constrained from exerting their own agency as to where and how they wanted to reside.

Massey, in her milestone book on the conceptualisation of relational space, argues that space is always 'a story-so-far and constitutive to identities, not prior to them' (Massey 2005: 8). For Bakhtin (1997), an individual is an inter-individual in his or her dialogical work. Personification is based on 'I', but I is related to other personalities – 'me and others' (Irvine 2012). These interconnected and supplemental visions of time, space and human experiences form the basis on which I aim to interpret return migration narratives as a dialogic work.

In a return migration narrative, people represent relations through an inner dialogue with themselves. Simultaneously, they refer to ideas and discourses that were and are prevalent in different times and places. Migrant children grew up and matured their identities along with emigration and return experiences; they borrow, cite and relate to various spatio-temporal references, ranging from everyday experiences in a new place to received discourses on how migration shapes people's identities (Ní Laoire *et al.* 2011). Therefore, although we can separate individual and social registers analytically, subjective experience can never be only individual. Co-experience is a new experience, born in a dialogue between a person who witnesses certain events and experiences in lives of other people and through his or her subjectivity, coming from his or her inner world (Bakhtin 1997: 91).

Finally, to conceptualise the return narratives of children and youth, we have to see a 'child' as an age-related, relational category that continually shifts both *within* and *across* cultures. 'Children and youth are expected to grow up in ways that represent the values of their communities ... seen as symbolic carriers of a changing world, embodying future and possibility' (Coe *et al.* 2011: 2). We have to take seriously the critique of the over-celebration of active agency and mobility of children as dogma in current literature (Vanderbeck 2008), recognising that in fact, childhood is 'the most intensively governed sector of existence over the life course (Rose 1999: 123). We should understand the limitations on exertion of agency that structural forces impose in the lives of children and adults, as *ideology* simultaneously builds on protection and recognises agency (Coe *et al.* 2011: 8–9).

The remainder of this chapter is built around interview excerpts from three young women: the child of a labour migrant, who represents, cites and engages with the wider dialogue of the return of the labour migrant; an 'exile' story, where a young woman frames her dialogue of return as an exile in her own homeland; and a 'cosmopolitan'. Other narrative voices are also included in shorter illustrative extracts.

Laura: 'if I want to live'

Laura, a young woman in her early twenties, was still living in England when we spoke last time in late 2014. She told me about her determination and preparations to relocate to Latvia in the near future. Laura's mother first went to England on her own, leaving an early-school-age girl with her extended family in Latvia. When the mother established herself in England, she took Laura, then aged 11, to live with her.

By the way, Laura is not her given name at birth.[2] The girl changed her Latvian name to a more 'international' one, which is also popular among Latvians, when she finished secondary school in England. The girl who arrived in England at the age of 11 to join her mother became an international Laura when she was 18. One of her reasons for changing her name was that some of her teachers were not able to pronounce it properly. However, there were more fundamental changes that she reflected upon in her narrative; some of them are told in her own words in this excerpt:

> Everything was different: food, school regime, not as much sports as I was
> used to at school in Latvia. I gained around eight pounds during the first
> year in England. The first year was a huge stress ... My weight was the only

thing I could control in my life. So I went for jogging several times, I weighed myself as often as each hour when I was at home, I wanted to see if I achieved some changes. A glass of yogurt and salads were enough for me for a whole day. I started feeling better ... I didn't notice much myself these changes though. But when I went back to Latvia for the summer, my grandmother noticed that I didn't look healthy. And then she and my aunts decided to take me to hospital for some tests.

During the first year in England, she was the only migrant child in her class, she did not have friends and she did not like her new life. Laura started experimenting with how to change her body, and went on a low-calorie diet and did frequent workouts. After her first return visit to Latvia, the teenage Laura made some health improvements, but when she came back to England, during her second and third years there, she went back on severe diets.

One day I fainted at school ... My mother decided to send me back to Latvia ... I will never forget what the doctor who treated me [in Latvia] told me: 'Had you stayed in the same situation as you were, you would not have survived more than two weeks'. I am so grateful to him, only then I understood that I have to do so something if I want to live ... and then progress began rapidly and it was such a great time! Whenever I was allowed to leave the hospital, I went to visit my aunt and my cousins, and it was a wonderful time together. I stayed for a school year in Latvia and it was the best time of all my schooling. Now, when I look back to what happened to me it almost seems as if I had planned my illness to return back to Latvia for a year.

In her memories, the young woman gives meaning to what a teenage girl did to cope on her terms with distress in a new environment as best she could. She integrates her later-obtained knowledge from a doctor, who played an important role in her life and helped her to understand her eating disorders. The way she narrated her story – in a constant dialogue with her own childhood and teenage experiences, also back in Latvia – and expressed her willingness to return to Latvia permanently evokes further thoughts on how these memories shape her inclination to return. Most importantly, she refers first to the doctor, who practically saved her life in Latvia and gave her the knowledge of how to live a healthy life; and second, she describes her satisfaction with the great time she had during a school year back in Latvia while she was recovering from illness. She sees it as a turning-point in growing up as a strong person who can achieve her life-plans anywhere in the world, but she particularly treasures the sense of belonging and experience of care and social contacts she enjoyed during a critical time in her life. It happened in Latvia. This is where she wants to return, and she highlights that this is a place where she really belongs.

The young woman, already called Laura, finished college in England and quickly found a well-paid job. She and her British boyfriend visit Latvia at least once a year. Although she says that 'during the past few years, I feel – how to describe that – much more grounded', Laura also often articulates slightly fatalistic thoughts such as 'in life, as the saying goes, you play the cards you are given'. With this phrase, she refers to the fact that her agency was highly constrained when her mother decided to take her abroad; instead, she is implying the power of destiny, which she did not choose herself. In her pragmatic plans, she states:

> I understand more and more that I want to belong to the society and the country where I was born. I know that I will definitely return to Latvia. Due to this thought of returning, it is easier for me to move ahead, to work hard, save, and earn more. [The idea of a permanent return] gives a whole meaning to my life because I know that I can return and belong [in Latvia] … Realistically, I know that I cannot go back without anything, I need a certain amount of money to launch my business in Latvia.

Even though Laura does work towards her pragmatic plans – for instance, she saves money for her return – she refers also to her uneasy memories of displacement as if imagining that a future permanent return, if it does take place in reality, may bring emotional distress too. In other words, her particular history of migration had profound psychosocial effects: she changed as a personality, and she senses that those who have not experienced migration themselves may not understand her:

> I look back to my experience as a lesson in life. I guess, the biggest thing is that my personality has changed, I have more empathy now. Maybe my soul needed these lessons … I guess, anybody who has lived abroad could understand [my story]. Can you?

As I have described elsewhere (Lulle 2014), many recent labour migrants narrate sensory, bodily pain and a longing for return to the homeland. They want to be understood and accepted after their migration experience, similarly to Laura. Also, like the experience of many other children, Laura's relatives were 'doing family', mobilising around the need to help her to overcome her health problems in ways that are widespread in migrant families but actually little known due to the prevalence of normative discourses of what a family is in contemporary societies (Baldassar *et al.* 2014: 155; see also Nelson 2006; Reynolds and Zontini 2014).

Imaginaries of return to the homeland are often somehow soothing, helping to enhance wellbeing in immigration countries before the physical relocation of return. To some extent, the fatalism of life's 'given cards' becomes an integral element of these meso-narratives of young people's returns. The permanent return itself may become a myth (Anwar 1979) or, rather, a fantasy (Bolognani 2015), but the mentality of a constant willingness to return features prominently in young people's stories. Typically, these narratives often actively engage with, but also contest, a patriotic discourse, which has been promoted in contemporary Latvian media. Namely, the return of recent labour migrants has been portrayed as a patriotic act in which an economic gain abroad is given up in the name of a desire to live in the environment where one really belongs.

In these personal stories, longing for the places of one's childhood is usually contrasted with broader ideas of what a young person in a globalised world could achieve if he or she remains mobile in their youth. Here, I want to bring in two other voices. Kate (20) works as a carer in England. She likes her job, but is sad that she did not obtain a full secondary education due to her uneasy relocation from her father in Latvia to her mother in England in late adolescence. Yet, she clearly expresses a 'youthful' joy, a sense of worldliness, gained through movement to different places:

> Words fail me to express how much I miss home, all those things I did in the countryside. Whenever I arrive back in Latvia, I look at all those trees – birches, oaks – and I really feel like crying. And then my grandmother tells me: 'Come home, you can live with me!' But I don't want to live in the countryside in my 20s. I want to see the world!

The transnational lifestyle due to higher income abroad characterises these narratives regardless of the employment sector. Karlina (24), who went to work in the banking sector in London immediately after university, narrated how the return idea impacts her transnational orientation in everyday life:

> That [idea of the return] is one more important motivation why I want to engage actively with Latvian professionals in London, because I want to keep ties with Latvia. I definitely want to return, but not permanently. I want to work with Latvia and for Latvia. I will be ready for return only when I have achieved greater material independence and will not worry that my income in Latvian professional circles is considerably smaller than I have in England.

Constantly present in these reflective narrative dialogues is a deep sense of national identity, 'Latvianness', which is rooted in long-nurtured discourses of an essentially peasant nation and closeness to nature, and affirmed continuously in song festivals, the practice of mid-summer celebrations and so forth.[3] These inner and interpersonal dialogues are both intimate and political; they influence greatly how people narrate their belonging and their possible return (Teo 2011).

For most Latvians abroad, the actual return practices are home visits, which bring new experiences and discourses of a continuous inner dialogue of a possible longer-term return (Lulle 2014). Read this in the words of Elza (23), who went to a boarding school in England when she was a teenager and now works as a brand manager in London. I interviewed her in Latvia:

The first time I came back it was because I felt so guilty about leaving my parents alone, and I am an only child, I know that they won't live forever ... the nostalgic sorrow was so strong that I nearly abandoned my studies and returned back home for good. But now ... I feel that I do not fit in here at all, I almost feel ashamed about my inability to fit into Latvian society again. My clothing style is too sporty, I don't wear make-up everyday, and when I buy a coffee in Latvia, I am greeted in English. And at the same time I know that I have THAT thought about my family in Latvia and maybe I could even find a Latvian husband and have Latvian children, and have Latvian song festivals. I miss, I miss all this. But I understand, and maybe it sounds arrogant but I don't think I can find such a person here who would be able to understand me.

Many migration scholars have argued that return imaginaries play an important role during migration (see, for instance, Anwar 1979; Black and King 2004; Rubenstein 1979). Such imaginaries can powerfully influence integration patterns, including a reluctance to integrate into the host society if the idea of return is always present (Cassarino 2004). Also, the difficulties of being accepted in a new place may create a pull back home, which might become idealised as a sort of 'refuge' place where one can really belong. Likewise, the return is another means of investing into transnational ties (Michail 2009). For labour migrants, return is one of the ongoing mobility options (Duval 2004; King and Christou 2011), not necessarily rationally planned but also not a failure, as it is sometimes described in everyday and academic discourses (Gmelch 1980).

Zanda: exiled return

Zanda (27) was 12 years old when her parents received a proposal to manage a large-scale project in Finland and Sweden. As she told me at the beginning of the interview, Zanda was aware that her parents would be able to earn considerably more and have a chance to develop their careers in ways that were not possible in Latvia at that time. She agreed to follow her parents, and as Zanda stressed, she felt a strong unity, especially with her mother, that they, as a team, had this money-earning and career-enhancing opportunity. But – crucially – it was always seen as a temporary project, and that there would be difficulties that would need to be endured. So she went with her parents, but throughout the three years abroad she waited for the day when she could return to Latvia. She still remembers a song she heard on the radio while being driven to the bus station in Riga to take the bus to Tallinn, Estonia, and then a ferry to Helsinki. 'Home, home, my father's home' – she sang me the first words of a popular Latvian pop song. Zanda articulates an exile's thoughts in her narrative of emigration and a return.

I remember my first year after the arrival [in Finland]. I often went to the harbour and there were ferries; almost every day I said to myself that one day I will embark on one of those ferries, I so much wanted to go home. That scene with the ferry is still bright in my memory … I was keeping in touch all the time with people in Latvia. I was comparing all the time. I knew that my home is there [in Latvia] and this thought helped me to survive all three years. My people are there [in Latvia] and I will definitely return as soon as I can. I felt tense, painfully distressed. I had no friends. I was called 'stinky' behind my back. It was quite traumatic. Even if I was not a star back in Latvia, I was well respected among my classmates … It became easier when I got friends outside school, also Latvians. But all the time I felt like in exile … Return to Latvia was like lifesaving to me.

Vathi and Duci (2016), in their research on Albanian migrant children, find that the psychosocial wellbeing of returning children reveals a strong link with their feelings of belongingness. From my informants I can confirm the same finding, but from a different angle: like Laura in England, also for Zanda prolonged sensory dissatisfaction and non-belonging in new places, and the inability to express all this in words, turned into eating disorders, but not in such a dramatic way. Zanda's family did not have the time or the financial means to travel back often to pay home visits in Latvia. The few times in those three years when Zanda did come back for vacations were remembered mainly as 'food-related' events to calm the ongoing distress due to separation from home. 'Without taking off my winter coat, I would run to the kitchen when I saw a roasted chicken on the table. Finally I could eat tasty food'. Just as a political refugee waits for a regime change, Zanda waited for the right moment in her education, just before the higher-secondary level, when she could exert her agency sufficiently convincingly that adults would accept it. She announced to her parents that she would move back to Latvia and live with her grandparents. Zanda's crucial decision illustrates further the significance of Vathi and Duci's (2016) work. Paying attention to the intersections of children's age and migration status – intra-EU vs third countries – in other words, the ability to move more freely between countries or restrictive mobility – reveals important contexts within which children themselves can exert their agency, persuade parents and choose where to live in order to ease the pressing psychosocial sense of non-belonging in an immigration place.

I was thinking that I am old enough to live quite independently. I missed out on my teenage years. I had to be strong in order to survive abroad, and when I returned I had to be a grown-up in order to deal with everything. I went to the doctors on my own, I solved all my school things. I returned back to my previous class and it was not simple at all. I had to pass all exams, routine tests, everything. But I so much wanted to continue with my class. I managed! But when the first few months passed, I realised that my classmates are not my people anymore and I am also a stranger to them. I sensed that I am not understood by them. They could not laugh about my jokes and nor could I about theirs. And to admit this to myself was even more painful than my experience abroad. I swallowed this [realisation of non-belonging] very consciously. At that time I understood already quite well that it is better to stay calm, not to say anything. I took the role of an observer. I became a boring person, I mainly stayed silent and listened. As a human being with my own feelings, I guess, I opened up only during my study times. Very, very slowly. But I still remain careful often – would people understand me, what would they think of me? ... I guess this [migration experience and the return] happened during the most important life stage. I can't see any other reason why I became so reserved, why I have such difficulties to express my emotions freely. I was suppressing them all those years and I continued to suppress and swallow everything ever since I came back.

In the above quote Zanda reflects on the linkages between life course, migration and wellbeing; an inner dialogue with herself with deep psychosocial content. Her teenage years, a time of intensive individual identity formation, coincided with experiences of diverse references to social identities in countries where she lived, and she had to re-evaluate her individual changes and social references once again when she returned to her homeland.

Coe *et al.* (2011) have argued that migration influences the pace of life for children – many need and want to grow up faster. The exilic feeling that Zanda maintained many years after returning to her homeland meant that, as she said, she became a different kind of person, much more reserved than she would have wanted to be. There is also a sense of victimhood, as she tried very hard to come back and reintegrate. She managed, but she was not appreciated for her efforts. In many such cases, returnee children are placed a year or two below their age in Latvian schools due to strict requirements for language proficiency. Returning to Latvian school was narrated as stressful in other interviews too, like 13-year-old Aleksandrs', who returned after three years abroad:

My memories [of a return] are of a very strange feeling. No school uniforms, everyone looking at me. A nervous feeling. I really disliked school that time, I was sad, I didn't like the fact that I had to stay at school longer than other children. It took me some time to improve my Latvian, to speak fluently again.

Zanda's and Aleksandrs' narratives about the education system in Latvian schools resonate strongly with what King and Kılınç (2014) have found about second-generation Turkish-German teenagers taken back to their parental homeland and the resultant traumatic experiences in Turkish school systems. The fact that Aleksandrs was the oldest child in the class was stigmatising for both him and his mother, and therefore the boy started taking private lessons to move to another school with a strong emphasis on foreign languages. Even when he improved the Latvian language to the native level again, he still felt a stranger and an outsider – always that older boy in the class.

King and Kılınç (2014: 131–132) also emphasised that those who experienced return with no input into the decision when they were teenagers still retained a sense of long-lasting bitterness. This could be overcome in the long adaptation process and thanks to other, empowering life events, such as a happy marriage and successful employment. However, Zanda's own decision to return and her prolonged discomfort point to the crucial role of age when the return happens, whether voluntary or imposed by parents. Moreover, Zanda's exertion of agency in insisting on her wish to return to Latvia in her teenage years deserves closer attention. I will do it here through a dialogue with a different case. Roberts was born in Sweden and was taken to his parental homeland when he was just six years old:

> I remember the very day when I was told that we are going to Latvia. I was in our kitchen and I was just simply told that we are moving to Latvia. It made me very angry. We arrived in late summer and I immediately had to go to school. I had an accent for several years.

However, he has good memories of his small, rural school. The insecurity mounted, when, in his early teenage years, he started at a new school in the capital city. By then he had no 'foreign' accent, and none of his classmates knew about his past, but:

> In Riga I felt quite insecure, I was a shy child who was sitting in a corner with a book. I decided to leave the secondary school, I wanted to do my own things and then my life changed completely.

Despite being a bright kid in languages and science, Roberts decided to drop out from school before he turned 18. His discontent was expressed towards the school system in general, where he did not feel he could develop his personality.

> I don't think [the return to Latvia] made me shyer and it is not the reason why I left school. However, it might have added to the fact that I became more reticent as I was not in my own environment. Had I stayed in Sweden I would have become a spoiled child most probably. Now I am thinking that it is a good thing that I had a chance to become a more humble person. I guess, one should always sacrifice something to gain a new experience. I know Latvia much better than Sweden, but I do have great sympathy for that country. When I went to visit it recently, the feeling comes back. Stockholm has its scent, all those landscapes which I haven't seen for years. I think I belong to both countries.

For Roberts, the feeling of exile is shifting, and I will return to his case in the next section on cosmopolitanism to demonstrate how polyvocality expresses itself as we grow older and reflect upon our experiences and what we want to be in the future. But here I want to take a moment to compare how both Roberts and Zanda reflected on their constrained agency when migration took place and on how they became reserved personalities out of a sense of insecurity. Zanda's inner dialogue reminds us of the relative invisibility of middle-class children or those coming from a relatively close cultural distance. As compared with refugees or the larger concentrations of 'visibly different' children in certain schools, the invisibility of middle-class children or those culturally not so distant may give the impression to teachers, parents and the children themselves that they 'naturally' belong to an environment where others, too, are white and middle-class. Upon return, they are nevertheless subjected to multiple 'othering' due to their migration experience. In order not to exhibit her difference after the return, Zanda chose to deliberately suppress her voice, while Roberts sat in his corner reading his book. On many occasions, children want to belong and fit into society, and if they cannot, they apply coping strategies, for example, trying to hide the difference when possible, which may cause long-term negative consequences for a person's emotional wellbeing.

Elizabete: cosmopolitan return

Elizabete (aged 21 when interviewed) was actually not born in Latvia and had lived in several countries outside her parental homeland for most of her life. But having just recently obtained a degree from a prestigious British university, she was nevertheless determined that she would come back to Latvia as soon as she completed her undergraduate studies. Elizabete also persuaded some other Latvian students at her university to come back to Riga. The young woman deliberately did not form a romantic partnership during her last study year in order to come back to Latvia more easily. She got a job as soon as she arrived, one that was directly related to her profession.

> When I decided that it was time to get a job I was pretty lucky, they took me pretty quickly. Actually all of my friends who came here got jobs in no time. If you have the right attitude and the right skills and you are applying for an opening for which you are well qualified, then it's easy. People say it's hard to find a job. They might be looking in the wrong place or having different expectations.

Elizabete talked about her feelings of belonging to a diaspora of Latvians in the UK. She had friends from different backgrounds, but she made extra effort to find Latvian friends, joined a Latvian association and sought out any Latvian freshmen in her university. 'I really did that because I wanted to fit with the Latvians'. Elizabete continues:

> Now I'm doing the opposite – I'm trying to find foreign people again [in Riga]. I made friends with people who are not from here and spend some time with them. When I came back to Latvia, I could feel the difference between me and the people who have lived their whole life here. Latvians

always ask about what school I finished; I believe the more important question is 'What university did you graduate from?' ... I'm pulled to foreign countries. And I feel annoyed when somebody asks me 'Where are you from?' I usually don't have a proper, short answer to this. But I really like it when I meet somebody who has a similar life-path to me. That's always so interesting and you understand each other.

Elizabete's switching strategies in different places represents the particular way she wants to live with difference – it is her cosmopolitan backbone.[4] She actively engages dialogic arguments in her narrative, which supports her main idea of Riga as a European city that can provide as good a quality of life for the highly skilled as many other places in Europe. And unlike labour migrants, Elizabete does not emphasise the role of money:

> Money is not a big obstacle. If you are 21 years old, your salary would be small whether you are in Great Britain or in Latvia. Maybe your salary will be comparatively bigger in Great Britain, but expenses also will be greater. I don't think that my quality of life is lower here. Quite the contrary, I think that my quality of life is much better in Riga. I have an acquaintance who stayed in Great Britain to work there after university. Maybe she earns a bit more, but socially ... I would never give up what I have socially here and take a bigger salary.

So, it seems that this young woman's experience of social integration and a diverse cultural life in Riga increases her psychosocial wellbeing, and she internally measures this feeling of satisfaction by comparing how other Latvian friends, currently living and working outside, feel. However, Elizabete does not over-idealise her opportunities in Riga. Rather, she draws on arguments that are not solely about the place where she lives at a given moment, but about the quality of certain aspects of life – socialising, housing, cultural life and a job. Here she recounts her critical rejection of an education opportunity, which she wanted to take in Riga, but gave up due to doubts over its quality:

> I went to the director of a [Master's] study programme but her attitude was like I am a nobody: wait for your turn when I am in the mood to talk to you. I understood that I am not ready for such kind of attitude. I was thinking that maybe I was very spoiled with my foreign education, all the professors were so accessible in England, and they were talking to you as an equal. I was really ready to study for a Master's degree in Latvia, but now I say – I will never do it.

Unlike Zanda, Elizabete is open to novelty seeking; she is flexible about staying in Riga for some time, or going abroad for the next stage of her studies when a good opportunity arises.

For Roberts, whom I introduced in the previous section, the main turning-point and exertion of his agency was when he left school. He can now more freely express his more cosmopolitan belonging. Of course, it is not only Latvian children who play with 'difference' when referring to their place of origin, bilingualism and belonging to two cultures. Ní Laoire *et al.* (2011: 148) have also described the same phenomenon in Irish children's return migration. Now Roberts' 'safe place' is outside the formal, nationalistic education system; it is people of different ages and ethnicities, whom he is socialising with and with whom he shares his future dreams:

> My dream is to travel around the world, to understand different cultures. I have a big wish to go to Paris and learn French properly. But it is not like a concrete plan. I can also do it here quite well. I want to learn and create something on my own and since I felt that it was oppressed in the traditional school system, I found it somewhere else. The circle of friends I made after I left school is fantastic and I hope these will be the people I will grow old with, wherever that would be.

In these two extracts from Roberts and Elizabete, cosmopolitanism is not only featured as belonging to the world, but both of them talk about openness and transforming the world into a better place (Glick Schiller and Irving 2015: 2). Belonging, for them, can be in Latvia, but it can also be elsewhere with people who share a similar mind-set. They argue for an understanding of a sense of 'global-local' place in contemporary Latvia, and nurture their social networks, where this sense of openness and diversity is valued.

Conclusion

In this chapter I chose to look at young Latvians' return experiences through the lens of an inner dialogue on actions taken, and on coping strategies and reflections. Doreen Massey critically encouraged scholars who aspire to inhabit a more just world to develop a global-local sense of place (Massey 1991), which echoes with Bakhtin's idea that the world's future model should become more dialogic (Bakhtin 1997: 351). The approach I have used in this chapter seeks to find ways of exploring and developing new discourses of the diversity of return experiences and outcomes.

The contribution of this chapter is twofold. First, thanks to a dynamic, dialogical approach, we can gain more in-depth insight into the life course and into the presumed notion of return migration as the 'end of migration cycle'. My informants experienced migration, imagined return and actually returned at different life-course turning-points, and the return itself, in turn, shaped their life course. This was especially visible in teenagers' experiences and in adults' memories of their teenage years. The link between return migration and psychosocial wellbeing here is paramount, shaping individual and social identity with references from different places, times and systems. Sometimes these multiple space-time references are interpreted as positive and creative; but equally, such profound changes can deeply disturb the sense of security and wellbeing. The coping strategies, which suppress difference, and the settings where socio-cultural differences cannot be freely played out and embraced have potentially harmful long-term consequences for psychosocial wellbeing.

This finding should be taken further by being accommodated into policies regarding the education and socio-cultural adaptation of returnee children. Parents, too, should engage in serious dialogue with their children when a decision to return has been taken. Moreover, I argue that it is not a child alone who needs to adapt; the state and its systems should be encouraged to recognise that 'difference' and mobility experiences constitute a prime human condition. By recognising that places in Europe nowadays are both local and global, we can create more ethical social systems, where a child is embraced to realise his or her potential and not just used as an object that fits or does not fit into the pre-determined standards of a certain grade in a school. When the compulsory school years are over, those with migration experience, like Elizabete, are freer to enjoy and even emphasise their cosmopolitan identity, a strategy that sits comfortably with her 'Latvianness' and leads to a more fulfilling psychosocial adaptation, either in Latvia or elsewhere.

Second, the chapter invites scholars to consider the important role of the internal dialogic work which young people continuously carry out in shaping their identities. I have demonstrated how return imaginaries are not only to be seen as indicators of integration and/or a transnational lifestyle. They are the intrinsic dialogic resource of a migrant, which helps to make sense of daily practices during migration and to provide refuge and a sense of belonging without necessarily involving an actual return. Such a rich and often emotional self-dialogue becomes internalised also in the inner dialogues of migrant children and youth who observe, feel and respond to their parents' anxieties over non-belonging. In the meantime, the figure of the émigré both engages and contests patriotism, a love for one's homeland, which is often exploited by various voices in political and media discourses and inflicts a guilt upon migrants who have left the country and whose 'duty' would be return and to contribute to its growth. Also, I showed how much and for how long return migrants may try to silence their inner insecurity due to various everyday media and political discourses about return, as well as pre-existing academic discourses of return migration. Presumably, this was because rather little was known or understood of the negative psychosocial impact on wellbeing, whereby both emigration and the return to the homeland can resemble a prolonged sense of exile, accompanied by the fear of not being accepted and understood. Therefore, this chapter also contributes to a better understanding of the 'exilic condition' among return migrants. It may become characteristic of some migrants, wherever they may be – it is constant, but manifested in different respects, both 'in migration' and 'at home, after return', as a rather permanent sense of exile (Said 2001).

Finally, I want to re-emphasise the third case study – return to parental homeland as a cosmopolitan choice (Elizabete) – to draw readers' attention to lesser-known returns in the post-Soviet Latvian context. Such returns are dialogically narrated in an active, argumentative and persuasive way as they seek to embed themselves into an accepted set of public discourses about returns. This young woman exemplifies polyvocality as a dialogue between individuals and the broader society and its structures, arguing for recognition of difference and an enriching engagement with modes of belonging beyond narrowly nationalistic ones. In the case presented here, it is also a very practical dialogue (or lack of it): Elizabete went to a high school and a university where dialogue between teachers and students was basic to the learning process. In Latvia, she realised that it is still rather rare that a teacher is willing to receive and engage in dialogue and also to receive constructive criticism from students.

The need to belong is entwined into multiple belongings – to an extended family and friends, to a vision of one's future, as well as place- and community-based sensory satisfactions such as the tastes, sights and sounds of 'home'. Simultaneously, a dialogic narrative practice itself exemplifies psychosocial efforts to give new meanings to various returns, which extend beyond a limited understanding of return as an idealised escape from the difficulties of integration, or simple failure in an immigration place, or the falsely teleological closure of the migration cycle as a return to the status quo ante.

Notes

1 The narratives analysed in this chapter are part of a larger ethnographic project, *Families on the Move: Children's Experiences of Migration in Europe*, funded by the Kone Foundation, Finland. The Principal Investigator of this project was Prof. Laura Assmuth, University of Eastern Finland.
2 Nor is Laura her real name – it is an analogous 'international' pseudonym. All other names are also pseudonyms.
3 For a closely similar comparison to the rural Irish return context, see Ní Laoire (2007).
4 For further case studies about migrant youth's cosmopolitan orientations in the context of 'East-West' migrations in Europe, see Polek *et al.* (2011); Vathi (2013).

References

Anwar, M. (1979) *The Myth of Return: Pakistanis in Britain*. London: Heinemann.
Bakhtin, M. (1986) *Speech Genres and Other Late Essays*. Austin, TX: University of Texas Press.
Bakhtin, M. (1997) *Collected Works 1940–Early 1960s*. Moscow: Russian Dictionaries (in Russian).
Baldassar, L., Kilkey, M., Merla, L. and Wilding, R. (2014) Transnational families, in J. Treas, J. Scott and M. Richards (eds) *The Wiley Blackwell Companion to the Sociology of Families*. Chichester: Wiley, 151–197.
Black, R. and King, R. (2004) Migration, return and development in West Africa, *Population, Space and Place* 10(2): 75–83.
Bolognani, M. (2015) From myth of return to return fantasy: a psychosocial interpretation of migration imaginaries. *Identities* 23(2): 193–209.
Cassarino, J. (2004) Theorising return migration: the conceptual approach to return migrants revisited, *International Journal on Multicultural Societies* 6(2): 253–279.

Central Statistical Bureau (2014) *Latvia, Emigration Trends 2001–2014*. Riga: CSB.

Coe, C., Reynolds, R.R., Boehm, D.A., Hess, J.M. and Rae-Espinoza, H. (2011) *Everyday Ruptures: Children, Youth, and Migration in Global Perspective*. Nashville, TN: Vanderbilt University Press.

Duval, D.T. (2004) Linking return visits and return migration among Commonwealth Eastern Caribbean migrants in Toronto, *Global Networks* 4(1): 51–67.

Glick Schiller, N. and Irving, A. (2015) Introduction. What's in the world? What's in a question? in N. Glick Schiller and A. Irving (eds) *Whose Cosmopolitanism?: Critical Perspectives, Relationalities and Discontents*. New York and Oxford: Berghahn, 1–22.

Gmelch, G. (1980) Return migration, *Annual Review of Anthropology* 9: 135–159.

Hazans, M. (2011) Latvijas emigrācijas mainīgā seja: 2000–2010 (The changing face of Latvia's emigration: 2000–2010), in B. Zepa and E. Klave (eds) *Latvia. Human Development Report 2010/2011*. Riga: University of Latvia, 70–91.

Irvine, M. (2012) *Mikhail Bakhtin: Main Theories: Dialogism, Polyphony, Heteroglossia, Open Interpretation. A Student's Guide. Georgetown University*. Published online: http://faculty.georgetown.edu/irvinem/theory/Bakhtin-MainTheory.html. Accessed 28 February 2016.

King, R. and Christou, A. (2011) Of counter-diaspora and reverse transnationalism: return mobilities to and from the ancestral homeland, *Mobilities* 6(4): 451–466.

King, R. and Kılınç, N. (2014) Routes to roots: second-generation Turks from Germany 'return' to Turkey, *Nordic Journal of Migration Research* 4(3): 126–133.

Lulle, A. (2014) Spaces of encounter-displacement: contemporary labour migrants' return visits to Latvia, *Geografiska Annaler, Series B* 96(2): 127–140.

Massey, D. (1991) A global local sense of place, *Marxism Today* 6: 24–29.

Massey, D. (2005) *For Space*. London: Sage.

Mellor, D., Stokes, M., Firth, L., Hayashi, Y. and Cummins, R. (2008) Need for belonging, relationship satisfaction, loneliness, and life satisfaction, *Personality and Individual Differences* 45(3): 213–218.

Michail, D. (2009) Working here, investing here and there: present economic practices, strategies of social inclusion and future plans for return among the Albanian immigrants in a Greek-Albanian border town, *Southeast European and Black Sea Studies* 9(4): 539–554.

Ministry of Foreign Affairs (2013) *Informational Report on Ministry of Foreign Affairs Cooperation with Diaspora in 2013–2015*. Riga: MFA.

Nabors, L.A. (2013) *Research Methods for Children*. New York: Nova Science Publishers.

Nelson, M.K. (2006) Single mothers 'do' family, *Journal of Marriage and Family* 68(4): 781–795.

Ní Laoire, C.N. (2007) The 'green green grass of home'? Return migration to rural Ireland, *Journal of Rural Studies* 23(3): 332–344.

Ní Laoire, C., Carpena-Mendez, F., Tyrrell, N. and White, A. (2011) *Childhood and Migration in Europe. Portraits of Mobility, Identity and Belonging in Contemporary Ireland*. Aldershot: Ashgate.

Piperno, F. (2011) The impact of female emigration on families and the welfare state in countries of origin: the case of Romania, *International Migration* 50(5): 189–204.

Polek, E., Van Oudenhoven, J.P. and Ten Berge, J.M.F. (2011) Evidence for a 'migrant personality': attachment styles of Poles in Poland and Polish immigrants in the Netherlands, *Journal of Immigrant and Refugee Studies* 9(4): 311–326.

Reynolds, T. and Zontini, E. (2014) Bringing transnational families from the margins to the centre of family studies in Britain, *Families, Relationships and Societies* 3(2): 251–268.

Rose, N. (1999) *Powers of Freedom: Reframing Political Thought.* Cambridge: Cambridge University Press.

Rubenstein, H. (1979) The return ideology in West Indian migration, *Papers in Anthropology* 20(1): 21–38.

Said, E. (2001) *Reflections on Exile: and Other Literary and Cultural Essays.* London: Granta.

Saracho, O.N. (ed.) (2014) *Handbook of Research Methods in Early Childhood Education: Research Methodologies.* Charlotte, NC: Information Age Publishing.

Teo, S.Y. (2011) 'The moon back home is brighter?' Return migration and the cultural politics of belonging, *Journal of Ethnic and Migration Studies* 37(5): 805–820.

Tisdall, K., Davis, J.M. and Gallagher, M. (2009) *Researching with Children and Young People.* London: Sage.

Vanderbeck, R.M. (2008) Reaching critical mass? Theory, politics and the culture of debate in children's geographies, *Area* 40(3): 292–300.

Vathi, Z. (2013) Transnational orientation, cosmopolitanism and integration among Albanian-origin teenagers in Tuscany, *Journal of Ethnic and Migration Studies* 39(6): 903–919.

Vathi, Z. and Duci, V. (2016). Making other dreams: the impact of migration on the psychosocial wellbeing of Albanian-origin children and young people upon their families' return to Albania, *Childhood* 23(1): 53–68.

12 Migration and return migration in later life to Albania

The pendulum between subjective wellbeing and place

Eralba Cela

Introduction

Return migration is currently one of the most widely debated dimensions of international mobility. It has gained a prominent role in the agenda of migration experts and politicians for its impact on both receiving and sending countries (Cassarino 2004). Nevertheless, empirical evidence has mainly focused on the economic element of return and its consequences in terms of development of migrants' countries of origin (see, for instance, Ammassari and Black 2001; Ghosh 2000; King 1986), whereas the underlying individual and contextual factors behind migrants' decision to return are still little researched (Hunter 2011). Also under-researched are the return experiences of older people, who are the specific demographic focus of this contribution.

Rather than seeing return as a kind of teleological end-point of the migration cycle – a definitive resettlement in the 'homeland' – my epistemological approach is to link return to the two main recent paradigms in migration theory, namely transnationalism (Glick Schiller *et al.* 1992) and the 'mobilities turn' (Sheller and Urry 2006). By embedding both migration and ageing in these two conceptual frameworks, we can more easily talk of 'transnational ageing' and 'return mobilities' as the key discursive containers within which my empirical research results can be analysed.

As far as return migration in later life and transnational ageing are concerned, the existing empirical literature shows that pendulism rather than definitive settlement is the preferred lifestyle for ageing migrants, especially when they are relatively young, living with their spouses and in good health (Fokkema *et al.* 2016). The decision whether to settle for good in the host country or to return to their country of origin tends to depend on the location of close family members (de Coulon and Wolff 2010), although some studies suggest that it is the children's location that really matters for the older generation's location (King *et al.* 2014). Moreover, the presence of other co-ethnics may well have an impact on the decision to settle abroad, as they might become important resources in providing support in later life (Bolzman *et al.* 2006).

In this chapter, I analyse the experiences of migration and return mobilities of older, ageing or soon-to-age Albanians who are living back and forth between

Italy and Albania, or have returned back home. I identify two generationally separate, but kinship-linked, groups for study: first-generation migrants who migrated from Albania to Italy around 20–25 years ago and who are now middle-aged or on the cusp of older age; and the parents, whom I call the 'zero generation', who are engaged in more recent and generally shorter-term mobility between Albania and Italy. By providing insights about both groups' perceptions of 'home' and belonging, I address issues around transnational ageing, wellbeing and vulnerability in later life, and the migrants' conceptions of space and place.

I mobilise two main key concepts within the ageing–mobility nexus. First, I highlight the importance of wellbeing in triggering migration and return mobilities. Wellbeing has been analysed from a variety of disciplines and standpoints (Wright 2012); it is a multidimensional concept and regards both objective conditions related to income, employment, housing and health, and subjective perspectives concerning individuals' assessment of the emotional, relational and mental aspects of their lives. Of course, these two dimensions are generally closely related. Wellbeing is shaped by the individual's characteristics, cultural aspects and contextual factors, and, in the case of international migration, wellbeing travels across borders according to the locations of family members. Place and space also have an important bearing on wellbeing, as many of the objective and subjective conditions – or, to put it another way, the different forms of capital (social, economic, cultural, political; cf. Bourdieu 1986) – are spatially circumscribed (Michielin and Mulder 2007). Having said this, it is also the case that some forms of capital (for instance, transnational social networks, or economic capital in the form of remittances) as well as some aspects of wellbeing (notably access to mobility) are embedded in transnational space and are not so spatially defined.

The second concept is related to the life-course approach, according to which the individual's life is characterised by a series of transitions or life events (Kulu and Milewski 2007). These are associated with status changes in different life domains like the family (marriage/divorce/widowhood, or childbirth and school enrolment), the domain of work (entering or exiting the labour market) and health (improvement/deterioration). They are all potential triggers of mobility, be it short or long distance, and may affect attachment to a specific location by increasing/decreasing the economic, social and psychological costs/benefits of staying or moving (Kley and Mulder 2010). Migration for many individuals is one of their main life events; it is a relational process that links people's lives over time and space (Findlay *et al.* 2015). The concept of linked lives, introduced by Elder (1994) within the life-course approach, is of crucial importance in understanding the relational dimensions of individuals' living and decision-making process in relation to migration also, as 'no principle of life course study is more central than the notion of interdependent lives' (Elder 1994: 6). Indeed, the decision of whether to move or to stay affects the lives of both the migrants and other individuals ('significant others') with whom they have important relations (Elder 1994; Findlay *et al.* 2015).

The chapter is structured as follows. Next, I describe the background of my study and the methodology used. Then, in the following two sections, I present the main findings that relate to the ageing and migration/mobility of the two study populations – first-generation migrants and the zero-generation 'older-old'. The concluding discussion relates the empirical results to key concepts and draws out implications for further research.

Background to Albanian migration

Contemporary Albanian migration dates to the early 1990s, when, after 45 years of communism and total isolation, during which time emigration was banned, a sudden, 'explosive' emigration occurred when the border was opened up and de-militarised (Barjaba and King 2005). Since then, Albania has experienced an intense population exodus over a short period of time, more dramatic than almost any other country in the world; by 2011, 1.4 million Albanians were estimated to be living abroad, mainly in Greece, Italy and the UK, compared with a population of 2.8 million living in Albania (INSTAT 2012).

This large-scale emigration resulted not only in the loss of labour force, as emigration was mainly dominated by young adults, but also in a process of demographic ageing due to the increased weight of older cohorts in an overall shrinking population. Moreover, with the process of emigration ongoing now for 25 years, the original migrants themselves are also ageing. Although migration has contributed, through a huge inflow of remittances, to alleviating poverty and improving households' living conditions, the other side of the coin concerns the social and human costs that are generated with the departure of entire families abroad.

The unbalanced nature of the initial Albanian emigration – young adults, mainly males, but also some couples and young families – separated family members in an abrupt manner, as it was impossible for both the younger and older generations to cross borders and visit each other.[1] This forced separation subsequently put enormous strain on traditional family solidarity based on intergenerational hands-on care and geographical proximity; the result was a care drain and the emergence of the phenomenon of 'orphan pensioners', who were made to feel 'abandoned' by their emigrant children. Psychologically, the parents of migrants were totally unprepared for the 'loss' of all of their children and grandchildren to emigration (King and Vullnetari 2006; King et al. 2014). In a second stage, the regularisation schemes that occurred in Italy in 1995, 1998 and 2002, in Greece in 1998 and 2001, and in the UK with a mini-regularisation in 2003 enabled many Albanians to reunite their families abroad, leading to a process of stabilisation and a rapid growth of the foreign-born second generation (Vathi and King 2011). As the first and second generations settled down in the host countries, a transnational family space emerged with regular bi-directional visits and longer periods of permanence for both younger and older generations to and from Albania (King et al. 2014).

In terms, then, of the particular chronology and typology of Albanian migration, and its interaction with the demographic ageing of both migrants and non-migrants, we observe a dualistic ageing–migration phenomenon. First, those migrants who left Albania as young adults during the peak migration years of the 1990s are now themselves middle-aged or approaching older age. And second, the parents of these migrants – the 'zero generation' – are witnessing the later stages of old age. Typically, the first-generation migrants are now in their forties, fifties and early sixties, while the zero generation are in their late sixties, seventies and eighties.

Methods

In this chapter, I draw on qualitative, in-depth interviews carried out between 2011 and 2015 with 25 zero-generation and 20 first-generation Albanians who have returned to Albania from Italy or engage in back-and-forth mobility between the two countries. I started to recruit participants through purposive sampling, utilising personal contacts, associations and workers in the social and healthcare sector. In Italy, the interviews were conducted in the Marche and Apulia regions (located on the eastern, or Adriatic, coast facing Albania), whereas in Albania I followed migrants in their origin villages/cities in different regions. The majority of migrants were interviewed two or three times, with many interviewees encountered in both countries in order to assess their wellbeing outcomes in different settings. Along with the interviews with older Albanian migrants, I also interviewed some other household members in Italy and Albania, thereby achieving a deeper understanding of gender and intergenerational relations within and across borders.

Migrants were interviewed face-to-face in private or public spaces such as their homes and cafés. The interviews were conducted in Albanian and/or Italian, depending on the participant's preference, and lasted from two to three hours. Thanks to my own Albanian background and fluency in both Albanian and Italian, I was able to switch between the two languages as needed. The interviews were audio-taped and transcribed. The follow-up interviews focused on migrants' return mobilities and perceptions about place and wellbeing. The names used in the quotes are pseudonyms in order to ensure confidentiality.

Given the exploratory nature of the study and its qualitative design, the sample cannot be claimed to be statistically representative of the older Albanian migrant population living in Italy and/or Albania. Accordingly, the findings cannot be generalised beyond the study sample. Nevertheless, my lifelong knowledge and personal experience of Albanian migration in Italy make me confident that the indicative findings presented in the rest of this chapter represent a reality that is widespread and not majorly distorted.

Mobility patterns in later life: the experience of the first-generation migrants

In this section, I analyse the experience of first-generation migrants who have spent their adult lives in Italy and have returned to Albania or are facing the decision of where to spend their old age. Three main typologies of return migration emerge from their narratives: 'forced' return due to the economic crisis, return triggered by a combination of life events, and the 'desired' return mobilities of those who live back and forth between Italy and Albania.

'Forced' return

According to Elder *et al.* (2003: 12), 'the life course of individuals is embedded and shaped by the historical times and places they experience over their life-time'. The long-lasting economic crisis has negatively affected migrants' integration in Italy, raising their unemployment rate from 8.1 per cent in 2008 to 14.1 per cent in 2012 and forcing many of them to leave the country (Bettin and Cela 2014). The effect of the crisis has, however, been gendered, as the most affected sectors are those where male migrants are traditionally employed, typically in the construction sector and manufacturing industries. By contrast, migrants' employment has increased in the service economy, due above all to the ongoing demand for female labour in the elderly and family care sector (Bettin and Cela 2014).

Being unemployed in later life is a negative life event that affects both objective and subjective wellbeing due to the loss of the family's economic mainstay and the difficulty of re-employment in older age. A main coping strategy for some of the first generation, at least in the short term, is the return to their home country – Albania. Agron (male, 58), for example, is one of them; he had lost his job in the factory where he was employed. At the time of the first interview in Italy in 2011, he was still confident that he would manage to find another job, as had already happened many times during his working life in Italy. Returning to Albania was absolutely not an option for him, because after 20 years of migration, he and his family were accustomed to the Italian lifestyle, and Albania was no longer the country he had left, in terms of his relationship to it.

> No, I will not return. I'll find another job as I always have done over the last 20 years. My life is in Italy, here I have raised my children, we are paying a mortgage on the house now, my path is here. Albania is where I was born. Going back for good would mean a new migration.

The role of the lives of 'significant others' (Elder 1994) was a key recurring topic in all migrants' narratives, as a trigger both of emigration and of return migration. In the case of Agron, for example, the future of his children was the main motivation to leave Albania, and the desire to stay close to them was the main pull factor of staying in Italy, reflecting not just the emotional dimension of living close to children and grandchildren, but also the cultural expectation of geographical proximity to the younger generations in later life. At the same time, the short geographical distance between Italy and Albania, and the ease of travel back and forth, become a further reason not to return to Albania.

> This is the place where I belong, where my family lives and I would like to live close to them until the very end. My kids would not go back either. It doesn't make sense. Tirana is one hour away by plane, why go back for good?

I had the opportunity to interview Agron again in 2014 in Albania, where he had, in the end, returned in 2013 in order to resume his work as a teacher. His family remained in Italy, where it had ultimately proved impossible to find a job at his age. Living in total economic dependency on his wife and children even for 'just a minimum amount of pocket money' had become for him an unsustainable psychological and economic burden, showing how psychosocial issues can act as a push factor to return. Although he was loved and sustained by his family, his decision to return to Albania in order to look for a job was 'a matter of dignity'. Return was intended as a temporary decision, although after two years in Albania he had the feeling that it was becoming a permanent 'temporary' arrangement. Agron returned to Albania thanks to his social networks, which supported him in finding a job. Although return to Albania could have been considered as a failure by his peer Albanians, he did not experience any discrimination; on the contrary, the solidarity of his friends, who warmly supported him, was crucial in his return.

> It is not like ten years ago when people were looking at your car and your wallet. Now they know how easy it has become to lose one's job in Italy or Greece. They see this news every day on television. I helped a lot of people here [in Albania] in the past. This time they have helped me.

At the beginning, returning home was not too painful, and life in Albania seemed pleasant because of starting a new job that was much more compatible with his background than any of the jobs he had done in Italy, although much less well remunerated. Regaining economic autonomy and spending time with old friends were positive factors that enhanced his self-esteem and improved his psychological wellbeing. The feeling of playing a role in society once again and supporting his family back in Italy with the mortgage payments was really rewarding. Over time, however, his perception of his psychosocial wellbeing changed. Returning to an 'empty home' in the evening brings to the surface his loneliness and sense of emptiness due to the lack of physical contact with his wife and children. Moreover, with the passage of time, the initial positive aspects of being back home have diminished, and negative thoughts now dominate his mind.

Albania is nice for holidays, but everyday life is tough. What I dislike the most is the mentality of the people, which has worsened. They have become aggressive, selfish, and arrogant. In Albania you have to hope that you never need to go to a public office, because that is there where your dignity is trashed.

Agron doesn't feel Albanian anymore and wants to return to be close to his family in Italy, but for the moment he needs to work for a number of years to at least gain the pension entitlement in Albania, 'hoping that loneliness won't kill me beforehand'.

Return as a combination of different life events

Long-term unemployment was the most common reason for returning for the first-generation male Albanians I interviewed between Italy and Albania. If, for Agron, return was an unexpected event, in the case of Mikel (63 years old), returning to his village had been his plan since the very beginning. His idea of returning was to invest the family savings into their farm and run it all together. During the first years of migration, his family had faced many difficulties in Italy – first because he and his wife were for a long period 'illegal' migrants, and afterwards they had severe economic difficulties that prolonged their stay in Italy. They kept going back and forth for holidays and special events and sending their children for three months during the summer holidays. Nevertheless, because of Mikel's strong desire to live in his village of origin, he did effectively return, but without his family. This was due to a combination of two life events: divorce and unemployment. When I initially interviewed him in 2011 in Bari, he talked a lot about the effect migration had had on his family and especially on his marriage – 'ruined by migration', as he often stated during the interview.

When Mikel started to talk to his family about returning to Albania, his marriage was already shaky, and gender and generational conflicts had undermined family dynamics. His wife's empowerment and independent lifestyle, thanks to her economic autonomy provided by employment, and her close relationship with their teenage daughters, who were enrolled in school and completely adapted to the Italian lifestyle, had generated an upside-down gender and generational equilibrium within the family. Mikel felt very uncomfortable and thought that, aside from his nostalgia for home, the return to Albania would save his marriage and restore his male position within the family. This did not happen, however. In 2012 they got divorced, and Mikel had to move out and find another flat. This situation generated a lot of stress and anxiety and worsened his economic position. He could no longer afford even to go to Albania as he used to do in the past.

Another year later, he was unemployed too, and this life event triggered his decision to move back to his home village for good. At the beginning, like many returnees, he thought life would be better at home, where he had other relatives who had remained there (brothers and their families). But he returned without any savings and after some failed attempts to find a job, he fell into poverty. His brothers, whom I also had the chance to interview, help him with food and some pocket money; he usually spends this on alcohol, which helps him 'escape the loneliness and desperation' for which he repeatedly blames his wife, even when referring to his situation of unemployment:

> This village is the best place of my life. Here I can be myself without being judged because I am unemployed (like my ex-wife did). Here I can live with bread and oil only, I will never starve here. Here is the place where I want to die. This is my home, Italy has never been my home. Italy exploited me and gave me nothing. Italy took my family away. I will never again return to Italy.

In 2014, I had the opportunity to interview one of Mikel's daughters in Bari, where I learned that Mikel had been hospitalised several times in Italy because of health problems related to alcoholism. At the moment, he is living back and forth between Albania and Italy and is supported by his family, both in Italy (mainly daughters) and in Albania (brothers), to deal with his health and alcohol issues.

If some of the male migrants have been affected by the economic crisis, all the female partners I have interviewed in Italy are employed in the domestic sector, primarily as informal or paid caregivers. Indeed, the Italian population is heavily affected by the ageing process and the demand for long-term care is expected to increase in the future. The co-existence of a welfare state oriented towards a family-based model of elderly care and social norms of filial responsibility that stigmatise the institutionalisation of the elderly attracts female immigrants to this sector (Bettio *et al.* 2006). As one of the interviewees states, 'there will always be elderly Italians in need of care, Italy is an old country and we are cheap'.

Return migration is not an option for the majority of women I interviewed; geographical proximity and having Italian citizenship enable them to move back and forth, and they consider Albania as the 'next-door neighbour'. There are, however, women who have decided to return, like Eda (62), in Bari, who wants to return for good after retirement. Eda arrived in Italy with her young daughter after divorcing her husband. Although she had a university degree, she has always worked as live-in caregiver. This arrangement has allowed her to work, take care of her daughter and save some money, which she has invested in property in Albania. But, at the same time, this living arrangement has prevented her from building a social network outside the domestic walls. Now that her daughter has moved out to study at university in northern Italy, and she is close to retirement, she is eager to return to her home city, where she still has her mother, friends and other relatives.

> I don't want to spend my whole life caring for others in Italy. I need to relax and enjoy life now while I am still in good health. I have invested in two small houses in Albania. I will live in one of them and benefit from the

rent of the other and I have a small Italian pension too. This will be enough for me to live well in Albania. Here if I had to pay the house rent [now she lives with the old Italian lady she is caring for], I would starve. I have Italian citizenship and can return to Italy whenever I want and whenever I need.

The desire to return for Eda is the result of a complex combination of life events (empty nest and retirement), personal circumstances (living alone) and social conditions (having all her social network in Albania) that all act as push factors, but also by her economic prospects of retirement in Italy. On the other hand, the presence of her mother, close relatives and friends in Albania becomes an incentive to return also, in anticipation of a decline in health in later life and the possibility of increased healthcare needs; her social network in Albania represents a safety-net for support in later life.

Desired return mobilities

At the moment, however, taking care of grandchildren and facilitating their children's participation in the labour market is the main priority for first-generation migrant women and men I interviewed in Italy:

We want to travel, otherwise I will be a perfect grandfather, with my home at the service of my daughters in Italy. I'm not saying we will stay in Italy, but we will go where our daughters go, not to take advantage of them, but to help them and make their lives as easy as possible. And when the grandchildren grow up we will be free to live back and forth between Albania and Italy.

(Ilir, 56 years old)

This quote opens the horizon of mobilities, not just in relation to the transnational space between Italy and Albania, but to a broader transnational social space where better life opportunities drive people's mobilities. Indeed, all the first generation I interviewed are also aware that their children might find it more advantageous to live in another European country, where there are more working opportunities and it is easier to achieve career mobility than in Italy. Their linked and interdependent lives will shape their future strategies of mobilities.

After retirement, in certain circumstances, such as good health, living as a couple and lack of family responsibilities, mobility would be the preferred condition; one of the interviewees coined the term 'family tourism', that is, visiting relatives and friends and together with them visiting Albania and the countries where their friends and relatives are located. This type of mobility can be considered as amenity driven – travelling and spending the hotter months in Albania, where they all have houses, relatives and friends, and spending the rest of the year in Italy, close to their (grand)children. This is the combination of mobility and residence considered by migrants as optimal in enhancing their quality of life:

> When we are retired, yes, I'd like to spend winter and a few days of spring here, then summer in Albania. This way of life would be a dream for me. Our life does not stop here. We also have a beautiful house in Albania, we bought it. Our wish is to live back and forth.
>
> (Besnik, 60 years old)

The optimum location and the challenges of returning or staying for the zero generation

The 'zero generation' have been called the 'forgotten subjects within the overall phenomenon of migration' (King *et al.* 2014: 728). They arrived in Italy under the family reunification provision of the Italian immigration law, which allowed Albanian families to enjoy being together without restrictions and to arrange mutual support when necessary.

There are two typologies of zero-generation migrants among the interviewees: the older-old, who are in their late seventies and older, and the younger-old, who arrived in Italy to join their children even before retirement. With the exception of two widows, they all arrived in Italy as couples. The main triggers of their migration are related both to life events of their family members, such as marriage, divorce and (anticipation of) childbirth, and to their own life-course stage, especially related to retirement, health deterioration and widowhood. In the first stage of their migration, they all co-reside with their children and are engaged full time in caring duties and household chores. The younger-old then usually move to an independent dwelling as soon as they are released from caring duties. This strategy of close-residing instead of co-residing allows them to engage in paid work and live independently, which also reflects one of their motivations for migration: as a way to cope with low wages in Albania.

Family reunification with older parents has finally restored the family configuration into a traditional multi-generational setting. This new situation has immediately improved older parents' emotional wellbeing; thanks to migration, they have regained their socially and culturally embedded grandparenting role, denied for a long time by the physical separation from their children. The zero-generation Albanians I have interviewed define their sense of wellbeing very much in relation to their role as (grand)parents; living surrounded by children and grandchildren gives them a sense of happiness and usefulness. During the interviews, they often recall the long years spent in Albania without having the possibility of seeing and hugging them or being present when grandchildren were born, during their birthdays or when they were ill. Being in Italy has also improved their objective wellbeing, due to both the better living conditions, especially for those coming from Albanian rural areas, and the better health services compared with Albania.

However, the positive impact on their wellbeing is not necessarily long-lasting, at least for the more dependent 'older-old' zero generation. Once released from caring duties, they have a lot of spare time, which, of course, they cannot spend with their children and grandchildren, who are engaged in work, school and after-school activities. The day for the zero generation lasts an eternity, and feelings of loneliness and uselessness arise. In Italy, they are totally isolated from the social context outside the domestic sphere. The first and foremost barrier is represented by language, which is difficult for older Albanians to learn. Moreover, contrary to Albania, where they were used to getting about on foot and meeting friends and kin casually, in these (and other) regions of Italy, they have few friends or social contacts nearby. There are no ethnic infrastructures for them to join, and they are nervous of using public transportation, which in many provincial areas of Italy is not well developed. All this means that they are more or less trapped at home and therefore totally dependent on their busy children and grandchildren for any outdoor activity. Sometimes, also, they find it difficult to meet other Albanians living in the same neighbourhood because of their children's distrust of other Albanians (King *et al.* 2014).

Another negative impact on their wellbeing is generated by the lack of financial means. The zero generation have no pension in Italy in the first years of their migration, so they are highly dependent on their children, who already have their own economic difficulties, which have only been exacerbated by the current economic crisis. On the other side, they miss their own home enormously, as well as their friends, their neighbourhoods and 'even the smell of the air' back in Albania. They are trapped between the desire to stay close to their family and their longing for their true home. Three typologies of coping strategies can be identified from their narratives: denied return, back-and-forth mobility and desired return.

Denied return

The older-old who are widowed or have experienced severe health deterioration feel really 'trapped' in Italy. A two-way concern of health and wellbeing drives their migration, which has often been imposed by their children, especially when the youngest son, who is traditionally responsible for the care of elderly parents, is already living in Italy. When I asked them to describe their meaning of 'home', some got emotional and started crying: 'I can't talk about it, I feel my heart is going to explode' (Fanije, 78 years old). Many interviewees found it difficult to discuss, as they are fully aware they will never return to Albania:

> Two years ago I had a stroke and my sons decided that I could no longer live on my own. So they brought me to Italy. I don't like it here, but at my age my opinion doesn't count anymore. I told them I want to be buried in my village. How awful the thought of dying without any friend or acquaintance crying for you. At least if I'm buried there [in Albania] they will come to visit me at the cemetery.

> (Marije, 83 years old)

Others, however, are aware that Italy is the place where they have definitively settled. They have accepted it, also because their children will never return to Albania and older parents cannot live far from them:

> We, elderly people, would like to remain in Albania; our place is there but we are forced to stay in Italy, close to our children, because we are getting older and we might need help, we could not live alone in Albania. The future is close to the children, if they were in Albania it would be better, but as they are in Italy we also should be here.
>
> (Bedrie, 68 years old)

They return to Albania at least once per year for holidays or on special occasions, such as weddings or funerals. The possibility of these occasional return trips, together with the ability to maintain ties through telephone and Skype, supports them in coping with their new 'home' in Italy.

The migration of the now-ageing first generation has the potential to erode intergenerational relations within the family, resulting in emotional hardship for the elderly parents. The situation of women, of both the first and the zero generation, is sometimes critical. In the case of the first generation, they have undergone a process of emancipation thanks to migration and involvement in paid work; but they are also embedded in culturally defined responsibilities and overloaded with the burden of caring for ailing or impaired older parents, as well as looking after children and sometimes also grandchildren. From the zero generation's point of view, having cared for children and grandchildren in the past, they expect to be supported by the younger generation in their older age. Being widowed and in poor health means, however, being totally dependent on their daughters-in-law; and this relationship is often a source of severe intergenerational tension. In a few cases, the zero generation suffers elderly abuse, which can be both physical and psychological.

Back-and-forth mobility

The majority of the zero generation I interviewed have adopted a transnational lifestyle to cope with both family and personal necessities, to find a right balance between their personal wellbeing and familial wellbeing. Of course, moving back and forth is not an affordable option for all the zero generation, but mainly for those who are still in good health and have the economic means (also thanks to their children's support) to travel.

An important factor in sustaining the regularity of transnational engagement is the financial situation; going back to Albania for longer periods becomes a strategy to cope with their limited financial resources in Italy, especially during the recent years of economic crisis. As stressed above, the majority of older migrants I interviewed do not have a pension in Italy and are usually economically dependent on their children. Returning home becomes an income-optimisation strategy, given the lower costs of living in Albania. At the same time, they do not feel the psychological pressure of being a burden on their children in Italy.

> My Albanian pension of about 100 euro [per month] is ridiculous here in Italy; what can I do with 100 euro? We save this money during the months that we live here so when we go to Albania there is no need for our children to help us and we can get by alone. In Albania, even with very little money you would not starve, whereas here, yes.
>
> (Besim, 84 years old)

Some of the zero generation benefit from a small pension (social allowance) in Italy, which represents, however, an important financial prop for them and accordingly, a lower economic burden for their children. Nevertheless, it is a social benefit, and as such it is linked to having permanent residence in Italy; older migrants are allowed to stay abroad for a maximum of four weeks, but not all Albanians in Italy know this rule. Even when they do know, it is difficult to prevent them from staying longer, which sometimes results in legal consequences.

> I cannot stay in Albania for more than three months otherwise I lose my Italian pension.... so we cannot do otherwise. We also need our children and here they can help us. If we had been healthier in Albania we would not have come to Italy.
>
> (Aferdita, 66 years old)

For the elderly, returning to Albania for longer periods means going 'home', spending time with their friends, taking care of their house and relatives, visiting the graveyards of their loved ones. Living back and forth generates a personal idea of 'home', which is a transnational space made of people, relations and resources in both the origin and destination countries.

Transnational ageing can have a very positive impact on the older generation's wellbeing. In some of the interviews with children of the zero generation, it emerged that spending part of the year in Albania is a way of coping with loneliness and depression that older migrants experience in Italy, as, for example, reported by Miranda (age 38, Italy):

> We are happy when they [her parents] return for a while to Albania, because we know they get bored here and what worries us more is that in Italy we are at the hospital all the time. When they go back to Albania they are dynamic like two teenagers and never complain about any physical pain.

So, if, on the one hand, better access to healthcare services is an important reason to bring parents to Italy, on the other hand, travelling back and forth seems to be beneficial for their health.

Desired return

With regard to definitive return, some empirical research shows that men are more likely to desire to return home than women, as a consequence of the downward employment mobility, loss of social status and diminished power within the family hierarchy that they undergo in Western host countries (Richter 2004). Women, being the main kin-keepers of the family, might be more likely to feel the social pressure of returning home for caring duties.

The zero generation whom I interviewed in Albania generally decided to return because of the unhappy situation of the men, who, unlike their female counterparts, who get fully engaged in child care and/or household chores, feel useless and bored. Accordingly, the pressure for returning home can be attributed to concerns for the husband's health – as this woman stated:

> It was my husband who decided when we had to return to Albania. He wanted to go back not only because in Albania he had things to keep him busy but also because we did not feel at home, we would stay one week at the home of each son, where we felt like guests and I was becoming worried for his health.

However, women easily get used to the idea of staying in Albania as well. Although they very much miss living close to their children and grandchildren in Italy, they admit that their home is Albania. Nevertheless, the choice of permanent settlement in Albania is not considered as an emotional detachment from their family, because they all have Italian documents and they know that they can return to Italy whenever they want. Again, the mobility perspective plays an important part in older individuals' wellbeing; it enhances the benefits of staying in a specific location by lowering the pain and emotional distress of physical separation from the family. Whether or not Albania will really be their final destination is a question for future research.

Discussion and conclusion

This chapter has focused on transnational ageing and the neglected return mobilities of two groups of older Albanian migrants: the first and zero generations. I have drawn on the frameworks of human wellbeing and the life-course approach to analyse the main drivers of migration and return mobilities in later life and address issues around migrants' conceptions of space, place and 'living well'.

Migration for all the generations is closely related to health and wellbeing, as every migrant (as opposed to a refugee) moves to improve both their own and their family's quality of life. The first-generation Albanians migrated to Italy for economic purposes and to generate better life opportunities for the younger generations; the zero generation migrated to Italy to achieve objective and subjective wellbeing by living close to their children and grandchildren. Family reunification determines family wellbeing and reflects its strategy to overcome geographical distance and ensure intergenerational care, which, in the case of Albanian migrants, has always been provided through physical co-presence. Wellbeing is therefore closely related to place, as many of the resources that determine it (like family and social networks, good healthcare, access to work and so on) are place specific. When some resources are lacking, mobility becomes a way of bringing to an equilibrium the cost–benefit of staying or moving. It is worth stressing, however, that migration/mobility is not just an individual decision; it very much involves the lives of the migrants' 'significant others'. This concept of interdependent lives is pivotal in understanding the idea of wellbeing, especially for migrants from collectivistic societies where the family represents the keystone of individuals' lives.

The decision-making process in relation to mobility and the stay/return dilemma for both older generations depends on a wide variety of factors. Their own life-stage and life events, the life events of family members, economic considerations, contextual factors on both sides of the Adriatic Sea, and emotional ties with home and host country; all these factors, whether singly or in combination, may trigger the decision to move or to stay put in Italy. However, the first-generation ageing migrants generally possess a greater degree of agency in the decisions to move – both for themselves and for their elderly parents. As we have seen, mobility is not an option for all the zero generation; in the case of widowhood and poor health conditions, denied mobility (both within Italy and to return to Albania) and consequently a strong sense of loneliness are often the main outcome. For those of the zero generation who have decided (temporarily) to settle in Albania, but who can, however, freely travel back and forth, the mobility perspective positively impacts their wellbeing, lowering the emotional impact of staying in Albania and reducing their perception of abandonment and isolation.

Regarding the first generation, the long economic downturn in Italy and other parts of Europe in recent years has deeply affected migrants' lives through unemployment and financial hardships, generating detrimental effects on their wellbeing. Unemployment is a life-course event that may generate changes in the perceived (financial and emotional) opportunities of living in one place instead of another and thus influence migration/mobility. The timing of life events has a crucial role in determining the effects of the events on individuals' lives. In particular, unemployment in later life is an 'off-time' life event that has disruptive effects on the migrants' family life; it has challenged their prior expectations of ageing in the host country. It is worth stressing, however, that return to the country of origin is gendered, with males more likely and more willing to return. Moreover, it becomes a feasible option only if the cost of living in Albania is lower than in the host country, and if migrants can count on the support of social and family networks that have been maintained over time through communication and remittances. Similarly to the first generation, the zero generation too have been affected by the negative vortex of the financial downturn, as being heavily dependent on their already stressed children has increased their perception of being a burden.

Besides contextual factors, retirement is another life event that triggers mobility between Italy and Albania, especially if coupled with the lack of care duties towards grandchildren. Mobility for the first generation is considered as a way of achieving wellbeing in later life, until life events related to the ageing process (health problems or widowhood) take place, and as a consequence prevent mobility. Their wish is to settle permanently close to their (grand)children in Italy and benefit from better healthcare services there. Contrary to the free choice of the first generation, the zero generation will probably (be forced to) settle in Italy close to their family, regardless of their desire to return home to die.

In conclusion, within a dual conceptual framework of transnational families and the (return) mobilities turn (King and Christou 2011; Sheller and Urry 2006), this chapter has demonstrated that it is essential to adopt a relational approach to the study of ageing and migration. Individuals' lives are continuously affected and shaped by a dynamic intersection of people of different generations, genders and relationships (Hopkins and Pain 2007: 288). Within the ageing–migration nexus, interaction, dependency, loneliness, conflict, support and cooperation all have material and psychosocial impacts on the lives and wellbeing of older people, and younger generations too, in the diverse spatial settings produced by migration. This chapter has demonstrated that, under positive economic, legal and health circumstances, transnational ageing offers the opportunity to enhance quality of life, improve psychosocial wellbeing and meet changing needs. But as the end-game of increasing frailty approaches, where the final resting-place will be remains a topic for future research.

Note

1 This was because of a dual problem: most of the early emigrants had an irregular status in Greece and Italy, having entered these countries clandestinely; and for the older generations left in Albania, access to visas to travel was extremely difficult.

References

Ammassari, S. and Black, R. (2001) *Harnessing the Potential of Migration and Return to Promote Development*. Geneva: IOM Research Series, 5.

Barjaba, K. and King, R. (2005) Introducing and theorizing Albanian migration, in R. King, N. Mai and S. Schwandner-Sievers (eds) *The New Albanian Migration*. Brighton: Sussex Academic Press, 1–28.

Bettin, G. and Cela, E. (2014) The evolution of migration flows in Europe and Italy, *Economia Marche/Journal of Applied Economics* 33(1): 37–63.

Bettio, F., Simonazzi A. and Villa, P. (2006) Change in care regimes and female migration: the 'care drain' in the Mediterranean, *Journal of European Social Policy* 16(3): 271–285.

Bolzman, C., Fibbi, R. and Vial M. (2006) What to do after retirement? Elderly migrants and the question of return, *Journal of Ethnic and Migration Studies* 32(8): 1359–1375.

Bourdieu, P. (1986) The forms of capital, in J.G. Richardson (ed.) *Handbook of Theory and Research for the Sociology of Education*. New York: Greenwood, 241–258.

Cassarino, J.P. (2004) Theorising return migration: the conceptual approach to return migrants revisited, *International Journal on Multicultural Societies* 6(2): 253–279.

de Coulon, A. and Wolff, F.C. (2010) Location intentions of immigrants at retirement: stay/return or go 'back and forth'? *Applied Economics* 42(26): 3319–3333.

Elder, G.H. (1994) Time, human agency, and social change: perspectives on the life course, *Social Psychology Quarterly* 57(1): 4–15.

Elder, G.H., Johnson, M.K. and Crosnoe, R. (2003) The emergence and development of life course theory, in J.T. Mortimer and M.J. Shanahan (eds) *Handbook of the Life Course*. New York: Kluwer Academic/Plenum Publishers, 3–19.

Findlay, A., McCollum, D., Coulter, R. and Gayle, V. (2015) New mobilities across the lifecourse: a framework for analysing demographically-linked drivers of migration, *Population, Space and Place* 21(4): 390–402.

Fokkema, T., Cela, E. and Witter, Y. (2016) Pendular migration of older adults: misconceptions and nuances, in C. Schweppe and V. Horn (eds) *Transnational Aging: Current Insights and Future Challenges*. New York: Routledge, 141–162.

Ghosh, B. (ed.) (2000) *Return Migration: Journey of Hope or Despair?* Geneva: IOM and UN.

Glick Schiller, N., Basch, L. and Blanc-Szanton, C. (1992) *Towards a Transnational Perspective on Migration: Race, Class, Ethnicity, and Nationalism Reconsidered*. New York: New York Academy of Sciences.

Hopkins, P. and Pain, R. (2007) Geographies of age: thinking relationally, *Area* 39(3): 287–294.

Hunter, A. (2011) Theory and practice of return migration at retirement: the case of migrant worker hostel residents in France, *Population, Space and Place* 17(2): 179–192.

INSTAT (2012) *Population and Housing Census in Albania 2011: Main Results*. Tirana: INSTAT.

King, R. (ed.) (1986) *Return Migration and Regional Economic Problems*. London: Croom Helm.

King, R. and Christou, A. (2011) Of counter-diaspora and reverse transnationalism: return mobilities to and from the ancestral homeland, *Mobilities* 6(4): 451–466.

King, R. and Vullnetari, J. (2006) Orphan pensioners and migrating grandparents: the impact of mass migration on older people in rural Albania, *Ageing and Society* 26(5): 783–816.

King, R., Cela, E., Fokkema, T. and Vullnetari, J. (2014) The migration and wellbeing of the zero generation: transgenerational care, grandparenting and loneliness amongst Albanian older people, *Population, Space and Place* 20(8): 728–738.

Kley, S.A. and Mulder, C.H. (2010) Considering, planning, and realizing migration in early adulthood: the influence of life-course events and perceived opportunities on leaving the city in Germany, *Journal of Housing and the Built Environment* 25(1): 73–94.

Kulu, H. and Milewski, N. (2007) Family change and migration in the life course: an introduction, *Demographic Research* 17(19): 567–590.

Michielin, F. and Mulder, C.H. (2007) Geographical distances between adult children and their parents in the Netherlands, *Demographic Research* 17(22): 655–678.

Richter, M. (2004) Contextualizing gender and migration: Galician immigration to Switzerland, *International Migration Review* 38(1): 263–286.

Sheller, M. and Urry, J. (2006) The new mobilities paradigm, *Environment and Planning A* 38: 207–226.

Vathi, Z. and King, R. (2011) Return visits of the young Albanian second generation in Europe: contrasting themes and comparative host-country perspectives, *Mobilities* 6(4): 503–518.

Wright, K. (2012) *International Migration, Development and Human Wellbeing.* Basingstoke: Palgrave Macmillan.

13 To stay or to go?

The motivations and experiences of older British returnees from Spain

Kelly Hall, Charles Betty and Jordi Giner

Introduction

Retirement is a time when people seek new opportunities away from the world of work, which for some includes international mobility. Within the EU, some retired people choose to exercise their rights and freedoms as EU citizens to move to another EU country. Spain is a popular retirement destination for older British and other Northern European people, due to its warm, sunny climate, which is attractive in itself as well as enabling a more active and outdoor life-style. While costs have gone up in recent years, Spain is still relatively cheap compared with the UK, enabling older people with a limited income to pursue some of the recreational activities in Spain that they could not afford to do in the UK. Most older migrants move following retirement when they are in the so-called 'third age' of life; they use retirement as an opportunity to seek new adventures, personal achievement and fulfilment (Laslett 1991). Retired migrants have been conceptualised as 'lifestyle migrants' (Benson and O'Reilly 2009), as they are seen as a group of relatively affluent individuals moving abroad full time or part time, permanently or temporarily, to improve their quality of life.

Research on the migration of retired people has been a fast-developing field of study over the past decade and more. Themes studied have included the reasons for moving, the lifestyles adopted and the social networks developed as part of a healthy retirement (Casado-Diaz 2009; Gustafson 2001; King *et al.* 2000). The focus of research to date has therefore been on the lifestyles and wellbeing of migrants within the country of migration – often Spain. However, more recently there has been a growing recognition that many retired migrants eventually return to their country of origin, especially following the onset of old age or the 'fourth age of life' (Hall and Hardill 2016). Return is often undertaken following a decline in health, in order to access health and social care services or financial support or to be close to family and friends. This chapter, therefore, explores the return migration of retired British migrants from Spain, focusing on health and psychosocial wellbeing as key factors in facilitating migration decisions and experiences, and the outcomes of these decisions for returnees' wellbeing. It utilises a holistic approach to wellbeing as including emotional, physical and social dimensions (Dodge *et al.* 2012) and draws on the broad definition offered by Gough and McGregor (2007), who refer to human wellbeing as a relational state of being with others that enables the pursuing of one's goals and ultimately the achievement of quality of life.

We draw on qualitative interview data collected by the authors, alongside data collected from online blogs and quantitative Spanish registry data. The chapter is structured as follows. After this brief introduction, the chapter details the research methods, followed by a discussion of the reasons for return organised around health and care, financial, and social reasons. The chapter then moves on to explore the process of returning from Spain and the structural, social and emotional challenges this can bring, including the financial difficulties of returning, the difficulties in accessing support from the British welfare state and the challenges of reintegrating.

The research studies

This chapter uses mixed methods by bringing together data from three studies on the return migration of older British people from Spain undertaken by each of the authors. The three studies together included five data sources. First, registry data were collected on the number of returnees. Second, narrative interviews were undertaken with 25 older British people in Spain who were planning a return move to the UK. Third, five narrative interviews were conducted with returnees who had resettled in the UK. Fourth, 24 semi-structured interviews were undertaken with representatives from organisations involved in supporting returning British migrants, including UK-based charities active in Spain, local government representatives and health workers in Spain. Fifth, 40 posts from online social media sites were gathered, including from the online forum for expatriates 'Eye on Spain'.

The research studies were undertaken between 2006 and 2015. Older people were defined as being over the age of 50, as this encompasses early retirees and those who have reached state pension age, as well as older 'fourth agers', which is a time associated with dependence and decline (Laslett 1991). The age of the migrant interviewees ranged from 51 to 93 years (the average was 76), and interviewees included those who had recently moved to Spain as well as those who had been living there for many years. Interviews were all transcribed and analysed thematically using a coding framework that was devised based both on the theoretical interests guiding the research questions and on the salient issues and recurring ideas that arose from the interviews (Attride-Stirling 2001). The qualitative social media data were also included within the coding framework and analysed alongside the interview data. The chapter uses quotes and case-study examples from these interviews to highlight some of the key issues uncovered around return migration and psychosocial wellbeing. The identity of individuals and their location in Spain have been disguised in order to ensure interviewees' confidentiality.

The lifestyles and movements of older British migrants

There has been a massive growth in the number of retired British people moving overseas in the past few decades. This form of lifestyle migration has been linked to wellbeing and a better way of life (Benson 2011). Long ago, Rogers discussed wellbeing in terms of 'the good life' (1961: 186), and many scholars have since linked wellbeing to having a purpose in life, personal growth, autonomy and positive relationships (Dodge *et al.* 2012; Ryff and Singer 2008). Lifestyle migration can, therefore, be directly linked to personal wellbeing, as such migrants consider that the place they are moving to offers greater personal fulfilment, quality of life, and physical and/or emotional health compared with the one left behind (Benson and O'Reilly 2009).

Retiring to Southern European destinations is particularly attractive to older British migrants and has been enabled through the interplay of individual experiences and structural factors underpinning international migration. Structural enablers include increased global interconnectivity, especially within the EU since the development of the Maastricht Treaty in 1992, which enabled the free movement of EU citizens, leading to a significant increase in intra-EU migration, including the migration of retirees (Huete *et al.* 2013; Warnes *et al.* 1999). In addition, improved international travel through the advent of regular and cheap flights, the growth in social media and the development of communication technology have enabled people to stay in touch regardless of time and space.

The Spanish 'Costas' in particular can offer enhanced wellbeing to older migrants, with a Mediterranean climate and lower living costs, combined with a well-established infrastructure catering to the needs of British people. This can offer physical, social and even cultural wellbeing to migrants. This infrastructure includes scores of purpose-built tourist and residential complexes, known as 'urbanisations', which have their own shops and restaurants that cater to British tastes, as well as personal service outlets that sell British products (King *et al.* 2000; O'Reilly 2000). There is also a vast array of British-run social clubs, which feature heavily in the social lives of retired migrants. Urbanisations are host to large British communities, who tend to be segregated from the local Spanish population. As such, levels of integration are generally low among older British people in Spain, with most speaking little or no Spanish and rarely interacting on more than a casual basis with Spanish people (Hall and Hardill 2016; O'Reilly 2000).

Many retired British people choose not to register their presence in Spain, making it difficult to know how many are living there. Spanish registry data, therefore, underestimate the number of older retirees in Spain. Figures from 2015 indicate that there are 161,306 registered British citizens over the age of 55 living in Spain, of whom 104,368 are over the age of 65 (Instituto Nacional de Estadística 2015). However, when non-registration is taken into account, it is estimated that there are around half a million British people over the age of 50 living in Spain, with 14 per cent of those being over 70 (Finch *et al.* 2010; Sriskandarajah and Drew 2006).

Older people choose not to register in Spain for two main reasons. The first is so that they can retain access to the British National Health Service and welfare system (as soon as someone registers as living in Spain they lose their entitlement to most welfare services in the UK; Coldron and Ackers 2007). Second, the lifestyles of many retired migrants are highly flexible and mobile, with some retirees calling multiple places 'home'. In addition, retired migrants may start off as holiday-makers, then become second-home owners, and finally make a permanent move to Spain following retirement. Retirement migration is, therefore, rarely a single move from one country to another, but may involve constant movement back and forth between the country of origin and the country of migration (as well as other places).

Subsequently, the growing body of literature on lifestyle migration recognises such forms of movement as an 'ongoing quest' in search of enhanced well-being or a better way of life (Benson 2011). Cohen *et al.* (2015), therefore, do not talk about lifestyle migration, but 'lifestyle mobilities'; while lifestyle migration indicates a move from one country to another, they instead refer to an ongoing lifestyle choice and mobility that blur the boundaries between travel, leisure and migration. This is especially the case for retired migrants, who are not constrained to a particular place by paid work and, subject to their financial means, have the opportunity to engage in onward mobility or to return at any time.

As a result, older British migrants in Spain have been labelled 'transmigrants', as they belong to two or more countries at the same time (Gustafson 2001; Hall and Hardill 2016; O'Reilly 2000). Their social relationships and personal attachments may span different countries, and their ongoing mobility practices may enable them to spend time in different locations. They may have multiple dwellings and create a 'home' in more than one place, so that their lifestyles and identities transcend the boundaries of multiple countries (Eimermann 2014). This involves not only travel back and forth between Spain and the UK but also the exchange of resources and information – including simple exchanges like someone bringing tea bags from the UK back to Spain for a friend. The concept of transnationalism has, therefore, grown out of a recognition that migrants do not necessarily substitute old homes for new in a straightforward transfer, but often create active fields between the two (Glick Schiller 2004). Transnational network theory can, therefore, help us to understand the increasingly fluid lifestyles of migrants, which span spatial and temporal boundaries and involve the flow of people as well as goods and cultural practices between the sending and receiving countries (Glick Schiller 2004; Wright 2012).

For the younger, healthy retired migrants, it was possible to live transnational lifestyles, and many split their time between Spain and the UK, returning regularly to visit family and friends. Those with the financial means had the advantage of owning homes in both countries, allowing them increased flexibility in their living arrangements. This was explained by one of our interviewees, a charity worker in Spain:

Many [retired migrants] have more than one home. That's because their financial state allowed them to have those two homes, and secondly, that may mean that they haven't really made the decision to move to Spain. They want the lifestyle when they want it, but they always want a safety-net at home, and they are very well off, they can afford it.

This level of flexibility and mobility was seen as a route to emotional, physical and social wellbeing. However, the onset of old age can also place a considerable constraint on post-retirement mobility. As migrants age, increased frailty and bodily decline result in greater immobility and physical and mental constraints. Age, therefore, brings a distinct dimension to mobility research; rather than a return move being part of ongoing mobilities, a return move for frail, vulnerable older migrants is often finite and indicates the end of their lifestyle and identity as a migrant.

There has been an increase in the return migration of older British people from Spain to the UK over the last decade or so. Return is often undertaken following the onset of advanced old age and is now evident within the baby boom population, who were the first generation to retire to Spain in the post-Franco era from the late 1980s. They are increasingly returning to the UK to access care and support in their old age. These reasons for return are discussed below, but first, we draw on Spanish registry data to explore the number of British older returnees from Spain.

Accurate statistics on the number of older people returning are even more difficult to obtain than the number living in Spain (Giner-Monfort *et al.* 2016). Difficulties arise as return migrants may not inform their local authority in Spain that they have moved out, and even fewer declare where they have moved to. Thus, even if we know someone has left Spain, it is not always clear whether they have returned to the UK or moved elsewhere. Spanish registry data do, however, include the return migration of those who register, and indicate that there are growing numbers of older British returnees, with 4,339 registered British people over the age of 55 returning to the UK between 2008 and 2013 (Instituto Nacional de Estadística 2015). Over 15,000 more British people over the age of 55 left Spain in this period, but the destination was unknown (although it can be assumed that many of them returned to the UK). The number of older returnees peaked in 2013, with 1,744 returnees to the UK reported in that year compared with only 236 in 2008.

Return migration is having a considerable effect on some towns and villages in Spain with large populations of British residents. In particular, those who remain in Spain lose vital social and support networks as their friends and neighbours return to the UK. Research by Giner (2015) indicates that 8 per cent of the older British population of one Spanish town returned to the UK between 2008 and 2013. He also found that 59 per cent of the same population would consider a return move, indicating the large return migration potential in some areas. The number of British returnees in 2013 also vastly exceeded the number of new arrivals, at a scale of 364 returns for every 100 arrivals (Giner 2015).

Therefore, the population of older British people in Spain appears to be declining.[1] The next section explores the reasons why older British people are returning to the UK from Spain.

To stay or to go? Reasons for return

While the initial move to Spain was undertaken as a means to enhance wellbeing, a change in physical or social circumstances has led some migrants to seek higher wellbeing by returning to the UK. Our interviewees indicated three key reasons for returning that are explored here: returning for care, returning for social support and returning for financial reasons. Migration scholars have indicated that international migrants tend to retain strong transnational bonds with their country of origin, and their daily-life activities and relationships often encapsulate both the country of migration and the country of origin (Glick Schiller 2004; Gustafson 2001). Furthermore, lifestyle migration can frequently involve ongoing mobility between the country of migration and the country of origin. However, making the decision to return to the UK permanently was not a straightforward process, as it effectively ended the migration journey. Return migration, therefore, involves the complex interplay of structural, social and individual emotional factors (Cassarino 2004). These include financial resources, social integration and networks, and individual expectations and aspirations.

For older migrants, the main reason for return is to access care and support in the country of origin. Evidence suggests that care features prominently in the reason for a return move, and the main reason older British people return from EU destinations is to use the national health and social care systems of their home country (Ackers and Dwyer 2002; Hall and Hardill 2016; Warnes *et al.* 1999). While British state pensioners are entitled to access health and care services in Spain to the same level as a Spanish national, there are considerable differences in the health and care systems between Spain and the UK. The most significant structural difference is the existence of a family model of care in Spain compared with a more individualist British model – meaning that in Spain, older people are largely the responsibility of the extended family rather than the state. Subsequently, there is very little state-funded care (community or institutional) in Spain, as explained by one female interviewee aged 79: 'When you come out of hospital, it doesn't matter how ill you are, you are on your own'.

Those who are fully integrated and speak Spanish appear much less likely to return, as they are in a better position to navigate health, care and support services in Spain. Having Spanish friends can also help, as they can be a vital source of support in navigating the bureaucracy and services, as well as providing translation during times of need. For those who do not speak Spanish (most of our interviewees), navigating health and care services can be extremely challenging, resulting in a negative impact on health and wellbeing.

Language and cultural differences cause two key problems: they prevent people from obtaining care in the first place; and if care is obtained, they cause communication barriers between the carer and the person needing care. While previous research indicates that many doctors do speak English in areas of Spain with large numbers of British migrants (King *et al.* 2000), our findings indicate that this is not always the case, and many interviewees could not access English-speaking doctors within the state-funded health and social care services. While translators are available, they may charge and will also be of limited use during hospital stays or for care at home. Therefore, when British migrants in Spain have complex care needs, they may find that they need to return to the UK. Therefore, the structural context of the welfare state and healthcare services can play a significant role in determining return migration decisions.

Experiences of lifestyle migration associated with living the 'good life' (Benson and O'Reilly 2009) can therefore change in the context of ageing and bodily decline. Health factors are often the initial stimulant for return; however, other, often related factors can become apparent following the onset of old age. This includes returning in order to reactivate personal social networks of friends and family who can provide care and support during old age. While scholars have highlighted the globalised and transnational nature of care networks (Baldassar 2014; Lawson 2007), providing care at a distance is not straightforward (Hall and Hardill 2016). Extended family ties, therefore, feature highly in the return reasoning for migrants of all ages (Eimermann 2014), but may be even more important for older, vulnerable people. Informal social support from family and friends is especially important in coping with a crisis, such as a rapid decline in health or the death of a partner. The socio-spatial context of migration, therefore, becomes important here, as the family of most retired migrants in Spain live in the UK. Returning to be close to family in the UK was cited as a key reason for return:

> We were very happy with living in Spain but unfortunately we are returning to the UK because my partner has the beginnings of dementia and I have heart problems. We have found the health care in Spain is good but our family have insisted that we return to the UK especially as there is little help for someone with dementia and we can't speak sufficient Spanish to access what little help there is, so we have decided our family are right, we will sell and return to the UK.
>
> (male interviewee in Spain, aged 71)

Returning to be near to family may either result directly from care needs or may be due to a more indirect pull, including, for example, the birth of a grandchild. Our findings indicated gender differences in return motivations, especially when it comes to returning for family reasons. Women in our study were much more likely to want to return to be close to family and especially grandchildren, as an interviewee from a charity in Spain explained:

> People tend to miss their grandchildren very much and that can ultimately be what takes them back. And there is usually ... one partner who wants to do that. The other one normally says: 'we can go there sometimes, and we

can see how it goes'. I see that is the greatest reason … and it is usually the woman who wants to go back and support the family.

Some of the older migrants in our study were able to create 'transnational families' (Baldassar 2014) through active participation in cross-border social activities and exchanges, to which children are often central. Transnational social networks were linked to wellbeing and could be achieved through visits, communication technology and social media, which, for some, allowed ongoing relationships with their families and especially grandchildren living in the UK. 'Transnational social fields' (Glick Schiller 2004), therefore, generate support and appear crucial to the enhancement of wellbeing in this case. However, other migrants felt that 'virtual communication' was not sufficient and subsequently experienced homesickness and a general decline in their social relationships with friends and relatives living in the UK. This, for some, had a negative impact on their wellbeing:

> Skype is wonderful but is no substitute for a hug. I think that you have to be a bit selfish and hard to cope with not being with the family. Homesickness is the price you pay for doing your own thing. Unless you make frequent flights back you will miss out on family occasions – happy and sad. I am sure that homesickness is a major factor in the decision of many expats who choose to go back to the UK.
>
> (blog post)

> I met a lady who said she had never bonded with her new grandchild as she lived in Spain and the baby was born in the UK.
>
> (blog post)

For these interviewees, return was undertaken to re-engage social networks and relationships. This was often based around the idea of 'home' being where family are based. Bolognani (2014) refers to romanticised imaginings and affective ideas of coming home, which, Eimermann (2014) argues, can gain momentum in return migration reasoning. Those who held these idealised images of UK as being 'home' often struggled to be happy in Spain. As also indicated by Betty and Hall (2014), some of our interviewees felt a longing for family, which resulted in loneliness and isolation, especially for women:

> Since I was divorced and living on my own I have become very lonely. Yes, my sons in the UK keep in touch with me by email and telephone calls, I have recently found out that the cancer which I had was in remission and now it has returned, so I will return to the UK so that I can be near my family. This will mean that I won't be lonely and I can get treatment in the UK.
>
> (female interviewee in Spain, 68)

The above-noted gender differences in return motivations can also potentially cause tension between couples when one wants to stay and the other wants to return. Prior research on the role of gender in migration decisions has been mixed, with some indicating that women are more likely to want to return (Burgelt *et al.* 2008), which supports our own findings; while other research indicates that women are more reluctant than men to return to their country of origin (Bocker and Gehring 2015). Other research indicates a relationship between decisions to migrate and preferences for return. For example, Burgelt *et al.* (2008) found that women may go along with their husband's decision to migrate in the first place, and as a result are more likely to experience poor well-being following migration and ultimately want to return. For those couples who cannot reach a decision about whether to stay or return, the result can be separation, as explained by one female interviewee:

> My husband retired and said England has had it and I am going to live in Spain. I said what about me? He said it's up to you. I thought I would find a place to live but as I hadn't a pension of my own I had to go with him. Since living in Spain I have been back to England many times to find a place to live – couldn't do it. I was told I shouldn't live alone and a care home is where I should go because I have cancer.

The final reason for return explored here relates to economic factors. Links between care and financial hardship have been previously noted (Betty and Hall 2014; Hall and Hardill 2016), and, as our interviewees indicated, paying for private care in Spain when state-funded care services are unavailable can quickly deplete financial resources. Furthermore, fluctuations in the value of the euro against the pound can impact on return decisions. Since 2008, the number of returnees may have also increased as a result of the recent economic crisis, as the value of the euro has sunk against the pound (Huete *et al.* 2013; Roberts 2013) and costs have risen.

> As the years have gone by, people that grow older, and because of the financial crisis money has to last longer, and the lifestyle that they had when they retired, is not now as it was.
>
> (charity representative in Spain)

> I dreamt of living out the rest of my days at my apartment in the sunshine. That dream has turned sour as every day I am consumed with total worry as I simply don't have enough money to live on. The pension's not enough and I can't receive more from the State so I must go back to the UK.
>
> (female interviewee, Spain, 65)

Therefore, the economic crisis (Huete *et al.* 2013), coupled with a general increase in costs of living in Spain, has led to a general decline in spending power. Some older migrants face financial hardship, while others have been forced to reduce their 'luxury' spending, including that on social and recreational activities, which ultimately has a negative impact on their social wellbeing. For some of our interviewees, returning to the UK was a rational financial decision made as a route to access financial support, including pension credit and housing benefits:

> I am finding it more and more difficult to manage on my pension plus my savings are rapidly disappearing. Electricity has gone up, the general cost of living has also risen. My community fees have increased. It seems that everything I need to enjoy my retirement in Spain has also gone up, so I intend to return to the UK where I may be able to get some help.
>
> (female interviewee, Spain, 78)

What is evident from the above discussion is that return migration can be either part of the retirement 'plan', and therefore pre-ordained and voluntary, or more 'forced' as a route to care or financial support in the wake of a crisis. There has been a clear distinction in the migration literature between 'forced' and 'voluntary' migration. While this normally refers to asylum-seekers and refugees (e.g. Castles 2003), we argue that similar distinctions can be applied within the context of lifestyle migration, ageing and wellbeing. While not 'forced' in the same way as those seeking refuge from war or persecution, retired lifestyle migrants may feel forced to return to the UK to seek welfare and support in their old age. There were clear links between return and wellbeing, with some people making the positive decision to return as they felt it was the right option for them following a change in their circumstances; as Ackers and Dwyer (2002) note, a return move for care may feature highly in the retirement 'plan' for older people living abroad. For other migrants, returning was not a plan as such, but presented itself as the result of a crisis and declining wellbeing in Spain. This included those who could no longer live independently but had no support systems in place. The following section, therefore, considers the level of choice and control exercised by older migrants when returning to the UK.

Return: a natural outcome or failed migration project?

Migration theories refer to return migration as either a 'failed migration experience' or as the 'natural outcome' of a successful migration project (Cassarino 2004). Referring to labour migrants, neoclassical economics sees return migration as a failure in the migration experience when the outcomes of migration do not live up to expectations. This is arguably linked to a lack of pre-migration planning, which, for retired migrants, may include a lack of planning for old age, especially a decline in health. Conversely, new economics of labour migration theories refer to return migration as the 'logical outcome of a calculated strategy' following the successful achievement of goals as part of a well-prepared migration project (Cassarino 2004: 256). Applying this to retired migrants, return migration can form part of the 'retirement project' for people who never intended to move permanently. Return migration from this perspective can be seen as being the 'natural' end-stage in the migration process and as constituting 'homecoming' (see Koliatis *et al.* 2003).

For some interviewees, returning to the UK was entirely voluntary and part of the retirement 'plan'. Return was undertaken by choice through the exercising of agency and linked to the enhancement of wellbeing that could be obtained from a lifestyle in the UK at a particular life-stage. Such 'strategic return reasoning' (Eimermann 2014) can form part of the flexible and mobile lifestyles undertaken by retired migrants and is highly indicative of lifestyle mobility – an ongoing journey with no clear end-point. Some of our interviewees talked about their life in Spain as a 'trial', and return was always on the cards:

> I think at some point I will have to go back to the UK but I knew that when I came here. But if we get some really nice weather and this arthritis eases up and I am able to do a bit more, I think I will leave it until next year ... I have put myself on trial to see if I am any better here in Spain than I was in England.
>
> (female interviewee, Spain, 68)

On the other hand, some of our interviewees felt 'forced' to return to the UK as a consequence of a considerable and rapid decline in health in either themselves or their partner. These 'forced' returnees tended to be those who experienced a crisis and, due to insufficient preparation or thinking ahead, had no coping strategies in place to deal with it. This can be linked to a mismatch between expectations and reality and has been termed 'post-migration ambivalence' (Benson and O'Reilly 2009; Eimermann 2014). For some of our interviewees, the expectations of care and welfare support in Spain did not live up to the reality; they expected a variety of care and other support services, but later realised that in Spain, the welfare system is less generous than in the UK, mainly because it is based on the 'South European model' of family-based care. Subsequently, they experienced a shock when they needed care or financial support for the first time, and it was not readily available to them. While some older migrants who experienced a decline in health made the decision to return, others were more reluctant to return, as explained by a charity worker in Spain:

> People phone me and they say they don't know what to do, and they think they ought to go back to the UK. And then, they say: 'or just wait and see if things get better'. Even when I talk to people from England and they are in Spain, I can tell on the phone things are not going to get better. It's a pipedream.

Returning for healthcare was tied up with returning for the practical and emotional care that could be provided by families in the UK. For those without family support in the UK, returning for health reasons was even more traumatic:

> A lot of the problems that we encounter is the fact that the people who don't have family in the UK feel they're going into a big black hole, and there's nobody to hold their hand or help them.
>
>   (charity representative, Spain)

Being forced to return made these respondents feel highly vulnerable, and had a considerable impact on their wellbeing. This includes unhappiness upon return and difficulties in reintegrating into the country of origin. Return migration has been linked by Cassarino (2004) to preparation and resilience. Vathi and Duci (2016) refer to some migrants as active agents in defining what for them is a crisis and in employing strategies to counter the negative effects of crises by developing strategies of resilience. Applying this to the retired migrants in this study, we found that those who were active agents in developing coping strategies for the negative effects of old age (including putting care and support in place) generally had a more positive wellbeing experience in old age and were able to choose whether to stay or return. Therefore, for some, this involved a planned return to the UK; and for those who did not want to return, the ability to stay in Spain was facilitated by appropriate care and support plans in place for old age. For some, this was provided by family who lived in Spain, while others had prepared for old age by exploring and establishing a care 'plan' such as finding sheltered accommodation (although this was quite expensive and was only available to those with a property or other financial assets). On the other hand, older migrants who were not active agents in anticipating and preparing for old age (or did not have the financial means to pay for care) were the most likely to encounter an unwanted return to the UK.

The process of return and reintegration

This section looks at how older migrants cope upon return to the UK, as well as the actual process of returning, which for some can be physically, emotionally and financially traumatic. We focus here on rights to welfare and support upon return, selling/buying property, and the social and emotional consequences of reintegration.

Structural constraints on return

Returning to the UK is not always straightforward. Residency restrictions, as well as the emotional and physical impacts of returning, can result in significant challenges to wellbeing for returnees. For example, accessing immediate support upon return to the UK can be difficult due to complex UK residency restrictions. Our interviewees referred to the 'safety-net' of the UK, and most assumed that, as they were British nationals, there was a range of welfare agencies waiting to offer support when they returned. However, in reality, if a British national decides to return to the UK permanently after taking up residency abroad, they may not be automatically eligible for any support. In order to claim income-related benefits (e.g. housing benefits or pension credit), someone must both have a right to reside and be 'habitually resident'. While returning British citizens automatically have the right to reside, to be classed as 'habitually resident' they must pass the Habitual Residence Test like any new immigrant to the UK. The Habitual Residency Test was introduced in August 1994, and only those who can demonstrate that they have a settled intention to stay can pass it.

Depending on individual circumstances, passing the Habitual Residency Test can take from as little as a few days to three months, and then applications for benefits can take an additional two to three weeks. For those returning for care, it can also be difficult to access care and support services immediately upon arrival, as any claimants must be living in the UK – i.e. applications should not be made from Spain. Even once they are living in the UK, there are long waiting lists for Social Services assistance, and new returnees may not be given priority. Therefore, the safety-net of the British welfare state was an unrealistic expectation for returnees, again demonstrating the tension between expectations and reality for returning migrants.

The financial impact of returning

As outlined above, contextual financial factors can trigger a return, including returning to the UK to access the British welfare system and its allied financial benefits. However, we also found that direct financial factors can play a considerable role in the actual process of return. In addition to the costs associated with returning (e.g. transport of possessions, cost of the flights), the property market in both countries was found to play a significant role in facilitating or obstructing return. A weak economy and a depressed property market in Spain posed a massive challenge for some of the returnees in our research. Many interviewees spoke of facing difficulties with selling their property in Spain and being forced to drop the selling price and lose money. A boom in the UK property market over the past few decades further exacerbates the financial consequences of this.

People who have lived in Spain for many years were unlikely to see the financial return on their property in Spain that they would have seen in the UK. Some were forced to downsize upon return to the UK or relocate to a different geographical area from the one they left, which had a negative impact on their wellbeing. One interviewee explained that, to return to the same village she had left around 15 years before, she would need financial help from her daughters:

> This house won't pay for a maisonette in England. The village I want to be in … It is about 200,000 for a one-bedroom. I want a two because [daughter] is going to help me. When I sell this, she is going to sell up to

give me the money to put towards the 100,000 to help me buy a place and then my two daughters want to try and have a small mortgage to pay the rest for me.

(female interviewee, Spain, 79)

Some of our interviewees who intended to return became 'stuck' in Spain due to the financial constraints associated with the property market. One lady explained that following the death of her husband she decided to return to be close to family and friends; however, when she looked into the value of her property in Spain and what her financial resources would buy her in the UK, she subsequently made the decision to stay:

I wouldn't be able to afford to go back. And certainly not into where I want to go because they are very, very expensive, very expensive, so I am afraid I will have to spend my last years here.

(female interviewee, Spain, 78)

For some people, the UK was seen as a safe haven both for welfare support and in terms of the property market, especially during times of economic crisis:

I think more and more are realising, especially during these times of crisis, that the UK isn't such a bad place if you are left with nothing. People have learnt they are very much on their own. Unfortunately, for some it is already too late, they are stuck in a country that they cannot escape due to the inability to sell property. Some have just thrown the keys into the bank and gone home.

(blog post)

Therefore, while viewed as a safety-net, the UK does not provide the plethora of welfare benefits and support expected by some returning migrants. In fact, retired British migrants are subject to many of the same regulations as all new immigrants to the UK, as discussed above.

Returning to a life that no longer exists

Upon returning to the UK, some older migrants reintegrate successfully and are able to re-establish meaningful ties with friends and family. The following quote from an older returnee couple highlights a situation where returning was the right decision and one that led to their enhanced wellbeing:

We have settled down nicely thank you and not missing Spain at all. We have had a lovely summer in the UK so it's not about the weather but being where we belong.

(male interviewee, UK, 71)

For some returnees, their social capital and networks are larger in the UK than in Spain, and these interviewees generally refer to 'home' as where their family live. Therefore, transnational networks, especially family relationships, are important facilitators for return. However, for others, the imagined return does not match up to the reality. Eimermann (2014) argues that imagined geographies of home can create high expectations of 'home' upon return; however, these may not be realised. Migrants are often ill prepared for their return, as they do not realise how their home country and personal relationships have changed since they left (Gmelch 1980: 143). Friends and family left behind have often moved on and developed new relationships and friendship groups, and so are not always enthusiastic about resuming old ties. This is referred to as 'reverse culture shock' (Kenny 1976; King 1977), after which some return migrants may consider re-migrating (Cassarino 2004; Gmelch 1980). Cassarino (2004) found that those migrants who are transnational and have retained ties with people in the home country are more likely to successfully reintegrate upon return. Conversely, those who do not retain links with the country of origin are often 'helpless' upon their return (Cassarino 2004: 260). This was explained by a charity representative:

> If we have a situation where usually the person is on their own, they may have relatives in the UK who may be very supportive and come over and help out. They may have relatives in the UK who want nothing to do with the person. You know? 'You have chosen to live in Spain? That's your problem'.

We also spoke to older returnees who returned to the UK because they missed family and friends or because of pressure from family to return; however, upon return, the returnees found that they had themselves moved on and started to remember why they had left the UK in the first place.

Conclusion

This chapter has explored the return migration of a subset of lifestyle migrants: those who are older and retired, many of whom are facing a decline in health and are in need of care and additional support. It has explored both the triggers and the consequences of return for these migrants and the impact this has on psychosocial wellbeing. While migration scholars have been researching return migration for many decades (Cassarino 2004; Gmelch 1980; King 1977), this has tended to focus on younger working-age migrants and the economic impacts of their return, while older migrants have been largely ignored.

The reasons for and experiences of migration for retired migrants are different from those of younger economic migrants. Retirees are not constrained by the need to work, and so migration is more flexible and provides an opportunity to seek new opportunities, a better quality of life and improved wellbeing through ongoing mobility (Benson and O'Reilly 2009). However, as retired migrants become older, a decline in health and increasing dependence and frailty bring increasing immobility. Therefore, even within the subset of retired migrants, there are distinct differences between younger (third-age) and older (fourth-age) migrants. Older migrants experience a gradual decline in emotional, physical and social wellbeing as a result of bodily decline, poor health and bereavement. This may force them to re-evaluate their lifestyles and their identity as a migrant, and therefore their country of residence. For many, return migration was used as a strategy to enhance emotional, physical and social wellbeing in older age.

For older migrants, care needs were the strongest driver of return. This was to access care services in the UK that were not available in Spain, or to be close to family. While transnational family care-giving from a distance may be appropriate for younger migrants, as Baldassar (2014) argues, there are stages in the life course when family need to physically 'be there'. This is especially the case during times of chronic illness, particularly during advanced old age, when hands-on care and immediate emotional care are the only way to satisfy wellbeing for both migrants and their family back home (Baldassar 2014).

We found that those who had retained strong ties with the UK, socially and culturally, were the most likely to return out of choice. Returning home to 'where one belongs' was part of the migration 'plan'. Those who felt forced to return were less likely to have maintained relationships with family and friends in the UK. Transnational connections are, therefore, important facilitators for return, and return is strongly related to social capital in both the country of origin and the destination country (Eimermann 2014). Returning to be close to family was often the natural end to the migration experience, but for those with little or no family, return was often unwanted and was seen as a failed migration project (Cassarino 2004). Return was, instead, structural: a route to care and financial support that was not available through the welfare state in Spain.

Transnationalism also plays a vital role in post-return belonging. Return is often not as simple as just 'going home', as feelings of belonging need to be renegotiated upon return (De Bree *et al.* 2010). Those who had maintained transnational ties were likely to reintegrate quickly; however, the high expectations of 'home' may not live up to the reality for some. Indeed, the 'home' left behind may have changed, and the return migrants themselves were likely to have changed. This disjuncture between expectations and reality upon return can have a negative impact on wellbeing, as a return move can be physically, emotionally and financially draining. The amount of agency exercised in the return decision has also been found to impact on creating a sense of home post return (De Bree *et al.* 2010), and so those forced to return when they could not access care or support in Spain were the least likely to reintegrate easily. This was likely to have a further detrimental impact on their health.

Structural barriers to health and care services caused further problems for returnees: as we have outlined, it is usually not possible to access care or financial benefits immediately upon arrival in the UK. As also recognised by Davies *et al.* (2011: 2), there is a gap in policies and programmes to address the health needs of returning migrants, and the UK does little to support the well-being of older migrants, including elderly British citizens who need immediate care or other support. Scholars have begun to consider migrants' preparation, coping strategies and resilience in relation to return migration (Vathi and Duci 2016), and it is important that policy-makers also consider the wellbeing of returnees.

Note

1 Whether this decline will continue in the light of Brexit and the fall in the value of the pound sterling remains to be seen, but seems likely.

References

Ackers, L. and Dwyer, P. (2002) *Senior Citizenship? Retirement, Migration and Welfare in the European Union.* Bristol: Policy Press.

Attride-Stirling, J. (2001) Thematic networks: an analytic tool for qualitative research, *Qualitative Research* 1(3): 385–405.

Baldassar, L. (2014) Too sick to move: distant 'crisis' care in transnational families, *International Review of Sociology* 24(3): 391–405.

Benson, M. (2011) The movement beyond (lifestyle) migration: mobile practices and the constitution of a better way of life, *Mobilities* 6(2): 221–235.

Benson, M. and O'Reilly, K. (eds) (2009) *Lifestyle Migration: Expectations, Aspirations and Experiences.* Aldershot: Ashgate.

Betty, C. and Hall, K. (2014) The myth of no return? Why British migrants return to the UK, in K. Torkington, I. David and J. Sardinha (eds) *Practising the Good Life: Lifestyle Migration in Practice.* Newcastle: Cambridge Scholars Publishing, 123–137.

Bocker, A. and Gehring, A. (2015) Returning 'home' after retirement? The role of gender in return migration decisions of Spanish and Turkish migrants, *Review of Social Studies* 2(1): 77–98.

Bolognani, M. (2014) The emergence of lifestyle reasoning in return considerations among British Pakistanis, *International Migration* 52(6): 31–42.

Burgelt, P., Morgan, M. and Pernice, R. (2008) Staying or returning: pre-migration influences on the migration process of German migrants to New Zealand, *Journal of Community and Applied Social Psychology* 18(4): 282–298.

Casado-Diaz, M. (2009) Social capital in the sun: bonding and bridging social capital among British retirees. In Benson, M. and O'Reilly, K. eds. *Lifestyle Migration: Expectations, Aspirations and Experiences.* Aldershot: Ashgate, 87–102.

Cassarino, J.P. (2004) Theorising return migration: the conceptual approach to return migration revisited, *International Journal on Multicultural Societies* 6(2): 253–279.

Castles, S. (2003) Towards a sociology of forced migration and social transformation, *Sociology* 37(1): 13–34.

Cohen, S.A., Duncan, T. and Thulemark, M. (2015) Lifestyle mobilities: the crossroads of travel, leisure and migration, *Mobilities* 10(1): 155–172.

Coldron, K. and Ackers, L. (2007) (Ab) Using European citizenship? EU retired migrants and the exercise of healthcare rights, *Maastricht Journal of European and Comparative Law* 14(3): 287–302.

Davies, A., Borland, R., Blake, C. and West, H. (2011) The dynamics of health and return migration, *PLoS Med* 8(6): 1–4.

De Bree, J., Davids, T. and De Haas, H. (2010) Post-return experiences and transnational belonging of return migrants: a Dutch–Moroccan case study, *Global Networks* 10(4): 489–509.

Dodge, R., Daly, A., Huyton, J. and Sanders, L. (2012) The challenge of defining wellbeing, *International Journal of Wellbeing* 2(3): 222–235.

Eimermann, M. (2014) Flying Dutchmen? Return reasoning among Dutch lifestyle migrants in rural Sweden, *Mobilities*, doi: 10.1080/17450101.2014.980128.

Finch, T., Andrew, H. and Latorre, M. (2010) *Global Brit: Making the Most of the British Diaspora*. London: Institute for Public Policy Research.

Giner, J. (2015) Retorn de Persones Retirades d'Origin Britanic Residents a la Marina Alta. València: PhD thesis, University of València.

Giner-Monfort, J., Hall, K. and Betty, C. (2016) Back to Brit: retired British migrants returning from Spain, *Journal of Ethnic and Migration Studies* 42(5): 797–815.

Glick Schiller, N. (2004) Transnationality, in D. Nugent and J. Vincent (eds) *A Companion to Anthropology of Politics*. London: Blackwell, 448–467.

Gmelch, G. (1980) Return migration, *Annual Review of Anthropology* 9: 135–159.

Gough, I. and McGregor, J.A. (eds) (2007) *Wellbeing in Developing Countries*. Cambridge: Cambridge University Press.

Gustafson, P. (2001) Retirement migration and transnational lifestyles, *Ageing and Society* 21(4): 371–394.

Hall, K. and Hardill, I. (2016) Retirement migration, the 'other' story: caring for frail elderly British citizens in Spain, *Ageing and Society* 6(3): 562–585.

Huete, R., Mantecon, A. and Estevez, J. (2013) Challenges in lifestyle migration: reflections and findings about the Spanish crisis, *Mobilities* 8(3): 331–348.

Instituto Nacional de Estadística (2015) *Explotación Estadística del Padrón* (Register Statistical Analysis) www.ine.es/jaxi/tabla.do?path=/t20/e245/p04/a2014/l1/&file=00000008. px&type=pcaxis&L=1. Accessed April 2015.

Kenny, M. (1976) Twentieth century Spanish expatriate ties with the homeland: remigration and its consequences, in J. Aceves and W. Douglass (eds) *The Changing Faces of Rural Spain*. New York: Schenkman, 97–121.

King, R. (1977) Problems of return migration: case study of Italians returning from Britain, *Tijdschrift voor Economische en Sociale Geografie* 68(4): 241–245.

King, R., Warnes, T. and Williams, A. (2000) *Sunset Lives: British Retirement Migration to the Mediterranean*. Oxford: Berg.

Koliatis, G., Tsiantis, J. and Madianos, M. (2003) Psychosocial adaptation of immigrant Greek children from the former Soviet Union, *European Child and Adolescent Psychiatry* 12(2): 67–74.

Laslett, P. (1991) *A Fresh Map of Life: The Emergence of the Third Age*. Cambridge, MA: Harvard University Press.

Lawson, V. (2007) Geographies of care and responsibility, *Annals of the Association of American Geographers* 97(1): 1–11.

O'Reilly, K. (2000) *The British on the Costa del Sol: Transnational Identities and Local Communities*. London: Routledge.

Roberts, E. (2013) The expat boom turns into a boomerang. *The Telegraph*, 28 May.

Rogers, C. (1961). *On Becoming a Person*. Boston: Houghton Mifflin.

Ryff, C. and Singer, B. (2008) Know thyself and become what you are: a eudaimonic approach to psychological wellbeing, *Journal of Happiness Studies* 9(1): 13–39.

Sriskandarajah, D. and Drew, C. (2006) *Brits Abroad: Mapping the Scale and Nature of British Emigration*. London: Institute for Public Policy Research.

Vathi, Z. and Duci, V. (2016) Making other dreams: the impact of migration on the psychosocial wellbeing of Albanian-origin children and young people upon return to Albania, *Childhood* 23(1): 53–68.

Warnes, A.M., King, R., Williams, A. and Patterson, G. (1999) The well-being of British expatriate retirees in southern Europe, *Ageing and Society* 19(6): 717–740.

Wright, K. (2012) Constructing human wellbeing across spatial boundaries: negotiating meanings in transnational migration, *Global Networks* 12(4): 467–484.

14 'Is this really where home is?'

Experiences of home in a revisited homeland among ageing Azorean returnees

Dora Sampaio

Introduction

While the challenges faced by immigrants in the host country have been extensively explored, much less has been written about the difficulties return migrants encounter when they return to their homeland (King 1978; Percival 2013). Whereas this lack of research can be linked to the assumption that, once immigrants return to their home country, they easily blend back into the local community they were once part of, several studies seem to suggest that migrants experience significant readjustment challenges when they return 'home' (Ní Laoire 2008a, 2008b; Tannenbaum 2007). Drawing from King's claim that 'return migration is the great unwritten chapter in the history of migration' (2000: 7), the fact that return migration in later life seems to be a particularly untouched subject is definitely a paradox needing to be solved in an era of ageing and ever-increasing mobility (Percival 2013; Warnes *et al.* 2004; Warnes and Williams 2006). Framed within this debate, and following from Gualda and Escriva's (2012) suggestion about the importance of better understanding the personal and social adjustments that migrants face upon return, especially at a later stage of life, this chapter explores the integration paths, experiences of home, and psychosocial wellbeing among ageing Azorean returnees. Taking a geographical perspective, I also delve into the role of place and of the multiple spatialities of home in shaping the integration process back in the homeland. My analysis is based on 36 in-depth life narrative interviews with ageing migrants who have relocated to the Azores, a Portuguese archipelago in the North Atlantic. Most of them are returning from the US and Canada, but a minority are moving back from Bermuda and Brazil.

Although the discussion is built upon the totality of information collected, a set of nine particularly insightful narratives are explored in further detail throughout the chapter. Bearing in mind the subjectivity inherent in the social construction of 'contentment' or 'wellbeing' (Black *et al.* 2004), particular attention is drawn to four dimensions: physical/material, health, psychosocial, and place attachment and belonging. The linkages between each one of these dimensions and the migrants' psychosocial wellbeing are especially touched upon throughout the chapter. As for the nine selected case histories, rather than representing hermetic categories, these stories aim to highlight a general tone within a particular narrative. Three such narrative types are distilled from the overall data and exemplified in the case studies. In some cases, the return 'home' represents successful self-realisation and the corollary of a hard-working life abroad, resulting in a deep sense of physical and emotional wellbeing. In others, loneliness and absence of family have led to narratives of disappointment and 'not quite belonging' (Ní Laoire 2008a). The third type is more complex and reflects ongoing changes resulting from major life events such as illness, the death of a spouse or the birth of a grandchild. As a result, an in-between situation arises, marked by a permanent renegotiation of 'here' and 'there' and a rehypothesising of later-in-life (im)mobility.

Having set the backdrop of the chapter, the following section provides a brief review of the literature on return, ageing and integration paths upon return; next, an overview of the Azorean migration context and a methodological section are outlined. The fourth section of the chapter – the longest – explores the multiple narratives of home among Azorean returnees. Concluding remarks are made on the complexities behind nuanced geographies of home, highlighting the role of individual, community and place-related dimensions in the different experiences and meanings of 'home' and wellbeing.

Experiences of home 'back home': return, ageing and multiple paths of integration

In a context of increasing international mobility, return migration can easily be described as a worldwide process, and, for the same reason, it consists of a stage, rather than necessarily the end, of the migration journey (Sussman 2000; Tannenbaum 2007). As suggested by different authors (Percival 2013; Stefansson 2004), it is crucial to further understand the reasons behind homecoming and integration upon return, particularly in later life. Indeed, as stressed by Gualda and Escriva (2012), older returnees add further complexity to the return phenomenon, given their often diverse financial, psychosocial and health conditions. To this could be added the challenges arising from rethinking ageing models back home and the socio-cultural challenges inherent in the redefinition of concepts of home and belonging (Percival 2013). In a seminal work, Gullahorn and Gullahorn (1963) suggested that return migrants are likely to experience periods of cultural shock upon return followed by acculturation and an affective, cognitive and socio-cultural readjustment to the homeland. While this theory certainly has the advantage of taking into account the fact that return often entails a period of disillusionment and readaptation, it has often been criticised for regarding return migration as an end-point per se (Percival 2013).

Looking particularly at the links between emigration and return, while some authors (e.g. Gualda and Escriva 2012) have stressed the positive association between a rapid integration abroad and a successful return experience, others (e.g. Tannenbaum 2007) contend that integration upon return is oftentimes a harder process due to the psychosocial changes experienced by the migrants while abroad and the confrontation between reality and idealised images of 'back home'. The idea of an 'inner compass' oriented towards the 'homeland' (Alsop 2002) can, therefore, often be blurred by the emigration and return experiences. As noted by Szkudlarek (2010) and Barrett and Mosca (2013), return migrants rarely anticipate (at least to the full extent) the readjustment challenges faced upon return, which often leads to feelings of estrangement back home. In addition, they tend to underestimate the impact of their experience abroad on their attitudes, behaviours and individual values (Sussman 2000), and are often seen as 'others' or 'newcomers' instead of 'homecomers' (Ní Laoire 2008a). The readjustment process can, in fact, seriously impact the physical and mental health of those who return, especially if no 'social field' (i.e. social networks of any kind) is available back home (Condon 2005).

Cases of physical debility, emotional distress, feelings of non-belonging and permanent shifting between 'here and there' have thus often been identified among return migrants (Alsop 2002; Cerase 1974; Christou 2006). While the dream of return is imbued in the geographies of home, there is a deep feeling of disappointment when the experience of return does not match the nostalgic and romanticised images of 'back home'. In light of this, a variety of studies (Barrett and Mosca 2013; Cerase 1974) have emphasised that the longer the period of time spent abroad, the harder the adaptation upon return. Other factors that seem to influence the degree of satisfaction and wellbeing back home include the experience of migration in the host country, frequency of contact/visit to the homeland, period of time since the return, and individual features such as gender and age. As highlighted by Gualda and Escriva (2012) in their study of return migrants to Andalusia, a key element in understanding migrants' contentment upon return is the relationship between objective and subjective or perceived wellbeing. According to Cerase (1974), different types of return migrants tend to follow different paths of integration back home. In his seminal work, Cerase identifies four types of returnees and links them to four different adaptation paths: *return of failure, return of conservatism, return of retirement* and *return of innovation. Return of conservatism*, including the migrants who never fully integrated into the host society and kept focused on working hard to afford a future return, and *return of retirement*, comprising the migrants who returned home to retire for either health, family or financial reasons, assume particular relevance in the Azorean case.

Adding to this scholarship, but focusing particularly on migrants' cultural identity, Sussman (2000) suggests that four types of identity shift can occur upon return: *subtractive, additive, affirmative* and *intercultural*. Especially important for the following discussion are the latter three. The *additive identity* is marked by a shift towards members and aspects of the host culture; the embracing of elements of the host society, even if also keeping the former identity, can lead to feelings of isolation and distress back home. The *affirmative identity* refers to preserving and strengthening the home culture while abroad; in this case, the differences between home and host societies are mostly unnoticed – this is, in Sussman's words, the 'grateful repatriate'. Finally, the *intercultural identity* alludes to migrants holding multiple cultural representations, leading, therefore, to low levels of distress back home and the search for a multicultural lifestyle. These identity shifts can be linked to different coping strategies upon return. The *intercultural identity* in particular seems to emerge as a sort of transnational living that can be related to Vertovec's concept of 'type of consciousness' – a mode of transnationalism characterised by dual or multiple identifications, a sense of being simultaneously 'home away from home' (1999: 450).

Home, away and back again: emigration and return to the Azores

The Azores is a Portuguese overseas territory (*Região Autónoma*) in the North Atlantic. The archipelago consists of nine islands located about 1,100 km from mainland Portugal and 3,200 km from New England, US. The islands have traditionally been characterised by geographical isolation and weak social ties with mainland Portugal, a fact that seems to have contributed to bolstering their links with the other side of the Atlantic (Williams and Fonseca 1999). This also helps to understand why the Azores have historically, since the nineteenth century, been a place of emigration. Although the islands have experienced migration outflows since the 1920s, in modern times, it was mostly from the early 1950s that emigration became significant. From the 1940s until the mid-1970s, the US stood out as the main destination for the Azoreans, followed by Canada and, in less significant numbers, Bermuda. From 1975 onwards there has been a gradual decline in the number of emigrants leaving the archipelago, especially with the end of the dictatorship in Portugal, the country's accession to the European Union in 1986, and the ensuing national and regional growth (Rocha *et al.* 2011).

Azorean migration to North America and Bermuda is linked to a desire to improve life from a material or financial point of view (Rocha *et al.* 2011). More localised in time, but not less importantly, natural disasters such as the volcanic eruptions and earthquakes in Faial Island in 1957 and in São Jorge Island in 1964 also contributed to the exodus from the Azores (Rocha *et al.* 2011; Williams and Fonseca 1999). In this context, the US Azorean Refugee Acts, extended until 1962, encouraged and fostered the arrival of Azorean migrants in the US. Three main features make the Azorean emigration distinctive: first, the high and constant level of emigration over a long period of time; second, its family character, which normally involved entire families and long periods of settlement in the destination countries;[1] and third, the remarkable geographical concentration of the migration flows in North America (Rocha *et al.* 2011).

Quantifying the return of Azoreans to the islands is not easy. Rocha *et al.* (2011) estimated that, between the late 1920s and roughly the mid-1940s, the return of Azoreans to the archipelago experienced a first peak. The highest figures were, however, registered for the period between 1986 and 1991, when approximately 4,730 individuals returned from North America – 65 per cent from the US and the remainder from Canada. Since the late 1990s, the return flows seem to have decelerated. This does not mean, however, that these movements have lost importance within the Azorean migration context. In fact, between 1996 and 2001, for every 100 legal emigrants leaving the archipelago, 152 individuals who had previously resided in the US or Canada settled back in the Azores (Rocha *et al.* 2011: 141). This relocation movement tends to be dominated by older people. According to a survey conducted by Rocha *et al.* (2011), the population of returnees in the Azores contains 60 per cent of individuals over the age of 60, and 80 per cent of returnees are over the age of 50. This signals the importance of drawing attention to the older cohorts of Azorean returnees.

Methodology

The empirical analysis presented is drawn upon 36 in-depth life narrative interviews with ageing Azorean returnees and a six-month period of ethnographic fieldwork in the Azores.[2] The interviews were collected in four of the archipelago's islands (including the most populated ones and those most affected by emigration flows), in both rural and urban settings, and include migrants aged 50 years old or more at the time of interview. Considering the conceptual intricacy around the definition of 'old age' (see Bytheway 2005), the age threshold selected attempts to fit into the Azorean reality covering the wide and diverse range of return migrants found on the islands. It should be noted, however, that differences in age may influence returnees' life experiences and accounts of being back home (Gualda and Escriva 2012). The majority of the interviewees emigrated from the Azores in the 1960s and 1970s. Abroad, Azorean migrants were mostly employed as farmers, construction and factory workers and cleaning personnel, and in most cases they returned throughout the 1980s and 1990s, having spent at least ten years abroad. The interviewees represent a gender-balanced group, including also six couples, and are mostly aged in their sixties and seventies. The majority are married, now retired, and returned to their home village or town.

For a more intuitive understanding of the stories collected, three 'ideal categories' were established, mirroring the Weberian concept of 'ideal types' (Heydebrand 1994); these narrative categories will act as the main framework of the chapter. The three broad categories are: '*narratives of contentment*', '*hybrid spaces of renegotiation and transitionality*' and '*narratives of discontent*'. It should be stressed once more that a '*narrative of contentment*' does not necessarily represent a unanimous account of satisfaction with the return experience back in the homeland; in the same way, a '*narrative of discontent*' does not necessarily represent a wholly negative experience of return to the Azores.

Integration paths in a (re)visited homeland: narratives of contentment, renegotiation and discontent

The multiplicity of narratives of belonging and different levels of satisfaction and wellbeing among Azorean returnees seem to be influenced by both the emigration project abroad and the return experience back home. While material achievements such as building a house or buying a plot of land play an important role in fostering socio-economic integration upon return, the subjective valuation of these accomplishments by the migrants themselves, family and neighbours and the successful reassimilation into the local community are fundamental in the readaptation process. Simultaneously, non-material dimensions such as social and health wellbeing as well as place attachment also contribute to smoothing the reintegration process upon return. The three categories of return narratives are, therefore, analysed according to four key dimensions: financial/material, health, psychosocial, and place attachment and sense of belonging.

Narratives of contentment

Consistently with the findings of Gualda and Escriva (2012), financial stability and material achievements proved to be very influential in the returnees' narratives of contentment and general life satisfaction in the Azores. The process of building a house or buying a piece of land seems to be particularly relevant from an economic and socio-cultural perspective, representing both local ownership for the family and a space for collective living, if possible with the extended family. As shown in previous studies (Gualda and Escriva 2012; Razum *et al.* 2005), there is a general understanding of how the tough period of work abroad was instrumental in allowing a comfortable life back home. Albertino's narrative is a typical example of how the migration experience improved his life and ageing experience back in the Azores. In the account of this 66-year-old man who returned from Canada in the late 1980s, material comfort seems to be intimately related to his ability to enjoy his time with family and keep himself active through his chosen 'leisure activities'. Reflecting on his material achievements and linking them to the period of work abroad, he remarks:

> We still have another house down by the coast, another one up there, a wine cellar ... I have vineyards, potatoes, banana trees. I own everything and I take care of everything myself ... If I hadn't been to Canada, I wouldn't have anything of what I have today.

However, and although it plays an important role, material wellbeing only partially explains the feelings of contentment back home. In addition, both physical and mental health are important for individual wellbeing, particularly at a later stage in life. In fact, in some of the narratives collected, access to practically free healthcare in the Azores compared with North America was an important factor leading to the choice of return. Again, Albertino's narrative is revealing of how a strong health condition, enhanced by the choice of return, helps him keep active at a later stage of life:

> To stop is to die; to work is to live. I have to wake up every day at 5 a.m.; I just cannot stay in bed. Even today, at 5 a.m., I was drinking my coffee ...

then my grandchildren come at 7.30 a.m. to go to school ... I go feed my animals, my chickens, and then I go to my vineyard. Today I went to the farmlands to work the land ... I always have something to do.

Following the same lines, Luísa, a 70-year-old woman back from Bermuda in the early 2000s, reinforces the link between life satisfaction and the ability to carry on some form of working the land:

I do everything in my farm. My son only ploughs the land and then I help to cut and prune the trees; I help with everything.

Most of the narratives of contentment link together the health dimension, psychosocial wellbeing and a strong attachment to the unique 'place' of the Azores, or the particular island. In fact, the small size of the Azores islands, where, despite recent urban growth in the largest islands of São Miguel and Terceira, traditional kinship ties are still very tight, tends to preserve the role of supporting networks and enhance feelings of belonging.[3] Although there is no consensus on the importance of family and social support for elderly wellbeing (Gualda and Escriva 2012), in the Azorean case this dimension assumes particular importance. Albertino, like other interviewees, was keen to describe the feasts they organise together with extended family and neighbours to celebrate traditional local and regional events such as religious holidays, the killing of the calf or the grape harvest. In most of the narratives collected, as in the case of Joaquim and Lúcia, a couple in their early seventies who returned from the US, the journey back to the homeland is pictured as a return to safety, familiarity and friendship:

I like it very much here [Joaquim] ... here is our place, now our home is here. Friends come over and we sit outside in the garage; we put some chairs outside, we sit down and chat ... they are very good friends. Sometimes I am sitting inside making lace [Lúcia], I hear them outside playing the harmonica and I laugh to myself; I really enjoy the atmosphere here. In the US we didn't have time for this.

The frequent narratives of return to the 'peace and quiet' of the Azores appear, then, to be based on rather defined constructions of home and away: the return home is narrated through discourses of traditionalism and the rural idyll, in opposition to the urban modernity and anomie experienced abroad. Furthermore, the shift from an active working life abroad to (pre-)retirement in the Azores assumes particular relevance in the returnees' perceptions of the life back in the homeland. A common feature in the narratives of contentment is also the long period of time elapsed since return. In fact, the majority of the migrants interviewed returned to the Azores more than 20 years ago, which has allowed them time to readjust to the life on the islands and calmly reassess the outcomes of their combined migration and return project.

Unlike Joaquim and Lúcia, who both cherish being back home, in some cases the positive experience of return is not generalisable to the couple. In Albertino's case (like other Azorean families), the man is the one prompting the return to the homeland.[4] The woman, on the other hand, often contests the idea of leaving the host country. Albertino's wife, for example, referred to feelings of alienation back on a small island, where she misses the big shopping malls and the noise of the city. Indeed, especially for women, the loss of anonymity back home can be compounded by a loss of independence after returning to a markedly patriarchal and traditional society.

Comparing the material dimension of return with more immaterial ones such as psychosocial wellbeing and place attachment, Warnes *et al.* (2004) argue that, as individuals grow older, social networks become less decisive than wealth and income in promoting quality of life. However, this perspective seems to overlook the role of cultural-geographical factors in the importance ascribed to family and friendship networks. The numerous 'narratives of contentment' that I found among my research participants, and the apparent easiness of their adaptation back home, can be linked to Cerase's typology of return migrants (1974). In fact, the majority of the Azorean returnees fall within his categories of '*return of conservatism*' and '*return of retirement*', therefore leaning towards accepting and preserving the local culture rather than changing it.

This can be further understood by looking at these migrants' migration projects abroad. Indeed, the majority of the Azoreans who later decided to return to the homeland lived within Portuguese/Azorean communities in North America; they always kept strong ties with the Azorean culture and way of living. They integrated to a 'comfortable minimum' into the receiving society, and always cherished the idea of an eventual return. In line with Cerase's (1974) findings for the Italians returning back from the US, Azorean returnees not only experience low levels of cultural shock back home but also help preserve local traditions and culture.

Sussman's (2000) 'cultural identity model' offers an interesting insight into the apparent easiness of readjustment experienced by the Azorean migrants. The *affirmative identity* as described by Sussman seems to fit the Azorean case well, since most of the Azorean returnees interviewed kept their links with the homeland through either sporadic travelling or writing, sometimes even strengthening the Azorean identity through the formation of tight-knit communities abroad. This can be seen as a mechanism of anticipating (or least not putting completely aside) an eventual return. The maintenance of the traditional Azorean culture associated with a sometimes long-planned, long-desired return seems, therefore, to explain the relatively smooth adaptation back home. It is, then, interesting to note that, contrary to what some other research has shown (Adler 1981; Tannenbaum 2007), in the Azorean case return is usually much more pleasant than the emigration experience in the first place. This becomes apparent, for example, in one of Albertino's comparisons between the Azores and Toronto, where he used to live:

> Here it's just peace and quiet … we leave the house and all doors are left unlocked. In Canada it was not like this.

And yet, not all interviewees experienced such an easy adaptation back home, as we see in the next subsection.

Narratives of discontent

A strong sense of accomplishment upon return is linked not only to material achievements but also to personally and socially created expectations; these are not only built around the individual and family but are also expressed in comparison with local reference groups such as the better-off, friends or other returnees (Gualda and Escriva 2012). In fact, it was common to find in some of the narratives of return, especially among migrants who returned at an earlier age, the feeling that a hard-working life abroad and investments made upon return were not enough to confront the necessities of living and ageing back in the Azores. As in some previous studies (Ní Laoire 2008a; Tannenbaum 2007), some Azorean returnees, too, shared experiences of not feeling welcome back home, which were contrary to their hopes and expectations. They found themselves experiencing jealousy from their neighbours, and facing multiple obstacles with the local authorities. In a sad but resigned tone, Fernando, a man in his late fifties who returned from the US in the early 2000s, summarises some of these experiences:

> and then things there [in the US] started to get worse and worse [in terms of jobs] and so I decided it was better to come back … I was only 43 back then. I brought with me a little boat with the idea of starting a tourism business here but it didn't work out. My initial idea was actually to buy a taxi but here they simply hold you back, anything you want to do becomes a problem, a difficulty … in the end I gave up.

Common among the Azorean returnees, regardless of age, gender or period of return, are narratives of discontent related, not only to a lack of financial success, but also to the frustration arising from recent decades' development in the Azores, which has allowed those who did not migrate to experience significant economic improvement. This often makes returnees see their life of sacrifice abroad as somehow minor or even unnecessary to their economic enhancement. In line with Gualda and Escriva's (2012) findings, the returnees whose narratives convey stronger feelings of disappointment are those who did not fully accomplish their material or social expectations or found their achievements too limited once they came back home. This is the case for José, a 78-year-old man who, after a period of working in Bermuda, decided to return to the Azores. Although he attempted to readapt to the life back home, he felt it hard to readjust and, at the age of 48, still feeling young and active, he decided to go back to Bermuda; he then returned to the Azores once again, after retirement. There are, thus, differences between ageing migrants, more specifically between those who return while still at an economically active age and those who return after retirement.

Local stereotypes can also strongly complicate the readaptation process. In the case of the Azorean returnees, the regional slang word '*Calafão*' [the one who returns to the Azores] conveys an image of the wealthy migrant who permanently glorifies the times spent in North America while criticising the way of life back on the islands. This is not so much the case for José, who kept strong ties with the Azores and even experienced a temporary period of return before his permanent move, but other returnees experienced strong feelings of resentment and frustration due to being treated as outsiders in the place they consider home. This was the case for Miguel and Florbela, a couple who returned from the US in the late 1990s:

> People here don't accept you. Although we live here now for all these years, we are still not accepted. The locals still call us the 'americanos' ... here it doesn't feel like home, this is not 'a home'.

As I am trying to understand the psychology of return, it is important to emphasise the role of the migration project abroad as a period of resocialisation and reshaping of migrants' identities, expectations and perceptions towards wellbeing. The cultural shock between pre-return expectations and the reality found back home can be particularly acute if the period abroad was long and without many visits to the homeland. Consistently with other studies (Gualda and Escriva 2012; Tannenbaum 2007), in the '*narratives of discontent*' of the Azorean returnees, the fact that return migrants rarely fully anticipated the difficulties of adjusting back home helps to explain some of the disappointment experienced upon return. On the one hand, there is the mismatch between idealised images of home and the reality encountered, and on the other, the unforeseen extent to which migrants changed their attitudes, values and behaviours while abroad and how those changes impact on their interactions back in the homeland (Cerase 1974; Sussman 2000). For many migrants, as in the cases of Fernando and José, although they did not feel completely disillusioned from a material or social point of view, they felt let down by the deeply ingrained power structure and the overall local culture of *laissez-faire, laissez-passer*. As a whole, the Azorean returnees tend to hold stronger negative views in terms of their objective contextual wellbeing, referring to a proper functioning and fair treatment by the local institutions, than in terms of their individual subjective welfare. In fact, the proximity to kinship and friendship networks and the markedly higher quality of life experienced in the Azores generally overcame, at least in the long term, the absence of close family ties or the lack of valued amenities characteristic of North American urban areas – the long and fast highways, the big supermarkets or the large shopping malls. Equally important here are the temporalities behind wellbeing perceptions. Indeed, initially critical views towards wellbeing back home tend to be softened over time as readaptation to the local reality takes place.

In some cases, however, feelings of disappointment and non-belonging are never fully overcome and can be worsened by a sense of obligation to return. This is evident in the case of José, whose return project was linked to the fact that his closest family – an ageing mother, a lonely wife and an only-child daughter – were patiently waiting for him 'back home'. In a similar vein, although the cultural shock and feelings of regret and non-belonging can be particularly acute among some returnees, fears of losing face or damaging one's reputation discourage a potential decision to re-migrate. This is clear in Fernando's account:

> My decision was to start over again back here; I sold everything I had in the US, I put everything in a big container and brought it here. I could not simply sell everything again and go back [talking about the shock faced upon return] ... and it's not only that; I felt I would lose face by going back after saying for so long that I was going back to my homeland.

Unlike previous studies that identified recurrent patterns of social isolation and loneliness among older return migrants (Barrett and Mosca 2013; Gualda and Escriva 2012), narratives of this kind were much less frequent among the Azorean returnees. Although several dimensions of disappointment have been identified above in the narratives of return, it is important to highlight that, as a whole, the majority of the accounts collected do not represent (at least presently) '*narratives of discontent*'. This may be explained by three main factors: first, the aforementioned long period of residence in the Azores after return, which allowed time for readaptation and reintegration into the local dynamics; second, the numerous visits to the homeland that normally preceded the permanent return, which frequently takes place as a family project (mostly couples or couples with non-adult children); and third, the strong local sense of community (and 'place'), which in most cases seems to promote a rapid integration back home, reducing feelings of loneliness and social isolation. Although in many cases, especially in later life, the return journey represents the closure of a migration cycle, the line between 'here and there' is sometimes blurred and the narratives of return embody a deep sense of 'in-betweenness', as shown below.

Hybrid spaces of renegotiation and transitionality

As previously emphasised, the Azorean return is often undertaken as a family project, which helps ease the transition back to the homeland and avoid feelings of loneliness and social isolation. In those cases in which migrants returned alone, neighbours and distant relatives played a reintegrating and accompanying role, especially for older returnees. This is evident in the case of Silvina, an 85-year-old widowed woman who, after going through a difficult ageing experience in the US, and without her son or daughter-in-law being able to care for her, decided to return in the mid-2000s to the Azores, where she could still rely on two sisters who had never left the islands and other nearby neighbours. This can be pictured within what Condon (2005) identifies as 'social field', a network of family, friends or, at its loosest, a sense of community, of place, where one is 'known' and in which return is conceptualised as a 'quest for anchorage' (Corcoran 2002). Underlying Silvina's narrative is also the ability to cope better with healthcare costs in the Azores. According to her,

> At my age it is better to be here [in the Azores] because everything is close by, while in America you have to get a car to go anywhere ... Here I can talk to my sister or I can just go and sit in the park in the afternoon when it gets cooler; the neighbours are kind too [...] If I was young, if I was working, if I still had my husband with me it would be different, but alone all these years ... I feel better here, that's how it's best for me, and here I don't feel scared of going outside....

In this case, although the traditional intergenerational care in old age seems to have been lost in the US, back in the Azores Silvina still finds the culturally accepted norm that close relatives will provide care and social support to each other. However, and despite the presence of siblings and other friends, Silvina's narrative unveils feelings of loneliness and longing for the family life left in the US – her only-child son, daughter-in-law, granddaughter and, recently, a great-grandson. In other cases, as in Silvina's, returnees make use of periodic travelling to the host country as a way of coping with a life back home that is to some extent emotionally incomplete. Unlike many migrants, whose return has been strongly influenced by the family's place of residence (Razum *et al.* 2005), Silvina's decision to return seems to balance the absence of her son with the familiarity of the Azores. For Silvina, place and the neighbourliness that it invokes proves to be a central element in the reintegration process back in the homeland and in the strengthening of feelings of home. But it remains an uneasy balance. In a similar vein, the case of Piedade, a 72-year-old woman who returned from Canada in the early 1990s, seems to epitomise the hybridity and permanent renegotiation of 'here and there' over the years. While for some returnees time has been key in adopting the Azores as an uncontested home, for Piedade the fact that her children are in Canada leads to a permanent feeling of 'in-betweenness':

> It is a mix of feelings, but here is my home ... it's been 23 years already! Here is my home, but I'm always staring at the phone; we go [to Canada] and stay one month, and I'm always looking forward to it ... [also] the day they [her daughters] come [to the Azores] I really can't sleep – I'm afraid that I will fall asleep in the morning and miss picking them up at the airport ... [she laughs]

Recalling Sussman's (2000) 'cultural identity model' and looking particularly at the *additive and intercultural identities*, the latter seems to fit particularly well with the hybrid narratives of belonging among Azorean returnees. A liminal or 'in-between' identity seems to emerge among some return migrants, whose lives and thoughts are permanently divided between 'here and there', and in their (re)construction of notions of 'home' and 'away' (Ahmed 1999). Further-more, as advocated in previous studies (Barrett and Mosca 2013; Gualda and Escriva 2012), feelings of social isolation and loneliness back home can be over-come by compensatory strategies such as living transnational lives and sharing time 'between homes' (Heikkinen and Lumme-Sandt 2013; Lamb 2002). Common coping strategies back in the homeland are then often framed around 'here and there', either by frequently travelling back and forth and thereby maintaining emotional and support networks in both places, or by getting locally involved in activities that somehow link the 'two worlds'. This is the case for Vasco, a 68-year-old man who, after returning from Canada in the late 1990s, developed a webpage and TV channel where he posts videos and information that helps to connect the Azores with the Azorean diaspora:

> I write, take photos, make videos, I spend many hours on Facebook, and I have my own channel on the satellite television ... it has more than 200 videos and people quite enjoy it, especially the elderly.

Within hybrid spaces of transitionality, Piedade and Vasco seem, then, to embody two different experiences of renegotiation of 'here and there' upon return. While Piedade shares her time between the Azores and Canada, receiv-ing frequent visits from her children and grandchildren, especially as she grows older, Vasco, whose close family is almost all in the Azores, keeps his links with the life back in Canada through social networks aimed at bridging the two places.

Concluding remarks

This contribution has explored the different paths of (re)integration among Azorean return migrants, placing particular emphasis on the experiences of ageing back in the homeland and the shifting meanings of home throughout the readaptation process. Framed around three main 'ideal categories' – '*narrat-ives of contentment*', '*hybrid spaces of renegotiation and transitionality*' and '*nar-ratives of discontent*' – this research has highlighted the individual and unique, but also joint and overlapping, nature of the narratives portrayed. Despite its attempt to simplify and make sense of the diversity of the narratives collected, this chapter has also unveiled the multiple temporalities and fluidity intrinsic to the narratives of return and experiences of home and wellbeing. What presently stands as a narrative of contentment might have been a narrative of discontent or renegotiation right after return. Similarly, not all migrants who are discon-tented at present were unhappy when they first arrived in the Azores. Hence, perceptions of wellbeing and happiness back home are often convoluted, multi-layered and continually reshaped. More than being circumscribed to a single box, which would be necessarily an oversimplification, migrants fluctuate between different realities as they readjust to new places, temporalities and stages in life. Furthermore, multiple and complex internal and external forces make certain that migrants' experiences of wellbeing back home are permanently in the making.

The diversity of stories found suggests the importance of further exploring the challenges faced by migrants upon return from both a research and a policy perspective. What role do individual, community and place-related factors play in the experiences of home among Azorean migrants? How do material (financial) and immaterial (health, psychosocial, place attachment and sense of belonging) dimensions interplay in these migrants' experiences back home? How should a successful integration and positive ageing experience back in the Azores be promoted? This research has stressed the importance of going beyond the objective and material side of (re)integration to further explore the role of community and place in shaping subjective dimensions such as health and psychosocial wellbeing.

The return to the Azores was a natural, non-policy-driven process. Drawing up policies for older returnees has been particularly challenging given the group's inner diversity. Key differences in the Azorean case are those of age, length of return and island of residence. Looking at the returnees' objective wellbeing, two measures are frequently pointed out as crucial in their narratives: first, the need to ensure that returnees' capacities acquired or improved while abroad are effectively mobilised back home; and second, the importance of supporting and promoting their entrepreneurial ability. Particularly relevant among 'younger' returnees, this represents an important valorisation of migrants' skills and has the potential to enhance their levels of wellbeing and feelings of belonging back in the homeland. Regarding psychosocial wellbeing, two actions emerge as central: first, the key role of promoting spaces for interaction among Azorean returnees – this was particularly highlighted by those who are older or have no close family ties in the Azores – and second, the importance of facilitating contact between older returnees and their families in North America via social networks. This would allow a much closer bridging between 'here and there', also potentially fostering the desire to visit the Azores among the younger Azoreans living abroad, and thereby ensure the strengthening of emotional ties and support, which would benefit the elderly returnees.

While most often the return narratives seem to embody stories of successful adaptation back home, they also entail experiences of cultural shock, disappointment, non-belonging (especially straight after return) and complex dichotomies such as the 'homecomer' vs the 'newcomer'. Hybrid transnational spaces bridging 'here and there' tend to be formed when the migrants have their family or close networks split between the 'two worlds', living emotionally fragmented lives back home. Permanent renegotiation and transnational belonging can be materialised in multiple ways – while Piedade travels to see her family in the host country and also enjoys their frequent visits, Vasco bridges the two places through social networks allowing him (and others) to keep in touch with the 'world' left behind. In light of the complexity of readjusting to life in the homeland, living transnational lives and permanently renegotiating 'two homes' proves essential to cope with the double-edged reality of return and separation.

In analysing four key dimensions of satisfaction and wellbeing back home – material/financial, health, psychosocial, and place attachment and sense of belonging – a set of individual, community and place-related factors has been identified as key to the understanding of the reintegration process of the Azorean returnees. From an individual perspective, the normally extended period of return to and living back in the Azores seems to be decisive in the successful adaptation to the local environment. As noted in Cerase's seminal work (1974), the longer the period back home, the greater the opportunity to blend into the local community, even if this occurs due to resignation rather than to the understanding or reincorporation of local values. Furthermore, the family character of the return project and the frequent visits preceding the permanent move are also important in fostering the integration process back home. From a community and place-related perspective, the small size of the Azores islands and the importance still ascribed to family and friendship ties prove to be vital for the less frequent narratives of loneliness and social isolation. Place emerges, then, as a central element in readjusting back home and developing a strong place attachment and sense of belonging.

Following from Tannenbaum's discussion (2007), can the 'inner compass' (Alsop 2002) be found only where we are born? Although it seems fair to say that the homeland will probably be perceived throughout our lives as a familiar and reassuring place compared with a foreign land, how should we frame this in light of return migrants who have spent a significant part of their lives elsewhere? Is there a way in which migrants can redefine and renegotiate their 'inner compasses' in 'multiple homes'? Or is 'home', the Azores, a unique entity that, despite prolonged absence and multiple experiences of integration, remains untouched? The need to rethink old-established categories such as 'local' or 'incomer' and 'home' or 'host' societies seems to be clear. Hence, return migrants can find themselves in an ambiguous place within the receiving society, playing the role of both the insider and the outsider, the 'newcomer' and the 'homecomer', and feeling permanently both at home and away.

Notes

1 This generalisation is less applicable to the destination of Bermuda.
2 This fieldwork forms part of my ongoing PhD research at the University of Sussex, which also includes interviews with two other older migrant categories – labour immigrants and lifestyle immigrants.
3 The ease with which Azorean returnees seemed to blend into the local community generally yielded positive feelings of emotional safety and belonging – unlike the findings of Ní Laoire (2007) in rural Ireland, where some returnees found the close-knit social environment threatening to their privacy.
4 See also Ní Laoire (2007) on Irish return migration, and Vlase (2013) on the Romanian case.

References

Adler, N. (1981) Reentry: managing cross-culture transitions, *Group and Organization Studies* 6(3): 341–356.

Ahmed, S. (1999) Home and away: narratives of migration and estrangement, *International Journal of Cultural Studies* 2(3): 329–347.

Alsop, C.K. (2002) Home and away: self-reflexive auto-ethnography, *Forum Qualitative Sozialforschung/Forum: Qualitative Social Research* 3(3): Art. 10. http://nbn-resolving.de/urn:nbn:de:0114-fqs0203105. Accessed 3 April 2015.

Barrett, A. and Mosca, I. (2013) Social isolation, loneliness and return migration: evidence from older Irish adults, *Journal of Ethnic and Migration Studies* 39(10): 1659–1677.

Black, R., Koser, K., Munk, K., Atfield, G., D'Onofrio, L. and Tiemoko, R. (2004) *Understanding Voluntary Return*. London: Home Office, Online Report 50/04. http://webarchive.nationalarchives.gov.uk/20110220105210/rds.homeoffice.gov.uk/rds/pdfs04/rdsolr5004.pdf. Accessed 3 April 2015.

Bytheway, B. (2005) Ageism and age categorization, *Journal of Social Issues* 61(2): 361–374.

Cerase, F. (1974) Expectations and reality: a case study of return migration from the United States to Southern Italy, *International Migration Review* 8(2): 245–262.

Christou, A. (2006) *Narratives of Place, Culture and Identity: Second-generation Greek-Americans Return 'Home'*. Amsterdam: Amsterdam University Press.

Condon, S. (2005) Transatlantic French Caribbean connections: return migration in the context of increasing circulation between France and the islands, in R.B. Potter, D. Conway and J. Phillips (eds.) *Experiences of Return Migration – Caribbean Perspectives*. Aldershot: Ashgate, 225–244.

Corcoran, M. (2002) The process of migration and the reinvention of self: the experiences of returning Irish emigrants, *Éire-Ireland* 37(1–2): 175–191.

Gualda, E. and Escriva, A. (2012) Diversity in return migration and its impact on old age: the expectations and experiences of returnees in Huelva (Spain), *International Migration* 52(5): 178–190.

Gullahorn, J.E. and Gullahorn, J.T. (1963) An extension of the U-curve hypothesis, *Journal of Social Issues* 19(3): 33–47.

Heikkinen, S. and Lumme-Sandt, K. (2013) Transnational connections of later-life migrants, *Journal of Aging Studies* 27(2): 198–206.

Heydebrand, W. (ed.) (1994) *Sociological Writings: Max Weber*. New York: Continuum.

King, R. (1978) Return migration: a neglected aspect of population geography, *Area* 10(3): 175–182.

King, R. (2000) Generalizations from the history of return migration, in B. Ghosh (ed.) *Return Migration: Journey of Hope or Despair?* Geneva: International Organization for Migration, 7–55.

Lamb, S. (2002) Intimacy in a transnational era: the remaking of aging among Indian Americans, *Diaspora: Journal of Transnational Studies* 11(3): 299–330.

Ní Laoire, C. (2007) The 'green green grass of home'? Return migration to rural Ireland, *Journal of Rural Studies* 23(3): 332–344.

Ní Laoire, C. (2008a) Complicating host-newcomer dualisms: Irish return migrants as home-comers or newcomers? *Translocations: Migration and Social Change* 4(1): 35–50.

Ní Laoire, C. (2008b) 'Settling back'? A biographical and life-course perspective on Ireland's recent return migration, *Irish Geography* 41(2): 195–210.

Percival, J. (2013) Charting the waters: return migration in later life, in J. Percival (ed.) *Return Migration in Later Life: International Perspectives*. Bristol: Policy Press, 1–20.

Razum, O., Sahin-Hodoglugil, N. and Polit, K. (2005) Health, wealth, or family ties? Why Turkish work migrants return from Germany, *Journal of Ethnic and Migration Studies* 31(4): 719–739.

Rocha, G., Ferreira, E. and Mendes, D. (2011) *Between Two Worlds. Emigration and Return to the Azores*. Azores: Regional Department of the Communities.

Stefansson, A.H. (2004) Homecomings to the future: from diasporic mythographies to social projects of return, in F. Markowitz and A.H. Stefansson (eds) *Homecomings. Unsettling Paths of Return*. Lanham, MD: Lexington Books, 2–20.

Sussman, N.M. (2000) The dynamic nature of cultural identity throughout cultural transitions: why home is not so sweet, *Personality and Social Psychology Review* 4(4): 355–373.

Szkudlarek, B. (2010) Reentry – A review of the literature, *International Journal of Intercultural Relations* 34(1): 1–21.

Tannenbaum, M. (2007) Back and forth: immigrants' stories of migration and return, *International Migration* 45(5): 147–175.

Vertovec, S. (1999) Conceiving and researching transnationalism, *Ethnic and Racial Studies* 22(2): 445–462.

Vlase, I. (2013) 'My husband is a patriot!': gender and Romanian family return migration from Italy, *Journal of Ethnic and Migration Studies* 39(5): 741–758.

Warnes, A. and Williams, A. (2006) Older migrants in Europe: a new focus for migration studies, *Journal of Ethnic and Migration Studies* 32(8): 1257–1281.

Warnes, A., Friedrich, K., Kellaher, L. and Torres, S. (2004) The diversity and welfare of older migrants in Europe, *Ageing and Society* 24(3): 307–326.

Williams, A. and Fonseca, L. (1999) The Azores: between Europe and North America, in R. King and J. Connell (eds) *Small Worlds, Global Lives. Islands and Migration*. London: Pinter, 55–76.

15 Conclusions

Exploring the multiple complexities of the return migration–psychosocial wellbeing nexus

Russell King

Introduction

In the opening sentence to an extensive historical review of the literature on return migration, I opined that return migration was 'the great unwritten chapter in the history of migration' (King 2000: 7). Nearly 20 years later, this statement is no longer quite so justified. In the new millennium, there has been a remarkable growth in the research literature on return migration, as there has been on most aspects of the broader migration process. However, there remain major gaps in research on return migration, which this volume has aspired to fill.

First, there has been little attempt to build comparative studies of return. Most of the existing 'return' literature consists of single case studies, which, even when they are brought together in edited books (e.g. Long and Oxfeld 2004; Markowitz and Stefansson 2004), are rarely fully integrated comparisons. This book avoids that shortcoming by being book-ended by Vathi's comprehensive overview in Chapter 1 and by this retrospective comparative synthesis.

Second, return migration has largely been seen as essentially a migration process, interpreted in the light of economic, demographic and sociological causes and effects. Little attention thus far has been given to the psychosocial dimensions and impacts of return, and filling this gap has been the main *raison d'être* of this book. Together, the editors and contributors of this book have explored some of the complex socio-cultural, emotional, ideological and political ramifications of the nexus between return migration and psychosocial wellbeing, and later in this chapter I will highlight the key findings.

Third, this book challenges the prevalent assumption in the literature that return migration is some kind of 'natural' conclusion to the migratory process in which the return 'home' closes the cycle of the migration trajectory (cf. Boyle *et al.* 1998: 35–36). A more mobile, transnational conceptualisation of migration sees return as part of an ongoing itinerary rather than a permanent resettlement back in the country of origin. Hence, there is a need to reconceptualise return – not so much as 'return migration' but more as 'return mobilities'.

Fourth and finally, almost no attention has been given to the psychosocial aspects of policies relating to return migration. Each of the authors of this book's chapters was asked to reflect on the policy implications of their research findings, and in the concluding section of this concluding chapter I will attempt to draw these policy reflections together.

Prior to that, and in light of the points made above, this chapter will first revisit the issue of return, then place the return migration–psychosocial wellbeing nexus within the broader 'emotional turn' within migration studies, and synthesise key findings from the chapters in terms of reconceptualising return migration and psychosocial wellbeing.

Problematising return: from return migration to return mobilities

It is a fair generalisation to say that research and writing on return migration have not kept pace with the broader reconceptualisations of migration as a whole. Instead, much of the literature on return migration remains confined by the straightjacket of statistical recording and conventional modes of migration analysis. The questions asked are restricted to a kind of standardised list. How many migrants return, and to where? What are the characteristics of returnees compared with non-returnees and non-migrants? Why do migrants return? What is the impact of their return in terms of development, employment, social class formation etc.? It is a striking paradox that while so much attention is paid in the international migration literature to the challenges of integration that migrants face in their new host countries, so little regard is paid to the challenges of (re)integration that returnees face when relocating to their country of origin.

This last statement links to a major critique of the way that return migration is traditionally conceptualised: as a 'return to base' that reinscribes the migrant in their 'rightful place' in the 'homeland' and restores the 'natural order of things' (Malkki 1995). This naturalistic view of return migration sees reintegration as unproblematic, as migrants relocate, or are relocated to, the place where it is alleged they 'naturally belong'. Four erroneous assumptions underpin this simplistic and conservative framing of return migration.

The first mistaken assumption is that the migrant has not been changed by his or her experience abroad, and that, therefore, reinsertion back 'home' is straightforward. Migrants *are* changed by living in a different society and culture, and therefore the reintegration process can be challenging for them (Cerase 1974). Only if the migrant has not integrated abroad (perhaps as a result of only a short stay, or alternatively because he or she has lived entirely within an ethnic enclave that reproduces 'home' society) can we envisage a more-or-less unproblematic reintegration upon return.

The second wrong assumption is that 'home' has not changed during the migrant's absence. Often it has, and in quite fundamental ways, which challenge the migrant's memory of how it was when they left. Occasional return visits for holidays and family celebrations are not sufficient to update these memories; indeed, they may well give a distorted picture, a kind of sugar-coated representation of home seen through the rose-tinted lens of summer weather, festive celebrations, and relatives and friends in relaxed holiday mood. Fundamentally, there is no going back in time or space: both the migrant and the place have changed. In this sense, the return home is phantasmagoric, created in the realm of dreams and the imagination, deceptive, illusionary and shifting as in a mirage (Christou 2016).

The phantasmagorias of the home-place are all the more powerful in the case of exiles, refugees and displaced people, for whom either the return is a space-time impossibility or, if it does take place, it is to a setting that has been so brutally changed as to be scarcely recognisable (see the chapter by Porobić on returns to Bosnia). Likewise, in the context of diasporic return, the move to the ancestral homeland (statistically not a true return migration) may involve a relocation to a mythical place that turns out to be very different from the picture imagined by the diaspora (chapters by Gońda, and Sardinha and Cairns; also the study on 'returning' second-generation Greeks by Christou and King 2014).

Third, there is the dubious assumption that the return to the home country is a definitive conclusion to the migration project. Just as cross-sectional comparative studies of migrants and non-migrants tend to overlook the possibility that non-migrants may become migrants in the future, so the return to the home country does not foreclose other future migrations. Such migration trajectories may take many forms – circulation back and forth, onward or serial migration to different destinations, combinations of international and internal moves – and can best be conceptualised not so much under the rubric of 'migration' but, rather, as 'mobility' or 'transnational living'. Rather than 'return migration', we should, therefore, speak of 'return mobilities' (King and Christou 2011). In sum, the engagement of migrants with the return phenomenon is characterised by a diversity of experiences, varying from imaginative returns to actual returns, from short visits to lifetime resettlement, as well as post-return mobilities and re-emigration. All these return mobility types are reflected in the preceding chapters, and all have diverse and cumulative impacts on the well-being of migrants and others.

Finally, there is a political and policy twist to the 'return migration is natural' discourse. Governments pursuing a policy of encouraging return – either by financial incentives to returnees and their countries of origin or through more explicit repatriation schemes – try to justify their actions by creating a discursive framing of the return as beneficial to the migrants: 'we are assisting them to return to where they really belong and where they want to be'. While this may be true in some cases, this rhetoric is disingenuous and often hides a different political and ideological agenda, which panders to an electorate that is somehow uneasy or hostile over immigration and wants to see it reduced. As several chapters in this book demonstrate (Bendixsen and Lidén; DeBono; Erdal and Oeppen; Kalir; Porobić), migrants generally prefer to continue their lives where their material and employment conditions are better, and where they (and especially their children) are putting down roots.

Rethinking the theorisation of return migration

Most of the chapters in this book pay homage to Jean-Pierre Cassarino's (2004) landmark paper on retheorising return migration. Cassarino correctly diagnosed return migration as under-theorised, and his article goes some way towards rectifying this by applying existing conceptual frameworks from international migration to the specific return situation. His successive application of neoclassical economics (returnees are 'failures' who have miscalculated the costs of migration), the new economics of labour migration (returnees are 'successes' who have achieved their targets), structural theory (returnees respond to the structural combination of opportunities in their home and host countries), transnationalism (returnees are agents of transnational practices and bearers of transnational identities) and social network theory (returnees are social actors involved in 'multiple relational ramifications') significantly advances our theoretical understanding of return migration. The insights of transnationalism, and social network theory in particular, help us to appreciate that return is no longer to be viewed as the culmination of the migration cycle but rather, as argued above, a stage in an ongoing migration process.

Additionally, Cassarino (2004: 270) points to the growing diversity of returnee types: not only 'traditional' labour migrants but also high-skilled migrants, student-migrants, asylum-seekers and refugees. Given the growing amount of recent research on second-generation and diasporic 'returnees' relocating to the ancestral homeland (chapters by Gońda; Sardinha and Cairns), this category, too, should be added. Each of these different types of returnee leads to potentially different psychological processes associated with return, as well as revealing intersectional differences relating to gender, age, ethnicity and so on.

Where Cassarino's revisitation of return migration moves closer to the second key theme of this book – psychosocial wellbeing – is in his fleeting remarks about transnational identity and social relations and in subsequent discussion (2004: 271–275; 2008: 101–103) on returnees' preparedness to return. However, Cassarino relates this preparedness largely to instrumental factors of resource endowment, willingness and readiness to return, and perception of the post-return possibilities, rather than to psychological preparedness, although there is a clear link between the material aspects of the preparedness to return and the psychosocial circumstances of the return decision and its outcome. Likewise, Cassarino makes no reference to the complex emotionalities that are almost inevitably imbricated in a migration or mobility event, especially a return move, which builds on earlier rounds of psychosocial experience, including trauma, that were bound up with the original migration, whether 'voluntary' or 'forced'.

Locating and exploring the return migration–psychosocial wellbeing nexus

It seems we live in the age of 'nexus thinking'. For migration scholars, the first major promotion of the term came with extensive discussion on the migration–development nexus in the early 2000s (see Van Hear and Sørensen 2003; also Faist 2008; Faist *et al.* 2011). In their recent book on ageing and migration, Lulle and King (2016) speak about the ageing–migration nexus and discuss at length the psychosocial aspects of what it is like to be both an older person and a migrant. The popularity of the 'nexus' notion was most recently confirmed by the overall title of the 2016 Royal Geographical Society Annual Conference: 'Nexus Thinking'.

For the purposes of the twin themes of this book, return migration and psychosocial wellbeing can be located within the broader nexus between migration and emotion (Boccagni and Baldassar 2015). The 'emotional turn' in migration studies draws inspiration from emerging literature on emotional geographies (Davidson *et al.* 2007; Smith *et al.* 2009) but is not limited to human geography, as the 'emotionalities' theme resonates across sociological, anthropological and psychological accounts of migration (e.g. Ewing 2007; Skrbis 2008; Svašek 2010; Zembylas 2012). The recency of this literature does not imply that emotion was ignored in early studies of migration. In fact, the emotions experienced and suffered by earlier generations of migrants were often described in evocative and empathetic ways; it is just that these earlier authors did not use terms like 'emotional geographies' or 'psychosocial wellbeing'. Two early migration classics that have rich descriptions of migrants' emotional reactions to their transplanted state are Oscar Handlin's *The Uprooted* (1951) and Theodore Saloutos' *They Remember America* (1956), about European migration to and return from the US, respectively, in the first half of the last century. Handlin describes the profound culture shock experienced by Southern and Eastern European migrants arriving in the US when everything – language, work, living conditions, food, climate – was very different and migrants realised the degree of their uprootedness from their country and village. Saloutos' is arguably the first in-depth study of return migration, and is a sensitive and occasionally humorous documentary about the 'reverse culture shock' experienced by returned Greek-Americans who struggled to reintegrate back into Greek life after so many years, often decades, in a very different country.

The chapters in the present book prioritise the emotional experiences of (return) migration as a challenge to the conventional framing of the migrant as *homo economicus*, but they do not signify the irrelevance of the material conditions of migration. Boccagni and Baldassar (2015: 77) argue compellingly that the economic and the emotional dimensions of migration cannot be productively separated, and they cite several empirical and theoretical studies that explicitly support this co-production of what they call *homo 'emotional' economicus* (Conradson and McKay 2007; Ho 2009, 2014; McKay 2007).

In a similar way, the broad notion of human wellbeing combines the economic/material domain, on the one hand, and perceptual and relational dimensions, on the other. Many of the chapters in this book follow the approach of Katie Wright and quote either her key paper (2012a) or her book (2012b) on the wellbeing of Peruvian migrants and of their non-migrant family members who are in receipt of financial and social remittances. While Wright does not focus on the wellbeing of returnees (reinforcing once again the importance of this book), she does lay out some useful 'meaning maps' of human and psycho-social wellbeing, which are reviewed by Vathi in Chapter 1 of this book and briefly recapped here.

Wright (2012a: 468) argues for greater holism in the study of the multifac-eted dimensions of human wellbeing as they are experienced by migrants and (via financial and social remittances and transnational care) their non-migrant family members. Wellbeing is culturally specific, and therefore it can 'travel' and be reshaped by migrants on the move and by the locations of their various family members and significant others. In her book, Wright (2012b: 10–11) disaggregates wellbeing into its objective/functional/material and subjective/ perceptual/emotional dimensions: the former entailing such mainly structural elements as income, housing, work and so on, which can be objectively meas-ured; the latter made up of more individual-scale factors such as values, percep-tions, mental health and personal relations. The holistic view stresses the interdependence of these two dimensions. In Chapter 1, Vathi makes the important distinction between psychosocial wellbeing as a person-centred concept that emphasises the value of social relations, and hence is an ongoing *process*, and the broader concept of human wellbeing more as a *state*, which can apply as much to aggregates of population as to individuals. As a summing-up definition in the concept of this book's focus on migrants, I would endorse and combine those offered by Bendixsen and Lidén in Chapter 2 and DeBono in Chapter 8. Psychosocial wellbeing is thus considered as an individual migrant's subjective assessment of his or her material and social conditions and possibility for agency. Such an assessment encompasses physical and mental health, social relationships and networks, autonomy and control, and personal and com-munity safety.

Highlights from the chapters

Starting with Chapter 2, I now highlight some of the key 'take-home' findings from each chapter, as regards both specific empirical results and the contribu-tion to the return migration–psychosocial wellbeing nexus. In doing so, I try to complement the more systematic overview of the chapters' themes made by Vathi in the opening chapter. Nevertheless, what follows is an inevitably sub-jective choice on my part.

Bendixsen and Lidén in Chapter 2 go straight to the core of what this book is about and exemplify several of the themes raised above about the nature of return migration and its relationship with psychosocial wellbeing. Their key framing device is the contrast between how the Norwegian government con-structs 'assisted return' (AR) of irregular migrants and failed asylum-seekers, and the meaning ascribed by the migrants themselves to their impending or actual return. In the government discourse, AR is presented, both to the migrants and to the wider Norwegian public, as a helpful facilitator (with attendant financial aid) for the migrants to 'go home' to continue and rebuild their lives in familiar surroundings. AR is also a means for the government to demonstrate 'control' over borders and to deter further irregular arrivals. What is lacking is any focus on migrants' psychosocial wellbeing. On the side of the migrants, reactions are mixed, but on the whole they do not match the rhetoric of the governmental view of the process. For many of those interviewed, return led to uncertainty, disillusionment, even stigmatisation as 'failures', or it is merely seen as a step towards moving subsequently to another country. Bendixsen and Lidén argue that this gap in the understanding and expectation of return – between the government's presentation of 'return with dignity' and the migrants' experience of 'return with shame' – has a strong influence on migrants' feelings of psychosocial wellbeing.

Chapter 3 is the only empirical chapter in the book to be explicitly comparative; Marta Bivand Erdal and Ceri Oeppen look at the psychosocial wellbeing of returnees to Afghanistan, Pakistan and Poland. This chapter also problematises the forced vs voluntary dichotomy in return migration through looking at the vulnerable wellbeing outcomes of those who are, by and large, 'forced' to return (to Afghanistan), those whose return is purely 'voluntary' (to Poland), and those whose return is theoretically voluntary but to an insecure political situation (Pakistan). Like the authors of Chapters 2 and 4, Erdal and Oeppen lean towards the suggestion that 'voluntary assisted return' is really a subset of forced migration. But they also question the dual assumption that forced return results in negative wellbeing and that voluntary return leads to positive wellbeing – largely because the latter group, having higher expectations, are more likely to feel let down by their actual return experience. Cassarino's (2008) important notion of 'return preparedness' is shown to be a key variable in the success of the return project; preparedness being broken down into three elements – resource accumulation, support of family members and others, and agency. The Polish data, however, question the very definition of return, since free intra-European mobility and an 'easy transnationalism' (King *et al.* 2015: 2) enable Poles to embody the notion of 'working abroad' but 'living at home'.

In Chapter 4, Barak Kalir switches the focus to Spain and to non-governmental organisations (NGOs) that intercede in the questionable process of assisted voluntary return (AVR). Kalir takes up Webber's (2011) polemical interrogation of AVR – 'how voluntary is voluntary return?' – and suggests that in reality it is a form of 'soft deportation'. NGO workers in organisations such as the Red Cross and the YMCA, who are usually motivated by genuine humanitarian principles, are nevertheless complicit in the implementation of return policies that reflect the neoliberalisation of migration governance and exclusion. Kalir uses such terms as 'cunning' and 'guileful' in persuasively alleging that the Spanish government's 'migration apparatus' is increasingly geared to removing 'illegalised' subjects for whom the Spanish state has absolved its own responsibility to help and support *in situ*. To quote directly from Kalir, in Spain the implementation of AVR by NGOs and civil-society organisations 'illustrates the triumph of the neoliberal state in creating a financial and ideological configuration under which repressive policies are executed by do-gooders'. As in many other countries, the ideological justification of AVR turns on a distinction between 'deserving' and 'non-deserving' migrants. On the one hand, 'healthy, fully employed, self-sustaining migrants' are 'allowed' to be 'incorporated' into (some sections) of Spanish society. On the other hand, 'failing' migrants, including those who have become ill, vulnerable, unemployed or irregular, often through no fault of their own (they are victims of the Spanish crisis and the country's fluctuating demand for cheap and flexible labour to sustain its agricultural, tourist, construction and care sectors), are thereby 'rejected' and must therefore be expelled.

'Burning without fire' is the strikingly evocative phrase used by one of Daniela DeBono's interviewees in Chapter 8 to describe life under the 'state of deportability' endured by failed asylum-seekers who have been 'condemned' to be returned to their home countries from Sweden. One of DeBono's main conclusions is that, notwithstanding the efforts of the Swedish authorities to make the forced migration process 'humane and dignified' and fully compliant with international human rights law, the migrants' psychosocial wellbeing is severely and negatively impacted. DeBono's research participants articulate extreme forms of anxiety over their impending return to a place where they may well face persecution and stigma; furthermore, few have any viable material resources or a proper 'home' on arrival. They feel that they have aged more rapidly during extensive periods in limbo in Sweden, often with no work, in hiding or in pre-return detention centres. In another striking phrase, they feel they are 'below zero', suffering a downward, fear-induced spiral of paranoia, insomnia, and other physical and mental manifestations. As in other chapters, DeBono reports particularly difficult situations for children undergoing protracted delays over decisions regarding the deportation of their families.

While Chapters 2–4 and 8 examined the psychosocial wellbeing of mostly 'irregular' migrants facing return or deportation, and hence reflected host-country perspectives (from Norway, Sweden, Spain and the UK), Chapters 5–7 and 9–11 take the perspective of those who have already returned to their supposed 'homeland'.

In Chapter 5, Marcin Gońda introduces the concept of 'roots migration' (Wessendorf 2007) to frame an evaluation of the psychosocial wellbeing experiences of Polish-descent students from the former Soviet Union who 'return' to their ancestral homeland of Poland to pursue their higher education. Gońda's chapter is one of the very few studies of the experiences of diasporic youth who study in the ancestral homeland. While, on the one hand, students might be regarded as an elite group, well resourced and well educated about their future life in a Polish university setting, on the other hand, their lack of direct experience of living in their ethnic homeland places them at a potential cognitive disadvantage. Through in-depth interviews with 60 such students, Gońda reveals the coping mechanisms of the diaspora students, and in particular their reactions to what is 'different', but also their reactions to the discovery that they themselves are seen as 'different' by local people. Hence, despite the fact that these 'return' migrations are both voluntary and incentivised (by scholarships, free healthcare etc.), as well as emotionally framed by a strong sense of ethnic Polish belonging, the psychosocial outcomes are far from positive. Quite apart from the normal challenges of moving out of the family home and living abroad for the first time at a young age (late teenage years), the students faced discrimination, labelled as 'poor *Ruskis*' and assumed to possess a range of negative characteristics associated with the Soviet 'East'. They are, to quote Gońda, 'strangers in the ancestral homeland'; yet, their reaction is to view themselves as 'true Poles', more faithful to Polish values than those Poles who have lived in Poland all their lives.

The theme of ancestral return migration introduced by Gońda in Chapter 5 is picked up by João Sardinha and David Cairns in Chapter 6, where they examine the impact of the post-2008 financial crisis on second-generation Portuguese born in France and Canada who had 'returned' to Portugal. In this case, the austerity-policy effects on incomes (falling) and unemployment (rising) had major impacts on these second-generationers' material and psychosocial wellbeing, including their very sense of identity and belonging in the diasporic homeland. This was, in the words of this chapter's title phrase, the 'trick' that Portugal had played on these returnees: in the first instance, welcoming them back during the 'good times' of economic growth and relative prosperity, but then making life so difficult that many had to leave again. Even without the crisis, however, the research subjects discovered previously unknown characteristics of life in Portugal – the stifling bureaucracy, poor public services, widespread corruption – that left them frustrated, angry and disillusioned, forcing them to consider moving back or moving on. The very definition of return migration is questioned by the empirical examples presented by Sardinha and Cairns: first, because they are not true returnees, having been born abroad; and second, because they may be forced to 're-return' to France or Canada or onward-migrate to a new country such as the UK.

In Chapter 7, Selma Porobić sheds new light on one of the most important return programmes of recent years in Europe – that of Bosnians from their refugee-country safe havens in Europe and North America in the wake of the Dayton Peace Accords. Porobić's focus, however, is rather specific: she studies the voluntary return of Bosnians who have acquired foreign citizenship and whose return is, or appears to be, genuinely driven by their own choice of return as a 'life project'. But here, too, we hear a now-familiar refrain: the disparity between, on the one hand, the framing of the return as a logical closure of the refugee-migration cycle and a restoration of the refugees to their 'natural' place in the homeland; and on the other, the harshness of some aspects of the returnees' experiences, due to unfavourable and unstable political and socio-economic conditions in the Bosnian 'home' environment. Among the key motivations for return, nurtured since the first displacement and maintained during ten or more years abroad, were nostalgia and the difficulty of establishing satisfactory social lives abroad; Bosnia offered a richer and more relaxed social environment, where feelings of patriotism and a desire to 'help' the home country could be put into practice. Among the key benefits of relocating to Bosnia were the everyday experiences of a warmer, family-centred social life, especially valued by older returnees, with renewal of the traditions of kindness and hospitality, and a reconnection with Bosnian culture and language. But the positive tone of Porobić's informants shifted to a much more negative one when they started talking about other aspects of their post-return lives, blighted by divisive ethnic homogenisation politics and corruption (cf. Paasche 2016). In a country where emigration is seen as the best route to advancement, returnees are regarded as abnormal, even 'out of their mind'. They face employment and education challenges, especially for their children, and many are tempted to re-emigrate. Meanwhile, the psychosocial trauma of the original displacement and uprooting is never erased, and is compounded by the further challenges of feeling alienated both abroad and back 'home' in a country that has changed so much in their absence.

With Chapter 9, by Nassim Majidi, we continue the theme of refugee returns, in this case from camps in Kenya to the 'home country', Somalia. Cassarino's (2004) earlier-discussed notion of preparedness for return is utilised to draw contrasts in psychosocial wellbeing outcomes for different categories of returnee and non-returnee. Lack of information on real-life conditions in Somalia is shown to be one of the main barriers to effective return decision-making. Majidi considers the refugee return process through the prism of women's experiences before departure and on return, and studies the consequences of their actions for both their own and their children's wellbeing. This is the chapter's unique contribution. Most existing research on refugee returns and repatriation programmes has focused on the male head of household or on vulnerable female-headed households, rather than on women as central social actors in return. Taking into account their diverse roles as mothers, wives, next-of-kin and workers, Majidi shows how refugee women both *choose* and *act*, but may also be forced to *endure*, return; they may also *resist* return, often for the sake of the children's education and safety. The explicit focus on children's psychosocial wellbeing in the return/non-return process is another novel aspect of this chapter (cf. Vathi and Duci 2016). If they return, women face tough challenges in negotiating their post-return transitions to a more tribal, patriarchal society, while their children face a dual adaptation process to their lives, both in the camps and in Somalia. Characteristic of the Kenyan-Somalian refugee return case is the phenomenon of 'staged' or 'split' family returns, whereby different family members return in different steps. Often the male head of the family returns first, to set up a base in Somalia, leaving his wife and children in the camp. Subsequently, the wife may return, with one or more children, leaving other children in Kenya in the care of relatives for a while, largely for educational reasons. But the children's return may also be gendered, with the daughters under pressure to return to get married as a priority.

Chapter 10 takes us to Armenia, and another political, historical and geographical setting for return migration – this time to a post-socialist space. Ine Lietaert, Eric Broekaert and Ilse Derluyn demonstrate the multi-phase, multi-layered nature of the return migration process, sometimes experienced as more difficult, with deeper and more complex material and psychosocial challenges, than the initial migration. The unique feature of this chapter is its longitudinal approach, using four in-depth biographical cases to illustrate the shifting nature of the return move, and above all the evolving post-return situation. As in Bosnia, strong emigration characterises post-independence Armenia, so that returnees encounter the same difficult socio-economic conditions that encourage others to leave – including political instability, widespread poverty, and unavailable or unaffordable healthcare. By interviewing each returnee three times – at the point of return departure (from Belgium) and at two junctures after return – the authors unveil dramatically shifting wellbeing outcomes over time, including improving, declining and unpredictably shifting wellbeing.

The highlight feature of Chapter 11 by Aija Lulle is her view of the return process and its associated psychosocial wellbeing as a continuous 'internal dialogue', which is used by young returnees to Latvia to understand their belonging to places (Latvia and emigration countries such as the UK and Norway) and people (their family and friends). Here, too, there are various and fluid returns, which challenge the unidirectional, naturalised understanding of a permanent return to one's homeland. Particularly for young Latvians who have spent some or all of their lives abroad, and whose multiple migration trajectories were shaped not by themselves but by the decision of others (typically their parents), a dialogic approach allows them to deconstruct and understand their own constrained agency. Along with Majidi (Chapter 9) and Vathi (Chapter 1; also Vathi and Duci 2016), Lulle pays attention to the psychological dimensions of children's 'return mobilities' (King and Christou 2011) in her attentive analysis of how her research participants narrate their sense of 'who they are' and 'where they are' in the different temporal and spatial contexts in which they are relationally embedded. Through three exemplary biographical case studies – Laura the labour migrant, Zanda the exile and Elizabete the cosmopolitan – we get an idea of the complexity and polyvocality of the inner dialogues of return processes of young Latvians.

From Latvia in Baltic Europe, Eralba Cela moves us in Chapter 12 to Balkan Europe, at the southern end of the post-socialist European space; and from a focus on young people in Latvia to older migrants in Albania. Chapter 12 is about the relatively new research topic of transnational ageing (cf. Walsh and Näre 2016), and more specifically about older migrants' conceptualisations of space, place, mobility, vulnerability and wellbeing in multiple contexts of return. For Albanian migrants, who have left their home country in droves since 1990, mainly for Italy and Greece, there are two older-age cohorts that intersect with migration and wellbeing: those who left Albania in the 1990s and who are now ageing (the 'first generation' or 'young-old'); and these migrants' left-behind parents (the 'zero generation' or 'older-old'). Both are faced with multiple options with regard to where they can maximise their wellbeing, which for them is linked to a combination of material living standards, personal satisfaction and dignity, healthcare access, and intergenerational care between parents, their children and these children's grandparents (the first, second and zero generations, respectively). Cela's stand-out finding is that, for these older Albanians, well-being is as much related to giving care as receiving it, thereby challenging the common view of ageing migrants as vulnerable care-receivers. But migration and return mobilities are multiple in the Albanian case. The first generation may want to return to Albania upon retirement, perhaps to look after their ageing, zero-generation parents. Alternatively, this oldest generation may follow their children in migration to Italy (where Cela did most of her fieldwork) in order to both receive care and access better health services than are available in Albania, but also to look after grandchildren – seen as their very *raison d'être* and, there-fore, key to their psychosocial wellbeing. For those who are financially able and have robust health, a kind of 'transnational pendulism' is the preferred option.

The triple nexus between ageing, return migration and wellbeing is con-tinued in the final two empirical chapters. In Chapter 13, Kelly Hall, Charles Betty and Jordi Giner examine the often difficult motivations and experiences of British retirees who return-migrate from Spain to the UK. These migrations – first to Spain and then back 'home' – are explicitly wellbeing driven. British reti-rees moved to Spain to enjoy happy, relaxed and fulfilling lives in a warm, sunny climate with lower living costs. However, continued ageing – from active 'young-old' to frail 'old-old' – brings with it increased vulnerability and chang-ing social and emotional needs, and hence deterioration in wellbeing. This chapter is one of the first studies to investigate the decisions and circumstances of return for older 'expats' in Spain, where the economic crisis has made life increasingly difficult. Key findings include evidence to support 'ageing return' from Spain as a growing phenomenon, shaped by health deterioration, bereave-ment and financial problems as 'push' factors, and by the desire to be close to family support and UK health services as 'pull' factors for return.

Chapter 14, by Dora Sampaio, is about retired labour migrants returning to the Azores archipelago after tough working lives in North America, where most worked in construction. As with the British retiree migrants in the previous chapter, this migration is largely amenity driven; returnees look forward to a relaxed later life in their island homes, with a mild climate and lush landscapes. An innovative feature of this chapter is its breakdown of the components of wellbeing into four dimensions – material, health, psychosocial, and place attachment – and the way that these elements interlink, both with each other and with interviewees' ongoing experiences post return. Three distinct narrative types are distilled from the interviews collected by Sampaio in several islands of the Azores: contentment; discontent; and renegotiation, transitionality and ambivalence. The first type reflects a successful reintegration and a deep sense of physical and psychosocial wellbeing, the reward for a hard life as a labour migrant. The second reflects unfulfilled expectations, loneliness and family separation, and lack of acceptance by locals, who tend to call returnees 'Americanos'. The third group of returnees articulates an ambivalent, fluctuat-ing type of narrative about their Azorean homecoming, shaped by changing events and continued uncertainty about belonging 'here' vs 'there'.

Policy implications

At the conclusion to Chapter 1, Vathi pre-announced a simple, main conclusion that has subsequently been echoed by most of the succeeding chapters, namely, that psychosocial issues should be incorporated into policies relating to returning migrants, at least for those who plan to stay long term in their country of origin. It is absolutely evident, both from the chapters in this book and from general surveys of return migration policy (Ghosh 2000; Koser 2000), that this recommendation has not been taken on board. First, Ghosh (2000: 182) reminds us that issues of return have received little attention from policy-makers and analysts. He stresses two key dimensions of return migration policy: returnees' potential contribution to the development of their countries of origin; and the personal success and welfare of the returning migrant as an individual, including their family (2000: 184). While this latter dimension edges close to considerations of psychosocial wellbeing, in fact it receives almost no further attention in his analysis of return migration policies. Meanwhile, in Koser's (2000) parallel review essay, the key elements of his systematic analysis are returnees' impact on economic development; the issue of brain drain and return; the return of asylum-seekers, trafficked persons and irregular migrants; readmission agreements and refugee repatriation; assistance to reintegration; citizenship issues; and 'ethnic' return migration. The only three points where Koser's review comes close to the main thrust of this book are where he argues for a longitudinal approach to the study and policy-framing of return migration, where he discusses the need for a more 'humane' approach to the return of irregular migrants, and where he highlights the social-welfare and counselling aspects of reintegration assistance (2000: 59, 66, 88).

From the 13 empirical chapters of this book, several concrete policy recommendations emerge. DeBono argues strongly for the inscription of a human-rights perspective among governments and other stakeholders dealing with return migration programmes, especially those that involve elements of heavy management and coercion. She puts forward a number of specific recommendations sourced from the Society for the Psychological Study of Social Issues, which can be 'tweaked' to apply to the case of returning migrants. These include incorporating psychosocial wellbeing as both a contribution to and an outcome of sustainable development (and, hence, 'sustainable return'; Black and Gent 2006); making high-quality mental healthcare accessible to all sectors of society, including mobile people and returnees; and ensuring that all social, health and welfare services are made available and implemented according to inclusive ethical principles that affirm the dignity of everyone. Another concrete policy recommendation comes from Lietaert *et al.*, who stress that psychosocial and other support for returnees needs to be available over a longer and sustained period of time, lasting from pre-return through the return move itself, and to continue for as long as needed into the post-return phase.

A second key policy recommendation endorsed by a number of chapter authors (Erdal and Oeppen; Kalir; Porobić) is the need to centre policy around an approach that recognises and respects the 'agency' of (return) migrants, in order to counter state policies of return, which victimise and marginalise irregular migrants and 'failed' asylum-seekers and often exacerbate the fragile psychosocial condition of these vulnerable people. Instead, to quote directly from Porobić's chapter, 'successful and meaningful return [should be] grounded in the social agency of [return] migrants and the gradual building of return projects … In these projects, social support and broader psychosocial wellbeing should be afforded more research and practical attention'.

A third important slant on policy is the specific need to safeguard the psychosocial wellbeing of women, children and older people, whose involvement in return movements, either 'voluntary' or 'forced', places them in positions of enhanced vulnerability and reduced, or zero, agency. For instance, Majidi argues for a policy protecting women and their children in refugee return situations: they need protection not only from the inflexible and authoritarian application of return programmes, but also from patriarchal structures, both in their refugee settings and in their countries of origin or return. 'Safe spaces' for them need to be created and protected. Majidi further campaigns for planning for women's skills, labour-market options and general agency, in order for them to transition to a sustainable and psychosocially satisfying position upon return.

Several chapters (Bendixsen and Lidén; Lulle; Majidi) emphasise the lack of involvement of children, both in the decisions about return (taken by their parents or repatriation agencies) and in policies directed towards return and resettlement. Both Bendixsen and Lidén, and Majidi, refer to cases (in Afghanistan, Iran, Somalia etc.) of children being returned to countries they hardly know or have never even visited, since they were born and brought up abroad, in camps or among labour-migrant, refugee or diaspora communities. While the parents may have prior experience of living in the 'homeland', their children may not. In Norway, according to Bendixsen and Lidén, a debate has started about the 'unfair' and 'inhumane' returns of children who had either been born in Norway or lived a substantial part of their lives there. In a similar vein, and based on the experience of young Latvian returnees still in education, Lulle recommends that more attention be paid to the schooling of such young mobile people, including their socio-cultural preparation for moves that are usually orchestrated by their parents' needs.

The final trio of chapters (Cela; Hall, Betty and Giner; Sampaio) are about the return experiences of older migrants, and raise interesting and often-overlooked aspects of policy surrounding the wellbeing of these older internationally mobile people. The fact that older returning migrants might be materially quite well off – including the British retirees returning from Spain for health, family or economic reasons – does not imply that they do not suffer threats to their psychosocial wellbeing, and this should be taken into account when they decide, or are forced by personal circumstances, to return 'home' (Hall *et al.*). Nevertheless, the psychosocial challenges posed by older-age labour migrants and refugees are generally greater, for they are returning to an origin country that is likely to be poorly equipped to deal with their needs. Cela's chapter on the two different older generations of Albanians reveals the gaps in health and social-care services in Albania and the dilemmas faced by ageing labour migrants and by the zero-generation 'oldest' generation. Here as elsewhere, the challenges to policy are multiple, yet constrained by the overall poverty of the country's finances, especially in the post-communist era when state guarantees to most sectors of the population have been slashed. Most return policies operated by migrant-sending countries are targeted towards attracting back young, healthy, entrepreneurial migrants (Lulle and King 2016: 127). Yet, many older migrants want to return home, above all for psychosocial reasons connected with nostalgia, familiarity and kinship. Returning older migrants should not be treated as a burden but as full citizens exercising their right either to be mobile or to return home to settle.

References

Black, R. and Gent, S. (2006) Sustainable return in post-conflict contexts, *International Migration* 44(3): 15–38.

Boccagni, P. and Baldassar, L. (2015) Emotions on the move: mapping the emergent field of emotion and migration, *Emotion, Space and Society* 16: 73–80.

Boyle, P., Halfacree, K. and Robinson, V. (1998) *Exploring Contemporary Migration*. London: Longman.

Cassarino, J.-P. (2004) Theorising return migration: the conceptual approach to return migrants revisited, *International Journal on Multicultural Societies* 6(2): 253–279.

Cassarino, J.-P. (2008) Conditions of modern return migrants, *International Journal on Multicultural Societies* 10(2): 95–105.

Cerase, F.P. (1974) Expectations and reality: a case study of return migration from the United States to Southern Italy, *International Migration Review* 8(2): 245–262.

Christou, A. (2016) Ageing 'phantasmagorically' in exile: the resilience of unbearable and unattainable homelands in the Jewish and Cuban imagination, in K. Walsh and L. Näre (eds) *Transnational Migration and Home in Older Age*. London: Routledge, 176–187.

Christou, A. and King, R. (2014) *Counter-diaspora: The Greek Second Generation Returns 'Home'*. Cambridge, MA: Harvard University Press.

Conradson, D. and McKay, D. (2007) Translocal subjectivities: mobility, connection, emotion, *Mobilities* 2(2): 167–174.

Davidson, J., Bondi, L. and Smith, M. (eds) (2007) *Emotional Geographies*. Aldershot: Ashgate.

Ewing, K.P. (2007) Immigrant identities and emotion, in C. Casey and R. Edgerton (eds) *A Companion to Psychological Anthropology*. Oxford: Blackwell, 225–240.

Faist, T. (2008) Migrants as transnational development agents: an inquiry into the newest round of the migration–development nexus, *Population, Space and Place* 14(1): 21–42.

Faist, T., Fauser, M. and Kivisto, P. (eds) (2011) *The Migration-Development Nexus: A Transnational Perspective*. Basingstoke: Palgrave Macmillan.

Ghosh, B. (2000) Return migration: reshaping policy approaches, in B. Ghosh (ed.) *Return Migration: Journey of Hope or Despair?* Geneva: International Organization for Migration and the United Nations, 181–226.

Handlin, O. (1951) *The Uprooted*. New York: Grosset & Dunlap.

Ho, E.L.-E. (2009) Constituting citizenship through emotions: Singaporean transmigrants in London, *Annals of the Association of American Geographers* 99(4): 788–804.

Ho, E.L.-E. (2014) The emotional economy of migration driving Mainland Chinese transnational sojourning across migration regimes, *Environment and Planning A* 46: 2212–2227.

King, R. (2000) Generalizations from the history of return migration, in B. Ghosh (ed.) *Return Migration: Journey of Hope or Despair?* Geneva: International Organization for Migration and the United Nations, 7–55.

King, R. and Christou, A. (2011) Of counter-diaspora and reverse transnationalism: return mobilities to and from the ancestral homeland, *Mobilities* 6(4): 451–466.

King, R., Lulle, A., Parutis, V. and Saar, M. (2015) Young Baltic Migrants Living and Working in London: From Peripheral Region to Escalator Region in Europe. Brighton: University of Sussex, Sussex Centre for Migration Research, Working Paper 82.

Koser, K. (2000) Return, readmission and reintegration: changing agendas, policy frameworks and operational programmes, in B. Ghosh (ed.) *Return Migration: Journey of Hope or Despair?* Geneva: International Organization for Migration and the United Nations, 57–99.

Long, L.D. and Oxfeld, E. (eds) (2004) *Coming Home? Refugees, Migrants, and Those Who Stayed Behind.* Philadelphia: University of Pennsylvania Press.

Lulle, A. and King, R. (2016) *Ageing, Gender, and Labour Migration.* Basingstoke: Palgrave Pivot.

McKay, D. (2007) 'Sending dollars shows feeling': emotions and economies in Filipino migration, *Mobilities* 2(2): 175–194.

Malkki, L. (1995) Refugees and exile: from 'refugee studies' to the national order of things, *Annual Review of Anthropology* 24: 495–523.

Markowitz, F. and Stefansson, A.H. (eds) (2004) *Homecomings: Unsettling Paths of Return.* Lanham, MD: Lexington Books.

Paasche, E. (2016) The role of corruption in reintegration: experiences of Iraqi Kurds upon return from Europe, *Journal of Ethnic and Migration Studies* 42(7): 1076–1093.

Saloutos, T. (1956) *They Remember America: The Story of the Repatriated Greek-Americans.* Cambridge, MA: Harvard University Press.

Skrbis, Z. (2008) Transnational families: theorising migration, emotions and belonging, *Journal of Intercultural Studies* 29(3): 213–230.

Smith, M., Davidson, J., Cameron, L. and Bondi, L. (eds) (2009) *Emotion, Place and Culture.* Farnham: Ashgate.

Svašek, M. (2010) On the move: emotions and human mobility, *Journal of Ethnic and Migration Studies* 36(6): 865–880.

Van Hear, N. and Sorensen, N.N. (eds) (2003) *The Migration–Development Nexus.* Geneva: International Organization for Migration.

Vathi, Z. and Duci, V. (2016) Making other dreams: the impact of migration on the psychosocial wellbeing of Albanian-origin children and young people upon their families' return to Albania, *Childhood* 23(1): 53–68.

Walsh, K. and Näre, L. (eds) (2016) *Transnational Migration and Home in Older Age.* London: Routledge.

Webber, F. (2011) How voluntary are voluntary returns? *Race and Class* 52: 98–107.

Wessendorf, S. (2007) 'Roots migration': transnationalism and 'return' among second-generation Italians in Switzerland, *Journal of Ethnic and Migration Studies* 33(7): 1083–1102.

Wright, K. (2012a) Constructing human wellbeing across spatial boundaries: negotiating meanings in transnational migration, *Global Networks* 12(4): 467–484.

Wright, K. (2012b) *International Migration, Development and Human Wellbeing.* Basingstoke: Palgrave Macmillan.

Zembylas, M. (2012) Transnationalism, migration and emotions, *Globalisation, Societies and Education* 10(2): 163–179.

Index

Taylor & Francis eBooks

Helping you to choose the right eBooks for your Library

Add Routledge titles to your library's digital collection today. Taylor and Francis ebooks contains over 50,000 titles in the Humanities, Social Sciences, Behavioural Sciences, Built Environment and Law.

Choose from a range of subject packages or create your own!

Benefits for you

» Free MARC records
» COUNTER-compliant usage statistics
» Flexible purchase and pricing options
» All titles DRM-free.

Benefits for your user

» Off-site, anytime access via Athens or referring URL
» Print or copy pages or chapters
» Full content search
» Bookmark, highlight and annotate text
» Access to thousands of pages of quality research at the click of a button.

REQUEST YOUR **FREE** INSTITUTIONAL TRIAL TODAY

Free Trials Available
We offer free trials to qualifying academic, corporate and government customers.

eCollections – Choose from over 30 subject eCollections, including:

Archaeology	Language Learning
Architecture	Law
Asian Studies	Literature
Business & Management	Media & Communication
Classical Studies	Middle East Studies
Construction	Music
Creative & Media Arts	Philosophy
Criminology & Criminal Justice	Planning
Economics	Politics
Education	Psychology & Mental Health
Energy	Religion
Engineering	Security
English Language & Linguistics	Social Work
Environment & Sustainability	Sociology
Geography	Sport
Health Studies	Theatre & Performance
History	Tourism, Hospitality & Events

For more information, pricing enquiries or to order a free trial, please contact your local sales team: www.tandfebooks.com/page/sales

 Routledge
Taylor & Francis Group

The home of
Routledge books

www.tandfebooks.com